DAS KAPITAL

DAS KAPITAL

A Critique of Political Economy

Karl Marx

Pacific Publishing Studio

Copyright © 2010 by Pacific Publishing Studio

All rights reserved.

Published in the United States by Madison Park, an imprint of Pacific Publishing Studio.

www.PacPS.com

ISBN is 145388632X

EAN-13 is 9781453886328

No part of this book may be reproduced in any form unless written permission is granted from the author or publisher. No electronic reproductions, information storage, or retrieval systems may be used or applied to any part of this book without written permission. Pacific Publishing Studio books are available at discounts for bulk purchases in the United States by institution, corporations, and other groups and organizations. For information on bulk purchases, contact Pacific Publishing Studio through the website at www.PacPS.com.

CONTENTS

Part One
Commodities and Money

Chapter 1
Commodities   1

Chapter 2
Exchange   29

Chapter 3
Money, or the Circulation of Commodities   35

Part Two
The Transformation of Money into Capital

Chapter 4
The General Formula for Capital   65

Chapter 5
Contradictions in the General Formula of Capital   71

Chapter 6
The Buying and Selling of Labour-Power

Part Three
The Production of Absolute Surplus-Value

Chapter 7
The Labour-Process and the Process of Producing Surplus-Value
83

Chapter 8
Constant Capital and Variable Capital   96

Chapter 9
The Rate of Surplus-Value   103

Chapter 10
The Working-Day   114

Chapter 11
Rate and Mass of Surplus Value   156

Part Four
Production of Relative Surplus Value

Chapter 12
The Concept of Relative Surplus-Value

Chapter 13
Co-operation   168

Chapter 14
Division of Labour and Manufacture   176

BOOK I.
CAPITALIST PRODUCTION

PART I.
COMMODITIES AND MONEY

CHAPTER I
COMMODITIES

Section 1. -- ; The Two Factors of a Commodity: Use-Value and Value (The Substance of Value and the Magnitude of Value)

The wealth of those societies in which the capitalist mode of production prevails, presents itself as "an immense accumulation of commodities," [1] its unit being a single commodity. Our investigation must therefore begin with the analysis of a commodity.

A commodity is, in the first place, an object outside us, a thing that by its properties satisfies human wants of some sort or another. The nature of such wants, whether, for instance, they spring from the stomach or from fancy, makes no difference. [2] Neither are we here concerned to know how the object satisfies these wants, whether directly as means of subsistence, or indirectly as means of production.

Every useful thing, as iron, paper, &c., may be looked at from the two points of view of quality and quantity. It is an assemblage of many properties, and may therefore be of use in various ways. To discover the various uses of things is the work of history. [3] So also is the establishment of socially-recognized standards of measure for the quantities of these useful objects. The diversity of these measures has its origin partly in the diverse nature of the objects to be measured, partly in convention.

The utility of a thing makes it a use-value. [4] But this utility is not a thing of air. Being limited by the physical properties of the commodity, it has no existence apart from that commodity. A commodity, such as iron, corn, or a diamond, is therefore, so far as it is a material thing, a use-value, something useful. This property of a commodity is independent of the amount of labour required to appropriate its useful qualities. When treating of use-value, we always assume to be dealing with definite quantities, such as dozens of watches, yards of linen, or tons of iron. The use-values of commodities furnish the material for a special study, that of the commercial knowledge of commodities.[5] Use-values become a reality only by use or consumption: they also constitute the substance of all wealth, whatever may be the social form of that wealth. In the form of society we are about to consider, they are, in addition, the material depositories of exchange-value.

Exchange-value, at first sight, presents itself as a quantitative relation, as the proportion in which values in use of one sort are exchanged for those of another sort,[6] a relation constantly changing with time and place. Hence exchange-value appears to be something accidental and purely relative, and consequently an intrinsic value, i.e., an exchange-value that is inseparably connected with, inherent in commodities, seems a contradiction in terms.[7] Let us consider the matter a little more closely.

A given commodity, e.g., a quarter of wheat is exchanged for x blacking, y silk, or z gold, &c. — in short, for other commodities in the most different proportions. Instead of one exchange-value, the wheat has, therefore, a great many. But since x blacking, y silk, or z gold &c., each represents the exchange-value of one quarter of wheat, x blacking, y silk, z gold, &c., must, as exchange-values, be replaceable by each other, or equal to each other. Therefore, first: the valid exchange-values of a given commodity express something equal; secondly, exchange-value, generally, is only the mode of expression, the phenomenal form, of something contained in it, yet distinguishable from it.

Let us take two commodities, e.g., corn and iron. The proportions in which they are exchangeable, whatever those proportions may be, can always be represented by an equation in which a given quantity of corn is equated to some quantity of iron: e.g., 1 quarter corn = x cwt. iron. What does this equation tell us? It tells us that in two different things — in 1 quarter of corn and x cwt. of iron, there exists in equal quantities something common to both. The two things must therefore be equal to a third, which in itself is neither the one nor the other. Each of them, so far as it is exchange-value, must therefore be reducible to this third.

A simple geometrical illustration will make this clear. In order to calculate and compare the areas of rectilinear figures, we decompose them into triangles. But the area of the triangle itself is expressed by something totally different from its visible figure, namely, by half the product of the base multiplied by the altitude. In the same way the exchange-values of commodities must be capable of being expressed in terms of something common to them all, of which thing they represent a greater or less quantity.

This common "something" cannot be either a geometrical, a chemical, or any other natural property of commodities. Such properties claim our attention only in so far as they affect the utility of those commodities, make them use-values. But the exchange of commodities is evidently an act characterised by a total abstraction from use-value. Then one use-value is just as good as another, provided only it be present in sufficient quantity. Or, as old Barbon says, "one sort of wares are as good as another, if the values be equal. There is no difference or distinction in things of equal value.... An hundred pounds' worth of lead or iron, is of as great value as one hundred pounds' worth of silver or gold."[8] As use-values, commodities are, above all, of different qualities, but as exchange-values they are merely different quantities, and consequently do not contain an atom of use-value.

If then we leave out of consideration the use-value of commodities, they have only one common property left, that of being products of labour. But even the product of labour itself has undergone a change in our hands. If we make abstraction from its use-value, we make abstraction at the same time from the material elements and shapes that make the product a use-value; we see in it no longer a table, a house, yarn, or any other useful thing. Its existence as a material thing is put out of sight. Neither can it any longer be regarded as the product of the labour of the joiner, the mason, the spinner, or of any other definite kind of productive labour. Along with the useful qualities of the products themselves, we put out of sight both the useful character of the various kinds of labour embodied in them, and the concrete forms of that labour; there is nothing left but what is common to them all; all are reduced to one and the same sort of labour, human labour in the abstract.

Let us now consider the residue of each of these products; it consists of the same unsubstantial reality in each, a mere congelation of homogeneous human labour, of labour-power expended without regard to the mode of its expenditure. All that these things now tell us is, that human labour-power has been expended in their production, that human labour is embodied in them. When looked at as crystals of this social substance, common to them all, they are — Values.

We have seen that when commodities are exchanged, their exchange-value manifests itself as something totally independent of their use-value. But if we abstract from their use-value, there remains their Value as defined above. Therefore, the common substance that manifests itself in the exchange-value of commodities, whenever they are exchanged, is their value. The progress of our investigation will show that exchange-value is the only form in which the value of commodities can manifest itself or be expressed. For the present, however, we have to consider the nature of value independently of this, its form.

A use-value, or useful article, therefore, has value only because human labour in the abstract has been embodied or materialised in it. How, then, is the magnitude of this value to be measured? Plainly, by the quantity of the value-creating substance, the labour, contained in the article. The quantity of labour, however, is measured by its duration, and labour-time in its turn finds its standard in weeks, days, and hours.

Some people might think that if the value of a commodity is determined by the quantity of labour spent on it, the more idle and unskilful the labourer, the more valuable would his commodity be, because more time would be required in its production. The labour, however, that forms the substance of value, is homogeneous human labour, expenditure of one uniform labour-power. The total labour-power of society, which is embodied in the sum total of the values of all commodities produced by that society, counts here as one homogeneous mass of human labour-power, composed though it be of innumerable individual units. Each of these units is the same as any other, so far as it has the character of the average labour-power of society, and takes effect as such; that is, so far as it requires for producing a commodity, no more time than is needed on an average, no more than is socially necessary. The labour-time socially necessary is that required to produce an article under the normal conditions of production, and with the average degree of skill and intensity prevalent at the time. The introduction of power-looms into England probably reduced by one-half the labour required to weave a given quantity of yarn into cloth. The hand-loom weavers, as a matter of fact, continued to require the same time as before; but for all that, the product of one hour of their labour represented after the change only half an hour's social labour, and consequently fell to one-half its former value.

We see then that that which determines the magnitude of the value of any article is the amount of labour socially necessary, or the labour-time socially necessary for its production.[9] Each individual commodity, in this connexion, is to be considered as an average sample of its class.[10] Commodities, therefore, in which equal quantities of labour are embodied, or which can be produced in the same time, have the same value. The value of one commodity is to the value of any other, as the labour-time necessary for the production of the one is to that necessary for the production of the other. "As values, all commodities are only definite masses of congealed labour-time."[11]

The value of a commodity would therefore remain constant, if the labour-time required for its production also remained constant. But the latter changes with every variation in the productiveness of labour. This productiveness is determined by various circumstances, amongst others, by the average amount of skill of the workmen, the state of science, and the degree of its practical application, the social organisation of production, the extent and capabilities of the means of production, and by physical conditions. For example, the same amount of labour in favourable seasons is embodied in 8 bushels of corn, and in unfavourable, only in four. The same labour extracts from rich mines more metal than from poor mines. Diamonds are of very rare occurrence on the earth's surface, and hence their discovery costs, on an average, a great deal of labour-time. Consequently much labour is represented in a small compass. Jacob doubts whether gold has ever been paid for at its full value. This applies still more to diamonds. According to Eschwege, the total produce of the Brazilian diamond mines for the eighty years, ending in 1823, had not realised the price of one and-a-half years' average produce of the sugar and coffee plantations of the same country, although the diamonds cost much more labour, and therefore represented more value. With richer mines, the same quantity of labour would embody itself in more diamonds, and their value would fall. If we could succeed at a small expenditure of labour, in converting carbon into diamonds, their value might fall below that of bricks. In general, the greater the productiveness of labour, the less is the labour-time required for the production of an article, the less is the amount of labour crystallised in that article, and the less is its value; and vice versâ, the less the productiveness of labour, the greater is the labour-time required for the production of an article, and the greater is its value. The value of a commodity, therefore, varies directly as the quantity, and inversely as the productiveness, of the labour incorporated in it.

A thing can be a use-value, without having value. This is the case whenever its utility to man is not due to labour. Such are air, virgin soil, natural meadows, &c. A thing can be useful, and the product of human labour, without being a commodity. Whoever directly satisfies his wants with the produce of his own labour, creates, indeed, use-values, but not commodities. In order to produce the latter, he must not only produce use-values, but use-values for others, social use-values. (And not only for others, without more. The mediaeval peasant produced quit-rent-corn for his feudal lord and tithe-corn for his parson. But neither the quit-rent-corn nor the tithe-corn became commodities by reason of the fact that they had been produced for others. To become a commodity a product must be transferred to another, whom it will serve as a use-value, by means of an exchange.) Lastly nothing can have value, without being an object of utility. If the thing is useless, so is the labour contained in it; the labour does not count as labour, and therefore creates no value.

Section 2. -- The TwoFold Charater of the Labour Embodied in Commodities

At first sight a commodity presented itself to us as a complex of two things-use-value and exchange-value. Later on, we saw also that labour, too, possesses the same two-fold nature; for, so far as it finds expression in value, it does not possess the same characteristics that belong to it as a creator of use-values. I was the first to point out and to examine critically this two-fold nature of the labour contained in commodities. As this point is the pivot on which a clear comprehension of Political Economy turns, we must go more into detail.

Let us take two commodities such as a coat and 10 yards of linen, and let the former be double the value of the latter, so that, if 10 yards of linen = W, the coat = 2W.

The coat is a use-value that satisfies a particular want. Its existence is the result of a special sort of productive activity, the nature of which is determined by its aim, mode of operation, subject, means, and result. The labour, whose utility is thus represented by the value in use of its product, or which manifests itself by making its product a use-value, we call useful labour In this connexion we consider only its useful effect.

As the coat and the linen are two qualitatively different use-values, so also are the two forms of labour that produce them, tailoring and weaving. Were these two objects not qualitatively different, not produced respectively by labour of different quality, they could not stand to each other in the relation of commodities. Coats are not exchanged for coats, one use-value is not exchanged for another of the same kind.

To all the different varieties of values in use there correspond as many different kinds of useful labour, classified according to the order, genus, species, and variety to which they belong in the social division of labour. This division of labour is a necessary condition for the production of commodities, but it does not follow, conversely, that the production of commodities is a necessary condition for the division of labour. In the primitive Indian community there is social division of labour, without production of commodities. Or, to take an example nearer home, in every factory the labour is divided according to a system, but this division is not brought about by the operatives mutually exchanging their individual products. Only such products can become commodities with regard to each other, as result from different kinds of labour, each kind being carried on independently and for the account of private individuals.

To resume, then: In the use-value of each commodity there is contained useful labour, i.e., productive activity of a definite kind and exercised with a definite aim. Use-values cannot confront each other as commodities, unless the useful labour embodied in them is qualitatively different in each of them. In a community, the produce of which in general takes the form of commodities, i.e., in a community of commodity producers, this qualitative difference between the useful forms of labour that are carried on independently of individual producers, each on their own account, develops into a complex system, a social division of labour.

Anyhow, whether the coat be worn by the tailor or by his customer, in either case it operates as a use-value. Nor is the relation between the coat and the labour that produced it altered by the circumstance that tailoring may have become a special trade, an independent branch of the social division of labour. Wherever the want of clothing forced them to it, the human race made clothes for thousands of years, without a single man becoming a tailor. But coats and linen, like every other element of material wealth that is not the spontaneous produce of Nature, must invariably owe their existence to a special productive activity, exercised with a definite aim, an activity that appropriates particular nature-given materials to particular human wants. So far therefore as labour is a creator of use-value, is useful labour, it is a necessary condition, independent of all forms of society, for the existence of the human race; it is an eternal nature-imposed necessity, without which there can be no material exchanges between man and Nature, and therefore no life.

The use-values, coat, linen, &c., i.e., the bodies of commodities, are combinations of two elements — matter and labour. If we take away the useful labour expended upon them, a material substratum is always left, which is furnished by Nature without the help of man. The latter can work only as Nature does, that is by changing the form of matter. [12] Nay more, in this work of changing the form he is constantly helped by natural forces. We see, then, that labour is not the only source of material wealth, of use-values produced by labour. As William Petty puts it, labour is its father and the earth its mother.

Let us now pass from the commodity considered as a use-value to the value of commodities.

By our assumption, the coat is worth twice as much as the linen. But this is a mere quantitative difference, which for the present does not concern us. We bear in mind, however, that if the value of the coat is double that of 10 yds. of linen, 20 yds. of linen must have the same value as one coat. So far as they are values, the coat and the linen are things of a like substance, objective expressions of essentially identical labour. But tailoring and weaving are, qualitatively, different kinds of labour. There are, however, states of society in which one and the same man does tailoring and weaving alternately, in which case these two forms of labour are mere modifications of the labour of the same individual, and no special and fixed functions of different persons, just as the coat which our tailor makes one day, and the trousers which he makes another day, imply only a variation in the labour of one and the same individual. oreover, we see at a glance that, in our capitalist society, a given portion of human labour is, in accordance with the varying demand, at one time supplied in the form of tailoring, at another in the form of weaving. This change may possibly not take place without friction, but take place it must.

Productive activity, if we leave out of sight its special form, viz., the useful character of the labour, is nothing but the expenditure of human labour-power. Tailoring and weaving, though qualitatively different productive activities, are each a productive expenditure of human brains, nerves, and muscles, and in this sense are human labour. They are but two different modes of expending human labour-power. Of course, this labour-power, which remains the same under all its modifications, must have attained a certain pitch of development before it can be expended in a multiplicity of modes. But the value of a commodity represents human labour in the abstract, the expenditure of human labour in general. And just as in society, a general or a banker plays a great part, but mere man, on the other hand, a very shabby part,[13] so here with mere human labour. It is the expenditure of simple labour-power, i.e., of the labour-power which, on an average, apart from any special development, exists in the organism of every ordinary individual. Simple average labour, it is true, varies in character in different countries and at different times, but in a particular society it is given. Skilled labour counts only as simple labour intensified, or rather, as multiplied simple labour, a given quantity of skilled being considered equal to a greater quantity of simple labour. Experience shows that this reduction is constantly being made. A commodity may be the product of the most skilled labour, but its value, by equating it to the product of simple unskilled labour, represents a definite quantity of the latter labour alone.[14] The different proportions in which different sorts of labour are reduced to unskilled labour as their standard. are established by a social process that goes on behind the backs of the producers, and, consequently, appear to be fixed by custom. For simplicity's sake we shall henceforth account every kind of labour to be unskilled, simple labour; by this we do no more than save ourselves the trouble of making the reduction.

Just as, therefore, in viewing the coat and linen as values, we abstract from their different use-values, so it is with the labour represented by those values: we disregard the difference between its useful forms, weaving and tailoring. As the use-values, coat and linen, are combinations of special productive activities with cloth and yarn, while the values, coat and linen, are, on the other hand, mere homogeneous congelations of undifferentiated labour, so the labour embodied in these latter values does not count by virtue of its productive relation to cloth and yarn, but only as being expenditure of human labour-power. Tailoring and weaving are necessary factors in the creation of the use-values, coat and linen, precisely because these two kinds of labour are of different qualities; but only in so far as abstraction is made from their special qualities, only in so far as both possess the same quality of being human labour, do tailoring and weaving form the substance of the values of the same articles.

Coats and linen, however, are not merely values, but values of definite magnitude, and according to our assumption, the coat is worth twice as much as the ten yards of linen. Whence this difference in their values? It is owing to the fact that the linen contains only half as much labour as the coat, and consequently, that in the production of the latter, labour-power must have been expended during twice the time necessary for the production of the former.

While, therefore, with reference to use-value, the labour contained in a commodity counts only qualitatively, with reference to value it counts only quantitatively, and must first be reduced to human labour pure and simple. In the former case, it is a question of How and What, in the latter of How much? How long a time? Since the magnitude of the value of a commodity represents only the quantity of labour embodied in it, it follows that all commodities, when taken in certain proportions, must be equal in value.

- all labor is equal
- labor should be measured quantitatively

If the productive power of all the different sorts of useful labour required for the production of a coat remains unchanged, the sum of the values of the coats produced increases with their number. If one coat represents x days' labour, two coats represent 2x days' labour, and so on. But assume that the duration of the labour necessary for he production of a coat becomes doubled or halved. In the first case one coat is worth as much as two coats were before; in the second case, two coats are only worth as much as one was before, although in both cases one coat renders the same service as before. and the useful labour embodied in it remains of the same quality. But the quantity of labour spent on its production has altered.

An increase in the quantity of use-values is an increase of material wealth. With two coats two men can be clothed, with one coat only one man. Nevertheless, an increased quantity of material wealth may correspond to a simultaneous fall in the magnitude of its value. This antagonistic movement has its origin in the two-fold character of labour. Productive power has reference, of course, only to labour of some useful concrete form, the efficacy of any special productive activity during a given time being dependent on its productiveness. Useful labour becomes, therefore, a more or less abundant source of products, in proportion to the rise or fall of its productiveness. On the other hand, no change in this productiveness affects the labour represented by value. Since productive power is an attribute of the concrete useful forms of labour, of course it can no longer have any bearing on that labour, so soon as we make abstraction from those concrete useful forms. However then productive power may vary, the same labour, exercised during equal periods of time, always yields equal amounts of value. But it will yield, during equal periods of time, different quantities of values in use; more, if the productive power rise, fewer, if it fall. The same change in productive power, which increases the fruitfulness of labour, and, in consequence, the quantity of use-values produced by that labour, will diminish the total value of this increased quantity of use-values, provided such change shorten the total labour-time necessary for their production; and vice versâ.

On the one hand all labour is, speaking physiologically, an expenditure of human labour-power, and in its character of identical abstract human labour, it creates and forms the value of commodities. On the other hand, all labour is the expenditure of human labour-power in a special form and with a definite aim, and in this, its character of concrete useful labour, it produces use-values.[15]

Section 3. -- ; The form of Value or Exchange Value

Commodities come into the world in the shape of use-values, articles, or goods, such as iron, linen, corn, &c. This is their plain, homely, bodily form. They are, however, commodities, only because they are something two-fold, both objects of utility, and, at the same time, depositories of value. They manifest themselves therefore as commodities, or have the form of commodities, only so far as they have two forms, a physical or natural form, and a value-form.

The reality of the value of commodities differs in this respect from Dame Quickly, that we don't know "where to have it." The value of commodities is the very opposite of the coarse materiality of their substance, not an atom of matter enters into its composition. Turn and examine a single commodity, by itself, as we will, yet in so far as it remains an object of value, it seems impossible to grasp it. If, however we bear in mind that the value of commodities has a purely social reality, and that they acquire this reality only in so far as they are expressions or embodiments of one identical social substance, viz., human labour, it follows as a matter of course, that value can only manifest itself in the social relation of commodity to commodity. In fact we started from exchange-value, or the exchange relation of commodities, in order to get at the value that lies hidden behind it. We must now return to this form under which value first appeared to us.

Every one knows, if he knows nothing else, that commodities have a value-form common to them all, and presenting a marked contrast with the varied bodily forms of their use-values. I mean their money-form. Here, however, a task is set us, the performance of which has never yet even been attempted by bourgeois economy, the task of tracing the genesis of this money-form, of developing the expression of value implied in the value-relation of commodities, from its simplest, almost imperceptible outline, to the

How do we assign money value?
 — not w/ use value

dazzling money-form. By doing this we shall, at the same time, solve the riddle presented by money.

The simplest value-relation is evidently that of one commodity to some one other commodity of a different kind. Hence the relation between the values of two commodities supplies us with the simplest expression of the value of a single commodity.

A. *Elementary or Accidental Form Of Value*

x commodity A = y commodity B, or

x commodity A is worth y commodity B.

20 yards of linen = 1 coat, or

20 Yards of linen are worth 1 coat.

1. *The two poles of the expression of value. Relative form and Equivalent form*

The whole mystery of the form of value lies hidden in this elementary form. Its analysis, therefore, is our real difficulty.

Here two different kinds of commodities (in our example the linen and the coat), evidently play two different parts. The linen expresses its value in the coat; the coat serves as the material in which that value is expressed. The former plays an active, the latter a passive, part. The value of the linen is represented as relative value, or appears in relative form. The coat officiates as equivalent, or appears in equivalent form.

The relative form and the equivalent form are two intimately connected, mutually dependent and inseparable elements of the expression of value; but, at the same time, are mutually exclusive, antagonistic extremes — i.e., poles of the same expression. They are allotted respectively to the two different commodities brought into relation by that expression. It is not possible to express the value of linen in linen. 20 yards of linen = 20 yards of linen is no expression of value. On the contrary, such an equation merely says that 20 yards of linen are nothing else than 20 yards of linen, a definite quantity of the use-value linen. The value of the linen can therefore be expressed only relatively — i.e., in some other commodity. The relative form of the value of the linen pre-supposes, therefore, the presence of some other commodity — here the coat — under the form of an equivalent. On the other hand, the commodity that figures as the equivalent cannot at the same time assume the relative form. That second commodity is not the one whose value is expressed. Its function is merely to serve as the material in which the value of the first commodity is expressed.

No doubt, the expression 20 yards of linen = 1 coat, or 20 yards of linen are worth 1 coat, implies the opposite relation. 1 coat = 20 yards of linen, or 1 coat is worth 20 yards of linen. But, in that case, I must reverse the equation, in order to express the value of the coat relatively; and. so soon as I do that the linen becomes the equivalent instead of the coat. A single commodity cannot, therefore, simultaneously assume, in the same expression of value, both forms. The very polarity of these forms makes them mutually exclusive.

Whether, then, a commodity assumes the relative form, or the opposite equivalent form, depends entirely upon its accidental position in the expression of value — that is, upon whether it is the commodity whose value is being expressed or the commodity in which value is being expressed.

2. *The Relative Form of value*

(a.) *The nature and import of this form*

In order to discover how the elementary expression of the value of a commodity lies hidden in the value-relation of two commodities, we must, in the first place, consider the latter entirely apart from its quantitative aspect. The usual mode of procedure is generally the reverse, and in the value-relation nothing is seen but the proportion between definite quantities of two different sorts of commodities that are considered equal to each other. It is apt to be forgotten that the magnitudes of different things can be compared quantitatively, only when those magnitudes are expressed in terms of the same unit. It is only as expressions of such a unit that they are of the same denomination, and therefore commensurable.[17]

Whether 20 yards of linen = 1 coat or = 20 coats or = x coats-that is, whether a given quantity of linen is worth few or many coats, every such statement implies that the linen and coats, as magnitudes of value, are expressions of the same unit, things of the same kind. Linen = coat is the basis of the equation.

But the two commodities whose identity of quality is thus assumed, do not play the same part. It is only the value of the linen that is expressed. And how? By its reference to the coat as its equivalent, as something that can be exchanged for it. In this relation the coat is the mode of existence of value, is value embodied, for only as such is it the same as the linen. On the other hand, the linen's own value comes to the front, receives independent expression, for it is only as being value that it is comparable with the coat as a thing of equal value, or exchangeable with the coat. To borrow an illustration from chemistry, butyric acid is a different substance from propyl formate. Yet both are made up of the same chemical substances, carbon (C), hydrogen (H), and oxygen (O), and that, too, in like proportions — namely, $C_4H_8O_2$. If now we equate butyric acid to propyl formate, then, in the first place, propyl formate would be, in this relation, merely a form of existence of $C_4H_8O_2$; and in the second place, we should be stating that butyric acid also consists of $C_4H_8O_2$. Therefore, by thus equating the two substances, expression would be given to their chemical composition, while their different physical forms would be neglected.

If we say that, as values, commodities are mere congelations of human labour, we reduce them by our analysis, it is true, to the abstraction, value; but we ascribe to this value no form apart from their bodily form. It is otherwise in the value-relation of one commodity to another. Here, the one stands forth in its character of value by reason of its relation to the other.

By making the coat the equivalent of the linen, we equate the labour embodied in the former to that in the latter. Now, it is true that the tailoring, which makes the coat, is concrete labour of a different sort from the weaving which makes the linen. But the act of equating it to the weaving, reduces the tailoring to that which is really equal in the two kinds of labour, to their common character of human labour. In this roundabout way, then, the fact is expressed, that weaving also, in so far as it weaves value, has nothing to distinguish it from tailoring, and, consequently, is abstract human labour. It is the expression of equivalence between different sorts of commodities that alone brings into relief the specific character of value-creating labour, and this it does by actually reducing the different varieties of labour embodied in the different kinds of commodities to their common quality of human labour in the abstract. [18]

There is, however, something else required beyond the expression of the specific character of the labour of which the value of the linen consists. Human labour-power in motion, or human labour, creates value, but is not itself value. It becomes value only in its congealed state, when embodied in the form of some object. In order to express the value of the linen as a congelation of human labour, that value must be expressed as having objective existence, as being a something materially different from the linen itself, and yet a something common to the linen and all other commodities. The problem is already solved.

When occupying the position of equivalent in the equation of value, the coat ranks qualitatively as the equal of the linen, as something of the same kind, because it is value. In this position it is a thing in which we see nothing but value, or whose palpable bodily form represents value. Yet the coat itself, the body of the commodity, coat, is a mere use-value. A coat as such no more tells us it is value, than does the first piece of linen we take hold of. This shows that when placed in value-relation to the linen, the coat signifies more than when out of that relation, just as many a man strutting about in a gorgeous uniform counts for more than when in mufti.

In the production of the coat, human labour-power, in the shape of tailoring, must have been actually expended. Human labour is therefore accumulated in it. In this aspect the coat is a depository of value, but though worn to a thread, it does not let this fact show through. And as equivalent of the linen in the value equation, it exists under this aspect alone, counts therefore as embodied value, as a body that is value. A, for instance, cannot be "your majesty" to B, unless at the same time majesty in B's eyes assumes the bodily form of A, and, what is more, with every new father of the people, changes its features, hair, and many other things besides.

Hence, in the value equation, in which the coat is the equivalent of the linen, the coat officiates as the form of value. The value of the commodity linen is expressed by the bodily form of the commodity coat, the value of one by the use-value of the other. As a use-value, the linen is something palpably different from the coat; as value, it is the same as the coat, and now has the appearance of a coat. Thus the linen acquires a value-form different from its physical form. The fact that it is value, is made manifest by its equality with the coat, just as the sheep's nature of a Christian is shown in his resemblance to the Lamb of God.

We see, then, all that our analysis of the value of commodities has already told us, is told us by the linen itself, so soon as it comes into communication with another commodity, the coat. Only it betrays its thoughts in that language with which alone it is familiar, the language of commodities. In order to tell us that its own value is created by labour in its abstract character of human labour, it says that the coat, in so far as it is worth as much as the linen, and therefore is value, consists of the same labour as the linen. In order to inform us that its sublime reality as value is not the same as its buckram body, it says that value has the appearance of a coat, and consequently that so far as the linen is value, it and the coat are as like as two peas. We may here remark, that the language of commodities has, besides Hebrew, many other more or less correct dialects. The German "Wertsein," to be worth, for instance, expresses in a less striking manner than the Romance verbs "valere," "valer," "valoir," that the equating of commodity B to commodity A, is commodity A's own mode of expressing its value. Paris vaut bien une messe.

By means, therefore, of the value-relation expressed in our equation, the bodily form of commodity B becomes the value-form of commodity A, or the body of commodity B acts as a mirror to the value of commodity A.[19] By putting itself in relation with commodity B, as value in *propriâ personâ*, as the matter of which human labour is made up, the commodity A converts the value in use, B, into the substance in which to express its, A's, own value. The value of A, thus expressed in the use-value of B, has taken the form of relative value.

(b.) Quantitative determination of Relative value

Every commodity, whose value it is intended to express, is a useful object of given quantity, as 15 bushels of corn, or 100 Ibs. of coffee. And a given quantity of any commodity contains a definite quantity of human labour. The value-form must therefore not only express value generally, but also value in definite quantity. Therefore, in the value-relation of commodity A to commodity B, of the linen to the coat, not only is the latter, as value in general, made the equal in quality of the linen, but a definite quantity of coat (1 coat) is made the equivalent of a definite quantity (20 yards) of linen.

The equation, 20 yards of linen = 1 coat, or 20 yards of linen are worth one coat, implies that the same quantity of value-substance (congealed labour) is embodied in both; that the two commodities have each cost the same amount of labour of the same quantity of labour-time. But the labour-time necessary for the production of 20 yards of linen or 1 coat varies with every change in the productiveness of weaving or tailoring. We have now to consider the influence of such changes on the quantitative aspect of the relative expression of value.

I. Let the value of the linen vary,[20] that of the coat remaining constant. If, say in consequence of the exhaustion of flax-growing soil, the labour-time necessary for the production of the linen be doubled, the value of the linen will also be doubled. Instead of the equation, 20 yards of linen = 1 coat, we should have 20 yards of linen = 2 coats, since 1 coat would now contain only half the labour-time embodied in 20 yards of linen. If, on the other hand, in consequence, say, of improved looms, this labour-time be reduced by one-half, the value of the linen would fall by one-half. Consequently, we should have 20 yards of linen = 1/2 coat. The relative value of commodity A, i.e., its value expressed in commodity B, rises and falls directly as the value of A, the value of B being supposed constant.

II. Let the value of the linen remain constant, while the value of the coat varies. If, under these circumstances, in consequence, for instance, of a poor crop of wool, the labour-time necessary for the production of a coat becomes doubled, we have instead of 20 yards of linen = 1 coat, 20 yards of linen = 1/2 coat. If, on the other hand, the value of the coat sinks by one-half, then 20 yards of linen = 2 coats. Hence, if the value of commodity A remain constant, its relative value expressed in commodity B rises and falls inversely as the value of B.

If we compare the different cases in I. and II., we see that the same change of magnitude in relative value may arise from totally opposite causes. Thus, the equation, 20 yards of linen = 1 coat, becomes 20 yards of linen = 2 coats, either, because the value of the linen has doubled, or because the value of the coat has fallen by one-half; and it becomes

20 yards of linen = 1/2 coat, either, because the value of the linen has fallen by one-half, or because the value of the coat has doubled.

III. Let the quantities of labour-time respectively necessary for the production of the linen and the coat vary simultaneously in the same direction and in the same proportion. In this case 20 yards of linen continue equal to 1 coat, however much their values may have altered. Their change of value is seen as soon as they are compared with a third commodity, whose value has remained constant. If the values of all commodities rose or fell simultaneously, and in the same proportion, their relative values would remain unaltered. Their real change of value would appear from the diminished or increased quantity of commodities produced in a given time.

IV. The labour-time respectively necessary for the production of the linen and the coat, and therefore the value of these commodities may simultaneously vary in the same direction, but at unequal rates or in opposite directions, or in other ways. The effect of all these possible different variations, on the relative value of a commodity, may be deduced from the results of I., II., and III.

Thus real changes in the magnitude of value are neither unequivocally nor exhaustively reflected in their relative expression, that is, in the equation expressing the magnitude of relative value. The relative value of a commodity may vary, although its value remains constant. Its relative value may remain constant, although its value varies; and finally, simultaneous variations in the magnitude of value and in that of its relative expression by no means necessarily correspond in amount.[21]

3. The Equivalent form of value

We have seen that commodity A (the linen), by expressing its value in the use-value of a commodity differing in kind (the coat), at the same time impresses upon the latter a specific form of value, namely that of the equivalent. The commodity linen manifests its quality of having a value by the fact that the coat, without having assumed a value-form different from its bodily form, is equated to the linen. The fact that the latter therefore has a value is expressed by saying that the coat is directly exchangeable with it. Therefore, when we say that a commodity is in the equivalent form, we express the fact that it is directly exchangeable with other commodities.

When one commodity, such as a coat, serves as the equivalent of another, such as linen, and coats consequently acquire the characteristic property of being directly exchangeable with linen, we are far from knowing in what proportion the two are exchangeable. The value of the linen being given in magnitude, that proportion depends on the value of the coat. Whether the coat serves as the equivalent and the linen as relative value, or the linen as the equivalent and the coat as relative value, the magnitude of the coat's value is determined, independently of its value-form, by the labour-time necessary for its production. But whenever the coat assumes in the equation of value, the position of equivalent, its value acquires no quantitative expression; on the contrary, the commodity coat now figures only as a definite quantity of some article.

For instance, 40 yards of linen are worth — what? 2 coats. Because the commodity coat here plays the part of equivalent, because the use-value coat, as opposed to the linen, figures as an embodiment of value, therefore a definite number of coats suffices to express the definite quantity of value in the linen. Two coats may therefore express the quantity of value of 40 yards of linen, but they can never express the quantity of their own value. A superficial observation of this fact, namely, that in the equation of value, the equivalent figures exclusively as a simple quantity of some article, of some use-value, has misled Bailey, as also many others, both before and after him, into seeing, in the expression of value, merely a quantitative relation. The truth being, that when a commodity acts as equivalent, no quantitative determination of its value is expressed.

The first peculiarity that strikes us, in considering the form of the equivalent, is this: use-value becomes the form of manifestation, the phenomenal form of its opposite, value.

The bodily form of the commodity becomes its value-form. But, mark well, that this quid pro quo exists in the case of any commodity B, only when some other commodity A enters into a value-relation with it, and then only within the limits of this relation. Since no commodity can stand in the relation of equivalent to itself, and thus turn its own bodily shape into the expression of its own value, every commodity is compelled to choose some other commodity for its equivalent, and to accept the use-value, that is to say, the bodily shape of that other commodity as the form of its own value.

One of the measures that we apply to commodities as material substances, as use-values, will serve to illustrate this point. A sugar-loaf being a body, is heavy, and therefore has weight: but we can neither see nor touch this weight. We then take various pieces of iron, whose weight has been determined beforehand. The iron, as iron, is no more the form of manifestation of weight, than is the sugar-loaf. Nevertheless, in order to express the sugar-loaf as so much weight, we put it into a weight-relation with the iron. In this relation, the iron officiates as a body representing nothing but weight. A certain quantity of iron therefore serves as the measure of the weight of the sugar, and represents, in relation to the sugar-loaf, weight embodied, the form of manifestation of weight. This part is played by the iron only within this relation, into which the sugar or any other body, whose weight has to be determined, enters with the iron. Were they not both heavy, they could not enter into this relation, and the one could therefore not serve as the expression of the weight of the other. When we throw both into the scales, we see in reality, that as weight they are both the same, and that, therefore, when taken in proper proportions, they have the same weight. Just as the substance iron, as a measure of weight, represents in relation to the sugar-loaf weight alone, so, in our expression of value, the material object, coat, in relation to the linen, represents value alone.

Here, however, the analogy ceases. The iron, in the expression of the weight of the sugar-loaf, represents a natural property common to both bodies, namely their weight; but the coat, in the expression of value of the linen, represents a non-natural property of both, something purely social, namely, their value.

Since the relative form of value of a commodity — the linen, for example — expresses the value of that commodity, as being something wholly different from its substance and properties, as being, for instance, coat-like, we see that this expression itself indicates that some social relation lies at the bottom of it. With the equivalent form it is just the contrary. The very essence of this form is that the material commodity itself — the coat — just as it is, expresses value, and is endowed with the form of value by Nature itself. Of course this holds good only so long as the value-relation exists, in which the coat stands in the position of equivalent to the linen.[22] Since, however, the properties of a thing are not the result of its relations to other things, but only manifest themselves in such relations, the coat seems to be endowed with its equivalent form, its property of being directly exchangeable, just as much by Nature as it is endowed with the property of being heavy, or the capacity to keep us warm. Hence the enigmatical character of the equivalent form which escapes the notice of the bourgeois political economist, until this form, completely developed, confronts him in the shape of money. He then seeks to explain away the mystical character of gold and silver, by substituting for them less dazzling commodities, and by reciting, with ever renewed satisfaction, the catalogue of all possible commodities which at one time or another have played the part of equivalent. He has not the least suspicion that the most simple expression of value, such as 20 yds. of linen = 1 coat, already propounds the riddle of the equivalent form for our solution.

The body of the commodity that serves as the equivalent, figures as the materialisation of human labour in the abstract, and is at the same time the product of some specifically useful concrete labour. This concrete labour becomes, therefore, the medium for expressing abstract human labour. If on the one hand the coat ranks as nothing but the embodiment of abstract human labour, so, on the other hand, the tailoring which is actually embodied in it, counts as nothing but the form under which that abstract labour is realised. In the expression of value of the linen, the utility of the tailoring consists, not in making clothes, but in making an object, which we at once recognise to be Value, and therefore to be a congelation of labour, but of labour indistinguishable from that realised in the value of the linen. In order to act as such a mirror of value, the labour of tailoring must reflect nothing besides its own abstract quality of being human labour generally.

In tailoring, as well as in weaving, human labour-power is expended. Both, therefore, possess the general property of being human labour, and may, therefore, in certain cases, such as in the production of value, have to be considered under this aspect alone. There is nothing mysterious in this. But in the expression of value there is a complete turn of the tables. For instance, how is the fact to be expressed that weaving creates the value of the linen, not by virtue of being weaving, as such, but by reason of its general property of being human labour? Simply by opposing to weaving that other particular form of concrete labour (in this instance tailoring), which produces the equivalent of the product of weaving. Just as the coat in its bodily form became a direct expression of value, so now does tailoring, a concrete form of labour, appear as the direct and palpable embodiment of human labour generally.

Hence, the second peculiarity of the equivalent form is, that concrete labour becomes the form under which its opposite, abstract human labour, manifests itself.

But because this concrete labour, tailoring in our case, ranks as, and is directly identified with, undifferentiated human labour, it also ranks as identical with any other sort of labour, and therefore with that embodied in the linen. Consequently, although, like all other commodity producing labour, it is the labour of private individuals, yet, at the same time, it ranks as labour directly social in its character. This is the reason why it results in a product directly exchangeable with other commodities. We have then a third peculiarity of the equivalent form, namely, that the labour of private individuals takes the form of its opposite, labour directly social in its form.

The two latter peculiarities of the equivalent form will become more intelligible if we go back to the great thinker who was the first to analyse so many forms, whether of thought, society, or Nature, and amongst them also the form of value. I mean Aristotle.

In the first place, he clearly enunciates that the money-form of commodities is only the further development of the simple form of value-i.e., of the expression of the value of one commodity in some other commodity taken at random; for he says -- ;:

5 beds = 1 house (ί   ἐ   ἀ   ì   ì

     ί   ) is not to be
distinguished from
5 beds = so much money.

(ί   ἐ   ἀ   ì   ì   ί...

ö   ί   ἐ   ί   )

He further sees that the value-relation which gives rise to this expression makes it necessary that the house should qualitatively be made the equal of the bed, and that, without such an equalisation, these two clearly different things could not be compared with each other as commensurable quantities. "Exchange," he says, "cannot take place

without equality, and equality not without commensurability". (ὔ   ' ì   ό

η̣   ῂ   ὔ   **η̣**   ί

). Here, however, he comes to a stop, and gives up the further analysis of the

form of value. "It is, however, in reality, impossible (ῇ   ἐ   ὔ   ἀ

η̣   ία ἀ   ύ   ), that such unlike things can
be commensurable" — i.e., qualitatively equal. Such an equalisation can only be something foreign to their real nature, consequently only "a makeshift for practical purposes."

Aristotle therefore, himself, tells us, what barred the way to his further analysis; it was the absence of any concept of value. What is that equal something, that common substance, which admits of the value of the beds being expressed by a house? Such a thing, in truth, cannot exist, says Aristotle. And why not? Compared with the beds, the house does represent something equal to them, in so far as it represents what is really equal, both in the beds and the house. And that is — human labour.

There was, however, an important fact which prevented Aristotle from seeing that, to attribute value to commodities, is merely a mode of expressing all labour as equal human labour, and consequently as labour of equal quality. Greek society was founded upon slavery, and had, therefore, for its natural basis, the inequality of men and of their labour-powers. The secret of the expression of value, namely, that all kinds of labour are equal and equivalent, because, and so far as they are human labour in general, cannot be deciphered, until the notion of human equality has already acquired the fixity of a popular prejudice. This, however, is possible only in a society in which the great mass of the produce of labour takes the form of commodities, in which, consequently, the dominant relation between man and man, is that of owners of commodities. The brilliancy of Aristotle's genius is shown by this alone, that he discovered, in the expression of the value of commodities, a relation of equality. The peculiar conditions of the society in which he lived, alone prevented him from discovering what, "in truth," was at the bottom of this equality.

4. The Elementary Form of value considered as a whole

The elementary form of value of a commodity is contained in the equation, expressing its value-relation to another commodity of a different kind, or in its exchange-relation to the-same. The value of commodity A, is qualitatively expressed, by the fact that commodity B is directly exchangeable with it. Its value is quantitatively expressed by the fact, that a definite quantity of B is exchangeable with a definite quantity of A. In other words, the value of a commodity obtains independent and definite expression, by taking the form of exchange-value. When, at the beginning of this chapter, we said, in common parlance, that a commodity is both a use-value and an exchange-value, we were, accurately speaking, wrong. A commodity is a use-value or object of utility, and a value. It manifests itself as this two-fold thing, that it is, as soon as its value assumes an independent form — viz., the form of exchange-value. It never assumes this form when isolated, but only when placed in a value or exchange relation with another commodity of a different kind. When once we know this, such a mode of expression does no harm; it simply serves as an abbreviation.

Our analysis has shown, that the form or expression of the value of a commodity originates in the nature of value, and not that value and its magnitude originate in the mode of their expression as exchange-value. This, however, is the delusion as well of the mercantilists and their recent revivers, Ferrier, Ganilh,[23] and others, as also of their antipodes, the modern bagmen of Free-trade, such as Bastiat. The mercantilists lay special stress on the qualitative aspect of the expression of value, and consequently on the equivalent form of commodities, which attains its full perfection in money. The modern hawkers of Free-trade, who must get rid of their article at any price, on the other hand, lay most stress on the quantitative aspect of the relative form of value. For them there consequently exists neither value, nor magnitude of value, anywhere except in its expression by means of the exchange relation of commodities, that is, in the daily list of prices current. Macleod, who has taken upon himself to dress up the confused ideas of Lombard Street in the most learned finery, is a successful cross between the superstitious mercantilists, and the enlightened Free-trade bagmen.

A close scrutiny of the expression of the value of A in terms of B, contained in the equation expressing the value-relation of A to B, has shown us that, within that relation, the bodily form of A figures only as a use-value, the bodily form of B only as the form or aspect of value. The opposition or contrast existing internally in each commodity between use-value and value, is, therefore, made evident externally by two commodities being placed in such relation to each other, that the commodity whose value it is sought to express, figures directly as a mere use-value, while the commodity in which that value is to be expressed, figures directly as mere exchange-value. Hence the elementary form of value of a commodity is the elementary form in which the contrast contained in that commodity, between use-value and value, becomes apparent.

Every product of labour is, in all states of society, a use-value; but it is only at a definite historical epoch in a society's development that such a product becomes a commodity, viz., at the epoch when the labour spent on the production of a useful article becomes expressed as one of the objective qualities of that article, i.e., as its value. It therefore follows that the elementary value-form is also the primitive form under which a product of labour appears historically as a commodity, and that the gradual transformation of such products into commodities, proceeds pari passu with the development of the value-form.

We perceive, at first sight, the deficiencies of the elementary form of value: it is a mere germ, which must undergo a series of metamorphoses before it can ripen into the price-form.

The expression of the value of commodity A in terms of any other commodity B, merely distinguishes the value from the use-value of A, and therefore places A merely in a relation of exchange with a single different commodity, B; but it is still far from expressing A's qualitative equality, and quantitative proportionality, to all commodities. To the elementary relative value-form of a commodity, there corresponds the single equivalent form of one other commodity. Thus, in the relative expression of value of the linen, the coat assumes the form of equivalent, or of being directly exchangeable, only in relation to a single commodity, the linen.

Nevertheless, the elementary form of value passes by an easy transition into a more complete form. It is true that by means of the elementary form, the value of a commodity A, becomes expressed in terms of one, and only one, other commodity. But that one may be a commodity of any kind, coat, iron, corn, or anything else. Therefore, according as A is placed in relation with one or the other, we get for one and the same commodity, different elementary expressions of value.[24] The number of such possible expressions is limited only by the number of the different kinds of commodities distinct from it. The isolated expression of A's value, is therefore convertible into a series, prolonged to any length, of the different elementary expressions of that value.

B. Total or Expanded Form of value

Com. A=u Com. B or=v Com. C or=w Com. D or=x Com. E or=&c.

(20 byards of linen=1 coat or=10 lb tea or=40 lb coffee or=1 quarter corn or=2 ounces gold or=1/2 ton iron or=&c.)

1. The Expanded Relative form of value

The value of a single commodity, the linen, for example, is now expressed in terms of numberless other elements of the world of commodities. Every other commodity now becomes a mirror of the linen's value.[25] It is thus, that for the first time, this value shows itself in its true light as a congelation of undifferentiated human labour. For the labour that creates it, now stands expressly revealed, as labour that ranks equally with every other sort of human labour, no matter what its form, whether tailoring, ploughing, mining, &c., and no matter, therefore, whether it is realised in coats, corn, iron, or gold. The linen, by virtue of the form of its value, now stands in a social relation, no longer with only one other kind of commodity, but with the whole world of commodities. As a commodity, it is a citizen of that world. At the same time, the interminable series of value equations implies, that as regards the value of a commodity, it is a matter of indifference under what particular form, or kind, of use-value it appears.

In the first form, 20 yds. of linen = 1 coat, it might, for ought that otherwise appears, be pure accident, that these two commodities are exchangeable in definite quantities. In the second form, on the contrary, we perceive at once the background that determines, and is essentially different from, this accidental appearance. The value of the linen remains unaltered in magnitude, whether expressed in coats, coffee, or iron, or in numberless different commodities, the property of as many different owners. The accidental relation between two individual commodity-owners disappears. It becomes plain, that it is not the exchange of commodities which regulates the magnitude of their value; but, on the contrary, that it is the magnitude of their value which controls their exchange proportions.

2. The particular Equivalent form

Each commodity, such as, coat, tea, corn, iron, &c., figures in the expression of value of the linen, as an equivalent, and, consequently, as a thing that is value. The bodily form of each of these commodities figures now as a particular equivalent form, one out of many. In the same way the manifold concrete useful kinds of labour, embodied in these different commodities, rank now as so many different forms of the realisation, or manifestation, of undifferentiated human labour.

3. Defects of the Total or Expanded form of value

In the first place, the relative expression of value is incomplete because the series representing it is interminable. The chain of which each equation of value is a link, is liable at any moment to be lengthened by each new kind of commodity that comes into existence and furnishes the material for a fresh expression of value. In the second place, it is a many-coloured mosaic of disparate and independent expressions of value. And lastly, if, as must be the case, the relative value of each commodity in turn, becomes expressed in this expanded form, we get for each of them a relative value-form, different in every case, and consisting of an interminable series of expressions of value. The defects of the expanded relative value-form are reflected in the corresponding equivalent form. Since the bodily form of each single commodity is one particular equivalent form amongst numberless others, we have, on the whole, nothing but fragmentary equivalent forms, each excluding the others. In the same way, also, the special, concrete, useful kind of labour embodied in each particular equivalent, is presented only as a particular kind of labour, and therefore not as an exhaustive representative of human labour generally. The latter, indeed, gains adequate manifestation in the totality of its manifold, particular, concrete forms. But, in that case, its expression in an infinite series is ever incomplete and deficient in unity.

The expanded relative value-form is, however, nothing but the sum of the elementary relative expressions or equations of the first kind, such as:

20 yards of linen = 1 coat 20 yards of linen = 10 Ibs. of tea, etc.

Each of these implies the corresponding inverted equation,

1 coat = 20 yards of linen 10 Ibs. of tea = 20 yards of linen, etc.

In fact, when a person exchanges his linen for many other commodities, and thus expresses its value in a series of other commodities, it necessarily follows, that the various owners of the latter exchange them for the linen, and consequently express the value of their various commodities in one and the same third commodity, the linen. If then, we reverse the series, 20 yards of linen = 1 coat or = 10 Ibs. of tea, etc., that is to say, if we give expression to the converse relation already implied in the series, we get,

C. The General Form of Value

1 coat 10 lbs. of tea 40 lbs. of coffee 1 quarter of corn 2 ounces of gold 1/2 a ton of iron x com. A., etc	= 20 yards of linen

1. The altered character of the form of value

All commodities now express their value (1) in an elementary form, because in a single commodity; (2) with unity, because in one and the same commodity. This form of value is elementary and the same for all, therefore general.

The forms A and B were fit only to express the value of a commodity as something distinct from its use-value or material form.

The first-form, A, furnishes such equations as the following: -- 1 coat = 20 yards of linen, 10 lbs. of tea = 1/2 ton of iron. The value of the coat is equated to linen, that of the tea to iron. But to be equated to linen, and again to iron, is to be as different as are linen and iron. This forms it is plain, occurs practically only in the first beginning, when the products of labour are converted into commodities by accidental and occasional exchanges.

The second form, B, distinguishes, in a more adequate manner than the first, the value of a commodity from its use-value, for the value of the coat is there placed in contrast under all possible shapes with the bodily form of the coat; it is equated to linen, to iron, to tea, in short, to everything else, only not to itself, the coat. On the other hand, any general expression of value common to all is directly excluded; for, in the equation of value of each commodity, all other commodities now appear only under the form of equivalents. The expanded form of value comes into actual existence for the first time so soon as a particular product of labour, such as cattle, is no longer exceptionally, but habitually, exchanged for various other commodities.

The third and lastly developed form expresses the values of the whole world of commodities in terms of a single commodity set apart for the purpose, namely, the linen, and thus represents to us their values by means of their equality with linen. The value of every commodity is now, by being equated to linen, not only differentiated from its own use-value, but from all other use-values generally, and is, by that very fact, expressed as that which is common to all commodities. By this form, commodities are, for the first time, effectively brought into relation with one another as values, or made to appear as exchange-values.

The two earlier forms either express the value of each commodity in terms of a single commodity of a different kind, or in a series of many such commodities. In both cases, it is, so to say, the special business of each single commodity to find an expression for its value, and this it does without the help of the others. These others, with respect to the former, play the passive parts of equivalents. The general form of value, C, results from the joint action of the whole world of commodities, and from that alone. A commodity can acquire a general expression of its value only by all other commodities, simultaneously with it, expressing their values in the same equivalent; and every new commodity must follow suit. It thus becomes evident that since the existence of commodities as values is purely social, this social existence can be expressed by the totality of their social relations alone, and consequently that the form of their value must be a socially recognised form.

All commodities being equated to linen now appear not only as qualitatively equal as values generally, but also as values whose magnitudes are capable of comparison. By expressing the magnitudes of their values in one and the same material, the linen, those magnitudes are also compared with each other For instance, 10 Ibs. of tea = 20 yards of linen, and 40 lbs. of coffee = 20 yards of linen. Therefore, 10 Ibs of tea = 40 Ibs. of coffee. In other words, there is contained in 1 lb. of coffee only one-fourth as much substance of value — labour — as is contained in 1 lb. of tea.

The general form of relative value, embracing the whole world of commodities, converts the single commodity that is excluded from the rest, and made to play the part of equivalent — here the linen — into the universal equivalent. The bodily form of the linen is now the form assumed in common by the values of all commodities; it therefore becomes directly exchangeable with all and every of them. The substance linen becomes the visible incarnation, the social chrysalis state of every kind of human labour. Weaving, which is the labour of certain private individuals producing a particular article, linen, acquires in consequence a social character, the character of equality with all other kinds of labour. The innumerable equations of which the general form of value is composed, equate in turn the labour embodied in the linen to that embodied in every other commodity, and they thus convert weaving into the general form of manifestation of undifferentiated human labour. In this manner the labour realised in the values of commodities is presented not only under its negative aspect, under which abstraction is made from every concrete form and useful property of actual work, but its own positive nature is made to reveal itself expressly. The general value-form is the reduction of all kinds of actual labour to their common character of being human labour generally, of being the expenditure of human labour-power.

The general value-form, which represents all products of labour as mere congelations of undifferentiated human labour, shows by its very structure that it is the social resume of the world of commodities. That form consequently makes it indisputably evident that in the world of commodities the character possessed by all labour of being human labour constitutes its specific social character.

2. The Interdependent Development of the Relative Form of Value, and of the Equivalent Form

The degree of development of the relative form of value corresponds to that of the equivalent form. But we must bear in mind that the development of the latter is only the expression and result of the development of the former.

The primary or isolated relative form of value of one commodity converts some other commodity into an isolated equivalent. The expanded form of relative value, which is the expression of the value of one commodity in terms of all other commodities, endows those other commodities with the character of particular equivalents differing in kind. And lastly, a particular kind of commodity acquires the character of universal equivalent, because all other commodities make it the material in which they uniformly express their value.

The antagonism between the relative form of value and the equivalent form, the two poles of the value-form, is developed concurrently with that form itself.

The first form, 20 yds. of linen = one coat, already contains this antagonism, without as yet fixing it. According as we read this equation forwards or backwards, the parts played by the linen and the coat are different. In the one case the relative value of the linen is expressed in the coat, in the other case the relative value of the coat is expressed in the linen. In this first form of value, therefore, it is difficult to grasp the polar contrast.

Form B shows that only one single commodity at a time can completely expand its relative value, and that it acquires this expanded form only because, and in so far as, all other commodities are, with respect to it, equivalents. Here we cannot reverse the equation, as we can the equation 20 yds. of linen = 1 coat, without altering its general character, and converting it from the expanded form of value into the general form of value.

Finally, the form C gives to the world of commodities a general social relative form of value, because, and in so far as, thereby all commodities, with the exception of one, are excluded from the equivalent form. A single commodity, the linen, appears therefore to have acquired the character of direct exchangeability with every other commodity because, and in so far as, this character is denied to every other commodity.[26]

The commodity that figures as universal equivalent, is, on the other hand, excluded from the relative value-form. If the linen, or any other commodity serving as universal equivalent, were, at the same time, to share in the relative form of value, it would have to serve as its own equivalent. We should then have 20 yds. of linen = 20 yds. of linen; this tautology expresses neither value, nor magnitude of value. In order to express the relative value of the universal equivalent, we must rather reverse the form C. This equivalent has no relative form of value in common with other commodities, but its value is relatively expressed by a never ending series of other commodities.

Thus, the expanded form of relative value, or form B, now shows itself as the specific form of relative value for the equivalent commodity.

3. Transition from the General Form of Value to the Money-Form

The universal equivalent form is a form of value in general. It can, therefore, be assumed by any commodity. On the other hand, if a commodity be found to have assumed the universal equivalent form (form C), this is only because and in so far as it has been excluded from the rest of all other commodities as their equivalent, and that by their own act. And from the moment that this exclusion becomes finally restricted to one particular commodity, from that moment only, the general form of relative value of the world of commodities obtains real consistence and general social validity.

The particular commodity, with whose bodily form the equivalent form is thus socially identified, now becomes the money-commodity, or serves as money. It becomes the special social function of that commodity, and consequently its social monopoly, to play within the world of commodities the part of the universal equivalent. Amongst the commodities which, in form B, figure as particular equivalents of the linen, and, in form C, express in common their relative values in linen, this foremost place has been attained by one in particular-namely, gold. If, then, in form C we replace the linen by gold, we get,

D. *The Money-Form*

20 yards of linen	=	
1 coat	=	
10 lb of tea	=	2 ounces of gold
40 lb of coffee	=	
1 qr. of corn	=	
1/2 a ton of iron	=	
x commodity A	=	

In passing from form A to form B, and from the latter to form C, the changes are fundamental. On the other hand, there is no difference between forms C and D, except that, in the latter, gold has assumed the equivalent form in the place of linen. Gold is in form D, what linen was in form C — the universal equivalent. The progress consists in this alone, that the character of direct and universal exchangeability — in other words, that the universal equivalent form — has now, by social custom, become finally identified with the substance, gold.

Gold is now money with reference to all other commodities only because it was previously, with reference to them, a simple commodity. Like all other commodities, it was also capable of serving as an equivalent, either as simple equivalent in isolated exchanges, or as particular equivalent by the side of others. Gradually it began to serve, within varying limits, as universal equivalent. So soon as it monopolises this position in the expression of value for the world of commodities, it becomes the money commodity, and then, and not till then, does form D become distinct from form C, and the general form of value become changed into the money-form.

The elementary expression of the relative value of a single commodity, such as linen, in terms of the commodity, such as gold, that plays the part of money, is the price-form of that commodity. The price-form of the linen is therefore

20 yards of linen = 2 ounces of gold, or, if 2 ounces of gold when coined are £2, 20 yards of linen = £2.

The difficulty in forming a concept of the money-form, consists in clearly comprehending the universal equivalent form, and as a necessary corollary, the general form of value, form C. The latter is deducible from form B, the expanded form of value, the essential component element of which, we saw, is form A, 20 yards of linen = 1 coat or x commodity A = y commodity B. The simple commodity-form is therefore the germ of the money-form.

Section 4 -- The Fetishism of Commodities and the Secret Thereof

A commodity appears, at first sight, a very trivial thing, and easily understood. Its analysis shows that it is, in reality, a very queer thing, abounding in metaphysical subtleties and theological niceties. So far as it is a value in use, there is nothing mysterious about it, whether we consider it from the point of view that by its properties it is capable of satisfying human wants, or from the point that those properties are the product of human labour. It is as clear as noon-day, that man, by his industry, changes the forms of the materials furnished by Nature, in such a way as to make them useful to him. The form of wood, for instance, is altered, by making a table out of it. Yet, for all that, the table continues to be that common, every-day thing, wood. But, so soon as it steps forth as a commodity, it is changed into something transcendent. It not only stands with its feet on the ground, but, in relation to all other commodities, it stands on its head, and evolves out of its wooden brain grotesque ideas, far more wonderful than "table-turning" ever was.

The mystical character of commodities does not originate, therefore, in their use-value. Just as little does it proceed from the nature of the determining factors of value. For, in the first place, however varied the useful kinds of labour, or productive activities, may be, it is a physiological fact, that they are functions of the human organism, and that each such function, whatever may be its nature or form, is essentially the expenditure of human brain, nerves, muscles, &c. Secondly, with regard to that which forms the ground-work for the quantitative determination of value, namely, the duration of that expenditure, or the quantity of labour, it is quite clear that there is a palpable difference between its quantity and quality. In all states of society, the labour-time that it costs to produce the means of subsistence, must necessarily be an object of interest to mankind, though not of equal interest in different stages of development. [27] And lastly, from the moment that men in any way work for one another, their labour assumes a social form.

Whence, then, arises the enigmatical character of the product of labour, so soon as it assumes the form of commodities? Clearly from this form itself. The equality of all sorts of human labour is expressed objectively by their products all being equally values; the measure of the expenditure of labour-power by the duration of that expenditure, takes the form of the quantity of value of the products of labour; and finally the mutual relations of the producers, within which the social character of their labour affirms itself, take the form of a social relation between the products.

A commodity is therefore a mysterious thing, simply because in it the social character of men's labour appears to them as an objective character stamped upon the product of that labour; because the relation of the producers to the sum total of their own labour is presented to them as a social relation, existing not between themselves, but between the products of their labour. This is the reason why the products of labour become commodities, social things whose qualities are at the same time perceptible and imperceptible by the senses. In the same way the light from an object is perceived by us not as the subjective excitation of our optic nerve, but as the objective form of something outside the eye itself. But, in the act of seeing, there is at all events, an actual passage of light from one thing to another, from the external object to the eye. There is a physical relation between physical things. But it is different with commodities. There, the existence of the things qua commodities, and the value-relation between the products of labour which stamps them as commodities, have absolutely no connexion with their physical properties and with the material relations arising therefrom. There it is a definite social relation between men, that assumes, in their eyes, the fantastic form of a relation between things. In order, therefore, to find an analogy, we must have recourse to the mist-enveloped regions of the religious world. In that world the productions of the human brain appear as independent beings endowed with life, and entering into relation both with one another and the human race. So it is in the world of commodities with the products of men's hands. This I call the Fetishism which attaches itself to the products of labour, so soon as they are produced as commodities, and which is therefore inseparable from the production of commodities.

This Fetishism of commodities has its origin, as the foregoing analysis has already shown, in the peculiar social character of the labour that produces them.

As a general rule, articles of utility become commodities, only because they are products of the labour of private individuals or groups of individuals who carry on their work independently of each other. The sum total of the labour of all these private individuals forms the aggregate labour of society. Since the producers do not come into social contact with each other until they exchange their products, the specific social character of each producer's labour does not show itself except in the act of exchange. In other words, the labour of the individual asserts itself as a part of the labour of society, only by means of the relations which the act of exchange establishes directly between the products, and indirectly, through them, between the producers. To the latter, therefore, the relations connecting the labour of one individual with that of the rest appear, not as direct social relations between individuals at work, but as what they really are, material relations between persons and social relations between things. It is only by being exchanged that the products of labour acquire, as values, one uniform social status, distinct from their varied forms of existence as objects of utility. This division of a product into a useful thing and a value becomes practically important, only when exchange has acquired such an extension that useful articles are produced for the purpose of being exchanged, and their character as values has therefore to be taken into account, beforehand, during production. From this moment the labour of the individual producer acquires socially a two-fold character. On the one hand, it must, as a definite useful kind of labour, satisfy a definite social want, and thus hold its place as part and parcel of the collective labour of all, as a branch of a social division of labour that has sprung up spontaneously. On the other hand, it can satisfy the manifold wants of the individual producer himself, only in so far as the mutual exchangeability of all kinds of useful private labour is an established social fact, and therefore the private useful labour of each producer ranks on an equality with that of all others. The equalisation of the most different kinds of labour can be the result only of an abstraction from their inequalities, or of reducing them to their common denominator, viz. expenditure of human labour-power or human labour in the abstract. The two-fold social character of the labour of the individual appears to him, when reflected in his brain, only under those forms which are impressed upon that labour in every-day practice by the exchange of products. In this way, the character that his own labour possesses of being socially useful takes the form of the condition, that the product must be not only useful, but useful for others, and the social character that his particular labour has of being the equal of all other particular kinds of labour, takes the form that all the physically different articles that are the products of labour. have one common quality, viz., that of having value.

Hence, when we bring the products of our labour into relation with each other as values, it is not because we see in these articles the material receptacles of homogeneous human labour. Quite the contrary: whenever, by an exchange, we equate as values our different products, by that very act, we also equate, as human labour, the different kinds of labour expended upon them. We are not aware of this, nevertheless we do it.[28] Value, therefore, does not stalk about with a label describing what it is. It is value, rather, that converts every product into a social hieroglyphic. Later on, we try to decipher the hieroglyphic, to get behind the secret of our own social products; for to stamp an object of utility as a value, is just as much a social product as language. The recent scientific discovery, that the products of labour, so far as they are values, are but material expressions of the human labour spent in their production, marks, indeed, an epoch in the history of the development of the human race, but, by no means, dissipates the mist through which the social character of labour appears to us to be an objective character of the products themselves. The fact, that in the particular form of production with which we are dealing, viz., the production of commodities, the specific social character of private labour carried on independently, consists in the equality of every kind of that labour, by virtue of its being human labour, which character, therefore, assumes in the product the form of value — this fact appears to the producers, notwithstanding the discovery above referred to, to be just as real and final, as the fact, that, after the discovery by science of the component gases of air, the atmosphere itself remained unaltered.

What, first of all, practically concerns producers when they make an exchange, is the question, how much of some other product they get for their own? in what proportions the products are exchangeable? When these proportions have, by custom, attained a certain stability, they appear to result from the nature of the products, so that, for instance, one ton of iron and two ounces of gold appear as naturally to be of equal value as a pound of gold and a pound of iron in spite of their different physical and chemical qualities appear to be of equal weight. The character of having value, when once impressed upon products, obtains fixity only by reason of their acting and re-acting upon each other as quantities of value. These quantities vary continually, independently of the will, foresight and action of the producers. To them, their own social action takes the form of the action of objects, which rule the producers instead of being ruled by them. It requires a fully developed production of commodities before, from accumulated experience alone, the scientific conviction springs up, that all the different kinds of private labour, which are carried on independently of each other, and yet as spontaneously developed branches of the social division of labour, are continually being reduced to the quantitative proportions in which society requires them. And why? Because, in the midst of all the accidental and ever fluctuating exchange-relations between the products, the labour-time socially necessary for their production forcibly asserts itself like an over-riding law of Nature. The law of gravity thus asserts itself when a house falls about our ears.[29] The determination of the magnitude of value by labour-time is therefore a secret, hidden under the apparent fluctuations in the relative values of commodities. Its discovery, while removing all appearance of mere accidentality from the determination of the magnitude of the values of products, yet in no way alters the mode in which that determination takes place.

Man's reflections on the forms of social life, and consequently, also, his scientific analysis of those forms, take a course directly opposite to that of their actual historical development. He begins, post festum, with the results of the process of development ready to hand before him. The characters that stamp products as commodities, and whose establishment is a necessary preliminary to the circulation of commodities, have already acquired the stability of natural, self-understood forms of social life, before man seeks to decipher, not their historical character, for in his eyes they are immutable, but their meaning. Consequently it was the analysis of the prices of commodities that alone led to the determination of the magnitude of value, and it was the common expression of all commodities in money that alone led to the establishment of their characters as values. It is, however, just this ultimate money-form of the world of commodities that actually conceals, instead of disclosing, the social character of private labour, and the social relations between the individual producers. When I state that coats or boots stand in a relation to linen, because it is the universal incarnation of abstract human labour, the absurdity of the statement is self-evident. Nevertheless, when the producers of coats and boots compare those articles with linen, or, what is the same thing, with gold or silver, as the universal equivalent, they express the relation between their own private labour and the collective labour of society in the same absurd form.

The categories of bourgeois economy consist of such like forms. They are forms of thought expressing with social validity the conditions and relations of a definite, historically determined mode of production, viz., the production of commodities. The whole mystery of commodities, all the magic and necromancy that surrounds the products of labour as long as they take the form of commodities, vanishes therefore, so soon as we come to other forms of production.

Since Robinson Crusoe's experiences are a favourite theme with political economists,[30] let us take a look at him on his island. Moderate though he be, yet some few wants he has to satisfy, and must therefore do a little useful work of various sorts, such as making tools and furniture, taming goats, fishing and hunting. Of his prayers and the like we take no account, since they are a source of pleasure to him, and he looks upon them as so much recreation. In spite of the variety of his work, he knows that his labour, whatever its form, is but the activity of one and the same Robinson, and consequently, that it consists of nothing but different modes of human labour. Necessity itself compels him to apportion his time accurately between his different kinds of work. Whether one kind occupies a greater space in his general activity than another, depends on the difficulties, greater or less as the case may be, to be overcome in attaining the useful effect aimed at. This our friend Robinson soon learns by experience, and having rescued a watch, ledger, and pen and ink from the wreck, commences, like a true-born Briton, to keep a set of books. His stock-book contains a list of the objects of utility that belong to him, of the operations necessary for their production; and lastly, of the labour-time that definite quantities of those objects have, on an average, cost him. All the relations between Robinson and the objects that form this wealth of his own creation, are here so simple and clear as to be intelligible without exertion, even to Mr. Sedley Taylor. And yet those relations contain all that is essential to the determination of value.

Let us now transport ourselves from Robinson's island bathed in light to the European middle ages shrouded in darkness. Here, instead of the independent man, we find everyone dependent, serfs and lords, vassals and suzerains, laymen and clergy. Personal dependence here characterises the social relations of production just as much as it does the other spheres of life organised on the basis of that production. But for the very reason that personal dependence forms the ground-work of society, there is no necessity for labour and its products to assume a fantastic form different from their reality. They take the shape, in the transactions of society, of services in kind and payments in kind. Here the particular and natural form of labour, and not, as in a society based on production of commodities, its general abstract form is the immediate social form of labour. Compulsory labour is just as properly measured by time, as commodity-producing labour; but every serf knows that what he expends in the service of his lord, is a definite quantity of his own personal labour-power. The tithe to be rendered to the priest is more matter of fact than his blessing. No matter, then, what we may think of the parts played by the different classes of people themselves in this society, the social relations between individuals in the performance of their labour, appear at all events as their own mutual personal relations, and are not disguised under the shape of social relations between the products of labour.

For an example of labour in common or directly associated labour, we have no occasion to go back to that spontaneously developed form which we find on the threshold of the history of all civilised races.[31] We have one close at hand in the patriarchal industries of a peasant family, that produces corn, cattle, yarn, linen, and clothing for home use. These different articles are, as regards the family, so many products of its labour, but as between themselves, they are not commodities. The different kinds of labour, such as tillage, cattle tending, spinning, weaving and making clothes, which result in the various products, are in themselves, and such as they are, direct social functions, because functions of the family, which, just as much as a society based on the production of commodities, possesses a spontaneously developed system of division of labour. The distribution of the work within the family, and the regulation of the labour-time of the several members, depend as well upon differences of age and sex as upon natural conditions varying with the seasons. The labour-power of each individual, by its very nature, operates in this case merely as a definite portion of the whole labour-power of the family, and therefore, the measure of the expenditure of individual labour-power by its duration, appears here by its very nature as a social character of their labour.

Let us now picture to ourselves, by way of change, a community of free individuals, carrying on their work with the means of production in common, in which the labour-power of all the different individuals is consciously applied as the combined labour-power of the community. All the characteristics of Robinson's labour are here repeated, but with this difference, that they are social, instead of individual. Everything produced by him was exclusively the result of his own personal labour, and therefore simply an object of use for himself. The total product of our community is a social product. One portion serves as fresh means of production and remains social. But another portion is consumed by the members as means of subsistence. A distribution of this portion amongst them is consequently necessary. The mode of this distribution will vary with the productive organisation of the community, and the degree of historical development attained by the producers. We will assume, but merely for the sake of a parallel with the production of commodities, that the share of each individual producer in the means of subsistence is determined by his labour-time. Labour-time would, in that case, play a double part. Its apportionment in accordance with a definite social plan maintains the proper proportion between the different kinds of work to be done and the various wants of the community. On the other hand, it also serves as a measure of the portion of the common labour borne by each individual, and of his share in the part of the total product destined for individual consumption. The social relations of the individual producers, with regard both to their labour and to its products, are in this case perfectly simple and intelligible, and that with regard not only to production but also to distribution.

The religious world is but the reflex of the real world. And for a society based upon the production of commodities, in which the producers in general enter into social relations with one another by treating their products as commodities and values, whereby they reduce their individual private labour to the standard of homogeneous human labour- for such a society, Christianity with its cultus of abstract man, more especially in its bourgeois developments, Protestantism, Deism, &c., is the most fitting form of religion. In the ancient Asiatic and other ancient modes of production, we find that the conversion of products into commodities, and therefore the conversion of men into producers of commodities, holds a subordinate place, which, however, increases in importance as the primitive communities approach nearer and nearer to their dissolution. Trading nations, properly so called, exist in the ancient world only in its interstices, like the gods of Epicurus in the Intermundia, or like Jews in the pores of Polish society. Those ancient social organisms of production are, as compared with bourgeois society, extremely simple and transparent. But they are founded either on the immature development of man individually, who has not yet severed the umbilical cord that unites him with his fellowmen in a primitive tribal community, or upon direct relations of subjection. They can arise and exist only when the development of the productive power of labour has not risen beyond a low stage, and when, therefore, the social relations within the sphere of material life, between man and man, and between man and Nature, are correspondingly narrow. This narrowness is reflected in the ancient worship of Nature, and in the other elements of the popular religions. The religious reflex of the real world can, in any case, only then finally vanish, when the practical relations of every-day life offer to man none but perfectly intelligible and reasonable relations with regard to his fellowmen and to Nature.

The life-process of society, which is based on the process of material production, does not strip off its mystical veil until it is treated as production by freely associated men, and is consciously regulated by them in accordance with a settled plan. This, however, demands for society a certain material ground-work or set of conditions of existence which in their turn are the spontaneous product of a long and painful process of development.

Political Economy has indeed analysed, however incompletely,[32] value and its magnitude, and has discovered what lies beneath these forms. But it has never once asked the question why labour is represented by the value of its product and labour-time by the magnitude of that value.[33] These formulae, which bear it stamped upon them in unmistakable letters that they belong to a state of society, in which the process of production has the mastery over man, instead of being controlled by him, such formulae appear to the bourgeois intellect to be as much a self-evident necessity imposed by Nature as productive labour itself. Hence forms of social production that preceded the bourgeois form, are treated by the bourgeoisie in much the same way as the Fathers of the Church treated pre-Christian religions. [34]

To what extent some economists are misled by the Fetishism inherent in commodities, or by the objective appearance of the social characteristics of labour, is shown, amongst other ways, by the dull and tedious quarrel over the part played by Nature in the formation of exchange-value. Since exchange-value is a definite social manner of expressing the amount of labour bestowed upon an object, Nature has no more to do with it, than it has in fixing the course of exchange.

The mode of production in which the product takes the form of a commodity, or is produced directly for exchange, is the most general and most embryonic form of bourgeois production. It therefore makes its appearance at an early date in history, though not in the same predominating and characteristic manner as now-a-days. Hence its Fetish character is comparatively easy to be seen through. But when we come to more concrete forms, even this appearance of simplicity vanishes. Whence arose the illusions of the monetary system? To it gold and silver, when serving as money, did not represent a social relation between producers, but were natural objects with strange social properties. And modern economy, which looks down with such disdain on the monetary system, does not its superstition come out as clear as noon-day, whenever it treats of capital? How long is it since economy discarded the physiocratic illusion, that rents grow out of the soil and not out of society?

But not to anticipate, we will content ourselves with yet another example relating to the commodity-form. Could commodities themselves speak, they would say: Our use-value may be a thing that interests men. It is no part of us as objects. What, however, does belong to us as objects, is our value. Our natural intercourse as commodities proves it. In the eyes of each other we are nothing but exchange-values. Now listen how those commodities speak through the mouth of the economist. "Value" — (i.e., exchange-value) "is a property of things, riches" — (i.e., use-value) "of man. Value, in this sense, necessarily implies exchanges, riches do not."[35] "Riches" (use-value) "are the attribute of men, value is the attribute of commodities. A man or a community is rich, a pearl or a diamond is valuable... A pearl or a diamond is valuable" as a pearl or a diamond.[36] So far no chemist has ever discovered exchange-value either in a pearl or a diamond. The economic discoverers of this chemical element, who by-the-by lay special claim to critical acumen, find however that the use-value of objects belongs to them independently of their material properties, while their value, on the other hand, forms a part of them as objects. What confirms them in this view, is the peculiar circumstance that the use-value of objects is realised without exchange, by means of a direct relation between the objects and man, while, on the other hand, their value is realised only by exchange, that is, by means of a social process. Who fails here to call to mind our good friend, Dogberry, who informs neighbour Seacoal, that, "To be a well-favoured man is the gift of fortune; but reading and writing comes by Nature."[37]

Footnotes

[1] Karl Marx, "Zur Kritik der Politischen Oekonomie." Berlin, 1859, p. 3.

[2] "Desire implies want, it is the appetite of the mind, and as natural as hunger to the body.... The greatest number (of things) have their value from supplying the wants of the mind." Nicholas Barbon: "A Discourse Concerning Coining the New Money Lighter. In Answer to Mr. Locke's Considerations," &c., London, 1696, pp. 2, 3.

[3] "Things have an intrinsick vertue" (this is Barbon's special term for value in use) "which in all places have the same vertue; as the loadstone to attract iron" (l.c., p. 6). The property which the magnet possesses of attracting iron, became of use only after by means of that property the polarity of the magnet had been discovered.

[4] "The natural worth of anything consists in its fitness to supply the necessities, or serve the conveniencies of human life." (John Locke, "Some Considerations on the Consequences of the Lowering of Interest, 1691," in Works Edit. Lond., 1777, Vol. II., p. 28.) In English writers of the 17th century we frequently find "worth" in the sense of value in use, and "value" in the sense of exchange-value. This is quite in accordance with the spirit of a language that likes to use a Teutonic word for the actual thing, and a Romance word for its reflexion.

[5] In bourgeois societies the economic fictio juris prevails, that every one, as a buyer, possesses an encyclopedic knowledge of commodities.

[6] "La valeur consiste dans le rapport d'echange qui se trouve entre telle chose et telle autre entre telle mesure d'une production et telle mesure d'une autre." (Le Trosne: "De l'Interet Social." Physiocrates, Ed. Daire. Paris, 1846. P. 889.)

[7] "Nothing can have an intrinsick value." (N. Barbon, t. c., p. 6); or as Butler says — "The value of a thing Is just as much as it will bring."

[8] N. Barbon, l.c., p. 53 and 7.

[9] "The value of them (the necessaries of life), when they are exchanged the one for another, is regulated by the quantity of labour necessarily required, and commonly taken in producing them." ("Some Thoughts on the Interest of Money in General, and Particularly in the Publick Funds, &." Lond., p. 36) This remarkable anonymous work written in the last century, bears no date. It is clear, however, from internal evidence that it appeared in the reign of George II, about 1739 or 1740.

[10] "Toutes les productions d'un meme genre ne forment proprement qu'une masse, dont le prix se determine en general et sans egard aux circonstances particulieres." (Le Trosne, l.c., p. 893.)

[11] K. Marx. l.c., p.6.

[13] Tutti i fenomeni dell'universo, sieno essi prodotti della mano dell'uomo, ovvero delle universali leggi della fisica, non ci danno idea di attuale creazione, ma unicamente di una modificazione della materia. Accostare e separare sono gli unici elementi che l'ingegno umano ritrova analizzando l'idea della riproduzione: e tanto e riproduzione di valore (value in use, although Verri in this passage of his controversy with the Physiocrats is not himself quite certain of the kind of value he is speaking of) e di ricchezze se la terra, l'aria e l'acqua ne' campi si trasmutino in grano, come se colla mano dell'uomo il glutine di un insetto si trasmuti in velluto ovvero alcuni pezzetti di metalio si organizzino a formare una ripetizione."-Pietro Verri, "Meditazioni sulla Economia Politica" [first printed in 1773] in Custodi's edition of the Italian Economists, Parte Moderna, t. XV., p. 22.

[14] Comp. Hegel, "Philosophie des Rechts." Berlin, 1840. P. 250

[15] The reader must note that we are not speaking here of the wages or value that the labourer gets for a given labour-time, but of the value of the commodity in which that labour-time is materialised. Wages is a category that, as yet, has no existence at the present stage of our investigation.

[16] In order to prove that labour alone is that all-sufficient and real measure, by which at all times the value of all commodities can be estimated and compared, Adam Smith says, "Equal quantities of labour must at all times and in all places have the same value for the labourer. In his normal state of health, strength, and activity, and with the average degree of skill that he may possess, he must always give up the same portion of his rest his freedom, and his happiness." ("Wealth of Nations," b. I. ch. V.) On the one hand Adam Smith here (but not everywhere) confuses the determination of value by means of the quantity of labour expended in the production of commodities, with the determination of the values of commodities by means of the value of labour, and seeks in consequence to prove that equal quantities of labour have always the same value. On the other hand he has a presentiment, that labour, so far as it manifests itself in the value of commodities, counts only as expenditure of labour-power, but he treats this expenditure as the mere sacrifice of rest, freedom, and happiness, not as at the same time the normal activity of living beings. But then, he has the modern wage-labourer in his eye. Much more aptly, the anonymous predecessor of Adam Smith, quoted above in Note 1, p. 39 [note 9 etext]. says "one man has employed himself a week in providing this necessary of life ... and he that gives him some other in exchange cannot make a better estimate of what is a proper equivalent, than by computing what cost him just as much labour and time which in effect is no more than exchanging one man's labour in one thing for a time certain, for another man's labour in another thing for the same time." (l.c., p. 39.) [The English language has the advantage of possessing different words for the two aspects of labour here considered. The labour which creates Use-Value, and counts qualitatively, is Work, as distinguished from Labour, that which creates Value and counts quantitatively, is Labour as distinguished from Work-Engels]

[17] The few economists, amongst whom is S. Bailey, who have occupied themselves with the analysis of the form of value, have been unable to arrive at any result, first, because they confuse the form of value with value itself; and second, because, under the coarse influence of the practical bourgeois, they exclusively give their attention to the

quantitative aspect of the question. "The command of quantity ... constitutes value." ("Money and its Vicissitudes." London, 1837, p. 11. By S. Bailey.)

[18] The celebrated Franklin, one of the first economists, after Wm. Petty, who saw through the nature of value, says: "Trade in general being nothing else but the exchange of labour for labour, the value of all things is ... most justly measured by labour." ("The works of B. Franklin, &c.," edited by Sparks. Boston, 1836, Vol. II., p. 267.) Franklin is unconscious that by estimating the value of everything in labour, he makes abstraction from any difference in the sorts of labour exchanged, and thus reduces them all to equal human labour. But although ignorant of this, yet he says it. He speaks first of "the one labour," then of "the other labour," and finally of "labour," without further qualification, as the substance of the value of everything.

[19] In a sort of way, it is with man as with commodities. Since he comes into the world neither with a looking glass in his hand, nor as a Fichtian philosopher, to whom "I am I" is sufficient, man first sees and recognises himself in other men. Peter only establishes his own identity as a man by first comparing himself with Paul as being of like kind. And thereby Paul, just as he stands in his Pauline personality, becomes to Peter the type of the genus homo.

[20] Value is here, as occasionally in the preceding pages, used in sense of value determined as to quantity, or of magnitude of value.

[21] This incongruity between the magnitude of value and its relative expression has, with customary ingenuity, been exploited by vulgar economists. For example-"Once admit that A falls, because B, with which it is exchanged, rises, while no less labour is bestowed in the meantime on A, and your general principle of value falls to the ground.... If he [Ricardo] allowed that when A rises in value relatively to B, B falls in value relatively to A, he cut away the ground on which he rested his grand proposition, that the value of a commodity is ever determined by the labour embodied in it, for if a change in the cost of A alters not only its own value in relation to B, for which it is exchanged, but also the value of B relatively to that of A, though no change has taken place in the quantity of labour to produce B, then not only the doctrine falls to the ground which asserts that the quantity of labour bestowed on an article regulates its value, but also that which affirms the cost of an article to regulate its value' (J. Broadhurst: "Political Economy," London, 1842, pp. 11 and 14.) Mr. Broadhurst might just as well say: consider the fractions 10/20, 10/50, 10/100, &c., the number 10 remains unchanged, and yet its proportional magnitude, its magnitude relatively to the numbers 20, 50, 100 &c., continually diminishes. Therefore the great principle that the magnitude of a whole number, such as 10, is "regulated" by the number of times unity is contained in it, falls to the ground. [The author explains in section 4 of this chapter, pp. 80-81, note 2 (note 33 etext), what he understands by "Vulgar Economy."-Engels]

[22] Such expressions of relations in general, called by Hegel reflex-categories, form a very curious class. For instance, one man is king only because other men stand in the relation of subjects to him. They, on the contrary, imagine that they are subjects because he is king.

[23] F. L. A. Ferrier, sous-inspecteur des douanes, "Du gouvernement considere dans ses rapports avec le commerce," Paris, 1805; and Charles Ganilh, "Des Systemes d'Economie Politique, — 2nd ed., Paris, 1821.

[24] In Homer, for instance, the value of an article is expressed in a series of different things II. Vll. 472-475.

[25] For this reason, we can speak of the coat-value of the linen when its value is expressed in coats, or of its corn-value when expressed in corn, and so on. Every such expression tells us, that what appears in the use-values, cost, corn, &c., is the value of the linen. "The value of any commodity denoting its relation in exchange, we may speak of it as ... corn-value, cloth-value, according to the commodity with which it is compared; and hence there are a thousand different kinds of value, as many kinds of value as there are commodities in existence, and all are equally real and equally nominal." ("A Critical Dissertation on the Nature, Measures and Causes of Value: chiefly in reference to the writings of Mr. Ricardo and his followers." By the author of "Essays on the Formation, &c., of Opinions. ' London, 1825, p. 39.) S. Bailey, the author of this anonymous work, a work which in its day created much stir in England, fancied that, by thus pointing out the various relative expressions of one and the same value, he had proved the impossibility of

any determination of the concept of value. However narrow his own views may have been, yet, that he laid his finger on some serious defects in the Ricardian Theory, is proved by the animosity with which he was attacked by Ricardo's followers. See the Westminster Review for example.

[26] It is by no means self-evident that this character of direct and universal exchangeability is, so to speak, a polar one, and as intimately connected with its opposite pole, the absence of direct exchangeability, as the positive pole of the magnet is with its negative counterpart. It may therefore be imagined that all commodities can simultaneously have this character impressed upon them, just as it can be imagined that all Catholics can be popes together. It is, of course, highly desirable in the eyes of the petit bourgeois, for whom the production of commodities is the nec plus ultra of human freedom and individual independence, that the inconveniences resulting from this character of commodities not being directly exchangeable, should be removed. Proudhon's socialism is a working out of this Philistine Utopia, a form of socialism which, as I have elsewhere shown, does not possess even the merit of originality. Long before his time, the task was attempted with much better success by Gray, Bray, and others. But, for all that, wisdom of this kind flourishes even now in certain circles under the name of "science." Never has any school played more tricks with the word science, than that of Proudhon, for

wo Begriffe fehlen,
Da stellt zur rechten Zeit ein Wort sich ein."

[27] Among the ancient Germans the unit for measuring land was what could be harvested in a day, and was called Tagwerk, Tagwanne (jurnale, or terra jurnalis, or diornalis), Mannsmaad, &c. (See G. L. von Maurer, "Einleitung zur Geschichte der Mark-, &c. Verfassung," Munchen, 1854, p. 129 sq.)

[28] When, therefore, Galiani says: Value is a relation between persons — "La Ricchezza e una ragione tra due persone," — he ought to have added: a relation between persons expressed as a relation between things. (Galiani: Della Moneta, p. 221, V. III. of Custodi's collection of "Scrittori Classici Italiani di Economia Politica." Parte Moderna, Milano 1803.)

[29] What are we to think of a law that asserts itself only by periodical revolutions? It is just nothing but a law of Nature, founded on the want of knowledge of those whose action is the subject of it." (Friedrich Engels: "Umrisse zu einer Kritik der Nationalokonomie," in the "Deutsch-Franzosische Jahrbucher," edited by Arnold Ruge and Karl arx. Paris. 1844.)

[30] Even Ricardo has his stories a la Robinson. "He makes the primitive hunter and the primitive fisher straightway, as owners of commodities, exchange fish and game in the proportion in which labour-time is incorporated in these exchange-values. On this occasion he commits the anachronism of making these men apply to the calculation, so far as their implements have to be taken into account, the annuity tables in current use on the London Exchange in the year 1817. The parallelograms of Mr. Owen' appear to be the only form of society, besides the bourgeois form, with which he was acquainted." (Karl Marx: "Zur Kritik, &c.." pp. 38, 39)

[31] 'A ridiculous presumption has latterly got abroad that common property in its primitive form is specifically a Slavonian, or even exclusively Russian form. It is the primitive form that we can prove to have existed amongst Romans, Teutons, and Celts, and even to this day we find numerous examples, ruins though they be, in India. A more exhaustive study of Asiatic, and especially of Indian forms of common property, would show how from the different forms of primitive common property, different forms of its dissolution have been developed. Thus, for instance, the various original types of Roman and Teutonic private property are deducible from different forms of Indian common property." (Karl Marx, "Zur Kritik, &c.," p. 10.)

[32] The insufficiency of Ricardo's analysis of the magnitude of value, and his analysis is by far the best, will appear from the 3rd and 4th books of this work. As regards value in general, it is the weak point of the classical school of Political Economy that it nowhere expressly and with full consciousness, distinguishes between labour, as it appears in the value of a product, and the same labour, as it appears in the use-value of that product. Of course the distinction is practically made, since this school treats labour, at one time under its quantitative aspect, at another under its qualitative aspect. But it has not the least idea, that when the difference between various kinds of labour is treated as purely quantitative,

their qualitative unity or equality, and therefore their reduction to abstract human labour, is implied. For instance, Ricardo declares that he agrees with Destutt de Tracy in this proposition: "As it is certain that our physical and moral faculties are alone our original riches, the employment of those faculties, labour of some kind, is our only original treasure, and it is always from this employment that all those things are created which we call riches.... It is certain, too, that all those things only represent the labour which has created them, and if they have a value, or even two distinct values, they can only derive them from that (the value) of the labour from which they emanate." (Ricardo, "The Principles of Pol. Econ.," 3 Ed. Lond. 1821, p. 334.) We would here only point out, that Ricardo puts his own more profound interpretation upon the words of Destutt. What the latter really says is, that on the one hand all things which constitute wealth represent the labour that creates them, but that on the other hand, they acquire their "two different values" (use-value and exchange-value) from "the value of labour." He thus falls into the commonplace error of the vulgar economists, who assume the value of one commodity (in this case labour) in order to determine the values of the rest. But Ricardo reads him as if he had said, that labour (not the value of labour) is embodied both in use-value and exchange-value. Nevertheless, Ricardo himself pays so little attention to the two-fold character of the labour which has a two-fold embodiment, that he devotes the whole of his chapter on "Value and Riches, Their Distinctive Properties," to a laborious examination of the trivialities of a J.B. Say. And at the finish he is quite astonished to find that Destutt on the one hand agrees with him as to labour being the source of value, and on the other hand with J. B. Say as to the notion of value.

[33] It is one of the chief failings of classical economy that it has never succeeded, by means of its analysis of commodities, and, in particular, of their value, in discovering that form under which value becomes exchange-value. Even Adam Smith and Ricardo, the best representatives of the school, treat the form of value as a thing of no importance, as having no connexion with the inherent nature of commodities. The reason for this is not solely because their attention is entirely absorbed in the analysis of the magnitude of value. It lies deeper. The value-form of the product of labour is not only the most abstract, but is also the most universal form, taken by the product in bourgeois production and stamps that production as a particular species of social production, and thereby gives it its special historical character. If then we treat this mode of production as one eternally fixed by Nature for every state of society, we necessarily overlook that which is the differentia specifica of the value-form, and consequently of the commodity-form, and of its further developments, money-form, capital-form, &c. We consequently find that economists, who are thoroughly agreed as to labour-time being the measure of the magnitude of value, have the most strange and contradictory ideas of money, the perfected form of the general equivalent. This is seen in a striking manner when they treat of banking, where the commonplace definitions of money will no longer hold water. This led to the rise of a restored mercantile system (Ganilh, &c.), which sees in value nothing but a social form, or rather the unsubstantial ghost of that form. Once for all I may here state, that by classical Political Economy, I understand that economy which, since the time of W. Petty, has investigated the real relations of production in bourgeois society in contradistinction to vulgar economy, which deals with appearances only, ruminates without ceasing on the materials long since provided by scientific economy, and there seeks plausible explanations of the most obtrusive phenomena, for bourgeois daily use, but for the rest, confines itself to systematising in a pedantic way, and proclaiming for everlasting truths, the trite ideas held by the self-complacent bourgeoisie with regard to their own world, to them the best of all possible worlds.

[34] "Les economistes ont une singuliere maniere de proceder. Il n'y a pour eux que deux sortes d'institutions, celles de l'art et celles de la nature. Les institutions de la feodalite sont des institutions artificielles celles de la bourgeoisie sont des institutions naturelles. Ils ressemblent en ceci aux theologiens, qui eux aussi etablissent deux sortes de religions. Toute religion qui n'est pas la leur, est une invention des hommes tandis que leur propre religion est une emanation de Dieu-Ainsi il y a eu de l'histoire, mais il n'y en a plus." (Karl Marx. isere de la Philosophie. Reponse a la Philosophie de la Misere par M. Proudhon, 1847, p. 113.) Truly comical is M. Bastiat, who imagines that the ancient Greeks and Romans lived by plunder alone. But when people plunder for centuries, there must always be something at hand for them to seize; the objects of plunder must be continually

reproduced. It would thus appear that even Greeks and Romans had some process of production, consequently, an economy, which just as much constituted the material basis of their world, as bourgeois economy constitutes that of our modern world. Or perhaps Bastiat means, that a mode of production based on slavery is based on a system of plunder. In that case he treads on dangerous ground. If a giant thinker like Aristotle erred in his appreciation of slave labour, why should a dwarf economist like Bastiat be right in his appreciation of wage-labour? I seize this opportunity of shortly answering an objection taken by a German paper in America, to my work, "Zur Kritik der Pol. Oekonomie, 1859." In the estimation of that paper, my view that each special mode of production and the social relations corresponding to it, in short, that the economic structure of society, is the real basis on which the juridical and political superstructure is raised and to which definite social forms of thought correspond; that the mode of production determines the character of the social, political, and intellectual life generally, all this is very true for our own times, in which material interests preponderate, but not for the middle ages, in which Catholicism, nor for Athens and Rome, where politics, reigned supreme. In the first place it strikes one as an odd thing for any one to suppose that these well-worn phrases about the middle ages and the ancient world are unknown to anyone else. This much, however, is clear, that the middle ages could not live on Catholicism, nor the ancient world on politics. On the contrary, it is the mode in which they gained a livelihood that explains why here politics, and there Catholicism, played the chief part. For the rest, it requires but a slight acquaintance with the history of the Roman republic, for example, to be aware that its secret history is the history of its landed property. On the other hand, Don Quixote long ago paid the penalty for wrongly imagining that knight errantry was compatible with all economic forms of society.

[35] "Observations on certain verbal disputes in Pol. Econ., particularly relating to value and to demand and supply" Lond., 1821, p. 16.

[36] S. Bailey, l.c., p. 165.

[37] The author of "Observations" and S. Bailey accuse Ricardo of converting exchange-value from something relative into something absolute. The opposite is the fact. He has explained the apparent relation between objects, such as diamonds and pearls, in which relation they appear as exchange-values, and disclosed the true relation hidden behind the appearances, namely, their relation to each other as mere expressions of human labour. If the followers of Ricardo answer Bailey somewhat rudely, and by no means convincingly, the reason is to be sought in this, that they were unable to find in Ricardo's own works any key to the hidden relations existing between value and its form, exchange-value.

Chapter Two: Exchange

It is plain that commodities cannot go to market and make exchanges of their own account. We must, therefore, have recourse to their guardians, who are also their owners Commodities are things, and therefore without power of resistance against man. If they are wanting in docility he can use force; in other words, he can take possession of them. [1] In order that these objects may enter into relation with each other as commodities, their guardians must place themselves in relation to one another, as persons whose will resides in those object, and must behave in such a way that each does not appropriate the commodity of the other, and part with his own, except by means of an act done by mutual consent. They must therefore, mutually recognise in each other the rights of private proprietors. This juridical relation, which thus expresses itself in a contract, whether such contract be part of a developed legal system or not, is a relation between two wills, and is but the reflex of the real economic relation between the two. It is this economic relation that determines the subject-matter comprised in each such juridical act. [2]

The persons exist for one another merely as representatives of, and, therefore. as owners of, commodities. In the course of our investigation we shall find, in general, that the characters who appear on the economic stage are but the personifications of the economic relations that exist between them.

What chiefly distinguishes a commodity from its owner is the fact, that it looks upon every other commodity as but the form of appearance of its own value. A born leveller and a cynic, it is always ready to exchange not only soul, but body, with any and every other commodity, be the same more repulsive than Maritornes herself. The owner makes up for this lack in the commodity of a sense of the concrete, by his own five and more senses. His commodity possesses for himself no immediate use-value. Otherwise, he would not bring it to the market. It has use-value for others; but for himself its only direct use-value is that of being a depository of exchange-value, and, consequently, a means of exchange.[3] Therefore, he makes up his mind to part with it for commodities whose value in use is of service to him. All commodities are non-use-values for their owners, and use-values for their non-owners. Consequently, they must all change hands. But this change of hands is what constitutes their exchange, and the latter puts them in relation with each other as values, and realises them as values. Hence commodities must be realised as values before they can be realised as use-values.

On the other hand, they must show that they are use-values before they can be realised as values. For the labour spent upon them counts effectively, only in so far as it is spent in a form that is useful for others. Whether that labour is useful for others, and its product consequently capable of satisfying the wants of others, can be proved only by the act of exchange.

Every owner of a commodity wishes to part with it in exchange only for those commodities whose use-value satisfies some want of his. Looked at in this way, exchange is for him simply a private transaction. On the other hand, he desires to realise the value of his commodity, to convert it into any other suitable commodity of equal value, irrespective of whether his own commodity has or has not any use-value for the owner of the other. From this point of view, exchange is for him a social transaction of a general character. But one and the same set of transactions cannot be simultaneously for all owners of commodities both exclusively private and exclusively social and general.

Let us look at the matter a little closer. To the owner of a commodity, every other commodity is, in regard to his own, a particular equivalent, and consequently his own commodity is the universal equivalent for all the others. But since this applies to every owner, there is, in fact, no commodity acting as universal equivalent, and the relative value of commodities possesses no general form under which they can be equated as values and have the magnitude of their values compared. So far, therefore, they do not confront each other as commodities, but only as products or use-values. In their difficulties our commodity owners think like Faust: "Im Anfang war die That." They therefore acted and transacted before they thought. Instinctively they conform to the laws imposed by the nature of commodities. They cannot bring their commodities into relation as values, and therefore as commodities, except by comparing them with some one other commodity as the universal equivalent. That we saw from the analysis of a commodity. But a particular commodity cannot become the universal equivalent except by a social act. The social action therefore of all other commodities, sets apart the particular commodity in which they all represent their values. Thereby the bodily form of this commodity becomes the form of the socially recognised universal equivalent. To be the universal equivalent, becomes, by this social process, the specific function of the commodity thus excluded by the rest. Thus it becomes—money. "Illi unum consilium habent et virtutem et potestatem suam bestiae tradunt. Et ne quis possit emere aut vendere, nisi qui habet characterem aut nomen bestiae aut numerum nominis ejus." (Apocalypse.)

Money is a crystal formed of necessity in the course of the exchanges, whereby different products of labour are practically equated to one another and thus by practice converted into commodities. The historical progress and extension of exchanges develops the contrast, latent in commodities, between use-value and value. The necessity for giving an external expression to this contrast for the purposes of commercial intercourse, urges on the establishment of an independent form of value, and finds no rest until it is once for all satisfied by the differentiation of commodities into commodities and money. At the same rate, then, as the conversion of products into commodities is being accomplished, so also is the conversion of one special commodity into money.[4]

The direct barter of products attains the elementary form of the relative expression of value in one respect, but not in another. That form is x Commodity A = y Commodity B. The form of direct barter is x use-value A = y use-value B.[5] The articles A and B in this case are not as yet commodities, but become so only by the act of barter. The first step made by an object of utility towards acquiring exchange-value is when it forms a non-use-value for its owner, and that happens when it forms a superfluous portion of some article required for his immediate wants. Objects in themselves are external to man, and consequently alienable by him. In order that this alienation may be reciprocal, it is only necessary for men, by a tacit understanding, to treat each other as private owners of those alienable objects, and by implication as independent individuals. But such a state of reciprocal independence has no existence in a primitive society based on property in common, whether such a society takes the form of a patriarchal family, an ancient Indian community, or a Peruvian Inca State. The exchange of commodities, therefore, first begins on the boundaries of such communities, at their points of contact with other similar communities, or with members of the latter. So soon, however, as products once become commodities in the external relations of a community, they also, by reaction, become so in its internal intercourse. The proportions in which they are exchangeable are at first quite a matter of chance. What makes them exchangeable is the mutual desire of their owners to alienate them. Meantime the need for foreign objects of utility gradually establishes itself. The constant repetition of exchange makes it a normal social act. In the course of time, therefore, some portion at least of the products of labour must be produced with a special view to exchange. From that moment the distinction becomes firmly established between the utility of an object for the purposes of consumption, and its utility for the purposes of exchange. Its use-value becomes distinguished from its exchange-value. On the other hand, the quantitative proportion in which the articles are exchangeable, becomes dependent on their production itself. Custom stamps them as values with definite magnitudes.

In the direct barter of products, each commodity is directly a means of exchange to its owner, and to all other persons an equivalent, but that only in so far as it has use-value for them. At this stage, therefore, the articles exchanged do not acquire a value-form independent of their own use-value, or of the individual needs of the exchangers. The necessity for a value-form grows with the increasing number and variety of the commodities exchanged. The problem and the means of solution arise simultaneously. Commodity-owners never equate their own commodities to those of others, and exchange them on a large scale, without different kinds of commodities belonging to different owners being exchangeable for, and equated as values to, one and the same special article. Such last-mentioned article, by becoming the equivalent of various other commodities, acquires at once, though within narrow limits, the character of a general social equivalent. This character comes and goes with the momentary social acts that called it into life. In turns and transiently it attaches itself first to this and then to that commodity. But with the development of exchange it fixes itself firmly and exclusively to particular sorts of commodities, and becomes crystallised by assuming the money-form. The particular kind of commodity to which it sticks is at first a matter of accident. Nevertheless there are two circumstances whose influence is decisive. The money-form attaches itself either to the most important articles of exchange from outside, and these in fact are primitive and natural forms in which the exchange-value of home products finds expression; or else it attaches itself to the object of utility that forms, like cattle, the chief portion of indigenous alienable wealth. Nomad races are the first to develop the money-form, because all their worldly goods consist of moveable objects and are therefore directly alienable; and because their mode of life, by continually bringing them into contact with foreign communities, solicits the exchange of products. Man has often made man himself, under the form of slaves, serve as the primitive material of money, but has never used land for that purpose. Such an idea could only spring up in a bourgeois society already well developed. It dates from the last third of the 17th century, and the first attempt to put it in practice on a national scale was made a century afterwards, during the French bourgeois revolution.

In proportion as exchange bursts its local bonds, and the value of commodities more and more expands into an embodiment of human labour in the abstract, in the same proportion the character of money attaches itself to commodities that are by Nature fitted to perform the social function of a universal equivalent. Those commodities are the precious metals.

The truth of the proposition that, "although gold and silver are not by Nature money, money is by Nature gold and silver,"[6] is shown by the fitness of the physical properties of these metals for the functions of money.[7] Up to this point, however, we are acquainted only with one function of money, namely, to serve as the form of manifestation of the value of commodities, or as the material in which the magnitudes of their values are socially expressed. An adequate form of manifestation of value, a fit embodiment of abstract, undifferentiated, and therefore equal human labour, that material alone can be whose every sample exhibits the same uniform qualities. On the other hand, since the difference between the magnitudes of value is purely quantitative, the money commodity must be susceptible of merely quantitative differences, must therefore be divisible at will, and equally capable of being reunited. Gold and silver possess these properties by Nature.

The use-value of the money-commodity becomes two-fold. In addition to its special use-value as a commodity (gold, for instance, serving to stop teeth, to form the raw material of articles of luxury, &c.), it acquires a formal use-value, originating in its specific social function.

Since all commodities are merely particular equivalents of money, the latter being their universal equivalent, they, with regard to the latter as the universal commodity, play the parts of particular commodities. [8]

We have seen that the money-form is but the reflex, thrown upon one single commodity, of the value relations between all the rest. That money is a commodity [9] is therefore a new discovery only for those who, when they analyse it, start from its fully developed shape. The act of exchange gives to the commodity converted into money, not its value, but its specific value-form. By confounding these two distinct things some writers have been led to hold that the value of gold and silver is imaginary. [10] The fact that money can, in certain functions, be replaced by mere symbols of itself, gave rise to that other mistaken notion, that it is itself a mere symbol. Nevertheless under this error lurked a presentiment that the money-form of an object is not an inseparable part of that object, but is simply the form under which certain social relations manifest themselves. In this sense every commodity is a symbol, since, in so far as it is value, it is only the material envelope of the human labour spent upon it.[11] But if it be declared that the social characters assumed by objects, or the material forms assumed by the social qualities of labour under the régime of a definite mode of production, are mere symbols, it is in the same breath also declared that these characteristics are arbitrary fictions sanctioned by the so-called universal consent of mankind. This suited the mode of explanation in favour during the 18th century. Unable to account for the origin of the puzzling forms assumed by social relations between man and man, people sought to denude them of their strange appearance by ascribing to them a conventional origin.

It has already been remarked above that the equivalent form of a commodity does not imply the determination of the magnitude of its value. Therefore, although we may be aware that gold is money, and consequently directly exchangeable for all other commodities, yet that fact by no means tells how much 10 lbs., for instance, of gold is worth. Money, like every other commodity, cannot express the magnitude of its value except relatively in other commodities. This value is determined by the labour-time required for its production, and is expressed by the quantity of any other commodity that costs the same amount of labour-time. [12] Such quantitative determination of its relative value takes place at the source of its production by means of barter. When it steps into circulation as money, its value is already given. In the last decades of the 17th century it had already been shown that money is a commodity, but this step marks only the infancy of the analysis. The difficulty lies, not in comprehending that money is a commodity, but in discovering how, why, and by what means a commodity becomes money. [13]

We have already seen, from the most elementary expression of value, x commodity A = y commodity B, that the object in which the magnitude of the value of another object is represented, appears to have the equivalent form independently of this relation, as a social property given to it by Nature. We followed up this false appearance to its final establishment, which is complete so soon as the universal equivalent form becomes identified with the bodily form of a particular commodity, and thus crystallised into the money-form. What appears to happen is, not that gold becomes money, in consequence of all other commodities expressing their values in it, but, on the contrary, txhat all other commodities universally express their values in gold, because it is money. The intermediate steps of the process vanish in the result and leave no trace behind. Commodities find their own value already completely represented, without any initiative on their part, in another commodity existing in company with them. These objects, gold and silver, just as they come out of the bowels of the earth, are forthwith the direct incarnation of all human labour. Hence the magic of money. In the form of society now under consideration, the behaviour of men in the social process of production is purely atomic. Hence their relations to each other in production assume a material character independent of their control and conscious individual action. These facts manifest themselves at first by products as a general rule taking the form of commodities. We have seen how the progressive development of a society of commodity-producers stamps one privileged commodity with the character of money. Hence the riddle presented by money is but the riddle presented by commodities; only it now strikes us in its most glaring form.

Footnotes

[1] In the 12th century, so renowned for its piety, they included amongst commodities some very delicate things. Thus a French poet of the period enumerates amongst the goods to be found in the market of Landit, not only clothing shoes, leather, agricultural implements, &c., but also "femmes folles de leur corps."

[2] Proudhon begins by taking his ideal of Justice, of "justice éternelle," from the juridical relations that correspond to the production of commodities: thereby, it may be noted, he proves, to the consolation of all good citizens, that the production of commodities is a form of production as everlasting as justice. Then he turns round and seeks to reform the actual production of commodities, and the actual legal system corresponding thereto, in accordance with this ideal. What opinion should we have of a chemist, who, instead of studying the actual laws of the molecular changes in the composition and decomposition of matter, and on that foundation solving definite problems, claimed to regulate the composition and decomposition of matter by means of the "eternal ideas," of "naturalité" and "affinité"? Do we really know any more about "usury," when we say it contradicts "justice éternelle," équité éternelle "mutualité éternelle," and other vérités éternelle than the fathers of the church did when they said it was incompatible with '-grâce éternelle," "foi éternelle," and "la volonté éternelle de Dieu"?

[3] "For two-fold is the use of every object.... The one is peculiar to the object as such, the other is not, as a sandal which may be worn, and is also exchangeable. Both are uses of the sandal, for even he who exchanges the sandal for the money or food he is in want of, makes use of the sandal as a sandal. But not in its natural way. For it has not been made for the sake of being exchanged." (Aristoteles, "De Rep." l. i. c. 9.)

[4] From this we may form an estimate of the shrewdness of the petit-bourgeois socialism. which, while perpetuating the production of commodities, aims at abolishing the "antagonism" between money and commodities, and consequently, since money exists only by virtue of this antagonism, at abolishing money itself. We might just as well try to retain Catholicism without the Pope. For more on this point see my work, "Zur Kritik der Pol. Oekon.", p. 61, sq.

[5] So long as, instead of two distinct use-values being exchanged, a chaotic mass of articles are offered as the equivalent of a single article, which is often the case with savages, even the direct barter of products is in its first infancy.

[6] Karl Marx, l. c., p. 135. "I metalli ... naturalmente moneta." (Galiani, "Della moneta" in Custodi's Collection: Parte Moderna t. iii.)

[7] For further details on this subject see in my work cited above, the chapter on "The precious metals."

[8] "Il danaro è la merce universale"(Verri, l. c., p. 16).

[9] "Silver and gold themselves (which we may call by the general name of bullion) are ... commodities ... rising and falling in ... value ... Bullion, then, may be reckoned to be of higher value where the smaller weight will purchase the greater quantity of the product or manufacture of the countrey," &c. ("A Discourse of the General Notions of Money, Trade, and Exchanges, as They Stand in Relation each to other." By a Merchant. Lond., 1695, p. 7.) "Silver and gold, coined or uncoined, though they are used for a measure of all other things, are no less a commodity than wine, oil, tobacco, cloth, or stuffs." ("A Discourse concerning Trade, and that in particular of the East Indies," &c. London, 1689, p. 2.) "The stock and riches of the kingdom cannot properly be confined to money, nor ought gold and silver to be excluded from being merchandise." ("The East-India Trade a Most Profitable Trade." London, 1677, p. 4.)

[10] "L'oro e l'argento hanno valore come metalli anteriore all'esser moneta." (Galiani, l. c.) Locke says, "The universal consent of mankind gave to silver, on account of its qualities which made it suitable for money, an imaginary value." Law, on the other hand. "How could different nations give an imaginary value to any single thing... or how could this imaginary value have maintained itself?" But the following shows how little he himself understood about the matter: "Silver was exchanged in proportion to the value in use it possessed, consequently in proportion to its real value. By its adoption as money it received an additional value (une valeur additionnelle)". (Jean Law: "Considérations sur le numéraire et le commerce" in E. Daire's Edit. of "Economistes Financiers du XVIII siècle," p. 470.)

[11] "L'Argent en (des denrées) est le signe." (V. de Forbonnais: "Elements du Commerce, Nouv. Edit. Leyde, 1766," t. II., p. 143.) "Comme signe il est attire par les denrées." (l. c., p. 155.) "L'argent est un signe d'une chose et la représente." (Montesquieu: "Esprit des Lois," (Oeuvres, Lond. 1767, t. II, p. 2.) "L'argent n'est pas simple signe, car il est lui-meme richesse, il ne représente pas les valeurs, il les équivaut." (Le Trosne, l. c., p. 910.) "The notion of value contemplates the valuable article as a mere symbol-the article counts not for what it is, but for what it is worth." (Hegel, l. c., p. 100.) Lawyers started long before economists the idea that money is a mere symbol, and that the value of the precious metals is purely imaginary. This they did in the sycophantic service of the crowned heads, supporting the right of the latter to debase the coinage, during the whole of the middle ages, by the traditions of the Roman Empire and the conceptions of money to be found in the Pandects. "Qu'aucun puisse ni doive faire doute," says an apt scholar of theirs Philip of Valois, in a decree of 1346, "que à nous et à notre majesté royale n'appartiennent seulement ... le mestier, le fait, l'état, la provision et toute l'ordonnance des monnaies, de donner tel cours, et pour tel prix comme il nous plait et bon nous semble." It was a maxim of the Roman Law that the value of money was fixed by decree of the emperor. It was expressly forbidden to treat money as a commodity. "Pecunias vero nulli emere fas erit, nam in usu publico constitutas oportet non esse mercem." Some good work on this question has been done by G. F. Pagnini: "Saggio sopra il giusto pregio delle cose, 1751"; Custodi "Parte Moderna," t. II. In the second part of his work Pagnini directs his polemics especially against the lawyers.

[12] "If a man can bring to London an ounce of Silver out of the Earth in Peru, in the same time that he can produce a bushel of Corn, then the one is the natural price of the

other; now, if by reason of new or more easier mines a man can procure two ounces of silver as easily as he formerly did one, the corn will be as cheap at ten shillings the bushel as it was before at five shillings, caeteris paribus." William Petty. "A Treatise of Taxes and Contributions." Lond., 1667, p. 32.

[13] The learned Professor Roscher, after first informing us that "the false definitions of money may be divided into two main groups: those which make it more, and those which make it less, than a commodity," gives us a long and very mixed catalogue of works on the nature of money, from which it appears that he has not the remotest idea of the real history of the theory; and then he moralises thus: "For the rest, it is not to be denied that most of the later economists do not bear sufficiently in mind the peculiarities-that distinguish money from other commodities" (it is then, after all, either more or less than a commodity!)... 'So far, the semi-mercantilist reaction of Ganilh is not altogether without foundation." (Wilhelm Roscher: "Die Grundlagen der Nationaloekonomie," 3rd Edn. 1858, pp. 207-210.) More! less! not sufficiently! so far! not altogether! What clearness and precision of ideas and language! And such eclectic professorial twaddle is modestly baptised by Mr. Roscher, "the anatomico-physiological method" of Political Economy! One discovery however, he must have credit for, namely, that money is "a pleasant commodity."

Chapter Three: Money, or the Circulation of Commodities

Section 1. The Measure of Values

Throughout this work, I assume, for the sake of simplicity, gold as the money-commodity.

The first chief function of money is to supply commodities with the material for the expression of their values, or to represent their values as magnitudes of the same denomination, qualitatively equal, and quantitatively comparable. It thus serves as a universal measure of value. And only by virtue of this function does gold, the equivalent commodity par excellence, become money.

It is not money that renders commodities commensurable. Just the contrary. It is because all commodities, as values, are realised human labour, and therefore commensurable, that their values can be measured by one and the same special commodity, and the latter be converted into the common measure of their values, i.e., into money. Money as a measure of value, is the phenomenal form that must of necessity be assumed by that measure of value which is immanent in commodities, labour-time. [1]

The expression of the value of a commodity in gold — x commodity A = y money-commodity — is its money-form or price. A single equation, such as 1 ton of iron = 2 ounces of gold, now suffices to express the value of the iron in a socially valid manner. There is no longer any need for this equation to figure as a link in the chain of equations that express the values of all other commodities, because the equivalent commodity, gold, now has the character of money. The general form of relative value has resumed its original shape of simple or isolated relative value. On the other hand, the expanded expression of relative value, the endless series of equations, has now become the form peculiar to the relative value of the money-commodity. The series itself, too, is now given, and has social recognition in the prices of actual commodities. We have only to read the quotations of a price-list backwards, to find the magnitude of the value of money expressed in all sorts of commodities. But money itself has no price. In order to put it on an equal footing with all other commodities in this respect, we should be obliged to equate it to itself as its own equivalent.

The price or money-form of commodities is, like their form of value generally, a form quite distinct from their palpable bodily form; it is, therefore, a purely ideal or mental form. Although invisible, the value of iron, linen and corn has actual existence in these very articles: it is ideally made perceptible by their equality with gold, a relation that, so to say, exists only in their own heads. Their owner must, therefore, lend them his tongue, or hang a ticket on them, before their prices can be communicated to the outside world. [2] Since the expression of the value of commodities in gold is a merely ideal act, we may use for this purpose imaginary or ideal money. Every trader knows, that he is far from having turned his goods into money, when he has expressed their value in a price or in imaginary money, and that it does not require the least bit of real gold, to estimate in that metal millions of pounds' worth of goods. When, therefore, money serves as a measure of value; it is employed only as imaginary or ideal money. This circumstance has given rise to the wildest theories. [3] But, although the money that performs the functions of a measure of value is only ideal money, price depends entirely upon the actual substance that is money. The value, or in other words, the quantity of human labour contained in a ton of iron, is expressed in imagination by such a quantity of the money-commodity as contains the same amount of labour as the iron. According, therefore, as the measure of value is gold, silver, or copper, the value of the ton of iron will be expressed by very different prices, or will be represented by very different quantities of those metals respectively.

If, therefore, two different commodities, such as gold and silver, are simultaneously measures of value, all commodities have two prices — one a gold-price, the other a silver-price. These exist quietly side by side, so long as the ratio of The value of silver to that of gold remains unchanged, say, at 15:1. Every change in their ratio disturbs the ratio which exists between the gold-prices and the silver-prices of commodities, and thus proves, by facts, that a double standard of value is inconsistent with the functions of a standard. [4]

Commodities with definite prices present themselves under the form; a commodity A = x gold; b commodity B = z gold; c commodity C = y gold, &c., where a, b, c, represent definite quantities of the commodities A, B, C and x, z, y, definite quantities of gold. The values of these commodities are, therefore, changed in imagination into so many different quantities of gold. Hence, in spite of the confusing variety of the commodities themselves, their values become magnitudes of the same denomination, gold-magnitudes. They are now capable of being compared with each other and measured, and the want becomes technically felt of comparing them with some fixed quantity of gold as a unit measure. This unit, by subsequent division into aliquot parts, becomes itself the standard or scale. Before they become money, gold, silver, and copper already possess such standard measures in their standards of weight, so that, for example, a pound weight, while serving as the unit, is, on the one hand, divisible into ounces, and, on the other, may be combined to make up hundredweights. [5] It is owing to this that, in all metallic currencies, the names given to the standards of money or of price were originally taken from the pre-existing names of the standards of weight.

As measure of Value, and as standard of price, money has two entirely distinct functions to perform. It is the measure of value inasmuch as it is the socially recognised incarnation of human labour; it is the standard of price inasmuch as it is a fixed weight of metal. As the measure of value it serves to convert the values of all the manifold commodities into prices, into imaginary quantities of gold; as the standard of price it measures those quantities of gold. The measure of values measures commodities considered as values; the standard of price measures, on the contrary, quantities of gold by a unit quantity of gold, not the value of one quantity of gold by the weight of another. In order to make gold a standard of price, a certain weight must be fixed upon as the unit. In this case, as in all cases of measuring quantities of the same denomination, the establishment of an unvarying unit of measure is all-important. Hence, the less the unit is subject to variation, so much the better does the standard of price fulfil its office. But only in so far as it is itself a product of labour, and, therefore, potentially variable in value, can gold serve as a measure of value. [6]

It is, in the first place, quite clear that a change in the value of gold does not, in any way, affect its function as a standard of price. No matter how this value varies, the proportions between the values of different quantities of the metal remain constant. However great the fall in its value, 12 ounces of gold still have 12 times the value of 1 ounce; and in prices, the only thing considered is the relation between different quantities of gold. Since, on the other hand, no rise or fall in the value of an ounce of gold can alter its weight, no alteration can take place in the weight of its aliquot parts. Thus gold always renders the same service as an invariable standard of price, however much its value may vary.

In the second place, a change in the value of gold does not interfere with its functions as a measure of value. The change affects all commodities simultaneously, and, therefore, caeteris paribus, leaves their relative values inter se, unaltered, although those values are now expressed in higher or lower gold-prices.

Just as when we estimate the value of any commodity by a definite quantity of the use-value of some other commodity, so in estimating the value of the former in gold, we assume nothing more than that the production of a given quantity of gold costs, at the given period, a given amount of labour. As regards the fluctuations of prices generally, they are subject to the laws of elementary relative value investigated in a former chapter.

A general rise in the prices of commodities can result only, either from a rise in their values — the value of money remaining constant — or from a fall in the value of money, the values of commodities remaining constant. On the other hand, a general fall in prices can result only, either from a fall in the values of commodities — the value of money remaining constant — or from a rise in the value of money, the values of commodities remaining constant. It therefore by no means follows, that a rise in the value of money necessarily implies a proportional fall in the prices of commodities; or that a fall in the value of money implies a proportional rise in prices. Such change of price holds good only in the case of commodities whose value remains constant. With those, for example, whose value rises, simultaneously with, and proportionally to, that of money, there is no alteration in price. And if their value rise either slower or faster than that of money, the fall or rise in their prices will be determined by the difference between the change in their value and that of money; and so on.

Let us now go back to the consideration of the price-form.

By degrees there arises a discrepancy between the current moneynames of the various weights of the precious metal figuring as money, and the actual weights which those names originally represented. This discrepancy is the result of historical causes, among which the chief are: — (1) The importation of foreign money into an imperfectly developed community. This happened in Rome in its early days, where gold and silver coins circulated at first as foreign commodities. The names of these foreign coins never coincide with those of the indigenous weights. (2) As wealth increases, the less precious metal is thrust out by the more precious from its place as a measure of value, copper by silver, silver by gold, however much this order of sequence may be in contradiction with poetical chronology. [7] The word pound, for instance, was the money-name given to an actual pound weight of silver. When gold replaced silver as a measure of value, the same name was applied according to the ratio between the values of silver and gold, to perhaps 1-15th of a pound of gold. The word pound, as a money-name, thus becomes differentiated from the same word as a weight-name. [8] (3) The debasing of money carried on for centuries by kings and princes to such an extent that, of the original weights of the coins, nothing in fact remained but the names. [9]

These historical causes convert the separation of the money-name from the weight-name into an established habit with the community. Since the standard of money is on the one hand purely conventional, and must on the other hand find general acceptance, it is in the end regulated by law. A given weight of one of the precious metals, an ounce of gold, for instance, becomes officially divided into aliquot parts, with legally bestowed names, such as pound, dollar, &c. These aliquot parts, which thenceforth serve as units of money, are then subdivided into other aliquot parts with legal names, such as shilling, penny, &c. [10] But, both before and after these divisions are made, a definite weight of metal is the standard of metallic money. The sole alteration consists in the subdivision and denomination.

The prices, or quantities of gold, into which the values of commodities are ideally changed, are therefore now expressed in the names of coins, or in the legally valid names of the subdivisions of the gold standard. Hence, instead of saying: A quarter of wheat is worth an ounce of gold; we say, it is worth £3 17s. 10 1/2d. In this way commodities express by their prices how much they are worth, and money serves as money of account whenever it is a question of fixing the value of an article in its money-form. [11]

The name of a thing is something distinct from the qualities of that thing. I know nothing of a man, by knowing that his name is Jacob. In the same way with regard to money, every trace of a value-relation disappears in the names pound, dollar, franc, ducat, &c. The confusion caused by attributing a hidden meaning to these cabalistic signs is all the greater, because these money-names express both the values of commodities, and, at the same time, aliquot parts of the weight of the metal that is the standard of money. [12] On the other hand, it is absolutely necessary that value, in order that it may be distinguished from the varied bodily forms of commodities, should assume this material and unmeaning, but, at the same time, purely social form. [13]

Price is the money-name of the labour realised in a commodity. Hence the expression of the equivalence of a commodity with the sum of money constituting its price, is a tautology, [14] just as in general the expression of the relative value of a commodity is a statement of the equivalence of two commodities. But although price, being the exponent of the magnitude of a commodity's value, is the exponent of its exchange-ratio with money, it does not follow that the exponent of this exchange-ratio is necessarily the exponent of the magnitude of the commodity's value. Suppose two equal quantities of socially necessary labour to be respectively represented by 1 quarter of wheat and £2 (nearly 1/2 oz. of gold), £2 is the expression in money of the magnitude of the value of the quarter of wheat, or is its price. If now circumstances allow of this price being raised to £3, or compel it to be reduced to £1, then although £1 and £3 may be too small or too great properly to express the magnitude of the wheat's value; nevertheless they are its prices, for they are, in the first place, the form under which its value appears, i.e., money; and in the second place, the exponents of its exchange-ratio with money. If the conditions of production, in other words, if the productive power of labour remain constant, the same amount of social labour-time must, both before and after the change in price, be expended in the reproduction of a quarter of wheat. This circumstance depends, neither on the will of the wheat producer, nor on that of the owners of other commodities.

Magnitude of value expresses a relation of social production, it expresses the connexion that necessarily exists between a certain article and the portion of the total labour-time of society required to produce it. As soon as magnitude of value is converted into price, the above necessary relation takes the shape of a more or less accidental exchange-ratio between a single commodity and another, the money-commodity. But this exchange-ratio may express either the real magnitude of that commodity's value, or the quantity of gold deviating from that value, for which, according to circumstances, it may be parted with. The possibility, therefore, of quantitative incongruity between price and magnitude of value, or the deviation of the former from the latter, is inherent in the price-form itself. This is no defect, but, on the contrary, admirably adapts the price-form to a mode of production whose inherent laws impose themselves only as the mean of apparently lawless irregularities that compensate one another.

The price-form, however, is not only compatible with the possibility of a quantitative incongruity between magnitude of value and price, i.e., between the former and its expression in money, but it may also conceal a qualitative inconsistency, so much so, that, although money is nothing but the value-form of commodities, price ceases altogether to express value. Objects that in themselves are no commodities, such as conscience, honour, &c., are capable of being offered for sale by their holders, and of thus acquiring, through their price, the form of commodities. Hence an object may have a price without having value. The price in that case is imaginary, like certain quantities in mathematics. On the other hand, the imaginary price-form may sometimes conceal either a direct or indirect real value-relation; for instance, the price of uncultivated land, which is without value, because no human labour has been incorporated in it.

Price, like relative value in general, expresses the value of a commodity (e.g., a ton of iron), by stating that a given quantity of the equivalent (e.g., an ounce of gold), is directly exchangeable for iron. But it by no means states the converse, that iron is directly exchangeable for gold. In order, therefore, that a commodity may in practice act effectively as exchange-value, it must quit its bodily shape, must transform itself from mere imaginary into real gold, although to the commodity such transubstantiation may be more difficult than to the Hegelian "concept," the transition from "necessity" to "freedom," or to a lobster the casting of his shell, or to Saint Jerome the putting off of the old Adam. [15] Though a commodity may, side by side with its actual form (iron, for instance), take in our imagination the form of gold, yet it cannot at one and the same time actually be both iron and gold. To fix its price, it suffices to equate it to gold in imagination. But to enable it to render to its owner the service of a universal equivalent, it must be actually replaced by gold. If the owner of the iron were to go to the owner of some other commodity offered for exchange, and were to refer him to the price of the iron as proof that it was already money, he would get the same answer as St. Peter gave in heaven to Dante, when the latter recited the creed —

"Assad bene e trascorsa
D'esta moneta gia la lega e'l peso,
dimmi se tu l'hai nella tua borsa."

A price therefore implies both that a commodity is exchangeable for money, and also that it must be so exchanged. On the other hand, gold serves as an ideal measure of value, only because it has already, in the process of exchange, established itself as the money-commodity. Under the ideal measure of values there lurks the hard cash.

Sections 2 The Medium of Circulation
A. The Metamorphosis of Commodities

We saw in a former chapter that the exchange of commodities implies contradictory and mutually exclusive conditions. The differentiation of commodities into commodities and money does not sweep away these inconsistencies, but develops a *modus vivendi*, a form in which they can exist side by side. This is generally the way in which real contradictions are reconciled. For instance, it is a contradiction to depict one body as constantly falling towards another, and as, at the same time, constantly flying away from it. The ellipse is a form of motion which, while allowing this contradiction to go on, at the same time reconciles it.

In so far as exchange is a process, by which commodities are transferred from hands in which they are non-use-values, to hands in which they become use-values, it is a social circulation of matter. The product of one form of useful labour replaces that of another. When once a commodity has found a resting-place, where it can serve as a use-value, it falls out of the sphere of exchange into that of consumption. But the former sphere alone interests us at present. We have, therefore, now to consider exchange from a formal point of view; to investigate the change of form or metamorphosis of commodities which effectuates the social circulation of matter.

The comprehension of this change of form is, as a rule, very imperfect. The cause of this imperfection is, apart from indistinct notions of value itself, that every change of form in a commodity results from the exchange of two commodities, an ordinary one and the money-commodity. If we keep in view the material fact alone that a commodity has been exchanged for gold, we overlook the very thing that we ought to observe — namely, what has happened to the form of the commodity. We overlook the facts that gold, when a mere commodity, is not money, and that when other commodities express their prices in gold, this gold is but the money-form of those commodities themselves.

Commodities, first of all, enter into the process of exchange just as they are. The process then differentiates them into commodities and money, and thus produces an external opposition corresponding to the internal opposition inherent in them, as being at once use-values and values. Commodities as use-values now stand opposed to money as exchange-value. On the other hand, both opposing sides are commodities, unities of use-value and value. But this unity of differences manifests itself at two opposite poles, and at each pole in an opposite way. Being poles they are as necessarily opposite as they are connected. On the one side of the equation we have an ordinary commodity, which is in reality a use-value. Its value is expressed only ideally in its price, by which it is equated to its opponent, the gold, as to the real embodiment of its value. On the other hand, the gold, in its metallic reality, ranks as the embodiment of value, as money. Gold, as gold, is exchange-value itself. As to its use-value, that has only an ideal existence, represented by the series of expressions of relative value in which it stands face to face with all other commodities, the sum of whose uses makes up the sum of the various uses of gold. These antagonistic forms of commodities are the real forms in which the process of their exchange moves and takes place.

Let us now accompany the owner of some commodity — say, our old friend the weaver of linen — to the scene of action, the market. His 20 yards of linen has a definite price, £2. He exchanges it for the £2, and then, like a man of the good old stamp that he is, he parts with the £2 for a family Bible of the same price. The linen, which in his eyes is a mere commodity, a depository of value, he alienates in exchange for gold, which is the linen's value-form, and this form he again parts with for another commodity, the Bible, which is destined to enter his house as an object of utility and of edification to its inmates. The exchange becomes an accomplished fact by two metamorphoses of opposite yet supplementary character — the conversion of the commodity into money, and the re-conversion of the money into a commodity. [16] The two phases of this metamorphosis are both of them distinct transactions of the weaver — selling, or the exchange of the commodity for money; buying, or the exchange of the money for a commodity; and, the unity of the two acts, selling in order to buy.

The result of the whole transaction, as regards the weaver, is this, that instead of being in possession of the linen, he now has the Bible; instead of his original commodity, he now possesses another of the same value but of different utility. In like manner he procures his other means of subsistence and means of production. From his point of view, the whole process effectuates nothing more than the exchange of the product of his labour for the product of some one else's, nothing more than an exchange of products.

The exchange of commodities is therefore accompanied by the following changes in their form.

Commodity — Money — Commodity.

C—————— M ———————C.

The result of the whole process is, so far as concerns the objects themselves, C − C, the exchange of one commodity for another, the circulation of materialised social labour. When this result is attained, the process is at an end.

C − M. First metamorphosis, or sale

The leap taken by value from the body of the commodity, into the body of the gold, is, as I have elsewhere called it, the salto mortale of the commodity. If it falls short, then, although the commodity itself is not harmed, its owner decidedly is. The social division of labour causes his labour to be as one-sided as his wants are many-sided. This is precisely the reason why the product of his labour serves him solely as exchange-value. But it cannot acquire the properties of a socially recognised universal equivalent, except by being converted into money. That money, however, is in some one else's pocket. In order to entice the money out of that pocket, our friend's commodity must, above all things, be a use-value to the owner of the money. For this, it is necessary that the labour expended upon it, be of a kind that is socially useful, of a kind that constitutes a branch of the social division of labour. But division of labour is a system of production which has grown up spontaneously and continues to grow behind the backs of the producers. The commodity to be exchanged may possibly be the product of some new kind of labour, that pretends to satisfy newly arisen requirements, or even to give rise itself to new requirements. A particular operation, though yesterday, perhaps, forming one out of the many operations conducted by one producer in creating a given commodity, may to-day separate itself from this connexion, may establish itself as an independent branch of labour and send its incomplete product to market as an independent commodity. The circumstances may or may not be ripe for such a separation. To-day the product satisfies a social want. Tomorrow the article may, either altogether or partially, be superseded by some other appropriate product. Moreover, although our weaver's labour may be a recognised branch of the social division of labour, yet that fact is by no means sufficient to guarantee the utility of his 20 yards of linen. If the community's want of linen, and such a want has a limit like every other want, should already be saturated by the products of rival weavers. our friend's product is superfluous, redundant, and consequently useless. Although people do not look a gift-horse in the mouth, our friend does not frequent the market for the purpose of making presents. But suppose his product turn out a real use-value, and thereby attracts money? The question arises, how much will it attract? No doubt the answer is already anticipated in the price of the article, in the exponent of the magnitude of its value. We leave out of consideration here any accidental miscalculation of value by our friend, a mistake that is soon rectified in the market. We suppose him to have spent on his product only that amount of labour-time that is on an average socially necessary. The price then, is merely the moneyname of the quantity of social labour realised in his commodity. But without the leave, and behind the back, of our weaver, the old-fashioned mode of weaving undergoes a change. The labour-time that yesterday was without doubt socially necessary to the production of a yard of linen, ceases to be so to-day, a fact which the owner of the money is only too eager to prove from the prices quoted by our friend's competitors. Unluckily for him, weavers are not few and far between. Lastly, suppose that every piece of linen in the market contains no more labour-time than is socially necessary. In spite of this, all these pieces taken as a whole, may have had superfluous labour-time spent upon them. If the market cannot stomach the whole quantity at the normal price of 2 shillings a yard, this proves that too great a portion of the total labour of the community has been expended in the form of weaving. The effect is the same as if each individual weaver had expended more labour-time upon his particular product than is socially necessary. Here we may say, with the German proverb: caught together, hung together. All the linen in the market counts but as one article of commerce, of which each piece is only an aliquot part. And as a matter of fact, the value also of each single yard is but the materialised form of the same definite and socially fixed quantity of homogeneous human labour.

We see then, commodities are in love with money, but "the course of true love never did run smooth." The quantitative division of labour is brought about in exactly the same spontaneous and accidental manner as its qualitative division. The owners of commodities therefore find out, that the same division of labour that turns them into independent private producers, also frees the social process of production and the relations of the individual producers to each other within that process, from all dependence on the will of those producers, and that the seeming mutual independence of the individuals is supplemented by a system of general and mutual dependence through or by means of the products.

The division of labour converts the product of labour into a commodity, and thereby makes necessary its further conversion into money. At the same time it also makes the accomplishment of this transubstantiation quite accidental. Here, however, we are only concerned with the phenomenon in its integrity, and we therefore assume its progress to be normal. Moreover, if the conversion take place at all, that is, if the commodity be not absolutely unsaleable, its metamorphosis does take place although the price realised may be abnormally above or below the value.

The seller has his commodity replaced by gold, the buyer has his gold replaced by a commodity. The fact which here stares us in the face is, that a commodity and gold, 20 yards of linen and £2, have changed hands and places, in other words, that they have been exchanged. But for what is the commodity exchanged? For the shape assumed by its own value, for the universal equivalent. And for what is the gold exchanged? For a particular form of its own use-value. Why does gold take the form of money face to face with the linen? Because the linen's price of £2, its denomination in money, has already equated the linen to gold in its character of money. A commodity strips off its original commodity-form on being alienated, i.e., on the instant its use-value actually attracts the gold, that before existed only ideally in its price. The realisation of a commodity's price, or of its ideal value-form, is therefore at the same time the realisation of the ideal use-value of money; the conversion of a commodity into money, is the simultaneous conversion of money into a commodity. The apparently single process is in reality a double one. From the pole of the commodity-owner it is a sale, from the opposite pole of the money-owner, it is a purchase. In other words, a sale is a purchase, C -- M is also M -- C. [18]

Up to this point we have considered men in only one economic capacity, that of owners of commodities, a capacity in which they appropriate the produce of the labour of others, by alienating that of their own labour. Hence, for one commodity-owner to meet with another who has money, it is necessary, either, that the product of the labour of the latter person, the buyer, should be in itself money, should be gold, the material of which money consists, or that his product should already have changed its skin and have stripped off its original form of a useful object. In order that it may play the part of money, gold must of course enter the market at some point or other. This point is to be found at the source of production of the metal, at which place gold is bartered, as the immediate product of labour, for some other product of equal value. From that moment it always represents the realised price of some commodity. [19] Apart from its exchange for other commodities at the source of its production, gold, in whose-so-ever hands it may be, is the transformed shape of some commodity alienated by its owner; it is the product of a sale or of the first metamorphosis C—-M. [20] Gold, as we saw, became ideal money, or a measure of values, in consequence of all commodities measuring their values by it, and thus contrasting it ideally with their natural shape as useful objects, and making it the shape of their value. It became real money, by the general alienation of commodities, by actually changing places with their natural forms as useful objects, and thus becoming in reality the embodiment of their values. When they assume this money-shape, commodities strip off every trace of their natural use-value, and of the particular kind of labour to which they owe their creation, in order to transform themselves into the uniform, socially recognised incarnation of homogeneous human labour. We cannot tell from the mere look of a piece of money, for what particular commodity it has been exchanged. Under their money-form all commodities look alike. Hence, money may be dirt, although dirt is not money. We will assume that the two gold pieces, in consideration of which our weaver has parted with his linen, are the metamorphosed shape of a quarter of wheat. The sale of the linen, C—-M, is at the same time its purchase, M—-C. But the sale is the first act of a process that ends with a transaction of an opposite nature, namely, the purchase of a Bible; the purchase of the linen, on the other hand, ends a movement that began with a transaction of an opposite nature, namely, with the sale of the wheat. C—-M (linen—-money), which is the first phase of C—-M'—-C (linen—-money—-Bible), is also M—-C (money—-linen), the last phase of another movement C—-M—-C (wheat—-money—-linen). The first metamorphosis of one commodity, its transformation from a commodity into money, is therefore also invariably the second metamorphosis of some other commodity, the retransformation of the latter from money into a commodity. [21]

M—-C, or purchase. The second and concluding metamorphosis of a commodity

Because money is the metamorphosed shape of all other commodities, the result of their general alienation, for this reason it is alienable itself without restriction or condition. It reads all prices backwards, and thus, so to say, depicts itself in the bodies of all other commodities, which offer to it the material for the realisation of its own use-value. At the same time the prices, wooing glances cast at money by commodities, define the limits of its convertibility, by pointing to its quantity. Since every commodity, on becoming money, disappears as a commodity, it is impossible to tell from the money itself, how it got into the hands of its possessor, or what article has been changed into it. Non olet, from whatever source it may come. Representing on the one hand a sold commodity, it represents on the other a commodity to be bought. [22]

M—-C, a purchase, is, at the same time, C—-M, a sale; the concluding metamorphosis of one commodity is the first metamorphosis of another. With regard to our weaver, the life of his commodity ends with the Bible, into which he has reconverted his £2. But suppose the seller of the Bible turns the £2 set free by the weaver into brandy M—-C, the concluding phase of C—-M—-C (linen—-money—-Bible), is also C—-M, the first phase of C—-M—-C (Bible—-money—-brandy). The producer of a particular commodity has that one article alone to offer; this he sells very often in large quantities, but his many and various wants compel him to split up the price realised, the sum of money set free, into numerous purchases. Hence a sale leads to many purchases of various articles. The concluding metamorphosis of a commodity thus constitutes an aggregation of first metamorphoses of various other commodities.

If we now consider the completed metamorphosis of a commodity, as a whole, it appears in the first place, that it is made up of two opposite and complementary movements, C—-M and M—-C. These two antithetical transmutations of a commodity are brought about by two antithetical social acts on the part of the owner, and these acts in their turn stamp the character of the economic parts played by him. As the person who makes a sale, he is a seller; as the person who makes a purchase, he is a buyer. But just as, upon every such transmutation of a commodity, its two forms, commodity-form and money-form, exist simultaneously but at opposite poles, so every seller has a buyer opposed to him, and every buyer a seller. While one particular commodity is going through its two transmutations in succession, from a commodity into money and from money into another commodity, the owner of the commodity changes in succession his part from that of seller to that of buyer. These characters of seller and buyer are therefore not permanent, but attach themselves in turns to the various persons engaged in the circulation of commodities.

The complete metamorphosis of a commodity, in its simplest form, implies four extremes, and three dramatic personae. First, a commodity comes face to face with money; the latter is the form taken by the value of the former, and exists in all its hard reality, in the pocket of the buyer. A commodity-owner is thus brought into contact with a possessor of money. So soon, now, as the commodity has been changed into money, the money becomes its transient equivalent-form, the use-value of which equivalent-form is to be found in the bodies of other commodities. Money, the final term of the first transmutation, is at the same time the starting-point for the second. The person who is a seller in the first transaction thus becomes a buyer in the second, in which a third commodity-owner appears on the scene as a seller. [23]

The two phases, each inverse to the other, that make up the metamorphosis of a commodity constitute together a circular movement, a circuit: commodity-form, stripping off of this form, and return to the commodity-form. No doubt, the commodity appears here under two different aspects. At the starting-point it is not a use-value to its owner; at the finishing point it is. So, too, the money appears in the first phase as a solid crystal of value, a crystal into which the commodity eagerly solidifies, and in the second, dissolves into the mere transient equivalent-form destined to be replaced by a use-value.

The two metamorphoses constituting the circuit are at the same time two inverse partial metamorphoses of two other commodities. One and the same commodity, the linen, opens the series of its own metamorphoses, and completes the metamorphosis of another (the wheat). In the first phase or sale, the linen plays these two parts in its own person. But, then, changed into gold, it completes its own second and final metamorphosis, and helps at the same time to accomplish the first metamorphosis of a third commodity. Hence the circuit made by one commodity in the course of its metamorphoses is inextricably mixed up with the circuits of other commodities. The total of all the different circuits constitutes the circulation of commodities.

The circulation of commodities differs from the direct exchange of products (barter), not only in form, but in substance. Only consider the course of events. The weaver has, as a matter of fact, exchanged his linen for a Bible, his own commodity for that of some one else. But this is true only so far as he himself is concerned. The seller of the Bible, who prefers something to warm his inside, no more thought of exchanging his Bible for linen than our weaver knew that wheat had been exchanged for his linen. B's commodity replaces that of A, but A and B do not mutually exchange those commodities. It may, of course, happen that A and B make simultaneous purchases, the one from the other; but such exceptional transactions are by no means the necessary result of the general conditions of the circulation of commodities. We see here, on the one hand, how the exchange of commodities breaks through all local and personal bounds inseparable from direct barter, and develops the circulation of the products of social labour; and on the other hand, how it develops a whole network of social relations spontaneous in their growth and entirely beyond the control of the actors. It is only because the farmer has sold his wheat that the weaver is enabled to sell his linen, only because the weaver has sold his linen that our Hotspur is enabled to sell his Bible, and only because the latter has sold the water of everlasting life that the distiller is enabled to sell his eau-de-vie, and so on.

The process of circulation, therefore, does not, like direct barter of products, become extinguished upon the use-values changing places and hands. The money does not vanish on dropping out of the circuit of the metamorphosis of a given commodity. It is constantly being precipitated into new places in the arena of circulation vacated by other commodities. In the complete metamorphosis of the linen, for example, linen — money — Bible, the linen first falls out of circulation, and money steps into its place. Then the Bible falls out of circulation, and again money takes its place. When one commodity replaces another, the money-commodity always sticks to the hands of some third person. [24] Circulation sweats money from every pore.

Nothing can be more childish than the dogma, that because every sale is a purchase, and every purchase a sale, therefore the circulation of commodities necessarily implies an equilibrium of sales and purchases. If this means that the number of actual sales is equal to the number of purchases, it is mere tautology. But its real purport is to prove that every seller brings his buyer to market with him. Nothing of the kind. The sale and the purchase constitute one identical act, an exchange between a commodity-owner and an owner of money, between two persons as opposed to each other as the two poles of a magnet. They form two distinct acts, of polar and opposite characters, when performed by one single person. Hence the identity of sale and purchase implies that the commodity is useless, if, on being thrown into the alchemistical retort of circulation, it does not come out again in the shape of money; if, in other words, it cannot be sold by its owner, and therefore be bought by the owner of the money. That identity further implies that the exchange, if it do take place, constitutes a period of rest, an interval, long or short, in the life of the commodity. Since the first metamorphosis of a commodity is at once a sale and a purchase, it is also an independent process in itself. The purchaser has the commodity, the seller has the money, i.e., a commodity ready to go into circulation at any time. No one can sell unless some one else purchases. But no one is forthwith bound to purchase, because he has just sold. Circulation bursts through all restrictions as to time, place, and individuals, imposed by direct barter, and this it effects by splitting up, into the antithesis of a sale and a purchase, the direct identity that in barter does exist between the alienation of one's own and the acquisition of some other man's product. To say that these two independent and antithetical acts have an intrinsic unity, are essentially one, is the same as to say that this intrinsic oneness expresses itself in an external antithesis. If the interval in time between the two complementary phases of the complete metamorphosis of a commodity become too great, if the split between the sale and the purchase become too pronounced, the intimate connexion between them, their oneness, asserts itself by producing — a crisis. The antithesis, use-value and value; the contradictions that private labour is bound to manifest itself as direct social labour, that a particularised concrete kind of labour has to pass for abstract human labour; the contradiction between the personification of objects and the representation of persons by things; all these antitheses and contradictions, which are immanent in commodities, assert themselves, and develop their modes of motion, in the antithetical phases of the metamorphosis of a commodity. These modes therefore imply the possibility, and no more than the possibility, of crises. The conversion of this mere possibility into a reality is the result of a long series of relations, that, from our present standpoint of simple circulation, have as yet no existence. [25]

B. The currency [26] of money

The change of form, C—-M—-C, by which the circulation of the material products of labour is brought about, requires that a given value in the shape of a commodity shall begin the process, and shall, also in the shape of a commodity, end it. The movement of the commodity is therefore a circuit. On the other hand, the form of this movement precludes a circuit from being made by the money. The result is not the return of the money, but its continued removal further and further away from its starting-point. So long as the seller sticks fast to his money, which is the transformed shape of his commodity, that commodity is still in the first phase of its metamorphosis, and has completed only half its course. But so soon as he completes the process, so soon as he supplements his sale by a purchase, the money again leaves the hands of its possessor. It is true that if the weaver, after buying the Bible, sell more linen, money comes back into his hands. But this return is not owing to the circulation of the first 20 yards of linen; that circulation resulted in the money getting into the hands of the seller of the Bible. The return of money into the hands of the weaver is brought about only by the renewal or repetition of the process of circulation with a fresh commodity, which renewed process ends with the same result as its predecessor did. Hence the movement directly imparted to money by the circulation of commodities takes the form of a constant motion away from its starting-point, of a course from the hands of one commodity-owner into those of another. This course constitutes its currency (cours de la monnaie).

The currency of money is the constant and monotonous repetition of the same process. The commodity is always in the hands of the seller; the money, as a means of purchase, always in the hands of the buyer. And money serves as a means of purchase by realising the price of the commodity. This realisation transfers the commodity from the seller to the buyer and removes the money from the hands of the buyer into those of the seller, where it again goes through the same process with another commodity. That this one-sided character of the money's motion arises out of the two-sided character of the commodity's motion, is a circumstance that is veiled over. The very nature of the circulation of commodities begets the opposite appearance. The first metamorphosis of a commodity is visibly, not only the money's movement, but also that of the commodity itself; in the second metamorphosis, on the contrary, the movement appears to us as the movement of the money alone. In the first phase of its circulation the commodity changes place with the money. Thereupon the commodity, under its aspect of a useful object, falls out of circulation into consumption. [27] In its stead we have its value-shape — the money. It then goes through the second phase of its circulation, not under its own natural shape, but under the shape of money. The continuity of the movement is therefore kept up by the money alone, and the same movement that as regards the commodity consists of two processes of an antithetical character, is, when considered as the movement of the money, always one and the same process, a continued change of places with ever fresh commodities. Hence the result brought about by the circulation of-commodities, namely, the replacing of one commodity by another, takes the appearance of having been effected not by means of the change of form of the commodities but rather by the money acting as a medium of circulation, by an action that circulates commodities, to all appearance motionless in themselves, and transfers them from hands in which they are non-use-values, to hands in which they are use-values; and that in a direction constantly opposed to the direction of the money. The latter is continually withdrawing commodities from circulation and stepping into their places, and in thus way continually moving further and further from its starting-point Hence although the movement of the money is merely the expression of the circulation of commodities, yet the contrary appears to be the actual fact,

and the circulation of commodities seems to be the result of the movement of the money.
28

Again, money functions as a means of circulation only because in it the values of commodities have independent reality. Hence its movement, as the medium of circulation, is, in fact, merely the movement of commodities while changing their forms. This fact must therefore make itself plainly visible in the currency of money. Thus the linen for instance, first of all changes its commodity-form into its moneyform. The second term of its first metamorphosis, C—-M, the money form, then becomes the first term of its final metamorphosis, M—-C, its re-conversion into the Bible. But each of these two changes of form is accomplished by an exchange between commodity and money, by their reciprocal displacement. The same pieces of coin come into the seller's hand as the alienated form of the commodity and leave it as the absolutely alienable form of the commodity. They are displaced twice. The first metamorphosis of the linen puts these coins into the weaver's pocket, the second draws them out of it. The two inverse changes undergone by the same commodity are reflected in the displacement, twice repeated, but in opposite directions, of the same pieces of coin.

If, on the contrary, only one phase of the metamorphosis is gone through, if there are only sales or only purchases, then a given piece of money changes its place only once. Its second change of place always expresses the second metamorphosis of the commodity, its re-conversion from money. The frequent repetition of the displacement of the same coins reflects not only the series of metamorphoses that a single commodity has gone through, but also the intertwining of the innumerable metamorphoses in the world of commodities in general. It is a matter of course, that all this is applicable to the simple circulation of commodities alone, the only form that we are now considering.

Every commodity, when it first steps into circulation, and undergoes its first change of form, does so only to fall out of circulation again and to be replaced by other commodities. Money, on the contrary, as the medium of circulation, keeps continually within the sphere of circulation, and moves about in it. The question therefore arises, how much money this sphere constantly absorbs?

In a given country there take place every day at the same time, but in different localities, numerous one-sided metamorphoses of commodities, or, in other words, numerous sales and numerous purchases. The commodities are equated beforehand in imagination, by their prices, to definite quantities of money. And since, in the form of circulation now under consideration, money and commodities always come bodily face to face, one at the positive pole of purchase, the other at the negative pole of sale, it is clear that the amount of the means of circulation required, is determined beforehand by the sum of the prices of all these commodities. As a matter of fact, the money in reality represents the quantity or sum of gold ideally expressed beforehand by the sum of the prices of the commodities. The equality of these two sums is therefore self-evident. We know, however, that, the values of commodities remaining constant, their prices vary with the value of gold (the material of money), rising in proportion as it falls, and falling in proportion as it rises. Now if, in consequence of such a rise or fall in the value of gold, the sum of the prices of commodities fall or rise, the quantity of money in currency must fall or rise to the same extent. The change in the quantity of the circulating medium is, in this case, it is true, caused by the money itself, yet not in virtue of its function as a medium of circulation, but of its function as a measure of value. First, the price of the commodities varies inversely as the value of the money, and then the quantity of the medium of circulation varies directly as the price of the commodities. Exactly the same thing would happen if, for instance, instead of the value of gold falling, gold were replaced by silver as the measure of value, or if, instead of the value of silver rising, gold were to thrust silver out from being the measure of value. In the one case, more silver would be current than gold was before; in the other case, less gold would be current than silver was before. In each case the value of the material of money, i. e., the value of the commodity that serves as the measure of value, would have undergone a change, and therefore so, too, would the prices of commodities which express their values in money, and so, too, would the quantity of money current whose function it is to realise those prices. We have already seen, that the sphere of circulation has an opening through which gold (or the material of money generally) enters into it as a commodity with a given value. Hence, when money enters on its functions as a measure of value, when it expresses prices, its value is already determined. If now its value fall, this fact is first evidenced by a change in the prices of those commodities that are directly bartered for the precious metals at the sources of their production. The greater part of all other commodities, especially in the imperfectly developed stages of civil society, will continue for a long time to be estimated by the former antiquated and illusory value of the measure of value. Nevertheless, one commodity infects another through their common value-relation, so that their prices, expressed in gold or in silver, gradually settle down into the proportions determined by their comparative values, until finally the values of all commodities are estimated in terms of the new value of the metal that constitutes money. This process is accompanied by the continued increase in the quantity of the precious metals, an increase caused by their streaming in to replace the articles directly bartered for them at their sources of production. In proportion therefore as commodities in general acquire their true prices, in proportion as their values become estimated according to the fallen value of the precious metal, in the same proportion the quantity of that metal necessary for realising those new prices is provided beforehand. A one-sided observation of the results that followed upon the discovery of fresh supplies of gold and silver, led some economists in the 17th, and particularly in the 18th century, to the false conclusion, that the prices of commodities had gone up in consequence of the increased quantity of gold and silver serving as means of circulation. Hence momentarily whenever we estimate the price of a commodity. On this supposition then, the quantity of the medium of circulation is determined by the sum of the prices that have to be realised. If now we further suppose the price of each commodity to be given, the sum of the prices clearly depends on the mass of commodities in circulation. It requires but little racking of brains to comprehend that if one quarter of wheat costs £2, 100 quarters will cost £200, 200 quarters £400, and so on, that consequently the quantity of money that changes place with the wheat, when sold, must increase with the quantity of that wheat.

If the mass of commodities remain constant, the quantity of circulating money varies with the fluctuations in the prices of those commodities. It increases and diminishes because the sum of the prices increases or diminishes in consequence of the change of price. To produce this effect, it is by no means requisite that the prices of all commodities should rise or fall simultaneously. A rise or a fall in the prices of a number of leading articles, is sufficient in the one case to increase, in the other to diminish, the sum of the prices of all commodities, and, therefore, to put more or less money in circulation. Whether the change in the price correspond to an actual change of value in the commodities, or whether it be the result of mere fluctuations in market-prices, the effect on the quantity of the medium of circulation remains the same. Suppose the following articles to be sold or partially metamorphosed simultaneously in different localities: say, one quarter of wheat, 20 yards of linen, one Bible, and 4 gallons of brandy. If the price of each article be £2, and the sum of the prices to be realised be consequently £8, it follows that £8 in money must go into circulation. If, on the other hand, these same articles are links in the following chain of metamorphoses: 1 quarter of wheat — £2 — 20 yards of linen — £2 — 1 Bible — £2 — 4 gallons of brandy — £2, a chain that is already well known to us, in that case the £2 cause the different commodities to circulate one after the other, and after realising their prices successively, and therefore the sum of those prices, £8, they come to rest at last in the pocket of the distiller. The £2 thus make four moves. This repeated change of place of the same pieces of money corresponds to the double change in form of the commodities, to their motion in opposite directions through two stages of circulation. and to the interlacing of the metamorphoses of different commodities. [29] These antithetic and complementary phases, of which the process of metamorphosis consists, are gone through, not simultaneously, but successively. Time is therefore required for the completion of the series. Hence the velocity of the currency of money is measured by the number of moves made by a given piece of money in a given time. Suppose the circulation of the 4 articles takes a day. The sum of the prices to be realised in the day is £8, the number of moves of the two pieces of money is four, and the quantity of money circulating is £2. Hence, for a given interval of time during the process of circulation, we have the following relation: the quantity of money functioning as the circulating medium is equal to the sum of the prices of the commodities divided by the number of moves made by coins of the same denomination. This law holds generally.

The total circulation of commodities in a given country during a given period is made up on the one hand of numerous isolated and simultaneous partial metamorphoses, sales which are at the same time purchases, in which each coin changes its place only once, or makes only one move; on the other hand, of numerous distinct series of metamorphoses partly running side by side, and partly coalescing with each other, in each of which series each coin makes a number of moves, the number being greater or less according to circumstances. The total number of moves made by all the circulating coins of one denomination being given, we can arrive at the average number of moves made by a single coin of that denomination, or at the average velocity of the currency of money. The quantity of money thrown into the circulation at the beginning of each day is of course determined by the sum of the prices of all the commodities circulating simultaneously side by side. But once in circulation, coins are, so to say, made responsible for one another. If the one increase its velocity, the other either retards its own, or altogether falls out of circulation; for the circulation can absorb only such a quantity of gold as when multiplied by the mean number of moves made by one single coin or element, is equal to the sum of the prices to be realised. Hence if the number of moves made by the separate pieces increase, the total number of those pieces in circulation diminishes. If the number of the moves diminish, the total number of pieces increases. Since the quantity of money capable of being absorbed by the circulation is given for a given mean velocity of currency, all that is necessary in order to abstract a given number of sovereigns from the circulation is to throw the same number of one-pound notes into it, a trick well known to all bankers.

Just as the currency of money, generally considered, is but a reflex of the circulation of commodities, or of the antithetical metamorphoses they undergo, so, too, the velocity of that currency reflects the rapidity with which commodities change their forms, the continued interlacing of one series of metamorphoses with another, the hurried social interchange of matter, the rapid disappearance of commodities from the sphere of circulation, and the equally rapid substitution of fresh ones in their places. Hence, in the velocity of the currency we have the fluent unity of the antithetical and complementary phases, the unity of the conversion of the useful aspect of commodities into their value-aspect, and their re-conversion from the latter aspect to the former, or the unity of the two processes of sale and purchase. On the other hand, the retardation of the currency reflects the separation of these two processes into isolated antithetical phases, reflects the stagnation in the change of form, and therefore, in the social interchange of matter. The circulation itself, of course, gives no clue to the origin of this stagnation; it merely puts in evidence the phenomenon itself. The general public, who, simultaneously with the retardation of the currency, see money appear and disappear less frequently at the periphery of circulation, naturally attribute this retardation to a quantitative deficiency in the circulating medium. [30]

The total quantity of money functioning during a given period as the circulating medium, is determined, on the one hand, by the sum of the prices of the circulating commodities, and on the other hand, by the rapidity with which the antithetical phases of the metamorphoses follow one another. On this rapidity depends what proportion of the sum of the prices can, on the average, be realised by each single coin. But the sum of the prices of the circulating commodities depends on the quantity, as well as on the prices, of the commodities. These three factors, however, state of prices, quantity of circulating commodities, and velocity of money-currency, are all variable. Hence, the sum of the prices to be realisedj and consequently the quantity of the circulating medium depending on that sum, will vary with the numerous variations of these three factors in combination. Of these variations we shall consider those alone that have been the most important in the history of prices.

While prices remain constant, She quantity of the circulating medium may increase owing to the number of circulating commodities increasing, or to the velocity of currency decreasing, or to a combination of the two. On the other hand the quantity of the circulating medium may decrease with a decreasing number of commodities, or with an increasing rapidity of their circulation.

With a general rise in the prices of commodities, the quantity of the circulating medium will remain constant, provided the number of commodities in circulation decrease proportionally to the increase in their prices, or provided the velocity of currency increase at the same rate as prices rise, the number of commodities in circulation remaining constant. The quantity of the circulating medium may decrease, owing to the number of commodities decreasing more rapidly; or to the velocity of currency rise.

With a general fall in the prices of commodities, the quantity of the circulating medium will remain constant, provided the number of commodities increase proportionally to their fall in price, or provided the velocity of currency decrease in the same proportion. The quantity of the circulating medium will increase, provided the number of commodities increase quicker, or the rapidity of circulation decrease quicker, than the prices fall.

The variations of the different factors may mutually compensate each other, so that notwithstanding their continued instability, the sum of the prices to be realised and the quantity of money in circulation remain constant; consequently, we find, especially if we take long periods into consideration, that the deviations from the average level, of the quantity of money current in any country, are much smaller than we should at first siht expect, apart of course from excessive perturbations periodically arising from industrial and commercial crises, or less frequently, from fluctuations in the value of money.

The law, that the quantity of the circulating medium is determined by the sum of the prices of the commodities circulating, and the average increasing more rapidly, than prices velocity of currency [31] may also be stated as follows: given the sum of the values of commodities, and the average rapidity of their metamorphoses, the quantity of precious metal current as money depends on the value of that precious metal. The erroneous opinion that it is, on the contrary, prices that are determined by the quantity of the circulating medium, and that the latter depends on the quantity of the precious metals in a country; [32] this opinion was based by those who first held it, on the absurd hypothesis that commodities are without a price, and money without a value, when they first enter into circulation, and that, once in the circulation, an aliquot part of the medley of commodities is exchanged for an aliquot part of the heap of precious metals. [33]

C. Coin and symbols of value

That money takes the shape of coin, springs from its function as the circulating medium. The weight of gold represented in imagination by the prices or money-names of commodities, must confront those commodities, within the circulation, in the shape of coins or pieces of gold of a given denomination. Coining, like the establishment of a standard of prices, is the business of the State. The different national uniforms worn at home by gold and silver as coins, and doffed again in the market of the world, indicate the separation between the internal or national spheres of the circulation of commodities, and their universal sphere.

The only difference, therefore, between coin and bullion, is one of shape, and gold can at any time pass from one form to the other. [34] But no sooner does coin leave the mint, than it immediately finds itself on the high-road to the melting pot. During their currency, coins wear away, some more, others less. Name and substance, nominal weight and real weight, begin their process of separation. Coins of the same denomination become different in value, because they are different in weight. The weight of gold fixed upon as the standard of prices, deviates from the weight that serves as the circulating medium, and the latter thereby ceases any longer to be a real equivalent of the commodities whose prices it realises. The history of coinage during the middle ages and down into the 18th century, records the ever renewed confusion arising from this cause. The natural tendency of circulation to convert coins into a mere semblance of what they profess to be, into a symbol of the weight of metal they are officially supposed to contain, is recognised by modern legislation, which fixes the loss of weight sufficient to demonetise a gold coin, or to make it no longer legal tender.

The fact that the currency of coins itself effects a separation between their nominal and their real weight, creating a distinction between them as mere pieces of metal on the one hand, and as coins with a definite function on the other — this fact implies the latent possibility of replacing metallic coins by tokens of some other material, by symbols serving the same purposes as coins. The practical difficulties in the way of coining extremely minute quantities of gold or silver, and the circumstance that at first the less precious metal is used as a measure of value instead of the-more precious, copper instead of silver, silver instead of gold, and that the less precious circulates as money until dethroned by the more precious — all these facts explain the parts historically played by silver and copper tokens as substitutes for gold coins. Silver and copper tokens take the place of gold in those regions of the circulation where coins pass from hand to hand most rapidly, and are subject to the maximum amount of wear and tear. This occurs where sales and purchases on a very small scale are continually happening. In order to prevent these satellites from establishing themselves permanently in the place of gold, positive enactments determine the extent to which they must be compulsorily received as payment instead of gold. The particular tracks pursued by the different species of coin in currency, run naturally into each other. The tokens keep company with gold, to pay fractional parts of the smallest gold coin; gold is, on the one hand, constantly pouring into retail circulation, and on the other hand is as constantly being thrown out again by being changed into tokens. [35]

The weight of metal in the silver and copper tokens is arbitrarily fixed by law. When in currency, they wear away even more rapidly than gold coins. Hence their functions are totally independent of their weight, and consequently of all value. The function of gold as coin becomes completely independent of the metallic value of that gold. Therefore things that are relatively without value, such as paper notes, can serve as coins in its place. This purely symbolic character is to a certain extent masked in metal tokens. In paper money it stands out plainly. In fact, ce n'est que le premier pas qui coûte.

We allude here only to inconvertible paper money issued by the State and having compulsory circulation. It has its immediate origin in the metallic currency. Money based upon credit implies on the other hand conditions, which, from our standpoint of the simple circulation of commodities, are as yet totally unknown to us. But we may affirm this much, that just as true paper money takes its rise in the function of money as the circulating medium, so money based upon credit takes root spontaneously in the function of money as the means of payment. [36]

The State puts in circulation bits of paper on which their various denominations, say £1, £5, &c., are printed. In so far as they actually take the place of gold to the same amount, their movement is subject to the laws that regulate the currency of money itself. A law peculiar to the circulation of paper money can spring up only from the proportion in which that paper money represents gold. Such a law exists; stated simply, it is as follows: the issue of paper money must not exceed in amount the gold (or silver as the case may be) which would actually circulate if not replaced by symbols. Now the quantity of gold which the circulation can absorb, constantly-fluctuates about a given level. Still, the mass of the circulating medium in a given country never sinks below a certain minimum easily ascertained by actual experience. The fact that this minimum mass continually undergoes changes in its constituent parts, or that the pieces of gold of which it consists are being constantly replaced by fresh ones, causes of course no change either in its amount or in the continuity of its circulation. It can therefore be replaced by paper symbols. If, on the other hand, all the conduits of circulation were to-day filled with paper money to the full extent of their capacity for absorbing money, they might to-morrow be overflowing in consequence of a fluctuation in the circulation of commodities. There would no longer be any standard. If the paper money exceed its proper limit, which is the amount in gold coins of the like denomination that can actually be current, it would, apart from the danger of falling into general disrepute, represent only that quantity of gold, which, in accordance with the laws of the circulation of commodities, is required, and is alone capable of being represented by paper. If the quantity of paper money issued be double what it ought to be, then, as a matter of fact, £1 would be the money-name not of 1/4 of an ounce, but of 1/8 of an ounce of gold. The effect would be the same as if an alteration had taken place in the function of gold as a standard of prices. Those values that were previously expressed by the price of £1 would now be expressed by the price of £2.

Paper money is a token representing gold or money. The relation between it and the values of commodities is this, that the latter are ideally expressed in the same quantities of gold that are symbolically represented by the paper. Only in so far as paper money represents gold, which like all other commodities has value, is it a symbol of value. [37]

Finally, some one may ask why gold is capable of being replaced by tokens that have no value? But, as we have already seen, it is capable of being so replaced only in so &r as it functions exclusively as coin, or as the circulating medium, and as nothing else. Now, money has other functions besides this one, and the isolated function of serving as the mere circulating medium is not necessarily the only one attached to gold coin, although this is the case with those abraded coins that continue to circulate. Each piece of money is a mere coin, or means of circulation, only so long as it actually circulates. But this is just the case with that minimum mass of gold, which is capable of being replaced by paper money. That mass remains constantly within the sphere of circulation, continually functions as a circulating medium, and exists exclusively for that purpose. Its movement therefore represents nothing but the continued alternation of the inverse phases of the metamorphosis C—-M—-C, phases in which commodities confront their value-forms, only to disappear again immediately. The independent existence of the exchange-value of a commodity is here a transient apparition, by means of which the commodity is immediately replaced by another commodity. Hence, in this process which continually makes money pass from hand to hand, the mere symbolical existence of money suffices. Its functional existence absorbs, so to say, its material existence. Being a transient and objective reflex of the prices of commodities, it serves only as a symbol of itself, and is therefore capable of being replaced by a token. [38] One thing is, however, requisite; this token must have an objective social validity of its own, and this the paper symbol acquires by its forced currency. This compulsory action of the State can take effect only within that inner sphere of circulation which is coterminous with the territories of the community, but it is also only within that sphere that money completely responds to its function of being the circulating medium, or becomes coin.

Section 3 Money

The commodity that functions as a measure of value, and, either in its own person or by a representative, as the medium of circulation, is money. Gold (or silver) is therefore money. It functions as money, on the one hand, when it has to be present in its own golden person. It is then the money-commodity, neither merely ideal, as in its function of a measure of value, nor capable of being represented, as in its function of circulating medium. On the other hand, it also functions as money, when by virtue of its function, whether that function be performed in person or by representative, it congeals into the sole form of value, the only adequate form of existence of exchange-value, in opposition to use-value, represented by all other commodities.

A. Hoarding

The continual movement in circuits of the two antithetical metamorphoses of commodities, or the never ceasing alternation of sale and purchase, is reflected in the restless currency of money, or in the function that money performs of a perpetuum mobile of circulation. But so soon as the series of metamorphoses is interrupted, so soon as sales are not supplemented by subsequent purchases, money ceases to be mobilised; it is transformed, as Boisguillebert says, from "meuble" into "immouble", from movable into immovable, from coin into money.

With the very earliest development of the circulation of commodities, there is also developed the necessity, and the passionate desire, to hold fast the product of the first metamorphosis. This product is the transformed shape of the commodity, or its gold-chrysalis. [39] Commodities are thus sold not for the purpose of buying others, but in order to replace their commodity-form by their money-form. From being the mere means of effecting the circulation of commodities, this change of form becomes the end and aim. The changed form of the commodity is thus prevented from functioning as its unconditionally alienable form, or as its merely transient money-form. The money becomes petrified into a hoard, and the seller becomes a hoarder of money.

In the early stages of the circulation of commodities, it is the surplus use-values alone that are converted into money. Gold and silver thus become of themselves social expressions for superfluity or wealth. This naive form of hoarding becomes perpetuated in those communities in which the traditional mode of production is carried on for the supply of a fixed and limited circle of home wants. It is thus with the people of Asia, and particularly of the East Indies. Vanderlint, who fancies that the prices of commodities in a country are determined by the quantity of gold and silver to be found in it, asks himself why Indian commodities are so cheap. Answer: Because the Hindus bury their money. From 1602 to 1734, he remarks, they buried 150 millions of pounds sterling of silver, which originally came from America to Europe. [40] In the 10 years from 1856 to 1866, England exported to India and China (120,000,000 in silver, which had been received in exchange for Australian gold. Most of the silver exported to China makes its way to India.

As the production of commodities further develops, every producer of commodities is compelled. to make sure of the nexus rerum or the social pledge. [41] His wants are constantly making themselves felt, and necessitate the continual purchase of other people's commodities, while the production and sale of his own goods require time, and depend upon circumstances. In order then to be able to buy without selling, he must have sold previously without buying. This operation, conducted on a general scale, appears to imply a contradiction. But the precious metals at the sources of their production are directly exchanged for other commodities. And here we have sales (by the owners of commodities) without purchases (by the owners of gold or silver). [42] And subsequent sales, by other producers, unfollowed by purchases, merely bring about the distribution of the newly produced precious metals among all the owners of commodities. In this way, all along the line of exchange, hoards of gold and silver of varied extent are accumulated. With the possibility of holding and storing up exchange-value in the shape of a particular commodity, arises also the greed for gold. Along with the extension of circulation, increases the power of money, that absolutely social form of wealth ever ready for use. "Gold is a wonderful thing! Whoever possesses it is lord of all he wants. By means of gold one can even get souls into Paradise." (Columbus in his letter from Jamaica, 1503.) Since gold does not disclose what has been transformed into it, everything, commodity or not, is convertible into gold. Everything becomes saleable and buyable. The circulation becomes the great social retort into which everything is thrown, to come out again as a gold-crystal. Not even are the bones of saints, and still less are more delicate res sacrosanctae, extra commercium hominum able to withstand this alchemy. [43] Just as every qualitative difference between commodities is extinguished in money, so money, on its side, like the radical leveller that it is, does away with all distinctions. [43a] But money itself is a commodity, an external object, capable of becoming the private property of any individual. Thus social power becomes the private power of private persons. The ancients therefore denounced money as subversive of the economic and moral order of things. [43b] Modern society, which, soon after its birth, pulled Plutus by the hair of his head from the bowels of the earth, [44] greets gold as its Holy Grail, as the glittering incarnation of the very principle of its own life.

A commodity, in its capacity of a use-value, satisfies a particular want, and is a particular element of material wealth. But the value of a commodity measures the degree of its attraction for all other elements of material wealth, and therefore measures the social wealth of its owner. To a barbarian owner of commodities, and even to a West-European peasant, value is the same as value-form, and therefore. to him the increase in his hoard of gold and silver is an increase in value. It is true that the value of money varies, at one time in consequence of a variation in its own value, at another, in consequence of a change in the values of commodities. But this, on the one hand, does not prevent 200 ounces of gold from still containing more value than 100 ounces, nor, on the other hand, does it hinder the actual metallic form of this article from continuing to be the universal equivalent form of all other commodities, and the immediate social incarnation of all human labour. The desire after hoarding is in its very nature unsatiable. In its qualitative aspect, or formally considered, money has no bounds to its efficacy, i.e., it is the universal representative of material wealth, because it is directly convertible into any other commodity. But, at the same time, every actual sum of money is limited in amount, and, therefore, as a means of purchasing, has only a limited efficacy. This antagonism between the quantitative limits of money and its qualitative boundlessness, continually acts as a spur to the hoarder in his Sisyphus-like labour of accumulating. It is with him as it is with a conqueror who sees in every new country annexed, only a new boundary.

In order that gold may be held as money, and made to form a hoard, it must be prevented from circulating, or from transforming itself into a means of enjoyment. The hoarder, therefore, makes a sacrifice of the lusts of the flesh to his gold fetish. He acts in earnest up to the Gospel of abstention. On the other hand, he can withdraw from circulation no more than what he has thrown into it in the shape of commodities. The more he produces, the more he is able to sell. Hard work, saving, and avarice are, therefore, his three cardinal virtues, and to sell much and buy little the sum of his political economy. [45]

By the side of the gross form of a hoard, we find also its aesthetic form in the possession of gold and silver articles. This grows with the wealth of civil society. "Soyons riches ou paraissons riches" (Diderot).

In this way there is created, on the one hand, a constantly extending market for gold and silver, unconnected with their functions as money, and, on the other hand, a latent source of supply, to which recourse is had principally in times of crisis and social disturbance.

Hoarding serves various purposes in the economy of the metallic circulation. Its first function arises out of the conditions to which the currency of gold and silver coins is subject. We have seen how, along with the continual fluctuations in the extent and rapidity of the circulation of commodities and in their prices, the quantity of money current unceasingly ebbs and flows. This mass must, therefore, be capable of expansion and contraction. At one time money must be attracted in order to act as circulating coin, at another, circulating coin must be repelled in order to act again as more or less stagnant money. In order that the mass of money, actually current, may constantly saturate the absorbing power of the circulation, it is necessary that the quantity of gold and silver in a country be greater than the quantity required to function as coin. This condition is fulfilled by money taking the form of hoards. These reserves serve as conduits for the supply or withdrawal of money to or from the circulation, which in this way never overflows its banks. [46]

B. Means of Payment

In the simple form of the circulation of commodities hitherto considered, we found a given value always presented to us in a double shape, as a commodity at one pole, as money at the opposite pole. The owners of commodities came therefore into contact as the respective representatives of what were already equivalents. But with the development of circulation, conditions arise under which the alienation of commodities becomes separated, by an interval of time, from the realisation of their prices. It will be sufficient to indicate the most simple of these conditions. One sort of article requires a longer, another a shorter time for its production. Again, the production of different commodities depends on different seasons of the year. One sort of commodity may be born on its own market place, another has to make a long journey to market. Commodity-owner No. 1, may therefore be ready to sell, before No. 2 is ready to buy. When the same transactions are continually repeated between the same persons, the conditions of sale are regulated in accordance with the conditions of production. On the other hand, the use of a given commodity, of a house, for instance, is sold (in common parlance, let) for a definite period. Here, it is only at the end of the term that the buyer has actually received the use-value of the commodity. He therefore buys it before he pays for it. The vendor sells an existing commodity, the purchaser buys as the mere representative of money, or rather of future money. The vendor becomes a creditor, the purchaser becomes a debtor. Since the metamorphosis of commodities, or the development of their value-form, appears here under a new aspect, money also acquires a fresh function; it becomes the means of payment.

The character of creditor, or of debtor, results here from the simple circulation. The change in the form of that circulation stamps buyer and seller with this new die. At first, therefore, these new parts are just as transient and alternating as those of seller and buyer, and are in turns played by the same actors. But the opposition is not nearly so pleasant, and is far more capable of crystallisation. [47] The same characters can, however, be assumed independently of the circulation of commodities. The class-struggles of the ancient world took the form chiefly of a contest between debtors and creditors, which in Rome ended in the ruin of the plebeian debtors. They were displaced by slaves. In the middle ages the contest ended with the ruin of the feudal debtors, who lost their political power together with the economic basis on which it was established. Nevertheless, the money relation of debtor and creditor that existed at these two periods reflected only the deeper-lying antagonism between the general economic conditions of existence of the classes in question.

Let us return to the circulation of commodities. The appearance of the two equivalents, commodities and money, at the two poles of the process of sale, has ceased to be simultaneous. The money functions now, first as a measure of value in the determination of the price of the commodity sold; the price fixed by the contract measures the obligation of the debtor, or the sum of money that he has to pay at a fixed date. Secondly, it serves as an ideal means of purchase. Although existing only in the promise of the buyer to pay, it causes the commodity to change hands. It is not before the day fixed for payment that the means of payment actually steps into circulation, leaves the hand of the buyer for that of the seller. The circulating medium was transformed into a hoard, because the process stopped short after the first phase, because the converted shape of the commodity, viz., the money, was withdrawn from circulation. The means of payment enters the circulation, but only after the commodity has left it. The money is no longer the means that brings about the process. It only brings it to a close, by stepping in as the absolute form of existence of exchange-value, or as the universal commodity. The seller turned his commodity into money, in order thereby to satisfy some want, the hoarder did the same in order to keep his commodity in its money-shape, and the debtor in order to be able to pay; if he do not pay, his goods will be sold by the sheriff. The value-form of commodities, money, is therefore now the end and aim of a sale, and that owing to a social necessity springing out of the process of circulation itself.

The buyer converts money back into commodities before he has turned commodities into money: in other words, he achieves the second metamorphosis of commodities before the first. The seller's commodity circulates, and realises its price, but only in the shape of a legal claim upon money. It is converted into a use-value before it has been converted into money. The completion of its first metamorphosis follows only at a later period. [48]

The obligations falling due within a given period, represent the sum of the prices of the commodities, the sale of which gave rise to those obligations. The quantity of gold necessary to realise this sum, depends, in the first instance, on the rapidity of currency of the means of payment. That quantity is conditioned by two circumstances: first the relations between debtors and creditors form a sort of chain, in such a way that A, when he receives money from his debtor B, straightway hands it over to C his creditor, and so on; the second circumstance is the length of the intervals between the different due-days of the obligations. The continuous chain of payments, or retarded first metamorphoses, is essentially different from that interlacing of the series of metamorphoses which we considered on a former page. By the currency of the circulating medium, the connexion between buyers and sellers, is not merely expressed. This connexion is originated by, and exists in, the circulation alone. Contrariwise, the movement of the means of payment expresses a social relation that was in existence long before.

The fact that a number of sales take place simultaneously, and side by side, limits the extent to which coin can be replaced by the rapidity of currency. On the other hand, this fact is a new lever in economising the means of payment. In proportion as payments are concentrated at one spot, special institutions and methods are developed for their liquidation. Such in the middle ages were the virements at Lyons. The debts due to A from B, to B from C, to C from A, and so on, have only to be confronted with each other, in order to annul each other to a certain extent like positive and negative quantities. There thus remains only a single balance to pay. The greater the amount of the payments concentrated, the less is this balance relatively to that amount, and the less is the mass of the means of payment in circulation.

The function of money as the means of payment implies a contradiction without a terminus medius. In so far as the payments balance one another, money functions only ideally as money of account, as a measure of value. In so far as actual payments have to be made, money does not serve as a circulating medium, as a mere transient agent in the interchange of products, but as the individual incarnation of social labour, as the independent form of existence of exchange-value, as the universal commodity. This contradiction comes to a head in those phases of industrial and commercial crises which are known as monetary crises. [49] Such a crisis occurs only where the ever-lengthening chain of payments, and an artificial system of settling them, has been fully developed. Whenever there is a general and extensive disturbance of this mechanism, no matter what its cause, money becomes suddenly and immediately transformed, from its merely ideal shape of money of account, into hard cash. Profane commodities can no longer replace it.

The use-value of commodities becomes valueless, and their value vanishes in the presence of its own independent form. On the eve of the crisis, the bourgeois, with the self-sufficiency that springs from intoxicating prosperity, declares money to be a vain imagination. Commodities alone are money. But now the cry is everywhere: money alone is a commodity! As the hart pants after fresh water, so pants his soul after money, the only wealth. [50] In a crisis, the antithesis between commodities and their value-form, money, becomes heightened into an absolute contradiction. Hence, in such events, the form under which money appears is of no importance. The money famine continues, whether payments have to be made in gold or in credit money such as bank-notes. [51]

If we now consider the sum total of the money current during a given period, we shall find that, given the rapidity of currency of the circulating medium and of the means of payment, it is equal to the sum of the prices to be realised, plus the sum of the payments falling due, minus the payments that balance each other, minus finally the number of circuits in which the same piece of coin serves in turn as means of circulation and of payment. Hence, even when prices, rapidity of currency, and the extent of the economy in payments, are given, the quantity of money current and the mass of commodities circulating during a given period, such as a day, no longer correspond. Money that represents commodities long withdrawn from circulation, continues to be current. Commodities circulate, whose equivalent in money will not appear on the scene till some future day. oreover, the debts contracted each day, and the payments falling due on the same day, are quite incommensurable quantities. [52]

Credit-money springs directly out of the function of money as a means of payment. Certificates of the debts owing for the purchased commodities circulate for the purpose of transferring those debts to others. On the other hand, to the same extent as the system of credit is extended, so is the function of money as a means of payment. In that character it takes various forms peculiar to itself under which it makes itself at home in the sphere of great commercial transactions. Gold and silver coin, on the other hand, are mostly relegated to the sphere of retail trade. [53]

When the production of commodities has sufficiently extended itself, money begins to serve as the means of payment beyond the sphere of the circulation of commodities. It becomes the commodity that is the universal subject-matter of all contracts. [54] Rents, taxes, and such like payments are transformed from payments in kind into money payments. To what extent this transformation depends upon the general conditions of production, is shown, to take one example, by the fact that the Roman Empire twice failed in its attempt to levy all contributions in money. The unspeakable misery of the French agricultural population under Louis XIV., a misery so eloquently denounced by Boisguillebert, Marshal Vauban, and others, was due not only to the weight of the taxes, but also to the conversion of taxes in kind into money taxes. [55] In Asia, on the other hand, the fact that state taxes are chiefly composed of rents payable in kind, depends on conditions of production that are reproduced with the regularity of natural phenomena. And this mode of payment tends in its turn to maintain the ancient form of production. It is one of the secrets of the conservation of the Ottoman Empire. If the foreign trade, forced upon Japan by Europeans, should lead to the substitution of money rents for rents in kind, it will be all up with the exemplary agriculture of that country. The narrow economic conditions under which that agriculture is carried on, will be swept away.

In every country, certain days of the year become by habit recognised settling days for various large and recurrent payments. These dates depend, apart from other revolutions in the wheel of reproduction, on conditions closely connected with the seasons. They also regulate the dates for payments that have no direct connexion with the circulation of commodities such as taxes, rents, and so on. The quantity of money requisite to make the-payments, falling due on those dates all over the country, causes periodical, though merely superficial, perturbations in the economy of the medium of payment. [56]

From the law of the rapidity of currency of the means of payment, it follows that the quantity of the means of payment required for all periodical payments, whatever their source, is in inverse [57] proportion to the length of their periods.

The development of money into a medium of payment makes it necessary to accumulate money against the dates fixed for the payment of the sums owing. While hoarding, as a distinct mode of acquiring riches, vanishes with the progress of civil society, the formation of reserves of the means of payment grows with that progress.

C. Universal Money

When money leaves the home sphere of circulation, it strips off the local garbs which it there assumes, of a standard of prices, of coin, of tokens, and of a symbol of value, and returns to its original form of bullion. In the trade between the markets of the world, the value of commodities is expressed so as to be universally recognised. Hence their independent value-form also, in these cases, confronts them under the shape of universal money. It is only in the markets of the world that money acquires to the full extent the character of the commodity whose bodily form is also the immediate social incarnation of human labour in the abstract. Its real mode of existence in this sphere adequately corresponds to its ideal concept.

Within the sphere of home circulation, there can be but one commodity which, by serving as a measure of value, becomes money. In the markets of the world a double measure of value holds sway, gold and silver. [59]

Money of the world serves as the universal medium of payment, as the universal means of purchasing, and as the universally recognised embodiment of all wealth. Its function as a means of payment in the settling of international balances is its chief one. Hence the watchword of the mercantilists, balance of trade. [60] Gold and silver serve as international means of purchasing chiefly and necessarily in those periods when the customary equilibrium in the interchange of products between different nations is suddenly disturbed. And lastly, it serves as the universally recognised embodiment of social wealth, whenever the question is not of buying or paying, but of transferring wealth from one country to another, and whenever this transference in the form of commodities is rendered impossible, either by special conjunctures in the markets or by the purpose itself that is intended. [61]

Just as every country needs a reserve of money for its home circulation so, too, it requires one for external circulation in the markets of the world. The functions of hoards, therefore, arise in part out of the function of money, as the medium of the home circulation and home payments, and in part out of its function of money of the world. [62] For this latter function, the genuine money-commodity, actual gold and silver, is necessary. On that account, Sir James Steuart, in order to distinguish them from their purely local substitutes, calls gold and silver "money of the world."

The current of the stream of gold and silver is a double one. On the one hand, it spreads itself from its sources over all the markets of the world, in order to become absorbed, to various extents, into the different national spheres of circulation, to fill the conduits of currency, to replace abraded gold and silver coins, to supply the material of articles of luxury, and to petrify into hoards. [63] This first current is started by the countries that exchange their labour, realised in commodities, for the labour embodied in the precious metals by gold and silver-producing countries. On the other hand, there is a continual flowing backwards and forwards of gold and silver between the different national spheres of circulation, a current whose motion depends on the ceaseless fluctuations in the course of exchange. [64]

Countries in which the bourgeois form of production is developed to a certain extent, limit the hoards concentrated in the strong rooms of the banks to the minimum required for the proper performance of their peculiar functions. [65] Whenever these hoards are strikingly above their average level, it is, with some exceptions, an indication of stagnation in the circulation of commodities, of an interruption in the even flow of their metamorphoses. [66]

Footnotes

[1] The question — Why does not money directly represent labour-time, so that a piece of paper may represent, for instance, x hours' labour, is at bottom the same as the question why, given the production of commodities, must products take the form of commodities? This is evident, since their taking the form of commodities implies their differentiation into commodities and money. Or, why cannot private labour — labour for the account of private individuals — be treated as its opposite, immediate social labour? I have elsewhere examined thoroughly the Utopian idea of "labour-money" in a society founded on the production of commodities (l. c., p. 61, seq.). On this point I will only say further, that

Owen's "labour-money," for instance, is no more "money" than a ticket for the theatre. Owen pre-supposes directly associated labour, a form of production that is entirely in consistent with the production of commodities. The certificate of labour is merely evidence of the part taken by the individual in the common labour, and of his right to a certain portion of the common produce destined for consumption. But it never enters into Owen's head to pre-suppose the production of commodities, and at the same time, by juggling with money, to try to evade the necessary conditions of that production.

[2] Savages and half-civilised races use the tongue differently. Captain Parry says of the inhabitants on the west coast of Baffin's Bay: "In this case (he refers to barter) they licked it (the thing represented to them) twice to their tongues, after which they seemed to consider the bargain satisfactorily concluded." In the same way, the Eastern Esquimaux licked the articles they received in exchange. If the tongue is thus used in the North as the organ of appropriation, no wonder that, in the South, the stomach serves as the organ of accumulated property, and that a Kaffir estimates the wealth of a man by the size of his belly. That the Kaffirs know what they are about is shown by the following: at the same time that the official British Health Report of 1864 disclosed the deficiency of fat-forming food among a large part of the working-class, a certain Dr. Harvey (not, however, the celebrated discoverer of the circulation of the blood), made a good thing by advertising recipes for reducing the superfluous fat of the bourgeoisie and aristocracy.

[3] See Karl Marx: "Zur Kritik, &c." "Theorien von der Masseinheit des Gelda," p. 53, seq.

[4] "Wherever gold and silver have by law been made to perform the function of money or of a measure of value side by side, it has always been tried, but in vain, to treat them as one and the same material. To assume that there is an invariable ratio between the quantities of gold and silver in which a given quantity of labour-time is incorporated, is to assume in fact, that gold and silver are of one and the same material, and that a given mass of the less valuable metal, silver, is a constant fraction of a given mass of gold. From the reign of Edward III. to the time of George II., The history of money in England consists of one long series of perturbations caused by the clashing of the legally fixed ratio between The values of gold and silver, with the fluctuations in their real values. At one time gold was too high, at another, silver. The metal that for the time being was estimated below its value, was withdrawn from circulation, mated and exported. The ratio between the two metals was then again altered by law, but the new nominal ratio soon came into conflict again with the real one. In our own times, the slight and transient fall in the value of gold compared with silver, which was a consequence of The Indo-Chinese demand for silver, produced on a far more extended scale in France the same phenomena, export of silver, and its expulsion from circulation by gold. During the years 1855, 1856 and 1857, the excess in France of gold-imports over gold-exports amounted to £41,580,000, while the excess of silver-exports over silver-imports was £14,704,000. In fact, in those countries in which both metals are legally measures of value, and therefore both legal tender so that everyone has the option of paying in either metal, the metal That rise in value is at a premium, and, like every other commodity, measures its price in the over-estimated metal which alone serve in reality as The standard of value. The result of all experience and history with regard to this equation is simply that, where two commodities perform by law the functions of a measure of value, in practice one alone maintains that position." (Karl Marx, l. c., pp. 52, 53.)

[5] The peculiar circumstance, that while the ounce of gold serves in England as the unit of the standard of money, the pound sterling does not form an aliquot part of it, has been explained as follows: "Our coinage was originally adapted to the employment of silver only, hence, an ounce of silver can always be divided into a certain adequate number of pieces of coin, but as gold was introduced at a later period into a coinage adapted only to silver, an ounce of gold cannot be coined into an aliquot number of pieces." Maclaren, "A Sketch of the History of the Currency." London, 1858, p. 16.

[6] With English writers the confusion between measure of value and standard of price (standard of value! is indescribable. Their functions, as well as their names, are constantly interchanged.

[7] Moreover, it has not general historical validity.

[8] It is thus that the pound sterling in English denotes less than one-third of its original weight; the pound Scot, before the union, only 1-36th; the French livre, 1-74th; the Spanish maravedi, less than 1-1,000th; and the Portuguese rei a still smaller fraction.

[9] "Le monete le quali oggi sono ideal) sono le più antiche d'ogni nazione, e tutte furono un tempo real), e perche erano reali con esse si contava" (Galiani: Della moneta, l. c., p. 153.)

[10] David Urquhart remarks in his "Familiar Words" on the monstrosity (!) that now-a-days a pound (sterling), which is the unit of the English standard of money, is equal to about a quarter of an ounce of gold. "This is falsifying a measure, not establishing a standard." He sees in this "false denomination" of the weight of gold, as in everything else. the falsifying hand of civilisation.

[11] When Anacharsis was asked for what purposes the Greeks used money, he replied, "For reckoning." (Ashen. Deipn. 1. iv. 49 v. 2. ed. Schweighauser, 1802.)

[12] "Owing to the fact that money, when serving as the standard of price, appears under the same reckoning names as do the prices of commodities, and that therefore the sum of £3 17s. 10 1/2d. may signify on the one hand an ounce weight of gold, and on the other, the value of a ton of iron, this reckoning name of money has been called its mint-price. Hence there sprang up the extraordinary notion, that the value of gold is estimated in its own material, and that, in contradistinction to all other commodities, its price is fixed by the State. It was erroneously thought that the giving of reckoning names to definite weights of gold, is the same thing as fixing the value of those weights." (Karl Marx, l. c., p. 52.)

[13] See "Theorien von der Masseinheit des Geldes" in "Zur Kritik der Poll Oekon. &c.," p. 53, seq. The fantastic notions about raising or lowering the mint-price of money by transferring to greater or smaller weights of gold or silver, the names already legally appropriated to fixed weights of those metals; such notions, at least in those cases in which they aim, not at clumsy financial operations against creditors, both public and private but at economic quack remedies, have been so exhaustively treated by Wm. Petty in his "Quantulumcunque concerning money: To the Lord Marquis of Halifax, 1682," that even his immediate followers, Sir Dudley North and John Locke, not to mention later ones, could only dilute him. "If the wealth of a nation " he remarks, "could be decupled by a proclamation, it were strange that such proclamations have not long since been made by our Governors." (l. c., p. 36.)

[14] "Ou bien, il faut consentir à dire qu'une valeur d'un million en argent vaut plus qu'une valeur égale en merchandises." (Le Troene, l. c., p. 919), which amounts to saying "qu'une valeur vaut plus qu'une valeur égale."

[15] Jerome had to wrestle hard, not only in his youth with the bodily flesh, as is shown by his fight in the desert with the handsome women of his imagination, but also in his old age with the spiritual flesh. "I thought," he says, "I was in the spirit before the Judge of the Universe." "Who art thou?" asked a voice. "I am a Christian." "Thou liest," thundered back the great Judge, "thou art nought but a Ciceronian."

[16] (F. Lassalle: ``Die Philosophie Herakleitos des Dunkeln." Berlin, 1858, Vol. I, p. 222.) Lassalle in his note on this passage, p. 224, n. 3., erroneously makes gold a mere symbol of value.

[17] "Toute vente est achat." (Dr. Quesnay: "Dialogues sur le Commerce et les Travaux des Artisans." Physiocrates ed. Daire I. Partie, Paris, 1846, p. 170), or as Quesnay in-his "Maximes générales" puts it, "Vendre est acheter."

[18] "Le prix d'une merchandise ne pouvant être payé que par le prix d'une autre merchandise" (Mercier de la Riviere: "L'Ordre naturel et essentiel de sociétés politiques." Physiocrates, ed. Daire II. Partie, p. 554.)

[19] "Pour avoir cet argent, il faut avoir vendu," l. c., p. 543.

[20] As before remarked, the actual producer of gold or silver forms an exception. He exchanges his product directly for another commodity, without having first sold it.

[21] "Si l'argent représente, dans nos mains, les choses que nous pouvons désirer d'acheter, il y représente aussi les choses que nous avons vendues pour cet argent." (Mercier de la Rivière, l. c., p. 586.)

[22] "Il y a donc ... quatre termes et trots contractants, dont l'un intervient deux foist" (Le Trosne, l. c., p. 909.)

[23] Self-evident as this may be, it is nevertheless for the most part unobserved by political economists, and especially by the "Free-trader Vulgaris."

[24] See my observations on James Mill in "Zur Kritik, &c.," pp. 74-76. With regard to this subject, we may notice two methods characteristic of apologetic economy. The first is the identification of the circulation of commodities with the direct barter of products, by simple abstraction from their points of difference; the second is, the attempt to explain away the contradictions of capitalist production, by reducing the relations between the persons engaged in that mode of production, to the simple relations arising out of the circulation of commodities. The production and circulation of commodities are however, phenomena that occur to a greater or less extent in modes of production the most diverse. If we are acquainted with nothing but the abstract categories of circulation, which are common to all these modes of production, we cannot possibly know anything of the specific points of difference of those modes, nor pronounce any judgment upon them. In no science is such a big fuss made with commonplace truisms as in Political Economy. For instance, J. B. Say sets himself up as a judge of crises, because, forsooth, he knows that a commodity is a product.

[25] *Translator's note.* — This word is here used in its original signification of the course or track pursued by money as it changes from hand to hand, a course which essentially differs from circulation.

[26] Even when the commodity is sold over and over again, a phenomenon that at present has no existence for us, it falls, when definitely sold for the last time, out of the sphere of circulation into that of consumption, where it serves either as means of subsistence or means of production.

[27] "Il (l'argent) n'a d'autre mouvement que celui qui lui est imprimé par les productions." (Le Trosne, l. c., p. 885.)

[28] "Ce sont les productions qui le (l'argent) mettent en mouvement et le font circuler ... La célérité de son mouvement (sc. de l'argent) supplée à sa quantité. Lorsqu'il en est besoin. il ne fait que glisser d'une main dans l'autre sans s'arrêter un instant." (Le Trosne, l. c.. pp. 915, 916.)

[29] "Money being ... the common measure of buying and selling, everybody who hath anything to sell, and cannot procure chapmen for it, is presently apt to think, that want of money in the. kingdom, or country, is the cause why his goods do not go off; and so, want of money is the common cry; which is a great mistake... What do these people want, who cry out for money? ... The farmer complains ... he thinks that were more money in the country; he should have a price for his goods. Then it seems money is not his want, but a price for his corn and cattel, which he would sell, but cannot... Why cannot he get a price? ... (1) Either there is too much corn and cattel in the country, so that most who come to market have need of selling, as he hash, and few of buying; or (2) There wants the usual vent abroad by transportation..., or (3) The consumption fails, as when men, by reason of poverty, do not spend so much in their houses as formerly they did; wherefore it is not the increase of specific money, which would at all advance the farmer's goods, but the removal of any of these three causes, which do truly keep down the market... The merchant and shopkeeper want money in the same manner, that is, they want a vent for the goods they deal in, by reason that the markets fail"... [A nation] "never thrives better, than when riches are tost from hand to hand." (Sir Dudley North: "Discourses upon Trade," Lond. 1691, pp. 11-15, passim.) Herrenschwand's fanciful notions amount merely to this, that the antagonism, which has its origin in the nature of commodities, and is reproduced in their circulation, can be removed by increasing the circulating medium. But if, on the one hand, it is a popular delusion to ascribe stagnation in production and circulation to insufficiency of the circulating medium, it by no means follows, on the other hand, that an actual paucity of the medium in consequence, e.g., of bungling legislative interference with the regulation of currency, may not give rise to such stagnation.

[30] "There is a certain measure and proportion of money requisite to drive the trade of a nation, more or less than which would prejudice the same. lust as there is a certain proportion of farthings necessary in a small retail trade, to change silver money, and to even such reckonings as cannot be adjusted with the smallest silver pieces.... Now, as the proportion of the number of farthings requisite in commerce is to be taken from the number of people, the frequency of their exchanges: as also, and principally, from the value of the smallest silver pieces of money; so in like manner, the proportion of money

[gold and silver specie] requisite in our trade, is to be likewise taken from the frequency of commutations, and from the bigness of the payments." (William Petty, "A Treatise of Taxes and Contributions." Lond. 1667, p. 17.) The Theory of Hume was defended against the attacks of J. Steuart and others, by A. Young, in his "Political Arithmetic," Lond; 1774, in which work there is a special chapter entitled "Prices depend on quantity of money, at p. 112, sqq. I have stated in "Zur Kritik, &c.," p. 149: "He (Adam Smith) passes over without remark the question as to the quantity of coin in circulation, and treats money quite wrongly as a mere commodity." This statement applies only in so far as Adam Smith, ex officio, treats of money. Now and then, however, as in his criticism of the earlier systems of Political Economy, he takes the right view. "The quantity of coin in every country is regulated by the value of the commodities which are to be circulated by It.... The value of the goods annually bought and sold in any country requires a certain quantity of money to circulate and distribute them to their proper consumers, and can give employment to no more. The channel of circulation necessarily draws to itself a sum sufficient to fill it, and never admits any more." ("Wealth of Nations." Bk. IV., ch. 1.) In like manner, ex officio, he opens his work with an apotheosis on the division of labour. Afterwards, in the last book which treats of the sources of public revenue, he occasionally repeats the denunciations of the division of labour made by his teacher, A. Ferguson.

[31] "The prices of things will certainly rise in every nation, as the gold and silver increase amongst the people, and consequently, where the gold and silver decrease in any nation, the prices of all things must fall proportionately to such decrease of money." (Jacob Vanderlint: "Money Answers all Things." Lond. 1734, p. 5.) A careful comparison of thus book with Hume's "Essays," proves to my mind without doubt that Hume was acquainted with and made use of Vanderlint's work, which is certainly an important one. The opinion that prices are determined by the quantity of the circulating medium, was also held by Barbon and other much earlier writers. "No inconvenience," says Vanderlint, "can arise by an unrestrained trade, but very great advantage; since, if the cash of the nation be decreased by it, which prohibitions are designed to prevent, those nations that get the cash will certainly find everything advance in price, as the cash increases amongst them. And ... our manufactures, and everything else, will soon become so moderate as to turn the balance of trade in our favour, and thereby fetch the money back again." (l. c.. pp. 43, 44.)

[32] That the price of each single kind of commodity forms a pan of the sum of the prices of all the commodities in circulation, is a self-evident proposition. But how use-values which are incommensurable with regard to each other, are to be exchanged, en masse for the total sum of gold and silver in a country, is quite incomprehensible. If we start from the notion that all commodities together form one single commodity, of which each is but an aliquot part, we get the following beautiful result: The total commodity = x cwt. of gold; commodity A = an aliquot part of the total commodity = the same liquot part of x cwt. of gold. This is stated in all seriousness by Montesquieu: "Si l'on compare la masse de l'or et de l'argent qui est dans le monde avec la somme des merchandises qui y vent il est cenain que chaque denrée ou merchandise, en paniculier, pourra être comparée à une certaine portion de la masse entière. Supposons qu'il n'y ait qu'une seule denrée ou marchandise dans le monde, ou qu'il n'y ait qu'une seule qui s'achète, et qu'elle se divise comme l'argent: Cette panic de cette marchandise répondra à une partie de la masee de l'argent; la moitié du total de l'une a la moitié du total de l'autre, &c.... I'établissement du prix des choses dépend tonjours fondamentalement de la raison du total des choses au total des signes." (Montesquieu, l. c. t. III, pp. 12, 13.) As to the further development of this theory by Ricardo and his disciples, James Mill, Lord Overstone, and others, see "Zur Kritik, &c.," pp. 140-146, and p. 150, sqq. John Stuart Mill, with his usual eclectic logic, understands how to hold at the same time the view of his father, James Mill, and the opposite view. On a comparison of the text of his compendium, "Principles of Poll Econ.," with his preface to the first edition, in which preface he announces himself as the Adam Smith of his day — we do not know whether to admire more the simplicity of the man, or that of the public, who took him, in good faith, for the Adam Smith he announced himself to be, although he bears about as much resemblance to Adam Smith as say General Williams, of Kars, to the Duke of Wellington. The original researches of r. J. S. Mill which are neither extensive nor profound, in the domain of Political Economy, will be found mustered in rank and file in his little work, "Some Unsettled Questions of Political Economy," which appeared in 1844. Locke asserts point blank the connexion between the

absence of value in gold and silver, and the determination of their values by quantity alone. "Mankind having consented to put an imaginary value upon gold and silver ... the intrinsic value, regarded in these metals, is nothing but the quantity." ("Some Considerations," &c., 1691, Works Ed. 1777, Vol. II., p. 15.)

[33] It lies of course, entirely beyond my purpose to take into consideration such details as the seigniorage on minting. I will, however, cite for the benefit of the romantic sycophant, Adam Muller, who admires the "generous liberality" with which the English Government coins gratuitously, the following opinion of Sir Dudley North: "Silver and gold, like other commodities, have their ebbings and flowings. Upon the arrival of quantities from Spain ... it is carried into the Tower, and coined. Not long after there will come a demand for bullion to be exported again. If there is none, but all happens to be in coin, what then? Melt it down again; there's no loss in it, for the coining costs the owner nothing. Thus the nation has been abused, and made to pay for the twisting of straw for asses to eat. If the merchant were made to pay the price of the coinage, he would not have sent his silver to the Tower without consideration, and coined money would always keep a value above uncoined silver. " (North, l. c., p. 18.) North was himself one of the foremost merchants in the reign of Charles II.

[34] "If silver never exceed what is wanted for the smaller payments it cannot be collected in sufficient quantities for the larger payments ... the use of gold in the main payments necessarily implies also Its use in the retail trade: those who have gold coin offering them for small purchases, and receiving with the commodity purchased a balance of silver in return; by which means the surplus of silver that would otherwise encumber the retail dealer, is drawn off and dispersed into general circulation. But if there is as much silver as will transact the small payments independent of gold, the retail trader must then receive silver for small purchases ; and it must of necessity accumulate in his hands." (David Buchanan; "Inquiry into the Taxation and Commercial Policy of Great Britain. " Edinburgh, 1844, pp. 248, 249.)

[35] The mandarin Wan-mao-in, the Chinese Chancellor of the Exchequer, took it into his head one day to lay before the Son of Heaven a proposal that secretly aimed at converting the assignats of the empire into convertible bank-notes. The assignats Committee, in its report of April, 1854, gives him a severe snubbing. Whether he also received the traditional drubbing with bamboos is not stated. The concluding part of the report is as follows: — "The Committee has carefully examined his proposal and finds that it is entirely in favour of the merchants, and that no advantage will result to the crown." ("Arbeiten der Kaiserlich Russischen Gesandtschaft zu Peking über China." Aus dem Russischen von Dr. K. Abel und F. A. Mecklenburg. Erster Band. Berlin, 1858, p. 47 sq.) In his evidence before the Committee of the House of Lords on the Bank Acts, a governor of the Bank of England says, with regard to the abrasion of gold coins during currency: "Every year a fresh class of sovereigns becomes too light. The class which one year passes with full weight, loses enough by wear and tear to draw the scales next year against it." (House of Lords' Committee, 1848, n. 429.)

[36] The following passage from Fullarton shows the want of clearness on the pan of even the best writers on money, in their comprehension of its various functions: "That, as far as concerns our domestic exchanges, all the monetary functions which are usually performed by gold and silver coins, may be performed as effectually by a circulation of inconvertible notes paying no value but that factitious and conventional value they derive from the law is a fact which admits, I conceive, of no denial. Value of this description may be made to answer all the purposes of intrinsic value, and supersede even the necessity for a standard, provided only the quantity of issues be kept under due limitation." (Fullerton: "Regulation of Currencies," London, 1845, p. 21.) Because the commodity that serves as money is capable of being replaced in circulation by mere symbols of value, therefore its functions as a measure of value and a standard of prices are declared to be superfluous!

[37] From the fact that gold and silver, so far as they are coins, or exclusively serve as the medium of circulation, become mere tokens of themselves, Nicholas Barbon deduces the right of Governments "to raise money," that is, to give to the weight of silver that is called a shilling the name of a greater weight, such as a crown; and so to pay creditors shillings, instead of crowns. "Money does wear and grow lighter by often telling over... It is the denomination and currency of the money that men regard in bargaining, and not the

quantity of silver...'Tis the public authority upon the metal that makes it money." (N. Barbon, l. c., pp. 29, 30, 25.)

[38] "Une richesse en argent n'est que ... richesse en productions, converties en argent." (Mercier de la Rivière, l. c.) "Une valeur en productions n'a fait que changer de forme." (Id., p. 486.)

[39] "'Tis by this practice' they keep all their goods and manufactures at such low rates." (Vanderlint, l. c., pp. 95, 96.)

[40] "Money ... is a pledge." (John Bellers: "Essays about the Poor, Manufactures, Trade, Plantations, and Immorality," Lond., 1699, p. 13.)

[41] A purchase. in a "categorical" sense, implies that gold and silver are already the converted form of commodities, or the product of a sale.

[42] Henry III., most Christian king of France, robbed cloisters of their relics, and turned them into money. It is well known what part the despoiling of the Delphic Temple, by the Phocians, played in the history of Greece. Temples with the ancients served as the dwellings of the gods of commodities. They were "sacred banks." With the Phoenicians, a trading people par excellence, money was the transmuted shape of everything. It was, therefore, quite in order that the virgins, who, at the feast of the Goddess of Love, gave themselves up to strangers, should offer to the goddess the piece of money they received.

"Gold, yellow, glittering, precious gold!
Thus much of this, will make black white, foul, fair;
Wrong, right; base, noble; old, young; coward, valiant.
... What this, you gods? Why, this
Will lug your priests and servants from your sides;
Pluck stout men's pillows from below their heads;
This yellow slave
Will knit and break religions; bless the accurs'd;
Make the hoar leprosy ador'd; place thieves,
And give them title, knee and approbation;
With senators on the bench, this is it;
That makes the wappen'd widow wed again:
... Come damned earth,
Though common whore of mankind."
(Shakespeare: Timon of Athens.)

[44] "Accrescere quanto più si può il numero de'venditori d'ogni merce, diminuere quanto più si puo il numero dei compratori, quest) sono i cardini sui quali si raggirano tutte le operazioni di economia politica." (Verri, l. c., p. 52.)

[45] "There is required for carrying on the trade of the nation a determinate sum of specifick money which varies, and is sometimes more, sometimes less, as the circumstances we are in require.... This ebbing and flowing of money supplies and accommodates itself, without any aid of Politicians.... The buckets work alternately; when money is scarce, bullion is coined; when bullion is scarce, money is melted." (Sir D. North, l. c., Postscript, p. 3.) John Stuart Mill, who for a long time was an official of the East India Company, confirms the fact that in India silver ornaments still continue to perform directly the functions of a hoard. The silver ornaments are brought out and coined when there is a high rate of interest, and go back again when the rate of interest falls. (1. S. Mill's Evidence "Reports on Bank Acts," 1857, 2084.) According to a Parliamentary document of 1864 on the gold and silver import and export of India, the import of gold and silver in 1863 exceeded the export by £19,367,764. During the 8 years immediately preceding 1864, the excess of imports over exports of the precious metals amounted to £109,652,917. During this century far more than £200,000,000 has been coined in India.

[46] The following shows the debtor and creditor relations existing between English traders at the beginning of the 18th century. "Such a spirit of crudity reigns here in England among the men of trade, that is not to be met with in any other society of men, nor in any other kingdom of the world." ("An Essay on Credit and the Bankrupt Act," Lond.,

[47] It will be seen from the following quotation from my book which appeared in 1859, why I take no notice in the text of an opposite form: "Contrariwise, in the process in M—-C, the money can be alienated as a real means of purchase, and in that way, the price of the commodity can be realised before the use-value of the money is realised and the commodity actually delivered. This occurs constantly under the every-day form of prepayments. And it is under this form, that the English government purchases opium from the ryots of India.... In these cases, however, the money always acts as a means of purchase.... Of course capital also is advanced in the shape of money.... This point of view, however, does not fall within the horizon of simple circulation." ("Zur Kritik, &c.," pp. 119, 120.)

[48] The monetary crisis referred to in the text, being a phase of every crisis, must be clearly distinguished from that particular form of crisis, which also is called a monetary crisis, but which may be produced by itself as an independent phenomenon in such a way as to react only indirectly on industry and commerce. The pivot of these crises is to be found in moneyed capital, and their sphere of direct action is therefore the sphere of that capital, viz., banking, the stock exchange, and finance.

[49] "The sudden reversion from a system of credit to a system of hard cash heaps theoretical fright on top of the practical panic; and the dealers by whose agency circulation is affected, shudder before the impenetrable mystery in which their own economic relations are involved" (Karl Marx, l. c., p. 126.) "The poor stand still, because the rich have no money to employ them, though they have the same land and hands to provide victuals and clothes, as ever they had; ...which is the true riches of a nation, and not the money." John Bellers, Proposals for Raising a College of Industry, London, 1696, p3.

[50] The following shows how such times are exploited by the "amis du commerce." "On one occasion (1839) an old grasping banker (in the city) in his private room raised the lid of the desk he sat over, and displayed to a friend rolls of bank-notes, saying with intense glee there were £600,000 of them, they were held to make money tight, and would all be let out after three o'clock on the same day." ("The Theory of Exchanges. The Bank Charter Act of 1844." Lond. 1864, p. 81). The Observer, a semi-official government organ, contained the following paragraph on 24th April, 1864: "Some very curious rumours are current of the means which have been resorted to in order to create a scarcity of banknotes.... Questionable as it would seem, to suppose that any trick of the kind would be adopted, the report has been so universal that it really deserves mention."

[51] "The amount of purchases or contracts entered upon during the course of any given day, will not affect the quantity of money afloat on that particular day, but, in the vast majority of cases, will resolve themselves into multifarious drafts upon the quantity of money which may be afloat at subsequent dates more or less distant.... The bills granted or credits opened, to-day, need have no resemblance whatever, either in quantity, amount or duration, to those granted or entered upon to-morrow or next day, nay, many of today's bills, and credits, when due, fall in with a mass of liabilities whose origins traverse a range of antecedent dates altogether indefinite, bills at 12, 6, 3 months or 1 often aggregating together to swell the common liabilities of one particular day...." ("The Currency Theory Reviewed; in a Letter to the Scottish People." By a Banker in England. Edinburgh, 1845, pp. 29, 30 passim.)

[52] As an example of how little ready money is required in true commercial operations, I give below a statement by one of the largest London houses of its yearly receipts and payments. Its transactions during the year 1856, extending to many millions of pounds sterling, are here reduced to the scale of one million.

Receipts		Payments	
Bankers's and Merchants' Bills payable after date	£533,596	Bills payable after date	£302,674
Cheques on Bankers, &c., payable on demand	357,715	Checks on London Bankers	663,672
Country Notes	9,627	Bank of England Notes	22,743

Bank of England Notes	68,554	Gold	9,427
Silver and Copper	1,486	Silver and Copper	1,484
Post Office Orders	933		
Total	£1,000,000	Total	£1,000,000

[53] "The course of trade being thus turned, from exchanging of goods for goods, or delivering and taking, to selling and paying, all the bargains ... are now stated upon the foot of a Price in money." ("An Essay upon Publick Credit." 3rd Ed. Lond., 1710, p. 8.)

[54] "L'argent ... est devenu le bourreau de toutes choses." Finance is the "alambic, qui a fait évaporer une quantité effroyable de biens et de denrees pour faire ce fatal précis." "L'argent déclare la guerre à tout le genre humain." (Boisguillebert: "Dissertation sur la nature des richesses, de l'argent et des tribute." Edit. Daire. Economistes financiers. Paris, 1843, t. i., pp. 413, 419, 417.)

[55] "On Whitsuntide, 1824," says Mr. Craig before the Commons' Committee of 1826, "there was such an immense demand for notes upon the banks of Edinburgh, that by 11 o'clock they had not a note left in their custody. They sent round to all the different banks to borrow, but could not get them, and many of the transactions were adjusted by slips of paper only; yet by three o'clock the whole of the notes were returned into the banks from which they had issued! It was a mere transfer from hand to hand. "Although the average effective circulation of bank-notes in Scotland is less than three millions sterling, yet on certain pay days in the year, every single note in the possession of the bankers, amounting in the whole to about £7,000,000, is called into activity. On these occasions the notes have a single and specific function to perform, and so soon as they have performed it, they flow back into the various banks from which they issued. (See John Fullarton, "Regulation of Currencies." Lond. 1845, p. 86, note.) In explanation it should be stated, that in Scotland, at the date of Fullarton's work, notes and not cheques were used to withdraw deposits.

[56] To the question, "If there were occasion to raise 40 millions p. a., whether the same 6 millions (gold) ... would suffice for such revolutions and circulations thereof, as trade requires," Petty replies in his usual masterly manner, "I answer yes: for the expense being 40 millions, if the revolutions were in such short circles, viz., weekly, as happens among poor artisans and labourers, who receive and pay every Saturday, then 40/52 parts of 1 million of money would answer these ends, but if the circles be quarterly, according to our custom of paying rent, and gathering taxes, then 10 millions were requisite. Wherefore, supposing payments in general to be of a mixed circle between one week and 13, then add 10 millions to 40/52, the half of which will be 5 1/2, so as if we have 5 1/2 millions we have enough." (William Petty: "Political Anatomy of Ireland." 1672, Edit.: Lond. 1691, pp. 13, 14.)

[58] Hence the absurdity of every law prescribing that the banks of a country shall form reserves of that precious metal alone which circulates at home. The "pleasant difficulties" thus self-created by the Bank of England, are well known. On the subject of the great epochs in the history of the changes in the relative value of gold and silver, see Karl Marx, l. c., p. 136 sq. Sir Robert Peel, by his Bank Act of 1844, sought to tide over the difficulty, by allowing the Bank of England to issue notes against silver bullion, on condition that the reserve of silver should never exceed more than one-fourth of the reserve of gold. The value of silver being for that purpose estimated at its price in the London market.

[59] The opponents, themselves, of the mercantile system, a system which considered the settlement of surplus trade balances in gold and silver as the aim of international trade, entirely misconceived the functions of money of the world. I have shown by the example of Ricardo in what way their false conception of the laws that regulate the quantity of the circulating medium, is reflected in their equally false conception of the international movement of the precious metals (l. c., pp. 150 sq.). His erroneous dogma: "An unfavourable balance of trade never arises but from a redundant currency.... The exportation of the coin is caused by its cheapness, and is not the effect, but the cause of an unfavourable balance," already occurs in Barbon: "The Balance of Trade, if there be one, is not the cause of sending away the money out of a nation; but that proceeds from the

difference of the value of bullion in every country." (N. Barbon; l. c., pp. 59, 60.) MacCulloch in "The Literature of Political Economy, a classified catalogue, Lond. 1845," praises Barbon for this anticipation, but prudently passes over the naive forms, in which Barbon clothes the absurd supposition on which the "currency principle" is based. The absence of real criticism and even of honesty, in that catalogue culminates in the sections devoted to the history of the theory of money; the reason is that MacCulloch in this part of the work is flattering Lord Overstone whom he calls "facile princeps argentanorum."

[60] For instance, in subsidies, money loans for carrying on wars or for enabling banks to resume cash payments, &c., it is the money-form, and no other, of value that may be wanted.

[61] "I would desire, indeed, no more convincing evidence of the competency of the machinery of the hoards in specie-paying countries to perform every necessary office of international adjustment, without any sensible aid from the general circulation, than the facility with which France, when but just recovering from the shock of a destructive foreign invasion, completed within the space of 27 months the payment of her forced contribution of nearly 20 millions to the allied powers, and a considerable proportion of the sum in specie, without any perceptible contraction or derangement of her domestic currency, or even any alarming fluctuation of her exchanges." (Fullerton, l. c., p. 141.) [Added in the 4th German edition. — We have a still more striking example in the facility with which the same France was able in 1871-73 to pay off within 30 months a forced contribution more than ten times as great, a considerable part of it likewise in specie. — F. E.]

[62] "L'argent se partage entre les nations relativement au besoin qu'elles en ont ... étant toujours attiré par les productions." (Le Trosne, l. c., p. 916.) "The mines which are continually giving gold and silver, do give sufficient to supply such a needful balance to every nation." (J. Vanderlint, l. c., p. 40.)

[63] "Exchanges rise and fall every week, and at some particular times in the year run high against a nation, and at other times run as high on the contrary." (N. Barbon, l. c., p. 39)

[64] These various functions are liable to come into dangerous conflict with one another whenever gold and silver have also to serve as a fund for the conversion of bank-notes.

[65] "What money is more than of absolute necessity for a Home Trade, is dead stock ... and brings no profit to that country it's kept in, but as it is transported in trade, as well as imported." (John Bellers, "Essays", p. 13.) "What if we have too much coin? We may melt down the heaviest and turn it into the splendour of plate, vessels or utensils of gold or silver, or send it out as a commodity, where the same is wanted or desired; or let it out at interest, where interest is high." (W. Petty: "Quantulumcunque," p. 39.) "Money is but the fat of the Body Politick, whereof too much cloth as often hinder its agility, as too little makes it sick ... as fat lubricates the motion of the muscles, feeds in want of victuals, fills up the uneven cavities, and beautifies the body; so cloth money in the state quicken its action, feeds from abroad in time of dearth at home, evens accounts ... and beautifies the whole; altho more especially the particular persons that have it in plenty." (W. Petty, "Political Anatomy of Ireland," p. 14.)

PART II.
The Transformation of Money into Capital

Chapter Four:
The General Formula for Capital

The circulation of commodities is the starting-point of capital. The production of commodities, their circulation, and that more developed form of their circulation called commerce, these form the historical ground-work from which it rises. The modern history of capital dates from the creation in the 16th century of a world-embracing commerce and a world-embracing market.

If we abstract from the material substance of the circulation of commodities, that is, from the exchange of the various use-values, and consider only the economic forms produced by this process of circulation, we find its final result to be money: this final product of the circulation of commodities is the first form in which capital appears.

As a matter of history, capital, as opposed to landed property, invariably takes the form at first of money; it appears as moneyed wealth, as the capital of the merchant and of the usurer. [1] But we have no need to refer to the origin of capital in order to discover that the first form of appearance of capital is money. We can see it daily under our very eyes. All new capital, to commence with, comes on the stage, that is, on the market, whether of commodities, labour, or money, even in our days, in the shape of money that by a definite process has to be transformed into capital.

The first distinction we notice between money that is money only, and money that is capital, is nothing more than a difference in their form of circulation.

The simplest form of the circulation of commodities is C-M-C, the transformation of commodities into money, and the change of the money back again into commodities; or selling in order to buy. But alongside of this form we find another specifically different form: M-C-M, the transformation of money into commodities, and the change of commodities back again into money; or buying in order to sell. Money that circulates in the latter manner is thereby transformed into, becomes capital, and is already potentially capital.

Now let us examine the circuit M-C-M a little closer. It consists, like the other, of two antithetical phases. In the first phase, M-C, or the purchase, the money is changed into a commodity. In the second phase, C-M, or the sale, the commodity is changed back again into money. The combination of these two phases constitutes the single movement whereby money is exchanged for a commodity, and the same commodity is again exchanged for money; whereby a commodity is bought in order to be sold, or, neglecting the distinction in form between buying and selling, whereby a commodity is bought with money, and then money is bought with a commodity. [2] The result, in which the phases of the process vanish, is the exchange of money for money, M-M. If I purchase 2,000 lbs. of cotton for £100, and resell the 2,000 lbs. of cotton for £110, I have, in fact, exchanged £100 for £110, money for money.

Now it is evident that the circuit M-C-M would be absurd and without meaning if the intention were to exchange by this means two equal sums of money, £100 for £100. The miser's plan would be far simpler and surer; he sticks to his £100 instead of exposing it to the dangers of circulation. And yet, whether the merchant who has paid £100 for his cotton sells it for £110, or lets it go for £100, or even £50, his money has, at all events, gone through a characteristic and original movement, quite different in kind from that which it goes through in the hands of the peasant who sells corn, and with the money thus set free buys clothes. We have therefore to examine first the distinguishing characteristics of the forms of the circuits M-C-M and C-M-C, and in doing this the real difference that underlies the mere difference of form will reveal itself.

Let us see, in the first place, what the two forms have in common.

Both circuits are resolvable into the same two antithetical phases, C-M, a sale, and M-C, a purchase. In each of these phases the same material elements-a commodity, and money, and the same economic dramatis personae, a buyer and a seller-confront one another. Each circuit is the unity of the same two antithetical phases, and in each case this unity is brought about by the intervention of three contracting parties, of whom one only sells, another only buys, while the third both buys and sells.

What, however, first and foremost distinguishes the circuit C-M-C from the circuit M-C-M, is the inverted order of succession of the two phases. The simple circulation of commodities begins with a sale and ends with a purchase, while the circulation of money as capital begins with a purchase and ends with a sale. In the one case both the starting-point and the goal are commodities, in the other they are money. In the first form the movement is brought about by the intervention of money, in the second by that of a commodity.

In the circulation C-M-C, the money is in the end converted into a commodity, that serves as a use-value; it is spent once for all. In the inverted form, M-C-M, on the contrary, the buyer lays out money in order that, as a seller, he may recover money. By the purchase of his commodity he throws money into circulation, in order to withdraw it again by the sale of the same commodity. He lets the money go, but only with the sly intention of getting it back again. The money, therefore, is not spent, it is merely advanced. [3]

In the circuit C-M-C, the same piece of money changes its place twice. The seller gets it from the buyer and pays it away to another seller. The complete circulation, which begins with the receipt, concludes with the payment, of money for commodities. It is the very contrary in the circuit M-C-M. Here it is not the piece of money that changes its place twice, but the commodity. The buyer takes it from the hands of the seller and passes it into the hands of another buyer. Just as in the simple circulation of commodities the double change of place of the same piece of money effects its passage from one hand into another, so here the double change of place of the same commodity brings about the reflux of the money to its point of departure.

Such reflux is not dependent on the commodity being sold for more than was paid for it. This circumstance influences only the amount of the money that comes back. The reflux itself takes place, so soon as the purchased commodity is resold, in other words, so soon as the circuit M-C-M is completed. We have here, therefore, a palpable difference between the circulation of money as capital, and its circulation as mere money.

The circuit C-M-C comes completely to an end, so soon as the money brought in by the sale of one commodity is abstracted again by the purchase of another.

If, nevertheless, there follows a reflux of money to its starting-point, this can only happen through a renewal or repetition of the operation. If I sell a quarter of corn for £3, and with this £3 buy clothes, the money, so far as I am concerned, is spent and done with. It belongs to the clothes merchant. If I now sell a second quarter of corn, money indeed flows back to me, not however as a sequel to the first transaction, but in consequence of its repetition. The money again leaves me, so soon as I complete this second transaction by a fresh purchase. Therefore, in the circuit C-M-C, the expenditure of money has nothing to do with its reflux. On the other hand, in M-C-M, the reflux of the money is conditioned by the very mode of its expenditure. Without this reflux, the operation fails, or the process is interrupted and incomplete, owing to the absence of its complementary and final phase, the sale.

The circuit C-M-C starts with one commodity, and finishes with another, which falls out of circulation and into consumption. Consumption, the satisfaction of wants, in one word, use-value, is its end and aim. The circuit M-C-M, on the contrary, commences with money and ends with money. Its leading motive, and the goal that attracts it, is therefore mere exchange-value.

In the simple circulation of commodities, the two extremes of the circuit have the same economic form. They are both commodities, and commodities of equal value. But they are also use-values differing in their qualities, as, for example, corn and clothes. The exchange of products, of the different materials in which the labour of society is embodied, forms here the basis of the movement. It is otherwise in the circulation -C-M, which at first sight appears purposeless, because tautological. Both extremes have the same economic form. They are both money, and therefore are not qualitatively different use-values; for money is but the converted form of commodities, in which their particular use-values vanish. To exchange £100 for cotton, and then this same cotton again for £100, is merely a roundabout way of exchanging money for money, the same for the same, and appears to be an operation just as purposeless as it is absurd. [4] One sum of money is distinguishable from another only by its amount. The character and tendency of the process M-C-M, is therefore not due to any qualitative difference between its extremes, both being money, but solely to their quantitative difference. More money is withdrawn from circulation at the finish than was thrown into it at the start. The cotton that was bought for £100 is perhaps resold for £100 + £10 or £100. The exact form of this process is therefore M-C-M', where M' = M + delta M = the original sum advanced, plus an increment. This increment or excess over the original value I call "surplus-value". The value originally advanced, therefore, not only remains intact while in circulation, but adds to itself a surplus-value or expands itself. It is this movement that converts it into capital.

Of course, it is also possible, that in C-M-C, the two extremes C-C, say corn and clothes, may represent different quantities of value. The farmer may sell his corn above its value, or may buy the clothes at less than their value. He may, on the other hand, "be done" by the clothes merchant. Yet, in the form of circulation now under consideration, such differences in value are purely accidental. The fact that the corn and the clothes are equivalents, does not deprive the process of all meaning, as it does in M-C-M. The equivalence of their values is rather a necessary condition to its normal course.

The repetition or renewal of the act of selling in order to buy, is kept within bounds by the very object it aims at, namely, consumption or the satisfaction of definite wants, an aim that lies altogether outside the sphere of circulation. But when we buy in order to sell, we, on the contrary, begin and end with the same thing, money, exchange-value; and thereby the movement becomes interminable. No doubt, M becomes M + delta , £100 become £110. But when viewed in their qualitative aspect alone, £110 are the same as £100, namely money; and considered quantitatively, £110 is, like £100, a sum of definite and limited value. If now, the £110 be spent as money, they cease to play their part. They eare no longer capital. Withdrawn from circulation, they become petrified into a hoard, and though they remained in that state till doomsday, not a single farthing would accrue to them. If, then, the expansion of value is once aimed at, there is just the same inducement to augment the value of the £110 as that of the £100; for both are but limited expressions for exchange-value, and therefore both have the same vocation to approach, by quantitative increase, as near as possible to absolute wealth. Momentarily, indeed, the value originally advanced, the £100 is distinguishable from the surplus-value of £10 that is annexed to it during circulation; but the distinction vanishes immediately. At the end of the process, we do not receive with one hand the original £100, and with the other, the surplus-value of £10. We simply get a value of £110, which is in exactly the same condition and fitness for commencing the expanding process, as the original £100 was. Money ends the movement only to begin it again. [5] Therefore, the final result of every separate circuit, in which a purchase and consequent sale are completed, forms of itself the starting-point of a new circuit. The simple circulation of commodities-selling in order to buy-is a means of carrying out a purpose unconnected with circulation, namely, the appropriation of use-valucs, thc satisfaction of wants. The circulation of money as capital is, on the contrary, an end in itself, for the expansion of value takes place only within this constantly renewed movement. The circulation of capital has therefore no limits. [6]

As the conscious representative of this movement, the possessor of money becomes a capitalist. His person, or rather his pocket, is the point from which the money starts and to which it returns. The expansion of value, which is the objective basis or main-spring of the circulation -C-M, becomes his subjective aim, and it is only in so far as the appropriation of ever more and more wealth in the abstract becomes the sole motive of his operations, that he functions as a capitalist, that is, as capital personified and endowed with consciousness and a will. Use-values must therefore never be looked upon as the real aim of the capitalist; [7] neither must the profit on any single transaction. The restless never-ending process of profit-making alone is what he aims at. [8] This boundless greed after riches, this passionate chase after exchange-value [9], is common to the capitalist and the miser; but while the miser is merely a capitalist gone mad, the capitalist is a rational miser. The never-ending augmentation of exchange-value, which the miser strives after, by seeking to save [10] his money from circulation, is attained by the more acute capitalist, by constantly throwing it afresh into circulation. [11]

The independent form, i.e., the money-form, which the value of commodities assumes in the case of simple circulation, serves only one purpose, namely, their exchange, and vanishes in the final result of the movement. On the other hand, in the circulation M-C-M, both the money and the commodity represent only different modes of existence of value itself, the money its general mode, and the commodity its particular, or, so to say, disguised mode. [12] It is constantly changing from one form to the other without thereby becoming lost, and thus assumes an automatically active character. If now we take in turn each of the two different forms which self-expanding value successively assumes in the course of its life, we then arrive at these two propositions: Capital is money: Capital is commodities. [13] In truth, however, value is here the active factor in a process, in which, while constantly assuming the form in turn of money and commodities, it at the same time changes in magnitude, differentiates itself by throwing off surplus-value from itself; the original value, in other words, expands spontaneously. For the movement, in the course of which it adds surplus-value, is its own movement, its expansion, therefore, is automatic expansion. Because it is value, it has acquired the occult quality of being able to add value to itself. It brings forth living offspring, or, at the least, lays golden eggs.

Value, therefore, being the active factor in such a process, and assuming at one time the form of money, at another that of commodities, but through all these changes preserving itself and expanding, it requires some independent form, by means of which its identity may at any time be established. And this form it possesses only in the shape of money. It is under the form of money that value begins and ends, and begins again, every act of its own spontaneous generation. It began by being £100, it is now £110, and so on. But the money itself is only one of the two forms of value. Unless it takes the form of some commodity, it does not become capital. There is here no antagonism, as in the case of hoarding, between the money and commodities. The capitalist knows that all commodities, however scurvy they may look, or however badly they may smell, are in faith and in truth money, inwardly circumcised Jews, and what is more, a wonderful means whereby out of money to make more money.

In simple circulation, C-M-C, the value of commodities attained at the most a form independent of their use-values, i.e., the form of money; but that same value now in the circulation M-C-M, or the circulation of capital, suddenly presents itself as an independent substance, endowed with a motion of its own, passing through a life-process of its own, in which money and commodities are mere forms which it assumes and casts off in turn. Nay, more: instead of simply representing the relations of commodities, it enters now, so to say, into private relations with itself. It differentiates itself as original value from itself as surplus-value; as the father differentiates himself from himself quâ the son, yet both are one and of one age: for only by the surplus-value of £10 does the £100 originally advanced become capital, and so soon as this takes place, so soon as the son, and by the son, the father, is begotten, so soon does their difference vanish, and they again become one, £110.

Value therefore now becomes value in process, money in process, and, as such, capital. It comes out of circulation, enters into it again, preserves and multiplies itself within its circuit, comes back out of it with expanded bulk, and begins the same round ever afresh. [14] -M', money which begets money, such is the description of Capital from the mouths of its first interpreters, the Mercantilists.

Buying in order to sell, or, more accurately, buying in order to sell dearer, M-C-M', appears certainly to be a form peculiar to one kind of capital alone, namely, merchants' capital. But industrial capital too is money, that is changed into commodities, and by the sale of these commodities, is re-converted into more money. The events that take place outside the sphere of circulation, in the interval between the buying and selling, do not affect the form of this movement. Lastly, in the case of interest-bearing capital, the circulation M-C-M' appears abridged. We have its result without the intermediate stage, in the form M-M', "en style lapidaire" so to say, money that is worth more money, value that is greater than itself.

M-C-M' is therefore in reality the general formula of capital as it appears prima facie within the sphere of circulation.

Footnotes

[1] The contrast between the power, based on the personal relations of dominion and servitude, that is conferred by landed property, and the impersonal power that is given by

money, is well expressed by the two French proverbs, "Nulle terre sans seigneur," and "L'argent n'a pas de maître."

[2] "Avec de l'argent on achète des marchandises et avec des marchandises on achète de l'argent." (Mercier de la Rivière: "L'ordre naturel et essentiel des sociétés politiques," p. 543.)

[3] "When a thing is bought in order to be sold again, the sum employed is called money advanced; when it is bought not to be sold, it may be said to be expended." — (James Steuart: "Works," &c. Edited by Gen. Sir James Steuart, his son. Lond., 1805, V. I., p. 274.)

[4] "On n'échange pas de l'argent contre de l'argent," says Mercier de la Rivière to the Mercantilists (l. c., p. 486.) In a work, which, ex professo treats of "trade" and "speculation," occurs the following: "All trade consists in the exchange of things of different kinds; and the advantage" (to the merchant?) "arises out of this difference. To exchange a pound of bread against a pound of bread ... would be attended with no advantage; ... Hence trade is advantageously contrasted with gambling, which consists in a mere exchange of money for money." (Th. Corbet, "An Inquiry into the Causes and Modes of the Wealth of Individuals; or the Principles of Trade and Speculation Explained." London, 1841, p. 5.) Although Corbet does not see that M-M, the exchange or money for money, is the characteristic form of circulation, not only of merchants' capital but of all capital, yet at least he acknowledges that this form is common to gambling and to one species of trade, viz., speculation: but then comes acCulloch and makes out, that to buy in order to sell, is to speculate, and thus the difference between Speculation and Trade vanishes. "Every transaction in which an individual buys produce in order to sell it again, is, in fact, a speculation." (MacCulloch: "A Dictionary Practical, &c., of Commerce." Lond., 1847, p. 1009.) With much more naiveté, Pinto, the Pindar of the Amsterdam Stock Exchange, remarks, "Le commerce est un jeu: (taken from Locke) et ce n'est pas avec des gueux qu'on peut gagner. Si l'on gagnait longtemps en tout avec tous, il faudrait rendre de bon accord les plus grandes parties du profit pour recommencer le jeu." (Pinto: "Traité de la Circulation et du Crédit." Amsterdam, 1771. p. 231,)

[5] "Capital is divisible ... into the original capital and the profit, the increment to the capital ... although in practice this profit is immediately turned into capital, and set in motion with the original." (F. Engels, "Umrisse zu einer Kritik der Nationalökonomie, in: Deutsch-Französische Jahrbücher, herausgegeben von Arnold Ruge und Karl Marx." Paris, 1844, p. 99.)

[6] Aristotle opposes Oeconomic to Chrematistic. He starts from the former. So far as it is the art of gaining a livelihood, it is limited to procuring those articles that are necessary to existence, and useful either to a household or the state. "True wealth (ὁ ἀ   ἦ

ὸ   ῦ) consists of such values in use; for the quantity of possessions of this kind, capable of making life pleasant, is not unlimited. There is, however, a second mode of acquiring things, to which we may by preference and with correctness give the name of Chrematistic, and in this case there appear to be no limits to riches and possessions. Trade (ἡ   ῆ   ἡ) is literally retail trade, and Aristotle takes this kind because in it values in use predominate) does not in its nature belong to Chrematistic, for here the exchange has reference only to what is necessary to themselves (the buyer or seller)." Therefore, as he goes on to show, the original form of trade was barter, but with the extension of the latter, there arose the necessity for money. On the discovery of money, barter of necessity developed into [

ῆ   ῆ], into trading in commodities, and this again, in opposition to its original tendency, grew into Chrematistic, into the art of making money. Now Chrematistic is distinguishable from Oeconomic in this way, that "in the case of

Chrematistic circulation is the source of riches (η̉   ὴ χ

η̉   ἀ   ...   ἀ χ   η̉   ἀ

η̃   ). Therefore also riches, such as Chrematistic strives for, are unlimited. Just as every art that is not a means to an end, but an end in itself, has no limit to its aims, because it seeks constantly to approach nearer and nearer to that end, while those arts that pursue means to an end, are not boundless, since the goal itself imposes a limit upon them, so with Chrematistic, there are no bounds to its aims, these aims being absolute wealth. Oeconomic not Chrematistic has a limit ... the object of the former is something different from money, of the latter the augmentation of money.... By confounding these two forms, which overlap each other, some people have been led to look upon the preservation and increase of money ad infinitum as the end and aim of Oeconomic." (Aristoteles, "De Rep." edit. Bekker, lib. l. c. 8, 9. passim.)

[7] "Commodities (here used in the sense of use-values) are not the terminating object of the trading capitalist, money is his terminating object." (Th. Chalmers, "On Pol. Econ. &c.," 2nd Ed., Glasgow, 1832, pp. 165, 166.)

[8] "Il mercante non conta quasi per niente il lucro fatto, ma mira sempre al futuro." (A. Genovesi, Lezioni di Economia Civile (1765), Custodi's edit. of Italian Economists. Parte Moderna t. viii, p. 139.)

[9] "The inextinguishable passion for gain, the auri sacra fames, will always lead capitalists." (MacCulloch: "The Principles of Polit. Econ." London, 1830, p. 179.) This view, of course, does not prevent the same MacCulloch and others of his kidney, when in theoretical difficulties, such, for example, as the question of over-production, from transforming the same capitalist into a moral citizen, whose sole concern is for use-values, and who even develops an insatiable hunger for boots, hats, eggs, calico, and other extremely familiar sorts of use-values.

[10] [greek: Sozein] is a characteristic Greek expression for hoarding. So in English to save has the same two meanings: sauver and épargner.

[11] "Questo infinito che le cose non hanno in progresso, hanno in giro." (Galiani.)

[12] Ce n'est pas la matière qui fait le capital, mais la valeur de ces matières. " (J. B. Say: "Traité d'Econ. Polit." 3ème éd. Paris, 1817, t. II., p. 429.)

[13] "Currency (!) employed in producing articles... is capital." (Macleod: "The Theory and Practice of Banking." London, 1855, v. 1, ch. i, p. 55.) "Capital is commodities." (James Mill: "Elements of Pol. Econ." Lond., 1821, p. 74.)

[14] Capital: "portion fructifiante de la richesse accumulée... valeur permanents, multipliante." (Sismondi: "Nouveaux Principes d'Econ. Polit.," t. i., p. 88, 89.)

Chapter Five:
Contradictions in the General Formula of Capital

The form which circulation takes when money becomes capital, is opposed to all the laws we have hitherto investigated bearing on the nature of commodities, value and money, and even of circulation itself. What distinguishes this form from that of the simple circulation of commodities, is the inverted order of succession of the two antithetical processes, sale and purchase. How can this purely formal distinction between these processes change their character as it were by magic?

But that is not all. This inversion has no existence for two out of the three persons who transact business together. As capitalist, I buy commodities from A and sell them again to B, but as a simple owner of commodities, I sell them to B and then purchase fresh ones from A. A and B see no difference between the two sets of transactions. They are merely buyers or sellers. And I on each occasion meet them as a mere owner of either money or commodities, as a buyer or a seller, and, what is more, in both sets of transactions, I am opposed to A only as a buyer and to B only as a seller, to the one only as money, to the other only as commodities, and to neither of them as capital or a capitalist, or as representative of anything that is more than money or commodities, or that can produce any effect beyond what money and commodities can. For me the purchase from A and the sale to B are part of a series. But the connexion between the two acts exists for me alone. A does not trouble himself about my transaction with B, nor does B about my business with A. And if I offered to explain to them the meritorious nature of my action in inverting the order of succession, they would probably point out to me that I was mistaken as to that order of succession, and that the whole transaction, instead of beginning with a purchase and ending with a sale, began, on the contrary, with a sale and was concluded with a purchase. In truth, my first act, the purchase, was from the standpoint of A, a sale, and my second act, the sale, was from the standpoint of B, a purchase. Not content with that, A and B would declare that the whole series was superfluous and nothing but Hokus Pokus; that for the future A would buy direct from B, and B sell direct to A. Thus the whole transaction would be reduced to a single act forming an isolated, non-complemented phase in the ordinary circulation of commodities, a mere sale from A's point of view, and from B's, a mere purchase. The inversion, therefore, of the order of succession, does not take us outside the sphere of the simple circulation of commodities, and we must rather look, whether there is in this simple circulation anything permitting an expansion of the value that enters into circulation, and, consequently, a creation of surplus-value.

Let us take the process of circulation in a form under which it presents itself as a simple and direct exchange of commodities. This is always the case when two owners of commodities buy from each other, and on the settling day the amounts mutually owing are equal and cancel each other. The money in this case is money of account and serves to express the value of the commodities by their prices, but is not, itself, in the shape of hard cash, confronted with them. So far as regards use-values, it is clear that both parties may gain some advantage. Both part with goods that, as use-values, are of no service to them, and receive others that they can make use of. And there may also be a further gain. A, who sells wine and buys corn, possibly produces more wine, with given labour-time, than farmer B could, and B on the other hand, more corn than wine-grower A could. A, therefore, may get, for the same exchange-value, more corn, and B more wine, than each would respectively get without any exchange by producing his own corn and wine. With reference, therefore, to use-value, there is good ground for saying that "exchange is a transaction by which both sides gain." [1] It is otherwise with exchange-value. "A man who has plenty of wine and no corn treats with a man who has plenty of corn and no wine; an exchange takes place between them of corn to the value of 50, for wine of the same value.This act produces no increase of exchange-value either for the one or the other; for each of them already possessed, before the exchange, a value equal to that which he acquired by means of that operation." [2] The result is not altered by introducing money, as a medium of circulation, between the commodities, and making the sale and the purchase two distinct acts. ³ The value of a commodity is expressed in its price before it goes into circulation, and is therefore a precedent condition of circulation, not its result. ⁴

Abstractedly considered, that is, apart from circumstances not immediately flowing from the laws of the simple circulation of commodities, there is in an exchange nothing (if we except the replacing of one use-value by another) but a metamorphosis, a mere change in the form of the commodity. The same exchange-value, i.e., the same quantity of incorporated social labour, remains throughout in the hands of the owner of the commodity, first in the shape of his own commodity, then in the form of the money for which he exchanged it, and lastly, in the shape of the commodity he buys with that money. This change of form does not imply a change in the magnitude of the value. But the change, which the value of the commodity undergoes in this process, is limited to a change in its money-form. This form exists first as the price of the commodity offered for sale, then as an actual sum of money, which, however, was already expressed in the price, and lastly, as the price of an equivalent commodity. This change of form no more implies, taken alone, a change in the quantity of value, than does the change of a £5 note into sovereigns, half sovereigns and shillings. So far therefore as the circulation of commodities effects a change in the form alone of their values, and is free from disturbing influences, it must be the exchange of equivalents. Little as Vulgar-Economy knows about the nature of value, yet whenever it wishes to consider the phenomena of circulation in their purity, it assumes that supply and demand are equal, which amounts to this, that their effect is nil. If therefore, as regards the use-values exchanged, both buyer and seller may possibly gain something, this is not the case as regards the exchange-values. Here we must rather say, "Where equality exists there can be no gain." ⁵ It is true, commodities may be sold at prices deviating from their values, but these deviations are to be considered as infractions of the laws of the exchange of commodities ⁶, which in its normal state is an exchange of equivalents, consequently, no method for increasing value. ⁷

Hence, we see that behind all attempts to represent the circulation of commodities as a source of surplus-value, there lurks a quid pro quo, a mixing up of use-value and exchange-value. For instance, Condillac says: "It is not true that on an exchange of commodities we give value for value. On the contrary, each of the two contracting parties in every case, gives a less for a greater value. ... If we really exchanged equal values, neither party could make a profit. And yet, they both gain, or ought to gain. Why? The value of a thing consists solely in its relation to our wants. What is more to the one is less to the other, and vice versâ. ... It is not to be assumed that we offer for sale articles required for our own consumption. ... We wish to part with a useless thing, in order to get one that we need; we want to give less for more. ... It was natural to think that, in an exchange, value was given for value, whenever each of the articles exchanged was of equal value with the same quantity of gold. ... But there is another point to be considered in our calculation. The question is, whether we both exchange something superfluous for something necessary." ⁸ We see in this passage, how Condillac not only confuses use-value with exchange-value, but in a really childish manner assumes, that in a society, in which the production of commodities is well developed, each producer produces his own means of subsistence, and throws into circulation only the excess over his own requirements. ⁹ Still, Condillac's argument is frequently used by modem economists, more especially when the point is to show, that the exchange of commodities in its developed form, commerce, is productive of surplus-value. For instance, "Commerce ... adds value to products, for the same products in the hands of consumers, are worth more than in the hands of producers, and it may strictly be considered an act of production." ¹⁰ But commodities are not paid for twice over, once on account of their use-value, and again on account of their value. And though the use-value of a commodity is more serviceable to the buyer than to the seller, its money-form is more serviceable to the seller. Would he otherwise sell it? We might therefore just as well say that the buyer performs "strictly an act of production," by converting stockings, for example, into money.

If commodities, or commodities and money, of equal exchange-value, and consequently equivalents, are exchanged, it is plain that no one abstracts more value from, than he throws into, circulation. There is no creation of surplus-value. And, in its normal form, the circulation of commodities demands the exchange of equivalents. But in actual practice, the process does not retain its normal form. Let us, therefore, assume an exchange of non-equivalents.

In any case the market for commodities is only frequented by owners of commodities, and the power which these persons exercise over each other, is no other than the power of their commodities. The material variety of these commodities is the material incentive to the act of exchange, and makes buyers and sellers mutually dependent, because none of them possesses the object of his own wants, and each holds in his hand the object of another's wants. Besides these material differences of their use-values, there is only one other difference between commodities, namely, that between their bodily form and the form into which they are converted by sale, the difference between commodities and money. And consequently the owners of commodities are distinguishable only as sellers, those who own commodities, and buyers, those who own money.

Suppose then, that by some inexplicable privilege, the seller is enabled to sell his commodities above their value, what is worth 100 for 110, in which case the price is nominally raised 10%. The seller therefore pockets a surplus-value of 10. But after he has sold he becomes a buyer. A third owner of commodities comes to him now as seller, who in this capacity also enjoys the privilege of selling his commodities 10% too dear. Our friend gained 10 as a seller only to lose it again as a buyer. [11] The net result is, that all owners of commodities sell their goods to one another at 10% above their value, which comes precisely to the same as if they sold them at their true value. Such a general and nominal rise of prices has the same effect as if the values had been expressed in weight of silver instead of in weight of gold. The nominal prices of commodities would rise, but the real relation between their values would remain unchanged.

Let us make the opposite assumption, that the buyer has the privilege of purchasing commodities under their value. In this case it is no longer necessary to bear in mind that he in his turn will become a seller. He was so before he became buyer; he had already lost 10% in selling before he gained 10% as buyer. [12] Everything is just as it was.

The creation of surplus-value, and therefore the conversion of money into capital, can consequently be explained neither on the assumption that commodities are sold above their value, nor that they are bought below their value. [13]

The problem is in no way simplified by introducing irrelevant matters after the manner of Col. Torrens: "Effectual demand consists in the power and inclination (!), on the part of consumers, to give for commodities, either by immediate or circuitous barter, some greater portion of ... capital than their production costs." [14] In relation to circulation, producers and consumers meet only as buyers and sellers. To assert that the surplus-value acquired by the producer has its origin in the fact that consumers pay for commodities more than their value, is only to say in other words: The owner of commodities possesses, as a seller, the privilege of selling too dear. The seller has himself produced the commodities or represents their producer, but the buyer has to no less extent produced the commodities represented by his money, or represents their producer. The distinction between them is, that one buys and the other sells. The fact that the owner of the commodities, under the designation of producer, sells them over their value, and under the designation of consumer, pays too much for them, does not carry us a single step further. [15]

To be consistent therefore, the upholders of the delusion that surplus-value has its origin in a nominal rise of prices or in the privilege which the seller has of selling too dear, must assume the existence of a class that only buys and does not sell, i.e., only consumes and does not produce. The existence of such a class is inexplicable from the standpoint we have so far reached, viz., that of simple circulation. But let us anticipate. The money with which such a class is constantly making purchases, must constantly flow into their pockets, without any exchange, gratis, by might or right, from the pockets of the commodity-owners themselves. To sell commodities above their value to such a class, is only to crib back again a part of the money previously given to it. [16] The towns of Asia Minor thus paid a yearly money tribute to ancient Rome. With this money Rome purchased from them commodities, and purchased them too dear. The provincials cheated the Romans, and thus got back from their conquerors, in the course of trade, a portion of the tribute. Yet, for all that, the conquered were the really cheated. Their goods were still paid for with their own money. That is not the way to get rich or to create surplus-value.

Let us therefore keep within the bounds of exchange where sellers are also buyers, and buyers, sellers. Our difficulty may perhaps have arisen from treating the actors as personifications instead of as individuals.

A may be clever enough to get the advantage of B or C without their being able to retaliate. A sells wine worth £40 to B, and obtains from him in exchange corn to the value of £50. A has converted his £40 into £50, has made more money out of less, and has converted his commodities into capital. Let us examine this a little more closely. Before the exchange we had £40 worth of wine in the hands of A, and £50 worth of corn in those of B, a total value of £90. After the exchange we have still the same total value of £90. The value in circulation has not increased by one iota, it is only distributed differently between A and B. What is a loss of value to B is surplus-value to A; what is "minus" to one is "plus" to the other. The same change would have taken place, if A, without the formality of an exchange, had directly stolen the £10 from B. The sum of the values in circulation can clearly not be augmented by any change in their distribution, any more than the quantity of the precious metals in a country by a Jew selling a Queen Anne's farthing for a guinea. The capitalist class, as a whole, in any country, cannot over-reach themselves. [17]

Turn and twist then as we may, the fact remains unaltered. If equivalents are exchanged, no surplus-value results, and if non-equivalents are exchanged, still no surplus-value. [18] Circulation, or the exchange of commodities, begets no value. [19]

The reason is now therefore plain why, in analysing the standard form of capital, the form under which it determines the economic organisation of modern society, we entirely left out of consideration its most popular, and, so to say, antediluvian forms, merchants' capital and money-lenders' capital.

The circuit M-C-M, buying in order to sell dearer, is seen most clearly in genuine merchants' capital. But the movement takes place entirely within the sphere of circulation. Since, however, it is impossible, by circulation alone, to account for the conversion of money into capital, for the formation of surplus-value, it would appear, that merchants' capital is an impossibility, so long as equivalents are exchanged; [20] that, therefore, it can only have its origin in the two-fold advantage gained, over both the selling and the buying producers, by the merchant who parasitically shoves himself in between them. It is in this sense that Franklin says, "war is robbery, commerce is generally cheating." [21] If the transformation of merchants' money into capital is to be explained otherwise than by the producers being simply cheated, a long series of intermediate steps would be necessary, which, at present, when the simple circulation of commodities forms our only assumption, are entirely wanting.

What we have said with reference to merchants' capital, applies still more to money-lenders' capital. In merchants' capital, the two extremes, the money that is thrown upon the market, and the augmented money that is withdrawn from the market, are at least connected by a purchase and a sale, in other words by the movement of the circulation. In money-lenders' capital the form M-C-M is reduced to the two extremes without a mean, M-M , money exchanged for more money, a form that is incompatible with the nature of money, and therefore remains inexplicable from the standpoint of the circulation of commodities. Hence Aristotle: "since chrematistic is a double science, one part belonging to commerce, the other to economic, the latter being necessary and praiseworthy, the former based on circulation and with justice disapproved (for it is not based on Nature, but on mutual cheating), therefore the usurer is most rightly hated, because money itself is the source of his gain, and is not used for the purposes for which it was invented. For it originated for the exchange of commodities, but interest makes out of money, more money. Hence its name ([greek: tokos] interest and offspring). For the begotten are like those who beget them. But interest is money of money, so that of all modes of making a living, this is the most contrary to Nature." [22]

In the course of our investigation, we shall find that both merchants' capital and interest-bearing capital are derivative forms, and at the same time it will become clear, why these two forms appear in the course of history before the modern standard form of capital.

We have shown that surplus-value cannot be created by circulation, and, therefore, that in its formation, something must take place in the background, which is not apparent in the circulation itself. [23] But can surplus-value possibly originate anywhere else than in circulation, which is the sum total of all the mutual relations of commodity-owners, as far as they are determined by their commodities? Apart from circulation, the commodity-owner is in relation only with his own commodity. So far as regards value, that relation is limited to this, that the commodity contains a quantity of his own labour, that quantity being measured by a definite social standard. This quantity is expressed by the value of the commodity, and since the value is reckoned in money of account, this quantity is also expressed by the price, which we will suppose to be £10. But his labour is not represented both by the value of the commodity, and by a surplus over that value, not by a price of 10 that is also a price of 11, not by a value that is greater than itself. The commodity owner can, by his labour, create value, but not self-expanding value. He can increase the value of his commodity, by adding fresh labour, and therefore more value to the value in hand, by making, for instance, leather into boots. The same material has now more value, because it contains a greater quantity of labour. The boots have therefore more value than the leather, but the value of the leather remains what it was; it has not expanded itself, has not, during the making of the boots, annexed surplus-value. It is therefore impossible that outside the sphere of circulation, a producer of commodities can, without coming into contact with other commodity-owners, expand value, and consequently convert money or commodities into capital.

It is therefore impossible for capital to be produced by circulation, and it is equally impossible for it to originate apart from circulation. It must have its origin both in circulation and yet not in circulation.

We have, therefore, got a double result.

The conversion of money into capital has to be explained on the basis of the laws that regulate the exchange of commodities, in such a way that the starting-point is the exchange of equivalents. [24] Our friend, Moneybags, who as yet is only an embryo capitalist, must buy his commodities at their value, must sell them at their value, and yet at the end of the process must withdraw more value from circulation than he threw into it at starting. His development into a full-grown capitalist must take place, both within the sphere of circulation and without it. These are the conditions of the problem. Hic Rhodus, hic salta!

Footnotes

[1] "L'échange est une transaction admirable dans laquelle les deux contractants gagnent-toujours (!)" (Destutt de Tracy: "Traité de la Volonté et de ses effets." Paris, 1826, p. 68.) This work appeared afterwards as "Traité d'Econ. Polit."

[2] "Mercier de la Rivière," l. c., p. 544.

[3] "Que l'une de ces deux valeurs soit argent, ou queues soient toutes deux marchandises usuelles, rien de plus indifférent en soi." ("Mercier de la Rivière," l. c., p. 543.)

[4] "Ce ne sont pas les contractants qui prononcent sur la valeur; elle est décidée avant la convention." (Le Trosne, p. 906.)

[5] "Dove è egualità non è lucro." (Galiani, "Della Moneta in Custodi, Parte Moderna," t. iv., p. 244.)

[6] "L'échange devient désavantageux pour l'une des parties, lorsque quelque chose étrangère vient diminuer ou exagérer le prix; alors l'égalité est blessée, mais la lésion procède de cette cause et non de l'échange." (Le Trosne, l. c., p. 904.)

[7] "L'échange est de sa nature un contrat d'égalité qui se fait de valeur pour valeur égale. Il n'est donc pas un moyen de s'enrichir, puisque l'on donne autant que l'on reçoit." (Le Trosne, l. c., p. 903.)

[8] Condillac: "Le Commerce et la Gouvernement" (1776). Edit. Daire et Molinari in the "Mélanges d'Econ. Polit." Paris, 1847, pp. 267, 291.

[9] Le Trosne, therefore, answers his friend Condillac with justice as follows: "Dans une ... société formée il n'y a pas de surabondant en aucun genre." At the same time, in a bantering way, he remarks: "If both the persons who exchange receive more to an equal amount, and part with less to an equal amount, they both get the same." It is because Condillac has not the remotest idea of the nature of exchange-value that he has been chosen by Herr Professor Wilhelm Roscher as a proper person to answer for the soundness of his own childish notions. See Roscher's "Die Grundlagen der Nationalökonomie, Dritte Auflage," 1858.

[10] S. P. Newman: "Elements of Polit. Econ." Andover and New York, 1835, p. 175.

[11] "By the augmentation of the nominal value of the produce... sellers not enriched... since what they gain as sellers, they precisely expend in the quality of buyers." ("The Essential Principles of the Wealth of Nations." &c., London, 1797, p. 66.)

[12] "Si l'on est forcé de donner pour 18 livres une quantité de telle production qui en valait 24, lorsqu'on employera ce même argent à acheter, on aura également pour 18 l. ce que l'on payait 24." (Le Trosne, I. c., p. 897.)

[13] "Chaque vendeur ne peut donc parvenir à renchérir habituellement ses marchandises, qu'en se soumettant aussi à payer habituellement plus cher les marchandises des autres vendeurs; et par la même raison, chaque consommateur ne peut payer habituellement moins cher ce qu 'il achète, qu'en se soumettant aussi à une diminution semblance sur le prix des choses qu'il vend." (Mercier de la Rivière, l. c., p. 555.)

[14] Torrens. "An Essay on the Production of Wealth." London, 1821, p. 349.

[15] The idea of profits being paid by the consumers, is, assuredly, very absurd. Who are the consumers?" (G. Ramsay: "An Essay on the Distribution of Wealth." Edinburgh, 1836, p. 183.)

[16] "When a man is in want of a demand, does Mr. Malthus recommend him to pay some other person to take off his goods?" is a question put by an angry disciple of Ricardo to Malthus, who, like his disciple, Parson Chalmers, economically glorifies this class of simple buyers or consumers. (See "An Inquiry into those Principles Respecting the Nature of Demand and the Necessity of Consumption, lately advocated by Mr. Malthus," &c. Lond., 1821, p. 55.)

[17] Destutt de Tracy, although, or perhaps because, he was a member of the Institute, held the opposite view. He says, industrial capitalists make profits because "they all sell for more than it has cost to produce. And to whom do they sell? In the first instance to one another." (I. c., p. 239.)

[18] "L'échange qui se fait de deux valeurs égales n'augmente ni ne diminue la masse des valeurs subsistantes dans la société. L'échange de deux valeurs inégales ... ne change rien non plus à la somme des valeurs sociales, bien qu'il ajoute à la fortune de l'un ce qu'il été de la fortune de l'autre." (J. B. Say, l. c., t. II, pp. 443, 444.) Say, not in the least troubled as to the consequences of this statement, borrows it, almost word for word, from the Physiocrats. The following example will show how Monsieur Say turned to account the writings of the Physiocrats, in his day quite forgotten, for the purpose of expanding the "value" of his own. His most celebrated saying, "On n'achète des produits qu'avec des produits" (I. c., t. II. p. 441.) runs as follows in the original physiocratic work: "Les productions ne se paient qu'avec des productions." (Le Trosne, . c., p. 899.)

[19] "Exchange confers no value at all upon products." (F. Wayland: "The Elements of Political Economy." Boston, 1843, p. 169.)

[20] Under the rule of invariable equivalents commerce would be impossible. (G. Opdyke: "A Treatise on Polit. Economy." New York, 1851, pp. 66-69.) "The difference between real value and exchange-value is based upon this fact, namely, that the value of a thing is different from the so-called equivalent given for it in trade, i.e., that this equivalent is no equivalent." (F. Engels, l. c., p. 96).

[21] Benjamin Franklin: Works, Vol. II, edit. Sparks in "Positions to be examined concerning National Wealth," p. 376.

[22] Aristotle, I. c., c. 10.

[23] "Profit, in the usual condition of the market, is not made by exchanging. Had it not existed before, neither could it after that transaction." (Ramsay, l. c., p. 184.)

[24] If prices actually differ from values, we must, first of all, reduce the former to the latter, in other words, treat the difference as accidental in order that the phenomena may be observed in their purity, and our observations not interfered with by disturbing circumstances that have nothing to do with the process in question. We know, moreover, that this reduction is no mere scientific process. The continual oscillations in prices, their rising and falling, compensate each other, and reduce themselves to an average price, which is their hidden regulator. It forms the guiding star of the merchant or the manufacturer in every undertaking that requires time. He knows that when a long period of time is taken, commodities are sold neither over nor under, but at their average price. If therefore he thought about the matter at all, he would formulate the problem of the formation of capital as follows: How can we account for the origin of capital on the supposition that prices are regulated by the average price, i. e., ultimately by the value of the commodities? I say "ultimately," because average prices do not directly coincide with the values of commodities, as Adam Smith, Ricardo, and others believe.

Chapter Six:
The Buying and Selling of Labour-Power

The change of value that occurs in the case of money intended to be converted into capital, cannot take place in the money itself, since in its function of means of purchase and of payment, it does no more than realise the price of the commodity it buys or pays for; and, as hard cash, it is value petrified, never varying. [1] Just as little can it originate in the second act of circulation, the re-sale of the commodity, which does no more than transform the article from its bodily form back again into its money-form. The change must, therefore, take place in the commodity bought by the first act, M-C, but not in its value, for equivalents are exchanged, and the commodity is paid for at its full value. We are, therefore, forced to the conclusion that the change originates in the use-value, as such, of the commodity, i.e., in its consumption. In order to be able to extract value from the consumption of a commodity, our friend, Moneybags, must be so lucky as to find, within the sphere of circulation, in the market, a commodity, whose use-value possesses the peculiar property of being a source of value, whose actual consumption, therefore, is itself an embodiment of labour, and, consequently, a creation of value. The possessor of money does find on the market such a special commodity in capacity for labour or labour-power.

By labour-power or capacity for labour is to be understood the aggregate of those mental and physical capabilities existing in a human being, which he exercises whenever he produces a use-value of any description.

But in order that our owner of money may be able to find labour-power offered for sale as a commodity, various conditions must first be fulfilled. The exchange of commodities of itself implies no other relations of dependence than those which, result from its own nature. On this assumption, labour-power can appear upon the market as a commodity, only if, and so far as, its possessor, the individual whose labour-power it is, offers it for sale, or sells it, as a commodity. In order that he may be able to do this, he must have it at his disposal, must be the untrammelled owner of his capacity for labour, i.e., of his person. [2] He and the owner of money meet in the market, and deal with each other as on the basis of equal rights, with this difference alone, that one is buyer, the other seller; both, therefore, equal in the eyes of the law. The continuance of this relation demands that the owner of the labour-power should sell it only for a definite period, for if he were to sell it rump and stump, once for all, he would be selling himself, converting himself from a free man into a slave, from an owner of a commodity into a commodity. He must constantly look upon his labour-power as his own property, his own commodity, and this he can only do by placing it at the disposal of the buyer temporarily, for a definite period of time. By this means alone can he avoid renouncing his rights of ownership over it. [3]

The second essential condition to the owner of money finding labour-power in the market as a commodity is this — that the labourer instead of being in the position to sell commodities in which his labour is incorporated, must be obliged to offer for sale as a commodity that very labour-power, which exists only in his living self.

In order that a man may be able to sell commodities other than labour-power, he must of course have the means of production, as raw material, implements, &c. No boots can be made without leather. He requires also the means of subsistence. Nobody — not even "a musician of the future" — can live upon future products, or upon use-values in an unfinished state; and ever since the first moment of his appearance on the world's stage, man always has been, and must still be a consumer, both before and while he is producing. In a society where all products assume the form of commodities, these commodities must be sold after they have been produced, it is only after their sale that they can serve in satisfying the requirements of their producer. The time necessary for their sale is superadded to that necessary for their production.

For the conversion of his money into capital, therefore, the owner of money must meet in the market with the free labourer, free in the double sense, that as a free man he can dispose of his labour-power as his own commodity, and that on the other hand he has no other commodity for sale, is short of everything necessary for the realisation of his labour-power.

The question why this free labourer confronts him in the market, has no interest for the owner of money, who regards the labour-market as a branch of the general market for commodities. And for the present it interests us just as little. We cling to the fact theoretically, as he does practically. One thing, however, is clear — Nature does not produce on the one side owners of money or commodities, and on the other men possessing nothing but their own labour-power. This relation has no natural basis, neither is its social basis one that is common to all historical periods. It is clearly the result of a past historical development, the product of many economic revolutions, of the extinction of a whole series of older forms of social production.

So, too, the economic categories, already discussed by us, bear the stamp of history. Definite historical conditions are necessary that a product may become a commodity. It must not be produced as the immediate means of subsistence of the producer himself. Had we gone further, and inquired under what circumstances all, or even the majority of products take the form of commodities, we should have found that this can only happen with production of a very specific kind, capitalist production. Such an inquiry, however, would have been foreign to the analysis of commodities. Production and circulation of commodities can take place, although the great mass of the objects produced are intended for the immediate requirements of their producers, are not turned into commodities, and consequently social production is not yet by a long way dominated in its length and breadth by exchange-value. The appearance of products as commodities pre-supposes such a development of the social division of labour, that the separation of use-value from exchange-value, a separation which first begins with barter, must already have been completed. But such a degree of development is common to many forms of society, which in other respects present the most varying historical features. On the other hand, if we consider money, its existence implies a definite stage in the exchange of commodities. The particular functions of money which it performs, either as the mere equivalent of commodities, or as means of circulation, or means of payment, as hoard or as universal money, point, according to the extent and relative preponderance of the one function or the other, to very different stages in the process of social production. Yet we know by experience that a circulation of commodities relatively primitive, suffices for the production of all these forms. Otherwise with capital. The historical conditions of its existence are by no means given with the mere circulation of money and commodities. It can spring into life, only when the owner of the means of production and subsistence meets in the market with the free labourer selling his labour-power. And this one historical condition comprises a world's history. Capital, therefore, announces from its first appearance a new epoch in the process of social production. [4]

We must now examine more closely this peculiar commodity, labour-power. Like all others it has a value. [5] How is that value determined?

The value of labour-power is determined, as in the case of every other commodity, by the labour-time necessary for the production, and consequently also the reproduction, of this special article. So far as it has value, it represents no more than a definite quantity of the average labour of society incorporated in it. Labour-power exists only as a capacity, or power of the living individual. Its production consequently pre-supposes his existence. Given the individual, the production of labour-power consists in his reproduction of himself or his maintenance. For his maintenance he requires a given quantity of the means of subsistence. Therefore the labour-time requisite for the production of labour-power reduces itself to that necessary for the production of those means of subsistence; in other words, the value of labour-power is the value of the means of subsistence necessary for the maintenance of the labourer. Labour-power, however, becomes a reality only by its exercise; it sets itself in action only by working. But thereby a definite quantity of human muscle, nerve. brain, &c., is wasted, and these require to be restored. This increased expenditure demands a larger income. [6] If the owner of labour-power works to-day, to-morrow he must again be able to repeat the same process in the same conditions as regards health and strength. His means of subsistence must therefore be sufficient to maintain him in his normal state as a labouring individual. His natural wants, such as food, clothing, fuel, and housing, vary according to the climatic and other physical conditions of his country. On the other hand, the number and extent of his so-called necessary wants, as also the modes of satisfying them, are themselves the product of historical development, and depend therefore to a great extent on the degree of civilisation of a country, more particularly on the conditions under which, and consequently on the habits and degree of comfort in which, the class of free labourers has been formed. [7] In contradistinction therefore to the case of other commodities, there enters into the determination of the value of labour-power a historical and moral element. Nevertheless, in a given country, at a given period, the average quantity of the means of subsistence necessary for the labourer is practically known.

The owner of labour-power is mortal. If then his appearance in the market is to be continuous, and the continuous conversion of money into capital assumes this, the seller of labour-power must perpetuate himself, "in the way that every living individual perpetuates himself, by procreation." [8] The labour-power withdrawn from the market by wear and tear and death, must be continually replaced by, at the very least, an equal amount of fresh labour-power. Hence the sum of the means of subsistence necessary for the production of labour-power must include the means necessary for the labourer's substitutes, i.e., his children, in order that this race of peculiar commodity-owners may perpetuate its appearance in the market. [9]

In order to modify the human organism, so that it may acquire skill and handiness in a given branch of industry, and become labour-power of a special kind, a special education or training is requisite, and this, on its part, costs an equivalent in commodities of a greater or less amount. This amount varies according to the more or less complicated character of the labour-power. The expenses of this education (excessively small in the case of ordinary labour-power), enter pro tanto into the total value spent in its production.

The value of labour-power resolves itself into the value of a definite quantity of the means of subsistence. It therefore varies with the value of these means or with the quantity of labour requisite for their production.

Some of the means of subsistence, such as food and fuel, are consumed daily, and a fresh supply must be provided daily. Others such as clothes and furniture last for longer periods and require to be replaced only at longer intervals. One article must be bought or paid for daily, another weekly, another quarterly, and so on. But in whatever way the sum total of these outlays may be spread over the year, they must be covered by the average income, taking one day with another. If the total of the commodities required daily for the production of labour-power = A, and those required weekly = B, and those required quarterly = C, and so on, the daily average of these commodities = $365A + 52B + 4C + \&c / 365$. Suppose that in this mass of commodities requisite for the average day there are embodied 6 hours of social labour, then there is incorporated daily in labour-power half a day's average social labour, in other words, half a day's labour is requisite for the daily production of labour-power. This quantity of labour forms the value of a day's labour-power or the value of the labour-power daily reproduced. If half a day's average social labour is incorporated in three shillings, then three shillings is the price corresponding to the value of a day's labour-power. If its owner therefore offers it for sale at three shillings a day, its selling price is equal to its value, and according to our supposition, our friend Moneybags, who is intent upon converting his three shillings into capital, pays this value.

The minimum limit of the value of labour-power is determined by the value of the commodities, without the daily supply of which the labourer cannot renew his vital energy, consequently by the value of those means of subsistence that are physically indispensable. If the price of labour-power fall to this minimum, it falls below its value, since under such circumstances it can be maintained and developed only in a crippled state. But the value of every commodity is determined by the labour-time requisite to turn it out so as to be of normal quality.

It is a very cheap sort of sentimentality which declares this method of determining the value of labour-power, a method prescribed by the very nature of the case, to be a brutal method, and which wails with Rossi that, "To comprehend capacity for labour (puissance de travail) at the same time that we make abstraction from the means of subsistence of the labourers during the process of production, is to comprehend a phantom (être de raison). When we speak of labour, or capacity for labour, we speak at the same time of the labourer and his means of subsistence, of labourer and wages." [10] When we speak of capacity for labour, we do not speak of labour, any more than when we speak of capacity for digestion, we speak of digestion. The latter process requires something more than a good stomach. When we speak of capacity for labour, we do not abstract from the necessary means of subsistence. On the contrary, their value is expressed in its value. If his capacity for labour remains unsold, the labourer derives no benefit from it, but rather he will feel it to be a cruel nature-imposed necessity that this capacity has cost for its production a definite amount of the means of subsistence and that it will continue to do so for its reproduction. He will then agree with Sismondi: "that capacity for labour ... is nothing unless it is sold." [11]

One consequence of the peculiar nature of labour-power as a commodity is, that its use-value does not, on the conclusion of the contract between the buyer and seller, immediately pass into the hands of the former. Its value, like that of every other commodity, is already fixed before it goes into circulation, since a definite quantity of social labour has been spent upon it; but its use-value consists in the subsequent exercise of its force. The alienation of labour-power and its actual appropriation by the buyer, its employment as a use-value, are separated by an interval of time. But in those cases in which the formal alienation by sale of the use-value of a commodity, is not simultaneous with its actual delivery to the buyer, the money of the latter usually functions as means of payment. [12] In every country in which the capitalist mode of production reigns, it is the custom not to pay for labour-power before it has been exercised for the period fixed by the contract, as for example, the end of each week. In all cases, therefore, the use-value of the labour-power is advanced to the capitalist: the labourer allows the buyer to consume it before he receives payment of the price; he everywhere gives credit to the capitalist. That this credit is no mere fiction, is shown not only by the occasional loss of wages on the bankruptcy of the capitalist, [13] but also by a series of more enduring consequences. [14] Nevertheless, whether money serves as a means of purchase or as a means of payment, this makes no alteration in the nature of the exchange of commodities. The price of the labour-power is fixed by the contract, although it is not realised till later, like the rent of a house. The labour-power is sold, although it is only paid for at a later period. It will, therefore, be useful, for a clear comprehension of the relation of the parties, to assume provisionally, that the possessor of labour-power, on the occasion of each sale, immediately receives the price stipulated to be paid for it.

We now know how the value paid by the purchaser to the possessor of this peculiar commodity, labour-power, is determined. The use-value which the former gets in exchange, manifests itself only in the actual usufruct, in the consumption of the labour-power. The money-owner buys everything necessary for this purpose, such as raw material, in the market, and pays for it at its full value. The consumption of labour-power is at one and the same time the production of commodities and of surplus-value. The consumption of labour-power is completed, as in the case of every other commodity, outside the limits of the market or of the sphere of circulation. Accompanied by Mr. Moneybags and by the possessor of labour-power, we therefore take leave for a time of this noisy sphere, where everything takes place on the surface and in view of all men, and follow them both into the hidden abode of production, on whose threshold there stares us in the face "No admittance except on business." Here we shall see, not only how capital produces, but how capital is produced. We shall at last force the secret of profit making.

This sphere that we are deserting, within whose boundaries the sale and purchase of labour-power goes on, is in fact a very Eden of the innate rights of man. There alone rule Freedom, Equality, Property and Bentham. Freedom, because both buyer and seller of a commodity, say of labour-power, are constrained only by their own free will. They contract as free agents, and the agreement they come to, is but the form in which they give legal expression to their common will. Equality, because each enters into relation with the other, as with a simple owner of commodities, and they exchange equivalent for equivalent. Property, because each disposes only of what is his own. And Bentham, because each looks only to himself. The only force that brings them together and puts them in relation with each other, is the selfishness, the gain and the private interests of each. Each looks to himself only, and no one troubles himself about the rest, and just because they do so, do they all, in accordance with the pre-established harmony of things, or under the auspices of an all-shrewd providence, work together to their mutual advantage, for the common weal and in the interest of all.

On leaving this sphere of simple circulation or of exchange of commodities, which furnishes the "Free-trader Vulgaris" with his views and ideas, and with the standard by which he judges a society based on capital and wages, we think we can perceive a change in the physiognomy of our dramatis personae. He, who before was the money-owner, now strides in front as capitalist; the possessor of labour-power follows as his labourer. The one with an air of importance, smirking, intent on business; the other, timid and holding back, like one who is bringing his own hide to market and has nothing to expect but — a hiding.

Footnotes

[1] "In the form of money ... capital is productive of no profit." (Ricardo: "'Princ. of Pol. Econ.," p. 267.)

[2] In encyclopaedias of classical antiquities we find such nonsense as this — that in the ancient world capital was fully developed, "except that the free labourer and a system of credit was wanting." Mommsen also, in his "History of Rome," commits, in this respect, one blunder after another.

[3] Hence legislation in various countries fixes a maximum for labour-contracts. Wherever free labour is the rule, the laws regulate the mode of terminating this contract. In some States, particularly in Mexico (before the American Civil War, also in the territories taken from Mexico, and also, as a matter of fact, in the Danubian provinces till the revolution effected by Kusa), slavery is hidden under the form of peonage. By means of advances, repayable in labour, which are handed down from generation to generation, not only the individual labourer, but his family, become, de facto, the property of other persons and their families. Juarez abolished peonage. The so-called Emperor aximilian re-established it by a decree, which, in the House of Representatives at Washington, was aptly denounced as a decree for the re-introduction of slavery into Mexico. "I may make over to another the use, for a limited time, of my particular bodily and mental aptitudes and capabilities; because in consequence of this restriction, they are impressed with a character of alienation with regard to me as a whole. But by the alienation of all my labour-time and the whole of my work, I should be converting the substance itself, in other words, my general activity and reality, my person, into the property of another." (Hegel, "Philosophie des Rechts." Berlin, 1840, p. 104, § 67.)

[4] The capitalist epoch is therefore characterised by this, that labour-power takes in the eyes of the labourer himself the form of a commodity which is his property; his labour consequently becomes wage-labour. On the other hand, it is only from this moment that the produce of labour universally becomes a commodity.

[5] "The value or worth of a man, is as of all other things his price — that is to say, so much as would be given for the use of his power." (Th. Hobbes: "Leviathan" in Works, Ed. Molesworth. Lond. 1839-44, v. iii. p. 76.)

[6] Hence the Roman Villicus, as overlooker of the agricultural slaves, received "more meagre fare than working slaves, because his work was lighter." (Th. Mommsen, Röm. Geschichte, 1856, p. 810.)

[7] Comparc W. Th. Thornton: "Over-population and its Remedy," Lond., 1846.

[8] Petty.

[9] "Its (labour's) natural price ... consists in such a quantity of necessaries and comforts of life, as, from the nature of the climate, and the habits of the country, are necessary to support the labourer, and to enable him to rear such a family as may preserve, in the market, an undiminished supply of labour." (R. Torrens: "An Essay on the External Corn Trade." Lond. 1815, p. 62.) The word labour is here wrongly used for labour-power.

[10] Rossi: "Cours d'Econ. Polit.," Bruxelles, 1842, p. 370.

[11] Sismondi: "Nouv. Princ. etc.," t. I, p. 112.

[12] "All labour is paid after it has ceased." ("An Inquiry into those Principles Respecting the Nature of Demand," &c., p. 104.) Le crédit commercial a dû commencer au moment où l'ouvrier, premier artisan de la production, a pu, au moyen de ses économies, attendre le salaire de son travail jusqu'à la fin de la semaine, de la quinzaine, du mois, du trimestre, &c." (Ch. Ganilh: "Des Systèmes d'Econ. Polit." 2éme édit. Paris, 1821, t. II, p. 150.)

[13] "L'ouvrier prête son industrie," but adds Storch slyly: he "risks nothing" except "de perdre son salaire ... l'ouvrier ne transmet rien de matériel." (Storch: "Cours d'Econ. Polit." Pétersbourg, 1815, t. II., p. 37.)

[14] One example. In London there are two sorts of bakers, the "full priced," who sell bread at its full value, and the "undersellers," who sell it under its value. The latter class comprises more than three-fourths of the total number of bakers. (p. xxxii in the Report of H. S. Tremenheere, commissioner to examine into "the grievances complained of by the journeymen bakers", &c., Lond. 1862.) The undersellers, almost without exception, sell bread adulterated with alum, soap, pearl ashes, chalk, Derbyshire stone-dust, and such like agreeable nourishing and wholesome ingredients. (See the above cited Blue book, as also the report of "the committee of 1855 on the adulteration of bread," and Dr. Hassall's "Adulterations Detected," 2nd Ed. Lond. 1861.) Sir John Gordon stated before the committee of 1855, that "in consequence of these adulterations, the poor man, who lives on two pounds of bread a day, does not now get one fourth part of nourishing matter, let alone the deleterious effects on his health." Tremenheere states (l. c., p. xlviii), as the reason, why a very large part of the working-class, although well aware of this adulteration, nevertheless accept the alum, stone-dust, &c., as part of their purchase: that it is for them "a matter of necessity to take from their baker or from the chandler's shop, such bread as they choose to supply." As they are not paid their wages before the end of the week, they in their turn are unable "to pay for the bread consumed by their families, during the week, before the end of the week", and Tremenheere adds on the evidence of witnesses, "it is notorious that bread composed of those mixtures, is made expressly for sale in this manner." In many English and still more Scotch agricultural districts, wages are paid fortnightly and even monthly; with such long intervals between the payments, the agricultural labourer is obliged to buy on credit.... He must pay higher prices, and is in fact tied to the shop which gives him credit. Thus at Horningham in Wilts, for example, where the wages are monthly, the same flour that he could buy elsewhere at 1s 10d per stone, costs him 2s 4d per stone. ("Sixth Report" on "Public Health" by "The Medical Officer of the Privy Council, &c., 1864," p.264.) "The block printers of Paisley and Kilmarnock enforced, by a strike, fortnightly, instead of monthly payment of wages." ("Reports of the Inspectors of Factories for 31st Oct., 1853," p. 34.) As a further pretty result of the credit given by the workmen to the capitalist, we may refer to the method current in many English coal mines, where the labourer is not paid till the end of the month, and in the meantime, receives sums on account from the capitalist, often in goods for which the miner is obliged to pay more than the market price (Truck-system). "It is a common practice with the coal masters to pay once a month, and advance cash to their workmen at the end of each intermediate week. The cash is given in the shop" (i.e., the Tommy shop which belongs to the master); "the men take it on one side and lay it out on the other." ("Children's Employment Commission, III. Report," Lond. 1864, p. 38, n. 192.)

Part III.
The Production of Absolute Surplus-Value

Chapter Seven:
The Labour-Process and the Process of Producing Surplus-Value

Section 1.
The Labour-Process or the Production of use-values

The capitalist buys labour-power in order to use it; and labour-power in use is labour itself. The purchaser of labour-power consumes it by setting the seller of it to work. By working, the latter becomes actually, what before he only was potentially, labour-power in action, a labourer. In order that his labour may re-appear in a commodity, he must, before all things, expend it on something useful, on something capable of satisfying a want of some sort. Hence, what the capitalist sets the labourer to produce, is a particular use-value, a specified article. The fact that the production of use-values, or goods, is carried on under the control of a capitalist and on his behalf, does not alter the general character of that production. We shall, therefore, in the first place, have to consider the labour-process independently of the particular form it assumes under given social conditions.

Labour is, in the first place, a process in which both man and Nature participate, and in which man of his own accord starts, regulates, and controls the material re-actions between himself and Nature. He opposes himself to Nature as one of her own forces, setting in motion arms and legs, head and hands, the natural forces of his body, in order to appropriate Nature's productions in a form adapted to his own wants. By thus acting on the external world and changing it, he at the same time changes his own nature. He develops his slumbering powers and compels them to act in obedience to his sway. We are not now dealing with those primitive instinctive forms of labour that remind us of the mere animal. An immeasurable interval of time separates the state of things in which a man brings his labour-power to market for sale as a commodity, from that state in which human labour was still in its first instinctive stage. We pre-suppose labour in a form that stamps it as exclusively human. A spider conducts operations that resemble those of a weaver, and a bee puts to shame many an architect in the construction of her cells. But what distinguishes the worst architect from the best of bees is this, that the architect raises his structure in imagination before he erects it in reality. At the end of every labour-process, we get a result that already existed in the imagination of the labourer at its commencement. He not only effects a change of form in the material on which he works, but he also realises a purpose of his own that gives the law to his modus operandi, and to which he must subordinate his will. And this subordination is no mere momentary act. Besides the exertion of the bodily organs, the process demands that, during the whole operation, the workman's will be steadily in consonance with his purpose. This means close attention. The less he is attracted by the nature of the work, and the mode in which it is carried on, and the less, therefore, he enjoys it as something which gives play to his bodily and mental powers, the more close his attention is forced to be.

The elementary factors of the labour-process are 1, the personal activity of man, i.e., work itself, 2, the subject of that work, and 3, its instruments.

The soil (and this, economically speaking, includes water) in the virgin state in which it supplies [1] man with necessaries or the means of subsistence ready to hand, exists independently of him, and is the universal subject of human labour. All those things which labour merely separates from immediate connexion with their environment, are subjects of labour spontaneously provided by Nature. Such are fish which we catch and take from their element, water, timber which we fell in the virgin forest, and ores which we extract from their veins. If, on the other hand, the subject of labour has, so to say, been filtered through previous labour, we call it raw material; such is ore already extracted and ready for washing. All raw material is the subject of labour, but not every subject of labour is raw material: it can only become so, after it has undergone some alteration by means of labour.

An instrument of labour is a thing, or a complex of things, which the labourer interposes between himself and the subject of his labour, and which serves as the conductor of his activity. He makes use of the mechanical, physical, and chemical properties of some substances in order to make other substances subservient to his aims. [2] Leaving out of consideration such ready-made means of subsistence as fruits, in gathering which a man's own limbs serve as the instruments of his labour, the first thing of which the labourer possesses himself is not the subject of labour but its instrument. Thus Nature becomes one of the organs of his activity, one that he annexes to his own bodily organs, adding stature to himself in spite of the Bible. As the earth is his original larder, so too it is his original tool house. It supplies him, for instance, with stones for throwing, grinding, pressing, cutting, &c. The earth itself is an instrument of labour, but when used as such in agriculture implies a whole series of other instruments and a comparatively high development of labour. [3] No sooner does labour undergo the least development, than it requires specially prepared instruments. Thus in the oldest caves we find stone implements and weapons. In the earliest period of human history domesticated animals, i.e., animals which have been bred for the purpose, and have undergone modifications by means of labour, play the chief part as instruments of labour along with specially prepared stones, wood, bones, and shells. [4] The use and fabrication of instruments of labour, although existing in the germ among certain species of animals, is specifically characteristic of the human labour-process, and Franklin therefore defines man as a tool-making animal. Relics of bygone instruments of labour possess the same importance for the investigation of extinct economic forms of society, as do fossil bones for the determination of extinct species of animals. It is not the articles made, but how they are made, and by what instruments, that enables us to distinguish different economic epochs. [5] Instruments of labour not only supply a standard of the degree of development to which human labour has attained, but they are also indicators of the social conditions under which that labour is carried on. Among the instruments of labour, those of a mechanical nature, which, taken as a whole, we may call the bone and muscles of production, offer much more decided characteristics of a given epoch of production, than those which, like pipes, tubs, baskets, jars, &c., serve only to hold the materials for labour, which latter class, we may in a general way, call the vascular system of production. The latter first begins to play an important part in the chemical industries.

In a wider sense we may include among the instruments of labour, in addition to those things that are used for directly transferring labour to its subject, and which therefore, in one way or another, serve as conductors of activity, all such objects as are necessary for carrying on the labour-process. These do not enter directly into the process, but without them it is either impossible for it to take place at all, or possible only to a partial extent. Once more we find the earth to be a universal instrument of this sort, for it furnishes a locus standi to the labourer and a field of employment for his activity. Among instruments that are the result of previous labour and also belong to this class, we find workshops, canals, roads, and so forth.

In the labour-process, therefore, man's activity, with the help of the instruments of labour, effects an alteration, designed from the commencement, in the material worked upon. The process disappears in the product, the latter is a use-value, Nature's material adapted by a change of form to the wants of man. Labour has incorporated itself with its subject: the former is materialised, the latter transformed. That which in the labourer appeared as movement, now appears in the product as a fixed quality without motion. The blacksmith forges and the product is a forging.

If we examine the whole process from the point of view of its result, the product, it is plain that both the instruments and the subject of labour, are means of production, [6] and that the labour itself is productive labour. [7]

Though a use-value, in the form of a product, issues from the labour-process, yet other use-values, products of previous labour, enter into it as means of production. The same-use-value is both the product of a previous process, and a means of production in a later process. Products are therefore not only results, but also essential conditions of labour.

With the exception of the extractive industries, in which the material for labour is provided immediately by Nature, such as mining, hunting, fishing, and agriculture (so far as the latter is confined to breaking up virgin soil), all branches of industry manipulate raw material, objects already filtered through labour, already products of labour. Such is seed in agriculture. Animals and plants, which we are accustomed to consider as products of Nature, are in their present form, not only products of, say last year's labour, but the result of a gradual transformation, continued through many generations, under man's superintendence, and by means of his labour. But in the great majority of cases, instruments of labour show even to the most superficial observer, traces of the labour of past ages.

Raw material may either form the principal substance of a product, or it may enter into its formation only as an accessory. An accessory may be consumed by the instruments of labour, as coal under a boiler, oil by a wheel, hay by draft-horses, or it may be mixed with the raw material in order to produce some modification thereof, as chlorine into unbleached linen, coal with iron, dye-stuff with wool, or again, it may help to carry on the work itself, as in the case of the materials used for heating and lighting workshops. The distinction between principal substance and accessory vanishes in the true chemical industries, because there none of the raw material re-appears, in its original composition, in the substance of the product. [8]

Every object possesses various properties, and is thus capable of being applied to different uses. One and the same product may therefore serve as raw material in very different processes. Corn, for example, is a raw material for millers, starch-manufacturers, distillers, and cattlebreeders. It also enters as raw material into its own production in the shape of seed; coal, too, is at the same time the product of, and a means of production in, coal-mining.

Again, a particular product may be used in one and the same process, both as an instrument of labour and as raw material. Take, for instance, the fattening of cattle, where the animal is the raw material, and at the same time an instrument for the production of manure.

A product, though ready for immediate consumption, may yet serve as raw material for a further product, as grapes when they become the raw material for wine. On the other hand, labour may give us its product in such a form, that we can use it only a's raw material, as is the case with cotton, thread, and yarn. Such a raw material, though itself a product, may have to go through a whole series of different processes: in each of these in turn, it serves, with constantly varying form, as raw material, until the last process of the series leaves it a perfect product, ready for individual consumption, or for use as an instrument of labour.

Hence we see, that whether a use-value is to be regarded as raw material, as instrument of labour, or as product, this is determined entirely by its function in the labour-process, by the position it there occupies: as this varies, so does its character.

Whenever therefore a product enters as a means of production into a new labour-process, it thereby loses its character of product, and becomes a mere factor in the process. A spinner treats spindles only as implements for spinning, and flax only as the material that he spins. Of course it is impossible to spin without material and spindles; and therefore the existence of these things as products, at the commencement of the spinning operation, must be presumed: but in the process itself, the fact that they are products of previous labour, is a matter of utter indifference; just as in the digestive process, it is of no importance whatever, that bread is the produce of the previous labour of the farmer, the miller, and the baker. On the contrary, it is generally by their imperfections as products, that the means of production in any process assert themselves in their character of products. A blunt knife or weak thread forcibly remind us of Mr. A., the cutler, or Mr. B., the spinner. In the finished product the labour by means of which it has acquired its useful qualities is not palpable, has apparently vanished.

A machine which does not serve the purposes of labour, is useless. In addition, it falls a prey to the destructive influence of natural forces. Iron rusts and wood rots. Yarn with which we neither weave nor knit, is cotton wasted. Living labour must seize upon these things and rouse them from their death-sleep, change them from mere possible use-values into real and effective ones. Bathed in the fire of labour, appropriated as part and parcel of labour's organism, and, as it were, made alive for the performance of their functions in the process, they are in truth consumed, but consumed with a purpose, as elementary constituents of new use-values, of new products, ever ready as means of subsistence for individual consumption, or as means of production for some new labour-process.

If then, on the one hand, finished products are not only results, but also necessary conditions, of the labour-process, on the other hand, their assumption into that process, their contact with living labour, is the sole means by which they can be made to retain their character of use-values, and be utilised.

Labour uses up its material factors, its subject and its instruments, consumes them, and is therefore a process of consumption. Such productive consumption is distinguished from individual consumption by this, that the latter uses up products, as means of subsistence for the living individual; the former, as means whereby alone, labour, the labour-power of the living individual, is enabled to act. The product, therefore, of individual consumption, is the consumer himself; the result of productive consumption, is a product distinct from the consumer.

In so far then, as its instruments and subjects are themselves products, labour consumes products in order to create products, or in other words, consumes one set of products by turning them into means of production for another set. But, just as in the beginning, the only participators in the labour-process were man and the earth, which latter exists independently of man, so even now we still employ in the process many means of production, provided directly by Nature, that do not represent any combination of natural substances with human labour.

The labour-process, resolved as above into its simple elementary factors, is human action with a view to the production of use-values, appropriation of natural substances to human requirements; it is the necessary condition for effecting exchange of matter between man and Nature; it is the everlasting Nature-imposed condition of human existence, and therefore is independent of every social phase of that existence, or rather, is common to every such phase. It was, therefore, not necessary to represent our labourer in connexion with other labourers; man and his labour on one side, Nature and its materials on the other, sufficed. As the taste of the porridge does not tell you who grew the oats, no more does this simple process tell you of itself what are the social conditions under which it is taking place, whether under the slave-owner's brutal lash, or the anxious eye of the capitalist, whether Cincinnatus carries it on in tilling his modest farm or a savage in killing wild animals with stones. [9]

Let us now return to our would-be capitalist. We left him just after he had purchased, in the open market, all the necessary factors of the labour-process-its objective factors, the means of production, as well as its subjective factor, labour-power. With the keen eye of an expert, he has selected the means of production and the kind of labour-power best adapted to his particular trade, be it spinning, bootmaking, or any other kind. He then proceeds to consume the commodity, the labour-power that he has just bought, by causing the labourer, the impersonation of that labour-power, to consume the means of production by his labour. The general character of the labour-process is evidently not changed by the fact, that the labourer works for the capitalist instead of for himself; moreover, the particular methods and operations employed in bootmaking or spinning are not immediately changed by the intervention of the capitalist. He must begin by taking the labour-power as he finds it in the market, and consequently be satisfied with labour of such a kind as would be found in the period immediately preceding the rise of capitalists. Changes in the methods of production by the subordination of labour to capital, can take place only at a later period, and therefore will have to be treated of in a later chapter.

The labour-process, turned into the process by which the capitalist consumes labour-power, exhibits two characteristic phenomena. First, the labourer works under the control of the capitalist to whom his labour belongs; the capitalist taking good care that the work is done in a proper manner, and that the means of production are used with intelligence, so that there is no unnecessary waste of raw material, and no wear and tear of the implements beyond what is necessarily caused by the work.

Secondly, the product is the property of the capitalist and not that of the labourer, its immediate producer. Suppose that a capitalist pays for a day's labour-power at its value; then the right to use that power for a day belongs to him, just as much as the right to use any other commodity, such as a horse that he has hired for the day. To the purchaser of a commodity belongs its use, and the seller of labour-power, by giving his labour, does no more, in reality, than part with the use-value that he has sold. From the instant he steps into the workshop, the use-value of his labour-power, and therefore also its use, which is labour, belongs to the capitalist. By the purchase of labour-power, the capitalist incorporates labour, as a living ferment, with the lifeless constituents of the product. From his point of view, the labour-process is nothing more than the consumption of the commodity purchased, i. e., of labour-power; but this consumption cannot be effected except by supplying the labour-power with the means of production. The labour-process is a process between things that the capitalist has purchased, things that have become his property. The product of this process belongs, therefore, to him, just as much as does the wine which is the product of a process of fermentation completed in his cellar. [10]

Section 2.
The Production of Surplus-Value

The product appropriated by the capitalist is a use-value, as yarn, for example, or boots. But, although boots are, in one sense, the basis of all social progress, and our capitalist is a decided "progressist," yet he does not manufacture boots for their own sake. Use-value is, by no means, the thing "qu'on aime pour lui-même" in the production of commodities. Use-values are only produced by capitalists, because, and in so far as, they are the material substratum, the depositories of exchange-value. Our capitalist has two objects in view: in the first place, he wants to produce a use-value that has a value in exchange, that is to say, an article destined to be sold, a commodity; and secondly, he desires to produce a commodity whose value shall be greater than the sum of the values of the commodities used in its production, that is, of the means of production and the labour-power, that he purchased with his good money in the open market. His aim is to produce not only a use-value, but a commodity also; not only use-value, but value; not only value, but at the same time surplus-value.

It must be borne in mind, that we are now dealing with the production of commodities, and that, up to this point, we have only considered one aspect of the process. Just as commodities are, at the same time, use-values and values, so the process of producing them must be a labour-process, and at the same time, a process of creating value. [11]

Let us now examine production as a creation of value.

We know that the value of each commodity is determined by the quantity of labour expended on and materialised in it, by the working-time necessary, under given social conditions, for its production. This rule also holds good in the case of the product that accrued to our capitalist, as the result of the labour-process carried on for him. Assuming this product to be 10 lbs. of yarn, our first step is to calculate the quantity of labour realised in it.

For spinning the yarn, raw material is required; suppose in this case 10 lbs. of cotton. We have no need at present to investigate the value of this cotton, for our capitalist has, we will assume, bought it at its full value, say of ten shillings. In this price the labour required for the production of the cotton is already expressed in terms of the average labour of society. We will further assume that the wear and tear of the spindle, which, for our present purpose, may represent all other instruments of labour employed, amounts to the value of 2s. If, then, twenty-four hours' labour, or two working-days, are required to produce the quantity of gold represented by twelve shillings, we have here, to begin with, two days' labour already incorporated in the yarn.

We must not let ourselves be misled by the circumstance that the cotton has taken a new shape while the substance of the spindle has to a certain extent been used up. By the general law of value, if the value of 40 lbs. of yarn = the value of 40 lbs. of cotton + the value of a whole spindle, i. e., if the same working-time is required to produce the commodities on either side of this equation, then 10 lbs. of yarn are an equivalent for 10 lbs. of cotton, together with one-fourth of a spindle. In the case we are considering the same working-time is materialised in the 10 lbs. of yarn on the one hand, and in the 10 lbs. of cotton and the fraction of a spindle on the other. Therefore, whether value appears in cotton, in a spindle, or in yarn, makes no difference in the amount of that value. The spindle and cotton, instead of resting quietly side by side, join together in the process, their forms are altered, and they are turned into yarn; but their value is no more affected by this fact than it would be if they had been simply exchanged for their equivalent in yarn.

The labour required for the production of the cotton, the raw material of the yarn, is part of the labour necessary to produce the yarn, and is therefore contained in the yarn. The same applies to the labour embodied in the spindle, without whose wear and tear the cotton could not be spun.

Hence, in determining the value of the yarn, or the labour-time required for its production, all the special processes carried on at various times and in different places, which were necessary, first to produce the cotton and the wasted portion of the spindle, and then with the cotton and spindle to spin the yarn, may together be looked on as different and successive phases of one and the same process. The whole of the labour in the yarn is past labour; and it is a matter of no importance that the operations necessary for the production of its constituent elements were carried on at times which, referred to the present, are more remote than the final operation of spinning. If a definite quantity of labour, say thirty days, is requisite to build a house, the total amount of labour incorporated in it is not altered by the fact that the work of the last day is done twenty-nine days later than that of the first. Therefore the labour contained in the raw material and the instruments of labour can be treated just as if it were labour expended in an earlier stage of the spinning process, before the labour of actual spinning commenced.

The values of the means of production, i. e., the cotton and the spindle, which values are expressed in the price of twelve shillings, are therefore constituent parts of the value of the yarn, or, in other words, of the value of the product.

Two conditions must nevertheless be fulfilled. First, the cotton and spindle must concur in the production of a use-value; they must in the present case become yarn. Value is independent of the particular use-value by which it is borne, but it must be embodied in a use-value of some kind. Secondly, the time occupied in the labour of production must not exceed the time really necessary under the given social conditions of the case. Therefore, if no more than I lb. of cotton be requisite to spin 11 lbs. of yarn, care must be taken that no more than this weight of cotton is consumed in the production of 11 lbs. of yarn; and similarly with regard to the spindle. Though the capitalist have a hobby, and use a gold instead of a steel spindle, yet the only labour that counts for anything in the value of the yarn is that which would be required to produce a steel spindle, because no more is necessary under the given social conditions.

We now know what portion of the value of the yarn is owing to the cotton and the spindle. It amounts to twelve shillings or the value of two days' work. The next point for our consideration is, what portion of the value of the yarn is added to the cotton by the labour of the spinner.

We have now to consider this labour under a very different aspect from that which it had during the labour-process; there, we viewed it solely as that particular kind of human activity which changes cotton into yarn; there, the more the labour was suited to the work, the better the yarn, other circumstances remaining the same. The labour of the spinner was then viewed as specifically different from other kinds of productive labour, different on the one hand in its special aim, viz., spinning, different, on the other hand, in the special character of its operations, in the special nature of its means of production and in the special use-value of its product. For the operation of spinning, cotton and spindles are a necessity, but for making rifled cannon they would be of no use whatever. Here, on the contrary, where we consider the labour of the spinner only so far as it is value-creating, i.e., a source of value, his labour differs in no respect from the labour of the man who bores cannon, or (what here more nearly concerns us), from the labour of the cotton-planter and spindle-maker incorporated in the means of production. It is solely by reason of this identity, that cotton planting, spindle making and spinning, are capable of forming the component parts differing only quantitatively from each other, of one whole, namely, the value of the yarn. Here, we have nothing more to do with the quality, the nature and the specific character of the labour, but merely with its quantity. And this simply requires to be calculated. We proceed upon the assumption that spinning is simple, unskilled labour, the average labour of a given state of society. Hereafter we shall see that the contrary assumption would make no difference.

While the labourer is at work, his labour constantly undergoes a transformation: from being motion, it becomes an object without motion; from being the labourer working, it becomes the thing produced. At the end of one hour's spinning, that act is represented by a definite quantity of yarn; in other words, a definite quantity of labour, namely that of one hour, has become embodied in the cotton. We say labour, i.e., the expenditure of his vital force by the spinner, and not spinning labour, because the special work of spinning counts here, only so far as it is the expenditure of labour-power in general, and not in so far as it is the specific work of the spinner.

In the process we are now considering it is of extreme importance, that no more time be consumed in the work of transforming the cotton into yarn than is necessary under the given social conditions. If under normal, i.e., average social conditions of production, a pounds of cotton ought to be made into b pounds of yarn by one hour's labour, then a day's labour does not count as 12 hours' labour unless 12 a pounds of cotton have been made into 12 b pounds of yarn; for in the creation of value, the time that is socially necessary alone counts.

Not only the labour, but also the raw material and the product now appear in quite a new light, very different from that in which we viewed them in the labour-process pure and simple. The raw material serves now merely as an absorbent of a definite quantity of labour. By this absorption it is in fact changed into yarn, because it is spun, because labour-power in the form of spinning is added to it; but the product, the yarn, is now nothing more than a measure of the labour absorbed by the cotton. If in one hour 1 2/3 lbs. of cotton can be spun into 1 2/3 lbs. of yarn, then 10 lbs. of yarn indicate the absorption of 6 hours' labour. Definite quantities of product, these quantities being determined by experience, now represent nothing but definite quantities of labour, definite masses of crystallised labour-time. They are nothing more than the materialisation of so many hours or so many days of social labour.

We are here no more concerned about the facts, that the labour is the specific work of spinning, that its subject is cotton and its product yarn, than we are about the fact that the subject itself is already a product and therefore raw material. If the spinner, instead of spinning, were working in a coal mine, the subject of his labour, the coal, would be supplied by Nature; nevertheless, a definite quantity of extracted coal, a hundredweight for example, would represent a definite quantity of absorbed labour.

We assumed, on the occasion of its sale, that the value of a day's labour-power is three shillings, and that six hours' labour is incorporated in that sum; and consequently that this amount of labour is requisite to produce the necessaries of life daily required on an average by the labourer. If now our spinner by working for one hour, can convert 1 2/3 lbs. of cotton into 1 2/3 lbs. of yarn, [12] it follows that in six hours he will convert 10 lbs. of cotton into 10 lbs. of yarn. Hence, during the spinning process, the cotton absorbs six hours' labour. The same quantity of labour is also embodied in a piece of gold of the value of three shillings. Consequently by the mere labour of spinning, a value of three shillings is added to the cotton.

Let us now consider the total value of the product, the 10 lbs. of yarn. Two and a half days' labour has been embodied in it, of which two days were contained in the cotton and in the substance of the spindle worn away, and half a day was absorbed during the process of spinning. This two and a half days' labour is also represented by a piece of gold of the value of fifteen shillings. Hence, fifteen shillings is an adequate price for the 10 lbs. of yarn, or the price of one pound is eighteenpence.

Our capitalist stares in astonishment. The value of the product is exactly equal to the value of the capital advanced. The value so advanced has not expanded, no surplus-value has been created, and consequently money has not been converted into capital. The price of the yarn is fifteen shillings, and fifteen shillings were spent in the open market upon the constituent elements of the product, or, what amounts to the same thing, upon the factors of the labour-process; ten shillings were paid for the cotton, two shillings for the substance of the spindle worn away, and three shillings for the labour-power. The swollen value of the yarn is of no avail, for it is merely the sum of the values formerly existing in the cotton, the spindle, and the labour-power: out of such a simple addition of existing values, no surplus-value can possibly arise. [13] These separate values are now all concentrated in one thing; but so they were also in the sum of fifteen shillings, before it was split up into three parts, by the purchase of the commodities.

There is in reality nothing very strange in this result. The value of one pound of yarn being eighteenpence, if our capitalist buys 10 lbs. of yarn in the market, he must pay fifteen shillings for them. It is clear that, whether a man buys his house ready built, or gets it built for him, in neither case will the mode of acquisition increase the amount of money laid out on the house.

Our capitalist, who is at home in his vulgar economy, exclaims: "Oh! but I advanced my money for the express purpose of making more money." The way to Hell is paved with good intentions, and he might just as easily have intended to make money, without producing at all. [14] He threatens all sorts of things. He won't be caught napping again. In future he will buy the commodities in the market, instead of manufacturing them himself. But if all his brother capitalists were to do the same, where would he find his commodities in the market? And his money he cannot eat. He tries persuasion. "Consider my abstinence; I might have played ducks and drakes with the 15 shillings; but instead of that I consumed it productively, and made yarn with it." Very well, and by way of reward he is now in possession of good yarn instead of a bad conscience; and as for playing the part of a miser, it would never do for him to relapse into such bad ways as that; we have seen before to what results such asceticism leads. Besides, where nothing is, the king has lost his rights; whatever may be the merit of his abstinence, there is nothing wherewith specially to remunerate it, because the value of the product is merely the sum of the values of the commodities that were thrown into the process of production. Let him therefore console' himself with the reflection that virtue is its own reward, But no, he becomes importunate. He says: "The yarn is of no use to me: I produced it for sale." In that case let him sell it, or, still better, let him for the future produce only things for satisfying his personal wants, a remedy that his physician MacCulloch has already prescribed as infallible against an epidemic of over-production. He now gets obstinate. "Can the labourer," he asks, "merely with his arms and legs, produce commodities out of nothing? Did I not supply him with the materials, by means of which, and in which alone, his labour could be embodied? And as the greater part of society consists of such ne'er-do-wells, have I not rendered society incalculable service by my instruments of production, my cotton and my spindle, and not only society, but the labourer also, whom in addition I have provided with the necessaries of life? And am I to be allowed nothing in return for all this service?" Well, but has not the labourer rendered him the equivalent service of changing his cotton and spindle into yarn? Moreover, there is here no question of service. [15] A service is nothing more than the useful effect of a use-value, be it of a commodity, or be it of labour. [16] But here we are dealing with exchange-value. The capitalist paid to the labourer a value of 3 shillings, and the labourer gave him back an exact equivalent in the value of 3 shillings, added by him to the cotton: he gave him value for value. Our friend, up to this time so purse-proud, suddenly assumes the modest demeanour of his own workman, and exclaims: "Have I myself not worked? Have I not performed the labour of superintendence and of overlooking the spinner? And does not this labour, too, create value?" His overlooker and his manager try to hide their smiles. Meanwhile, after a hearty laugh, he re-assumes his usual mien. Though he chanted to us the whole creed of the economists, in reality, he says, he would not give a brass farthing for it. He leaves this and all such like subterfuges and juggling tricks to the professors of Political Economy, who are paid for it. He himself is a practical man; and though he does not always consider what he says outside his business, yet in his business he knows what he is about.

Let us examine the matter more closely. The value of a day's labour-power amounts to 3 shillings, because on our assumption half a day's labour is embodied in that quantity of labour-power, i.e., because the means of subsistence that are daily required for the production of labour-power, cost half a day's labour. But the past labour that is embodied in the labour-power, and the living labour that it can call into action; the daily cost of maintaining it, and its daily expenditure in work, are two totally different things. The former determines the exchange-value of the labour-power, the latter is its use-value. The fact that half a day's labour is necessary to keep the labourer alive during 24 hours, does not in any way prevent him from working a whole day. Therefore, the value of labour-power, and the value which that labour-power creates in the labour-process, are two entirely different magnitudes; and this difference of the two values was what the capitalist had in view, when he was purchasing the labour-power. The useful qualities that labour-power possesses, and by virtue of which it makes yarn or boots, were to him nothing more than a conditio sine qua non; for in order to create value, labour must be expended in a useful manner. What really influenced him was the specific use-value which this commodity possesses of being a source not only of value, but of more value than it has itself. This is the special service that the capitalist expects from labour-power, and in this transaction he acts in accordance with the "eternal laws" of the exchange of commodities. The seller of labour-power, like the seller of any other commodity, realises its exchange-value, and parts with its use-value. He cannot take the one without giving the other. The use-value of labour-power, or in other words, labour, belongs just as little to its seller, as the use-value of oil after it has been sold belongs to the dealer who has sold it. The owner of the money has paid the value of a day's labour-power; his, therefore, is the use of it for a day; a day's labour belongs to him. The circumstance, that on the one hand the daily sustenance of labour-power costs only half a day's labour, while on the other hand the very same labour-power can work during a whole day, that consequently the value which its use during one day creates, is double what he pays for that use, this circumstance is, without doubt, a piece of good luck for the buyer, but by no means an injury to the seller.

Our capitalist foresaw this state of things, and that was the cause of his laughter. The labourer therefore finds, in the workshop, the means of production necessary for working, not only during six, but during twelve hours. Just as during the six hours' process our 10 lbs. of cotton absorbed six hours' labour, and became 10 lbs. of yarn, so now, 20 lbs. of cotton will absorb 12 hours' labour and be changed into 20 lbs. of yarn. Let us now examine the product of this prolonged process. There is now materialised in this 20 lbs. of yarn the labour of five days, of which four days are due to the cotton and the lost steel of the spindle, the remaining day having been absorbed by the cotton during the spinning process. Expressed in gold, the labour of five days is thirty shillings. This is therefore the price of the 20 lbs. of yarn, giving, as before, eighteenpence as the price of a pound. But the sum of the values of the commodities that entered into the process amounts to 27 shillings. The value of the yarn is 30 shillings. Therefore the value of the product is 1/9 greater than the value advanced for its production; 27 shillings have been transformed into 30 shillings; a surplus-value of 3 shillings has been created. The trick has at last succeeded; money has been converted into capital.

Every condition of the problem is satisfied, while the laws that regulate the exchange of commodities, have been in no way violated. Equivalent has been exchanged for equivalent. For the capitalist as buyer paid for each commodity, for the cotton, the spindle and the labour-power, its full value. He then did what is done by every purchaser of commodities; he consumed their use-value. The consumption of the labour-power, which was also the process of producing commodities, resulted in 20 lbs. of yarn, having a value of 30 shillings. The capitalist, formerly a buyer, now returns to market as a seller, of commodities. He sells his yarn at eighteenpence a pound, which is its exact value. Yet for all that he withdraws 3 shillings more from circulation than he originally threw into it. This metamorphosis, this conversion of money into capital, takes place both within the sphere of circulation and also outside it; within the circulation, because conditioned by the purchase of the labour-power in the market; outside the circulation, because what is done within it is only a stepping-stone to the production of surplus-value, a process which is entirely confined to the sphere of production. Thus "tout est pour le mieux dans le meflleur des mondes possibles."

By turning his money into commodities that serve as the material elements of a new product, and as factors in the labour-process, by incorporating living labour with their dead substance, the capitalist at the same time converts value, i.e., past, materialised, and dead labour into capital, into value big with value, a live monster that is fruitful and multiplies.

If we now compare the two processes of producing value and of creating surplus-value, we see that the latter is nothing but the continuation of the former beyond a definite point. If on the one hand the process be not carried beyond the point, where the value paid by the capitalist for the labour-power is replaced by an exact equivalent, it is simply a process of producing value; if, on the other hand, it be con tinued beyond that point, it becomes a process of creating surplus-value.

If we proceed further, and compare the process of producing value with the labour-process, pure and simple, we find that the latter consists of the useful labour, the work, that produces use-values. Here we contemplate the labour as producing a particular article; we view it under its qualitative aspect alone, with regard to its end and aim. But viewed as a value-creating process, the same labour-process presents itself under its quantitative aspect alone. Here it is a question merely of the time occupied by the labourer in doing the work; of the period during which the labour-power is usefully expended. Here, the commodities that take part in the process, do not count any longer as necessary adjuncts of labour-power in the production of a definite, useful object. They count merely as depositories of so much absorbed or materialised labour; that labour, whether previously embodied in the means of production, or incorporated in them for the first time during the process by the action of labour-power, counts in either case only according to its duration; it amounts to so many hours or days as the case may be.

Moreover, only so much of the time spent in the production of any article is counted, as, under the given social conditions, is necessary. The consequences of this are various. In the first place, it becomes necessary that the labour should be carried on under normal conditions. If a self-acting mule is the implement in general use for spinning, it would be absurd to supply the spinner with a distaff and spinning wheel. The cotton too must not be such rubbish as to cause extra waste in being worked, but must be of suitable quality. Otherwise the spinner would be found to spend more time in producing a pound of yarn than is socially necessary, in which case the excess of time would create neither value nor money. But whether the material factors of the process are of normal quality or not, depends not upon the labourer, but entirely upon the capitalist. Then again, the labour-power itself must be of average efficacy. In the trade in which it is being employed, it must possess the average skill, handiness and quickness prevalent in that trade, and our capitalist took good care to buy labour-power of such normal goodness. This power must be applied with the average amount of exertion and with the usual degree of intensity; and the capitalist is as careful to see that this is done, as that his workmen are not idle for a single moment. He has bought, the use of the labour-power for a definite period, and he insists upon his rights. He has no intention of being robbed. Lastly, and for this purpose our friend has a penal code of his own, all wasteful consumption of raw material or instruments of labour is strictly forbidden, because what is so wasted, represents labour superfluously expended, labour that does not count in the product or enter into its value. [17]

We now see, that the difference between labour, considered on the one hand as producing utilities, and on the other hand, as creating value, a difference which we discovered by our analysis of a commodity, resolves itself into a distinction between two aspects of the process of production.

The process of production, considered on the one hand as the unity of the labour-process and the process of creating value, is production of commodities; considered on the other hand as the unity of the labour-process and the process of producing surplus-value, it is the capitalist process of production, or capitalist production of commodities.

We stated, on a previous page, that in the creation of surplus-value it does not in the least matter, whether the labour appropriated by the capitalist be simple unskilled labour of average quality or more complicated skilled labour. All labour of a higher or more complicated character than average labour is expenditure of labour-power of a more costly kind, labour-power whose production has cost more time and labour, and which therefore has a higher value, than unskilled or simple labour-power. This power being higher-value, its consumption is labour of a higher class, labour that creates in equal times proportionally higher values than unskilled labour does. Whatever difference in skill there may be between the labour of a spinner and that of a jeweller, the portion of his labour by which the jeweller merely replaces the value of his own labour-power, does not in any way differ in quality from the additional portion by which he creates surplus-value. In the making of jewellery, just as in spinning, the surplus-value results only from a quantitative excess of labour, from a lengthening-out of one and the same labour-process, in the one case, of the process of making jewels, in the other of the process of making yarn. [18]

But on the other hand, in every process of creating value, the reduction of skilled labour to average social labour, e.g., one day of skilled to six days of unskilled labour, is unavoidable. [19] We therefore save ourselves a superfluous operation, and simplify our analysis, by the assumption, that the labour of the workman employed by the capitalist is unskilled average labour.

Footnotes

[1] "The earth's spontaneous productions being in small quantity, and quite independent of man, appear, as it were, to be furnished by Nature, in the same way as a small sum is given to a young man, in order to put him in a way of industry, and of making his fortune." (James Stueart: "Principles of Polit. Econ." edit. Dublin, 1770, v. I, p.116.)

[2] "Reason is just as cunning as she is powerful. Her cunning consists principally in her mediating activity, which, by causing objects to act and re-act on each other in accordance with their own nature, in this way, without any direct interference in the process, carries out reason's intentions." (Hegel: "Enzyklopädie, Erster Theil, Die Logik," Berlin, 1840, p. 382.)

[3] In his otherwise miserable work ("Théorie de I'Econ. Polit." Paris, 1815), Ganilh enumerates in a striking manner in opposition to the "Physiocrats" the long series of previous processes necessary before agriculture properly so called can commence.

[4] Turgot in his "Réflexions sur la Formation et la Distribution des Richesses" (1766) brings well into prominence the importance of domesticated animals to early civilisation.

[5] The least important commodities of all for the technological comparison of different epochs of production are articles of luxury, in the strict meaning of the term. However little our written histories up to this time notice the development of material production, which is the basis of all social life, and therefore of all real history, yet prehistoric times have been classified in accordance with the results, not of so-called historical, but of materialistic investigations. These periods have been divided, to correspond with the materials from which their implements and weapons were made, viz., into the stone, the bronze, and the iron ages.

[6] It appears paradoxical to assert, that uncaught fish, for instance, are a means of production in the fishing industry. But hitherto no one has discovered the art of catching fish in waters that contain none.

[7] This method of determining, from the standpoint of the labour-process alone, what is productive labour, is by no means directly applicable to the case of the capitalist process of production.

[8] Storch calls true raw materials "matières," and accessory material "matériaux." Cherbuliez describes accessories as "matières instrumentales."

[9] By a wonderful fcat of logical acumen, Colonel Torrens has discovered, in this stone of the savage the origin of capital. "In the first stone which he [the savage] flings at the wild animal he pursues, in the first stick that he seizes to strike down the fruit which hangs above his reach, we see the appropriation of one article for the purpose of aiding in the acquisition of another, and thus discover the origin of capital." (R. Torrens: "An Essay on the Production of Wealth," &c., pp. 70-71.)

[10] "Products are appropriated before they are converted into capital; this conversion does not secure them from such appropriation." (Cheibuliez: "Richesse on Pauvreté," edit. Paris, 1841, p. 54.) "The Proletarian, by selling his labour for a definite quantity of the necessaries of life, renounces all claim to a share in the product. The mode of appropriation of the products remains the same as before; it is in no way altered by the bargain we have mentioned. The product belongs exclusively to the capitalist, who supplied the raw material and the necessaries of life; and this is a rigorous consequence of the law of appropriation, a law whose fundamental principle was the very opposite, namely, that every labourer has an exclusive right to the ownership of what he produces." (l. c., p. 58.) "When the labourers receive wages for their labour ... the capitalist is then the owner not of the capital only" (he means the means of production) "but of the labour also. If what is paid as wages is included, as it commonly is, in the term capital, it is absurd to talk of labour separately from capital. The word capital as thus employed includes labour and capital both." (James Mill: "Elements of Pol. Econ.," &c., Ed. 1821, pp. 70, 71.)

[11] As has been stated in a previous note, the English language has two different expressions for these two different aspects of labour: in the Simple Labour-process, the process of producing Use-Values, it is Work; in the process of creation of Value, it is Labour, taking the term in its strictly economic sense. — F. E.

[12] These figures are quite arbitrary.

[13] This is the fundamental proposition on which is based the doctrine of the Physiocrats as to the unproductiveness of all labour that is not agriculture: it is irrefutable for the orthodox economist. "Cette façon d'imputer à une seule chose la valeur de plusieurs autres" (par exemple au lin la consommation du tisserand), "d'appliquer, pour ainsi dire, couche sur couche, plusieurs valcurs sur une seule, fait que celle-ci grossit d'autant.... Le terme d'addition peint trés-bien la maniere dont se forme le prix des ouvrages de maind'oeuvre; ce prix n'est qu'un total de plusieurs valeurs consommées et additionnées ensemble; or, additionner n'est pas multiplier." ("Mercier de la Rivière," l. c., p. 599.)

[14] Thus from 1844-47 he withdrew part of his capital from productive employment, in order to throw it away in railway speculations; and so also, during the American Civil War, he closed his factory, and turned his work-people into the streets, in order to gamble on the Liverpool cotton exchange.

[15] "Extol thyself, put on finery and adorn thyself ... but whoever takes more or better than he gives, that is usury, and is not service, but wrong done to his neighbour, as when one steals and robs. All is not service and benefit to a neighbour that is called service and benefit. For an adulteress and adulterer do one another great service and pleasure. A horseman does an incendiary a great service, by helping him to rob on the highway, and pillage land and houses. The papists do ours a great service, in that they don't drown, burn, murder all of them, or let them all rot in prison; but let some live, and only drive them out, or take from them what they have. The devil himself does his servants inestimable service.... To sum up, the world is full of great, excellent, and daily service and benefit." (Martin Luther: "An die Pfarrherrn wider den Wucher zu predigen," Wittenberg, 1540.)

[16] In "Zur Kritik der Pol. Oek.," p. 14, I make the following remark on this point — "It is not difficult to understand what 'service' the category 'service' must render to a class of economists like J. B. Say and F. Bastiat."

[17] This is one of the circumstances that makes production by slave labour such a costly process. The labourer here is, to use a striking expression of the ancients, distinguishable only as instrumentum vocale, from an animal as instrumentum semi-vocale, and from an implement as instrumentum mutum. But he himself takes care to let both beast and implement feel that he is none of them,'but is a man. He convinces himself with immense satisfaction, that he is a different being, by treating the one unmercifully and damaging the other con amore. Hence the principle, univerially applied in this method of production, only to employ the rudest and heaviest implements and such as are difficult to damage owing to their sheer clumsiness. In the slave-statcs bordering on the Gulf of Mexico, down to the date of the civil war, ploughs constructed on old Chinese models, which turned up the soil like a hog or a mole, instead of making furrows, were alone to be found. Conf. J. E. Cairnes. "The Slave Power," London, 1862, p. 46 sqq. In his "Sea Board Slave States," Olmsted tells us: "I am here shown tools that no man in his senses, with us, would allow a labourcr, for whom he was paying wages, to be encumbered with; and the excessive weight and clumsiness of which, I would judge, would make work at least ten per cent greater than with those ordinarily used with us. And I am assured that, in the careless and clumsy way they must be used by the slaves, anything lighter or less rude could not be fumished them with good economy, and that such tools as we constantly give our labourers and find our profit in giving them, would not last out a day in a Virginia comficid-much lighter and more free from stones though it be than ours. So, too, when I ask why mules are so universally substituted for horses on the farm, the first reason given, and confessedly the most conclusive one, is that horses cannot bear the treatment that they always must get from negroes; horses are always soon foundered or crippled by them, while mules will bear cudgelling, or lose a meal or two now and then, and not be materially injured, and they do not take cold or get sick, if neglected or overworked. But I do not need to go further than to the window of the room in which I am writing, to see at almost any time, treatment of cattle that would ensure the immediate discharge of the driver by almost any farmer owning them in the North."

[18] The distinction between skilled and unskilled labour rests in part on pure illusion, or, to say the least, on distinctions that have long since ceased to be real, and that survive only by virtue of a traditional convention; in part on the helpless condition of some groups of the working-class, a condition that prevents themfrom exacting equally with the rest the value of their labour-power. Accidental circumstances here play so great a part, that these

two forms of labour sometimes change places. Where, for instance, the physique of the working-class has deteriorated, and is, relatively speaking, exhausted, which in the case in all countries with a well developed capitalist production, the lower forms of labour, which demand great expenditure of muscle, are in general considered as skilled, compared with much more delicate forms of labour; the latter sink down to the level of unskilled labour. Take as an example the labour of a bricklayer, which in England occupies a much higher level than that of a damask-weaver. Again, although the labour of a fustian cutter demands great bodily exertion, and is at the same time unhealthy, yet it counts only as unskilled labour. And then, we must not forget, that the so-called skilled labour does not occupy a large space in the field of national labour. Laing estimates that in England (and Wales) the livelihood of 11,300,000 people depends on unskilled labour. If from the total population of 18,000,000 living at the time when he wrote, we deduct 1,000,000 for the "genteel population," and 1,500,000 for paupers, vagrants, criminals, prostitutes, &c., and 4,650,000 who compose the middle-class, there remain the above mentioned 11,000,000. But in his middle-class he includes people that live on the interest of small investments, officials, men of letters, artists, schoolmasters and the like, and in order to swell the number he also includes in these 4,650,000 the better paid portioti of the factory operatives! The bricklayers, too, figure amongst them. (S. Laing: "National Distress," &c., London, 1844). "The great class who have nothing to give for food but ordinary labour, are the great bulk of the people." (James Mill, in art.:"Colony," Supplement to the Encyclop. Brit., 1831.)

[19] "Where reference is made to labour as a measure of value, it necessarily implies labour of one particular kind ... the proportion which the other kinds bear to it being easily ascertained." ("Outlines of Pol. Econ.," Lond., 1832, pp. 22 and 23.)

Chapter Eight:
Constant Capital and Variable Capital

The various factors of the labour-process play different parts in forming the value of the product.

The labourer adds fresh value to the subject of fiis labour by expending upon it a given amount of additional labour, no matter what the specific character and utility of that labour may be. On the other hand, the values of the means of production used up in the process are preserved, and present themselves afresh as constituent parts of the value of the product; the values of the cotton and the spindle, for instance, re-appear again in the value of the yarn. The value of the means of production is therefore preserved, by being transferred to the product. This transfer takes place during the conversion of those means into a product, or in other words, during the labour-process. It is brought about by labour; but how?

The labourer does not perform two operations at once, one in order to add value to the cotton, the other in order to preserve the value of the means of production, or, what amounts to the same thing, to transfer to the yarn, to the product, the value of the cotton on which he works, and part of the value of the spindle with which he works. But, by the very act of adding new value, he preserves their former values. Since, however, the addition of new value to the subject of his labour, and the preservation of its former value, are two entirely distinct results, produced simultaneously by the labourer, during one operation, it is plain that this two-fold nature of the result can be explained only by the two-fold nature of his labour; at one and the same time, it must in one character create value, and in another character preserve or transfer value.

Now, in what manner does every labourer add new labour and consequently new value? Evidently, only by labouring productively in a particular way; the spinner by spinning, the weaver by weaving, the smith by forging. But, while thus incorporating labour generally, that is value, it is by the particular form alone of the labour, by the spinning, the weaving and the forging respectively, that the means of production, the cotton and spindle, the yarn and loom, and the iron and anvil become constituent elements of the product, of a new use-value. [1] Each use-value disappears, but only to re-appear under a new form in a new use-value. Now, we saw, when we were considering the process of creating value, that, if a use-value be effectively consumed in the production of a new use-value, the quantity of labour expended in the production of the consumed article, forms a portion of the quantity of labour necessary to produce the new use-value; this portion is therefore labour transferred from the means of production to the new product. Hence, the labourer preserves the values of the consumed means of production, or transfers them as portions of its value to the product, not by virtue of his additional labour, abstractedly considered, but by virtue of the particular useful character of that labour, by virtue of its special productive form. In so far then as labour is such specific productive activity, in so far as it is spinning, weaving, or forging, it raises, by mere contact, the means. of production from the dead, makes them living factors of the labour-process, and combines with them to form the new products.

If the special productive labour of the workman were not spinning, he could not convert the cotton into yarn, and therefore could not transfer the values of the cotton and spindle to the yarn. Suppose the same workman were to change his occupation to that of a joiner, he would still by a day's labour add value to the material he works upon. Consequently, we see, first, that the addition of new value takes place not by virtue of his labour being spinning in particular, or joinering in particular, but because it is labour in the abstract, a portion of the total labour of society; and we see next, that the value added is of a given definite amount, not because his labour has a special utility, but because it is exerted for a definite time. On the one hand, then, it is by virtue of its general character, as being expenditure of human labour-power in the abstract, that spinning adds new value to the values of the cotton and the spindle; and on the other hand, it is by virtue of its special character, as being a concrete, useful process, that the same labour of spinning both transfers the values of the means of production to the product, and preserves them in the product. Hence at one and the same time there is produced a two-fold result.

By the simple addition of a certain quantity of labour, new value is added, and by the quality of this added labour, the original values of the means of production are preserved in the product. This two-fold effect, resulting from the two-fold character of labour, may be traced in various phenomena.

Let us assume, that some invention enables the spinner to spin as much cotton in 6 hours as he was able to spin before in 36 hours. His labour is now six times as effective as it was, for the purposes of useful production. The product of 6 hours' work has increased six-fold, from 6 lbs. to 36 lbs. But now the 36 lbs. of cotton absorb only the same amount of labour as formerly did the 6 lbs. One-sixth as much new labour is absorbed by each pound of cotton, and consequently, the value added by the labour to each pound is only one-sixth of what it formerly was. On the other hand, in the product, in the 36 lbs. of yarn, the value transferred from the cotton is six times as great as before. By the 6 hours' spinning, the value of the raw material preserved and transferred to the product is six times as great as before, although the new value added by the labour of the spinner to each pound of the very same raw material is one-sixth what it was formerly. This shows that the two properties of labour, by virtue of which it is enabled in one case to preserve value, and in the other to create value, are essentially different. On the one hand, the longer the time necessary to spin a given weight of cotton into yarn, the greater is the new value added to the material; on the other hand, the greater the weight of the cotton spun in a given time, the greater is the value preserved, by being transferred from it to the product.

Let us now assume, that the productiveness of the spinner's labour, instead of varying, remains constant, that he therefore requires the same time as he formerly did, to convert one pound of cotton into yarn, but that the exchange-value of the cotton varies, either by rising to six times its former value or falling to one-sixth of that value. In both these cases, the spinner puts the same quantity of labour into a pound of cotton, and therefore adds as much value, as he did before the change in the value: he also produces a given weight of yarn in the same time as he did before. Nevertheless, the value that he transfers from the cotton to the yarn is either one-sixth of what it was before the variation, or, as the case may be, six times as much as before. The same result occurs when the value of the instruments of labour rises or falls, while their useful efficacy in the process remains unaltered.

Again, if the technical conditions of the spinning process remain unchanged, and no change of value takes place in the means of production, the spinner continues to consume in equal working-times equal quantities of raw material, and equal quantities of machinery of unvarying value. The value that he preserves in the product is directly proportional to the new value that he adds to the product. In two weeks he incorporates twice as much labour, and therefore twice as much value, as in one week, and during the same time he consumes twice as much material, and wears out twice as much machinery, of double the value in each case: he therefore preserves, in the product of two weeks, twice as much value as in the product of one week. So long as the conditions of production remain the same, the more value the labourer adds by fresh labour, the more value he transfers and preserves; but he does so merely because this addition of new value takes place under conditions that have not varied and are independent of his own labour. Of course, it may be said in one sense, that the labourer preserves old value always in proportion to the quantity of new value that he adds. Whether the value of cotton rise from one shilling to two shillings, or fall to sixpence, the workman invariably preserves in the product of one hour only one half as much value as he preserves in two hours. In like manner, if the productiveness of his own labour varies by rising or falling, he will in one hour spin either more or less cotton, as the case may be, than he did before, and will consequently preserve in the product of one hour, more or less value of cotton; but, all the same, he will preserve by two hours' labour twice as much value as he will by one.

Value exists only in articles of utility, in objects: we leave out of consideration its purely symbolical representation by tokens. (Man himself, viewed as the impersonation of labour-power, is a natural object, a thing, although a living conscious thing, and labour is the manifestation of this power residing in him.) If therefore an article loses its utility, it also loses its value. The reason why means of production do not lose their value, at the same time that they lose their use-value, is this: they lose in the labour-process the original form of their use-value, only to assume in the product the form of a new use-value. But, however important it may be to value, that it should have some object of utility to embody itself in, yet it is a matter of complete indifference what particular object serves this purpose; this we saw when treating of the metamorphosis of commodities. Hence it follows that in the labour-process the means of production transfer their value to the product only so far as along with their use-value they lose also their exchange-value. They give up to the product that value alone which they themselves lose as means of production. But in this respect the material factors of the labour-process do not all behave alike.

The coal burnt under the boiler vanishes without leaving a trace; so, too, the tallow with which the axles of wheels are greased. Dye stuffs and other auxiliary substances also vanish but re-appear as properties of the product. Raw material forms the substance of the product, but only after it has changed its form. Hence raw material and auxiliary substances lose the characteristic form with which they are clothed on entering the labour-process. It is otherwise with the instruments of labour. Tools, machines, workshops, and vessels, are of use in the labour-process, only so long as they retain their original shape, and are ready each morning to renew the process with their shape unchanged. And just as during their lifetime, that is to say, during the continued labour-process in which they serve, they retain their shape independent of the product, so, too, they do after their death. The corpses of machines, tools, workshops, &c., are always separate and distinct from the product they helped to turn out. If we now consider the case of any instrument of labour during the whole period of its service, from the day of its entry into the workshop, till the day of its banishment into the lumber room, we find that during this period its use-value has been completely consumed, and therefore its exchange-value completely transferred to the product. For instance, if a spinning machine lasts for 10 years, it is plain that during that working period its total value is gradually transferred to the product of the 10 years. The lifetime of an instrument of labour, therefore, is spent in the repetition of a greater or less number of similar operations. Its life may be compared with that of a human being. Every day brings a man 24 hours nearer to his grave: but how many days he has still to travel on that road, no man can tell accurately by merely looking at him. This difficulty, however, does not prevent life insurance offices from drawing, by means of the theory of averages, very accurate, and at the same time very profitable conclusions. So it is with the instruments of labour. It is known by experience how long on the average a machine of a particular kind will last. Suppose its use-value in the labour-process to last only six days. Then, on the average, it loses each day one-sixth of its use-value, and therefore parts with one-sixth of its value to the daily product. The wear and tear of all instruments, their daily loss of use-value, and the corresponding quantity of value they part with to the product, are accordingly calculated upon this basis.

It is thus strikingly clear, that means of production never transfer more value to the product than they themselves lose during the labour-process by the destruction of their own use-value. If such an instrument has no value to lose, if, in other words, it is not the product of human labour, it transfers no value to the product. It helps to create use-value without contributing to the formation of exchange-value. In this class are included all means of production supplied by Nature without human assistance, such as land, wind, water, metals in situ, and timber in virgin forests.

Yet another interesting phenomenon here presents itself. Suppose a machine to be worth £1,000, and to wear out in 1,000 days. Then one thousandth part of the value of the machine is daily transferred to the day's product. At the same time, though with diminishing vitality, the machine as a whole continues to take part in the labour-process. Thus it appears, that one factor of the labour-process, a means of production, continually enters as a whole into that process, while it enters into the process of the formation of value by fractions only. The difference between the two processes is here reflected in their material factors, by the same instrument of production taking part as a whole in the labour-process, while at the same time as an element in the formation of value, it enters only by fractions. [2]

On the other hand, a means of production may take part as a whole in the formation of value, while into the labour-process it enters only bit by bit. Suppose that in spinning cotton, the waste for every 115 lbs. used amounts to 15 lbs., which is converted, not into yarn, but into "devil's dust." Now, although this 15 lbs. of cotton never becomes a constituent element of the yarn, yet assuming this amount of waste to be normal and inevitable under average conditions of spinning, its value is just as surely transferred to the value of the yarn, as is the value of the 100 lbs. that form the substance of the yarn. The use-value of 15 lbs. of cotton must vanish into dust, before 100 lbs. of yarn can be made. The destruction of this cotton is therefore a necessary condition in the production of the yarn. And because it is a necessary condition, and for no other reason, the value of that cotton is transferred to the product. The same holds good for every kind of refuse resulting from a labour-process, so tar at least as such refuse cannot be further employed as a means in the production of new and independent use-values. Such an employment of refuse may be seen in the large machine works at Manchester, where mountains of iron turnings are carted away to the foundry in the evening, in order the next morning to re-appear in the workshops as solid masses of iron.

We have seen that the means of production transfer value to the new product, so far only as during the labour-process they lose value in the shape of their old use-value. The maximum loss of value that they can suffer in the process, is plainly limited by the amount of the original value with which they came into the process, or in other words, by the labour-time necessary for their production. Therefore, the means of production can never add more value to the product than they themselves possess independently of the process in which they assist. However useful a given kind of raw material, or a machine, or other means of production may be, though it may cost £150, or, say, 500 days' labour, yet it cannot, under any circumstances, add to the value of the product more than £150. Its value is determined not by the labour-process into which it enters as a means of production, but by that out of which it has issued as a product. In the labour-process it only serves as a mere use-value, a thing with useful properties, and could not, therefore, transfer any value to the product, unless it possessed such value previously. [3]

While productive labour is changing the means of production into constituent elements of a new product, their value undergoes a metempsychosis. It deserts the consumed body, to occupy the newly created one. But this transmigration takes place, as it were, behind the back of the labourer. He is unable to add new labour, to create new value, without at the same time preserving old values, and this, because the labour he adds must be of a specific useful kind; and he cannot do work of a useful kind, without employing products as the means of production of a new product, and thereby transferring their value to the new product. The property therefore which labour-power in action, living labour, possesses of preserving value, at the same time that it adds it, is a gift of Nature which costs the labourer nothing, but which is very advantageous to the capitalist inasmuch as it preserves the existing value of his capital. [4] So long as trade is good, the capitalist is too much absorbed in money-grubbing to take notice of this gratuitous gift of labour. A violent interruption of the labour-process by a crisis, makes him sensitively aware of it. [5]

As regards the means of production, what is really consumed is their use-value, and the consumption of this use-value by labour results in the product. There is no consumption of their value, [6] and it would therefore be inaccurate to say that it is reproduced. It is rather preserved; not by reason of any operation it undergoes itself in the process; but because the article in which it originally exists, vanishes, it is true, but vanishes into some other article. Hence, in the value of the product, there is a reappearance of the value of the means of production, but there is, strictly speaking, no reproduction of that value. That which is produced is a new use-value in which the old exchange-value reappears. [7]

It is otherwise with the subjective factor of the labour-process, with labour-power in action. While the labourer, by virtue of his labour being of a specialised kind that has a special object, preserves and transfers to the product the value of the means of production, he at the same time, by the mere act of working, creates each instant an additional or new value. Suppose the process of production to be stopped just when the workman has produced an equivalent for the value of his own, labour-power, when, for example, by six hours' labour, he has added a value of three shillings. This value is the surplus, of the total value of the product, over the portion of its value that is due to the means of production. It is the only original bit of value formed during this process, the only portion of the value of the product created by this process. Of course, we do not forget that this new value only replaces the money advanced by the capitalist in the purchase of the labour-power, and spent by the labourer on the necessaries of life. With regard to the money spent, the new value is merely a reproduction; but, nevertheless, it is an actual, and not, as in the case of the value of the means of production, only an apparent, reproduction. The substitution of one value for another, is here effected by the creation of new value.

We know, however, from what has gone before, that the labour-process may continue beyond the time necessary to reproduce and incorporate in the product a mere equivalent for the value of the labour-power. Instead of the six hours that are sufficient for the latter purpose, the process may continue for twelve hours. The action of labour-power, therefore, not only reproduces its own value, but produces value over and above it. This surplus-value is the difference between the value of the product and the value of the elements consumed in the formation of that product, in other words, of the means of production and the labour-power.

By our explanation of the different parts played by the various factors of the labour-process in the formation of the product's value, we have, in fact, disclosed the characters of the different functions allotted to the different elements of capital in the process of expanding its own value. The surplus of the total value of the product, over the sum of the values of its constituent factors, is the surplus of the expanded capital over the capital originally advanced. The means of production on the one hand, labour-power on the other, are merely the different modes of existence which the value of the original capital assumed when from being money it was transformed into the various factors of the labour-process. That part of capital then, which is represented by the means of production, by the raw material, auxiliary material and the instruments of labour does not, in the process of production, undergo any quantitative alteration of value. I therefore call it the constant part of capital, or, more shortly, constant capital.

On the other hand, that part of capital, represented by labour-power, does, in the process of production, undergo an alteration of value. It both reproduces the equivalent of its own value, and also produces an excess, a surplus-value, which may itself vary, may be more or less according to circumstances. This part of capital is continually being transformed from a constant into a variable magnitude. I therefore call it the variable part of capital, or, shortly, variable capital. The same elements of capital which, from the point of view of the labour-process, present themselves respectively as the objective and subjective factors, as means of production and labour-power, present themselves, from the point of view of the process of creating surplus-value, as constant and variable capital.

The definition of constant capital given above by no means excludes the possibility of a change of value in its elements. Suppose the price of cotton to be one day sixpence a pound, and the next day, in consequence of a failure of the cotton crop, a shilling a pound. Each pound of the cotton bought at sixpence, and worked up after the rise in value, transfers to the product a value of one shilling; and the cotton already spun before the rise, and perhaps circulating in the market as yarn, likewise transfers to the product twice its, original value. It is plain, however, that these changes of value are independent of the increment or surplus-value added to the value of the cotton by the spinning itself. If the old cotton had never been spun, it could, after the rise, be resold at a shilling a pound instead of at sixpence. Further, the fewer the processes the cotton has gone through, the more certain is this result. We therefore find that speculators make it a rule when such sudden changes in value occur, to speculate in that material on which the least possible quantity of labour has been spent: to speculate, therefore, in yarn rather than in cloth, in cotton itself, rather than in yarn. The change of value in the case we have been considering, originates, not in the process in which the cotton plays the part of a means of production, and in which it therefore functions as constant capital, but in the process in which the cotton itself is produced. The value of a commodity, it. is true, is determined by the quantity of labour contained in it, but this quantity is itself limited by social conditions. If the time socially necessary for the production of any commodity alters — and a given weight of cotton represents, after a bad harvest, more labour than after a good one — all previously existing commodities of the same class are affected, because they are, as it were, only individuals of the species, [8] and their value at any given time is measured by the labour socially necessary, i.e., by the labour necessary for their production under the then existing social conditions.

As the value of the raw material may change, so, too, may that of the instruments of labour, of the machinery, &c., employed in the process; and consequently that portion of the value of the product transferred to it from them, may also change. If in consequence of a new invention, machinery of a particular kind can be produced by a diminished expenditure of labour, the old machinery becomes depreciated more or less, and consequently transfers so much less value to the product. But here again, the change in value originates outside the process in which the machine is acting as a means of production. Once engaged in this process, the machine cannot transfer more value than it possesses apart from the process.

Just as a change in the value of the means of production, even after they have commenced to take a part in the labour-process, does not alter their character as constant capital, so, too, a change in the proportion of constant to variable capital does not affect the respective functions of these two kinds of capital. The technical conditions of the labour-process may be revolutionised to such an extent, that where formerly ten men using ten implements of small value worked up a relatively small quantity of raw material, one man may now, with the aid of one expensive machine, work up one hundred times as much raw material. In the latter case we have an enormous increase in the constant capital, that is represented by the total value of the means of production used, and at the same time a great reduction in the variable capital, invested in labour-power. Such a revolution, however, alters only the quantitative relation between the constant and the variable capital, or the proportions in which the total capital is split up into its constant and variable constituents; it has not in the least degree affected the essential difference between the two.

Footnotes

[1] "Labour gives a new creation for one extinguished." ("An Essay on the Polit. Econ. of Nations," London, 1821, p. 13.)

[2] The subject of repairs of the implements of labour does not concern us here. A machine that is undergoing repair, no longer plays the part of an instrument, but that of a subject of labour. Work is no longer done with it, but upon it. It is quite permissible for our purpose to assume, that the labour expended on the repairs of instruments is included in the labour necessary for their original production. But in the text we deal with that wear and tear, which no doctor can cure, and which little by little brings about death, with "that kind of wear which cannot be repaired from time to time, and which, in the case of a knife, would ultimately reduce it to a state in which the cutler would say of it, it is not worth a new blade." We have shewn in the text, that a machine takes part in every labour-process as an integral machine, but that into the simultaneous process of creating value it enters only bit by. bit. How great then is the confusion of ideas exhibited in the following extract! "Mr. Ricardo says a portion of the labour of the engineer in making [stocking] machines" is contained for example in the value of a pair of stockings. "Yet the total labour, that produced each single pair of stockings ... includes the whole labour of the engineer, not a portion; for one machine makes many pairs, and none of those pairs could have been done without any part of the machine." ("Obs. on Certain Verbal Disputes in Pol. Econ., Particularly Relating to Value," p. 54.1 The author, an uncommonly self-satisfied wiseacre, is right in his confusion and therefore in his contention, to this extent only, that neither Ricardo nor any other economist, before or since him, has accurately distinguished the two aspects of labour, and still less, therefore, the part played by it under each of these aspects in the formation of value.

[3] From this we may judge of the absurdity of J. B. Say, who pretends to account for surplus-value (Interest, Profit, Rent), by the "services productifs" which the means of production, soil, instruments, and raw material, render in the labour-process by means of their use-values. Mr. Wm. Roscher who seldom loses an occasion of registering, in black and white, ingenious apologetic fancies, records the following specimen:-"J. B. Say (Traité, t. 1, ch. 4) very truly remarks: the value produced by an oil mill, after deduction of all costs, is something new, something quite different from the labour by which the oil mill itself was erected." (l. c., p. 82, note.) Very true, Mr. Professor! the oil produced by the oil mill is indeed something very different from the labour expended in constructing the mill! By value, Mr. Roscher understands such stuff as "oil," because oil has value, notwithstanding that "Nature" produces petroleum, though relatively "in small quantities," a fact to which he seems to refer in his further observation: "It (Nature) produces scarcely any exchange-value." Mr. Roscher's "Nature" and the exchange-value it produces are rather like the

foolish virgin who admitted indeed that she had had a child, but "it was such a little one." This "savant sérieux" in continuation remarks: "Ricardo's school is in the habit of including capital as accumulated labour under the head of labour. This is unskilful work, because, indeed, the owner of capital, after all, does something more than the merely creating and preserving of the same: namely, the abstention from the enjoyment of it, for which he demands, e.g., interest." (l. c.) How very "skilful" is this "anatomico-physiological method" of Political Economy, which, "indeed," converts a mere desire "after all' into a source of value.

[4] "Of all the instruments of the farmers' trade, the labour of man ... is that on which he is most to rely for the repayment of his capital. The other two ... the working stock of the cattle and the ... carts, ploughs, spades, and so forth, without a given portion of the first, are nothing at all." (Edmund Burke: "Thoughts and Details on Scarcity, originally presented to the Right Hon. W. Pitt, in the month of November 1795," Edit. London, 1800, p. 10.)

[5] In The Times of 26th November, 1862, a manufacturer, whose mill employed 800 hands, and consumed, on the average, 150 bales of East Indian, or 130 bales of American cotton, complains, in doleful manner, of the standing expenses of his factory when not working. He estimates them at £6,000 a year. Among them are a number of items that do not concern us here, such as rent, rates, and taxes, insurance, salaries of the manager, book-keeper, engineer, and others. Then he reckons £150 for coal used to heat the mill occasionally, and run the engine now and then. Besides this, he includes the wages of the people employed at odd times to keep the machinery in working order. Lastly, he puts down £1,200 for depreciation of machinery, because "the weather and the natural principle of decay do not suspend their operations because the steam-engine ceases to revolve." He says, emphatically, he does not estimate his depreciation at more than the small sum of £1,200, because his machinery is already nearly worn out.

[6] "Productive consumption ... where the consumption of a commodity is a part of the process of production. ... In these instances there is no consumption of value." (S. P. Newman, l. c., p. 296.)

[7] In an American compendium that has gone through, perhaps, 20 editions, this passage occurs: "It matters not in what form capital re-appears;" then after a lengthy enumeration of all the possible ingredients of production whose value re-appears in the product, the passage concludes thus: "The various kinds of food, clothing, and shelter, necessary for the existence and comfort of the human being, are also changed. They are consumed from time to time, and their value re-appears in that new vigour imparted to his body and mind, forming fresh capital, to be employed again in the work of production." (F. Wayland, l. c., pp. 31, 32.) Without noticing any other oddities, it suffices to observe, that what re-appears in the fresh vigour, is not the bread's price, but its bloodforming substances. What, on the other hand, re-appears in the value of that vigour, is not the means of subsistence, but their value. The same necessaries of life, at half the price, would form just as much muscle and bone, just as much vigour, but not vigour of the same value. This confusion of "value" and "vigour" coupled with our author's pharisaical indefiniteness, mark an attempt, futile for all that, to thrash out an explanation of surplus-value from a mere re-appearance of pre-existing values.

[8] "Toutes les productions d'un même — genre ne forment proprement qu'une masse, dont le prix se détermine en général et sans égard aux circonstances particulières." (Le Trosne, 1. c., p. 893.)

Chapter Nine: The Rate of Surplus-Value

Section 1.
The Degree of Exploration of Labour-Power

The surplus-value generated in the process of production by C, the capital advanced, or in other words, the self-expansion of the value of the capital C, presents itself for our consideration, in the first place, as a surplus, as the amount by which the value of the product exceeds the value of its constituent elements.

The capital C is made up of two components, one, the sum of money c laid out upon the means of production, and the other, the sum of money v expended upon the labour-power; c represents the portion that has become constant capital, and v the portion that has become variable capital. At first then, C = c + v: for example, if £500 is the capital advanced, its components may be such that the £500 = £410 const. + £90 var. When the process of production is finished, we get a commodity whose value = (c + v) + s, where s is the surplus-value; or taking our former figures, the value of this commodity may be (£410 const. + £90 var.) + £90 surpl. The original capital has now changed from C to C', from £500 to £590. The difference is s or a surplusvalue of £90, Since the value of the constituent elements of the product is equal to the value of the advanced capital, it is mere tautology to say, that the excess of the value of the product over the value of its constituent elements, is equal to the expansion of the capital advanced or to the surplus-value produced.

Nevertheless, we must examine this tautology a little more closely. The two things compared are, the value of the product and the value of its constituents consumed in the process of production. Now we have seen how that portion of the constant capital which consists of the instruments of labour, transfers to the production only a fraction of its value, while the remainder of that value continues. to reside in those instruments. Since this remainder plays no part in the formation of value, we may at present leave it on one side. To introduce it into the calculation would make no difference. For instance, taking our former example, c = £410: suppose this sum to consist of £312 value of raw material, £44 value of auxiliary material, and £54 value of the machinery worn away in the process; and suppose that the total value of the machinery employed is £1,054. Out of this latter sum, then, we reckon as advanced for the purpose of turning out the product, the sum of £54 alone, which the machinery loses by wear and tear in the process; for this is all it parts with to the product. Now if we also reckon the remaining £1,000, which still continues in the machinery, as transferred to the product, we ought also to reckon it as part of the value advanced, and thus make it appear on both sides of our calculation. [1] We should, in this way, get £1,500 on one side and £1,590 on the other. The difference of these two sums, or the surplus-value, would still be £90. Throughout this Book therefore, by constant capital advanced for the production of value, we always mean, unless the context is repugnant thereto, the value of the means of production actually consumed in the process, and that value alone.

This being so, let us return to the formula C = c + v, which we saw was transformed into C' = (c + v) + s, C becoming C'. We know that the value of the constant capital is transferred to, and merely re-appears in the product. The new value actually created in the process, the value produced, or value-product, is therefore not the same as the value of the product; it is not, as it would at first sight appear (c + v) + s or £410 const. + £90 var. + £90 surpl.; but v + s or £90 var. + £90 surpl., not £590 but £180. If c = 0, or in other words, if there were branches of industry in which the capitalist could dispense with all means of production made by previous labour, whether they be raw material, auxiliary material, or instruments of labour, employing only labour-power and materials supplied by Nature, in that case, there would be no constant capital to transfer to the product. This component of the value of the product, i.e., the £410 in our example, would be eliminated, but the sum of £180, the amount of new value created, or the value produced, which contains £90 of surplus-value, would remain just as great as if c represented the highest value imaginable. We should have C = (0 + v) = v or C' the expanded capital = v + s and therefore C'-C = s as before. On the other hand, if s = 0, or in other words, if the labour-power, whose value is advanced in the form of variable capital, were to produce only its equivalent, we should have C = c + v or C' the value of the product — (c + v) + 0 or C = C'. The capital advanced would, in this case, not have expanded its value.

From what has gone before, we know that surplus-value is purely the result of a variation in the value of v, of that portion of the capital which is transformed into labour-power; consequently, v + s = v + v, or v plus an increment of v. But the fact that it is v alone that varies, and the conditions of that variation, are obscured by the circumstance that in consequence of the increase in the variable component of the capital, there is also an increase in. the sum total of the advanced capital. It was originally £500 and becomes £590. Therefore in order that our investigation may lead to accurate results, we must make abstraction from that portion of the value of the product, in which constant capital alone appears, and consequently must equate the constant capital to zero or make c = 0. This is merely an application of a mathematical rule, employed whenever we operate with constant and variable magnitudes, related to each other by the symbols of addition and subtraction only.

A further difficulty is caused by the original form of the variable capital. In our example, C' = £410 const. + £90 var. + £90 surpl.; but £90 is a given and therefore a constant quantity; hence it appears absurd to treat it as variable. But in fact, the term £90 var. is here merely a symbol to show that this value undergoes a process. The portion of the capital invested in the purchase of labour-power is a definite quantity of materialised labour, a constant value like the value of the labour-power purchased. But in the process of production the place of the £90 is taken by the labour-power in action, dead labour is replaced by living labour, something stagnant by something flowing, a constant by a variable. The result is the reproduction of v plus an increment of v. From the point of view then of capitalist production, the whole process appears as the spontaneous variation of the originally constant value, which is transformed into labour-power. Both the process and its result, appear to be owing to this value. If, therefore, such expressions as "£90 variable capital," or "so much self-expanding value", appear contradictory, this is only because they bring to the surface a contradiction immanent in capitalist production.

At first sight it appears a strange proceeding, to equate the constant capital to zero. Yet it is what we do every day. If, for example, we wish to calculate the amount of England's profits from the cotton industry, we first of all deduct the sums paid for cotton to the United States, India, Egypt and other countries; in other words, the value of the capital that merely re-appears in the value of the product, is put = 0.

Of course the ratio of surplus-value not only to that portion of the capital from which it immediately springs, and whose change of value it represents, but also-to the sum total of the capital advanced is economically of very great importance. We shall, therefore, in the third book, treat of this ratio exhaustively. In order to enable one portion of a capital to expand its value by being converted into labour-power, it is necessary that another portion be converted into means of production. In order that variable capital may perform its function, constant capital must be advanced in proper proportion, a proportion given by the special technical conditions of each labour-process. The circumstance, however, that retorts and other vessels, are necessary to a chemical process, does not compel the chemist to notice them in the result of his analysis. If we look at the means of production, in their relation to the creation of value, and to the variation in the quantity of value, apart from anything else, they appear simply as the material in which labour-power, the value-creator, incorporates itself. Neither the nature, nor the value of this material is of any importance. The only requisite is that there be a sufficient supply to absorb the labour expended in the process of production. That supply once given, the material may rise or fall in value, or even be, as land and the sea, without any value in itself; but this will have no influence on the creation of value or on the variation in the quantity of value. [2]

In the first place then we equate the constant capital to zero. The capital advanced is consequently reduced from c + v to v, and instead of the value of the product (c + v) + s we have now the value produced (v + s). Given the new value produced = £180, which sum consequently represents the whole labour expended during the process, then subtracting from it £90 the value of the variable capital, we have remaining £90, the amount of the surplus-value. This sum of £90 or s expresses the absolute quantity of surplus-value produced. The relative quantity produced, or the increase per cent of the variable capital, is determined, it is plain, by the ratio of the surplus-value to the variable capital, or is expressed by s/v. In our example this ratio is 90/90, which gives an increase of 100%. This relative increase in the value of the variable capital, or the relative magnitude of the surplus-value, I call, "The rate of surplus-value." [3]

We have seen that the labourer, during one portion of the labour-process, produces only the value of his labour-power, that is, the value of his means of subsistence. Now since his work forms part of a system, based on the social division of labour, he does not directly produce the actual necessaries which he himself consumes; he produces instead a particular commodity, yarn for example, whose value is equal to the value of those necessaries or of the money with which they can be bought. The portion of his day's labour devoted to this purpose, will be greater or less, in proportion to the value of the necessaries that he daily requires on an average, or, what amounts to the same thing, in proportion to the labour-time required on an average to produce them. If the value of those necessaries represent on an average the expenditure of six hours' labour, the workman must on an average work for six hours to produce that value. If instead of working for the capitalist, he worked independently on his own account, he would, other things being equal, still be obliged to labour for the same number of hours, in order to produce the value of his labour-power, and thereby to gain the means of subsistence necessary for his conservation or continued reproduction. But as we have seen, during that portion of his day's labour in which he produces the value of his labour-power, say three shillings, he produces only an equivalent for the value of his labour-power already advanced [4] by the capitalist; the new value created only replaces the variable capital advanced. It is owing to this fact, that the production of the new value of three shillings takes the semblance of a mere reproduction. That portion of the working-day, then, during which this reproduction takes place, I call "necessary" labour-time, and the labour expended during that time I call "necessary" labour [5] Necessary, as regards the labourer, because independent of the particular . 2 social form of his labour; necessary, as regards capital, and the world of capitalists, because on the continued existence of the labourer depends their existence also.

During the second period of the labour-process, that in which his labour is no longer necessary labour, the workman, it is true, labours, expends labour-power; but his labour, being no longer necessary labour, he creates no value for himself. He creates surplus-value which, for the capitalist, has all the charms of a creation out of nothing. This portion of the working-day, I name surplus labour-time, and to the labour expended during that time, I give the name of surplus-labour. It is every bit as important, for a correct understanding of surplus-value, to conceive it as a mere congelation of surplus labour-time, as nothing but materialised surplus-labour, as it is, for a proper comprehension of value, to conceive it as a mere congelation of so many hours of labour, as nothing but materialised labour. The essential difference between the various economic forms of society, between, for instance, a society based on slave-labour, and one based on wage-labour, lies only in the mode in which this surplus-labour is in each case extracted from the actual producer, the labourer. [6]

Since, on the one hand, the values of the variable capital and of the labour-power purchased by that capital are equal, and the value of this labour-power determines the necessary portion of the working-day; and since, on the other hand, the surplus-value is determined by the surplus portion of the working-day, it follows that surplus-value bears the same ratio to variable capital, that surplus-labour does to necessary labour, or in other words, the rate of surplus-value

$$ \frac{s}{v} = \frac{\text{surplus-labour}}{\text{necessary labour}} $$

Both ratios, s/v and surplus-labour/necessary-labour, express the same thing in different ways; in the one case by reference to materialised, incorporated labour, in the other by reference to living, fluent labour.

The rate of surplus-value is therefore an exact expression for the degree of exploitation of labour-power by capital, or of the labourer by the capitalist. [7]

We assumed in our example, that the value of the product £410 const. + £90 var. + £90 surpl., and that the capital advanced = £500. Since the surplus-value = £90, and the advanced capital = £500, we should, according to the usual way of reckoning, get as the rate of surplus-value (generally confounded with rate of profits) 18%, a rate so low as possibly to cause a pleasant surprise to Mr. Carey and other harmonisers. But in truth, the rate of surplus-value is not equal to s/C or s/C+v: thus it is not 90/500 but 90/500 or 100%, which is more than five times the apparent degree of exploitation. Although, in the case we have supposed, we are ignorant of the actual length of the working-day, and of the duration in days or weeks of the labour-process, as also of the number of labourers employed, yet the rate of surplus-value s/v accurately discloses to us, by means of its equivalent expression, surplus-labour/necessary labour the relation between the two parts of the working-day. This relation is here one of equality, the rate being 100%. Hence, it is plain, the labourer, in our example, works one half of the day for himself, the other half for the capitalist.

The method of calculating the rate of surplus-value is therefore, shortly, as follows. We take the total value of the product and put the constant capital which merely re-appears in it, equal to zero. What remains, is the only value that has, in the process of producing the commodity, been actually created. If the amount of surplus-value be given, we have only to deduct it from this remainder, to find the variable capital. And vice versâ, if the latter be given, and we require to find the surplus-value. If both be given, we have only to perform the concluding operation, viz., to calculate s/v, the ratio of the surplus-value to the v variable capital.

Though the method is so simple, yet it may not be amiss, by means of a few examples, to exercise the reader in the application of the novel principles underlying it.

First we will take the case of a spinning mill containing 10,000 mule spindles, spinning No. 32 yarn from American cotton, and producing 1 lb. of yarn weekly per spindle. We assume the waste to be 6%: under these circumstances 10,600 lbs. of cotton are consumed weekly, of which 600 lbs. go to waste. The price of the cotton in April, 1871, was 7 3/4d. per lb.; the raw material therefore costs in round numbers £342. The 10,000 spindles, including preparation-machinery, and motive power, cost, we will assume, £1 per spindle, amounting to a total of £10,000. The wear and tear we put at 10%, or £1,000 yearly = £20 weekly. The rent of the building we suppose to be £300 a year, or £6 a week. Coal consumed (for 100 horse-power indicated, at 4 lbs. of coal per horse-power per hour during 60 hours, and inclusive of that consumed in heating the mill), 11 tons a week at 8s. 6 d. a ton, amounts to about £4 1/2 a week: gas, £1 a week, oil, &c., £4 1/2 a week. Total cost of the above auxiliary materials, £10 weekly. Therefore the constant portion of the value of the week's product is £378. Wages amount to £52 a week. The price of the yarn is 12 1/4d. per. lb. which gives for the value of 10,000 lbs. the sum of £510. The surplus-value is therefore in this case £510-£430 = £80. We put the constant part of the value of the product = 0, as it plays no part in the creation of value. There remains £132 as the weekly value created, which = £52 var. + £80 surpl. The rate of surplus-value is therefore 80/52 = 153 11/13%. In a working-day of 10 hours with average labour the result is: necessary labour = 3 31/33 hours, and surplus-labour = 6 2/33. [8]

One more example. Jacob gives the following calculation for the year 1815. Owing to the previous adjustment of several items it is very imperfect; nevertheless for our purpose it is sufficient. In it he assumes the price of wheat to be 8s. a quarter, and the average yield per acre to be 22 bushels.

Value Produced Per Acre

Seed	-	£1	9		Tithes, Rates, Taxes	-	£1	1	c
Manure	-	2	10		Rent,	-	1	8	c
Wages	-	3	10		Farmer's profit and Interest,	-	1	2	c
	Total	£7	9		Total	£3	11	0	

Assuming that the price of the product is the same as its value, we here find the surplus-value distributed under the various heads of profit, interest, rent, &c. We have. nothing to do with these in detail; we simply add them together, and the sum is a surplus-value of £3 11s. 0d. The sum of £3 19s. 0d., paid for seed and manure, is constant capital, and we put it equal to zero. There is left the sum of £3 10s. 0d., which is the variable capital advanced: and we see that a new value of £3 10s. 0d + £3 11s. 0d. has been produced in its place. Therefore ' s/v = £3 11s. 0d. / £3 10s. 0d., giving a rate of surplus-value of more than 100%. The labourer employs more than one half of his working-day in producing the surplus-value, which different persons, under different pretexts, share amongst themselves. [9]

Section 2.
The Representation of the Components of the Value of the Product by Corresponding Proportional Parts of the Product Itself

Let us now return to the example by which we were shown how the capitalist converts money into capital.

The product of a working-day of 12 hours is 20 lbs. of yarn, having a value of 30s. No less than 8/10ths of this value, or 24s., is due to mere re-appearance in it, of the value of the means of production (20 lbs. of cotton, value 20s., and spindle worn away, 4s.): it is therefore constant capital. The remaining 2/10ths or 6s. is the new value created during the spinning process: of this one half replaces the value of the day's labour-power, or the variable capital, the remaining half constitutes a surplus-value of 3s. The total value then of the 20 lbs. of yarn is made up as follows: 30s. value of yarn = 24s. const. + 3s. var. + 3s. surpl.

Since the whole of this value is contained in the 20 lbs. of yarn produced, it follows that the various component parts of this value, can be represented as being contained respectively in corresponding parts of the product.

If the value of 30s. is contained in 20 lbs. of yarn, then 8/10ths of this value, or the 24s. that form its constant part, is contained in 8/10ths of the product or in 16 lbs. of yarn. Of the latter 13 1/3 lbs. represent the value of the raw material, the 20s. worth of cotton spun, and 2 2/3 lbs. represent the 4s. worth of spindle, &c., worn away in the process.

Hence the whole of the cotton used up in spinning the 20 lbs. of yarn, is represented by 13 1/3 lbs. of yarn. This latter weight of yarn contains, it is true, by weight, no more than 13 1/3 lbs. of cotton, worth 13 1/3 shillings; but the 6 2/3 shillings additional value contained in it, are the equivalent for the cotton consumed in spinning the remaining 6 2/3 lbs. of yarn. The effect is the same as if these 6 2/3 lbs. of yarn contained no cotton at all, and the whole 20 lbs. of cotton were concentrated in the 13 1/3 lbs. of yarn. The latter weight, on the other hand, does not contain an atom either of the value of the auxiliary materials and implements, or of the value newly created in the process.

In the same way, the 2 2/3 lbs. of yarn, in which the 4s., the remainder of the constant capital, is embodied, represents nothing but the value of the auxiliary materials and instruments of labour consumed in producing the 20 lbs. of yarn.

We have, therefore, arrived at this result: although eight-tenths of the product, or 16 lbs. of yarn, is, in its character of an article of utility, just as much the fabric of the spinner's labour, as the remainder of the same product, yet when viewed in this connexion, it does not contain, and has not absorbed any labour expended during the process of spinning. It is just as if the cotton had converted itself into yarn, without help; as if the shape it had assumed was mere trickery and deceit: for so soon as our capitalist sells it for 24s., and with the money replaces his means of production, it becomes evident that this 16 lbs. of yarn is nothing more than so much cotton and spindle-waste in disguise.

On the other hand, the remaining 2/10 ths of the product, or 4 lbs. of yarn, represent nothing but the new value of 6s., created during the 12 hours' spinning process. All the value transferred to those 4 lbs., from the raw material and instruments of labour consumed, was, so to say, intercepted in order to be incorporated in the 16 lbs. first spun. In this case, it is as if the spinner had spun 4 lbs. of yarn out of air, or, as if he had spun them with the aid of cotton and spindles, that, being the spontaneous gift of Nature, transferred no value to the product.

Of this 4 lbs. of yarn, in which the whole of the value newly created during the process, is condensed, one half represents the equivalent for the value of the labour consumed, or the 3s. variable capital, the other half represents the 3s. surplus-value.

Since 12 working-hours of the spinner are embodied in 6s., it follows that in yarn of the value of 30s., there must be embodied 60 working-hours. And this quantity of labour-time does in fact exist in the 20 lbs. of yarn; for in 8/10ths or 16 lbs. there are materialised the 48 hours of 10 labour expended, before the commencement of the spinning process, on the means of production; and in the remaining 2 ths or 4 lbs. there 10 are materialised the 12 hours' work done during the process itself.

On a former page we saw that the value of the yarn is equal to the sum of the new value created during the production of that yarn plus the value previously existing in the means of production.

It has now been shown how the various component parts of the value of the product, parts that differ functionally from each other, may be represented by corresponding proportional parts of the product itself.

To split up in this manner the product into different parts, of which one represents only the labour previously spent on the means of production, or the constant capital, another, only the necessary labour spent during the process of production, or the variable capital, and another and last part, only the surplus-labour expended during the same process, or the surplus-value; to do this, is, as will be seen later on from its application to complicated and hitherto unsolved problems, no less important than it is simple.

In the preceding investigation we have treated the total product as the final result, ready for use, of a working-day of 12 hours. We can however follow this total product through all the stages of its production; and in this way we shall arrive at the same result as before, if we represent the partial products, given off at the different stages, as functionally different parts of the final or total product.

The spinner produces in 12 hours 20 lbs. of yarn, or in I hour 1 2/3 lbs; consequently he produces in 8 hours 13 2/3 lbs., or a partial product equal in value to all the cotton that is spun in a whole day. In like manner the partial product of the next period of 1 hour and 36 minutes, is 2 2/3 lbs. of yarn: this represents the value of the instruments of labour that are consumed in 12 hours. In the following hour and 12 minutes, the spinner produces 2 lbs. of yarn worth 3 shillings, a value equal to the whole value he creates in his 6 hours' necessary labour. Finally, in the last hour and 12 minutes he produces another 2 lbs. of yarn, whose value is equal to the surplus-value, created by his surplus-labour during half a day. This method of calculation serves the English manufacturer for every-day use; it shows, he will say, that in the first 8 hours, or 2/3 of the working-day, he gets back the value of his cotton; and so on for the remaining hours. It is also a perfectly correct method: being in fact the first method given above with this difference, that instead of being applied to space, in which the different parts of the completed product lie side by side, it deals with time, in which those parts are suc cessively produced. But it can also be accompanied by very barbarian notions, more especially in the heads of those who are as much interested, practically, in the process of making value beget value, as they are in misunderstanding that process theoretically. Such people may get the notion into their heads, that our spinner, for example, produces or replaces in the first 8 hours of his working-day the value of the cotton; in the following hour and 36 minutes the value of the instruments of labour worn away; in the next hour and 12 minutes the value of the wages; and that he devotes to the production of surplus-value for the manufacturer, only that well known "last hour." In this way the poor spinner is made to perform the two-fold miracle not only of producing cotton, spindles, steam-engine, coal, oil, &c., at the same time that he spins with them, but also of turning one working-day into five; for, in the example we are considering, the production of the raw material and instruments of labour demands four working-days of twelve hours each, and their conversion into yarn requires another such day. That the love of lucre induces an easy belief in such miracles, and that sycophant doctrinaires are never wanting to prove them, is vouched for by the following incident of historical celebrity.

Section 3.
Senior's "Last Hour"

One fine morning, in the year 1836, Nassau W. Senior, who may be called the bel-esprit of English economists, well known, alike for his economic "science," and for his beautiful style, was summoned from Oxford to Manchester, to learn in the latter place, the Political Economy that he taught in the former. The manufacturers elected him as their champion, not only against the newly passed Factory Act, but against the still more menacing Ten-hours' agitation. With their usual practical acuteness, they had found out that the learned Professor "wanted a good deal of finishing;" it was this discovery that caused them to write for him. On his side the Professor has embodied the lecture he received from the Manchester manufacturers, in a pamphlet, entitled: "Letters on the Factory Act, as it affects the cotton manufacture." London, 1837. Here we find, amongst others, the following edifying passage: "Under the present law, no mill in which persons under 18 years of age are employed, ... can be worked more than 11 1/2 hours a day, that is 12 hours for 5 days in the week, and nine on Saturday.

"Now the following analysis (!) will show that in a mill so worked, the whole net profit is derived from the last hour. I will suppose a manufacturer to invest £100,000: — £80,000 in his mill and machinery, and £20,000 in raw material and wages. The annual return of that mill, supposing the capital to be turned once a year, and gross profits to be 15 per cent., ought to be goods worth £15,000.... Of this £115,000, each of the twenty-three half-hours of work produces 5-115ths or one twenty-third. Of these 23-23rds (constituting the whole £115,000) twenty, that is to say £100,000 out of the £115,000, simply replace the capital; — one twenty-third (or £5,000 out of the £115,000) makes up for the deterioration of the mill and machinery. The remaining 2-23rds, that is, the last two of the twenty-three half-hours of every day, produce the net profit of 10 per cent. If, therefore (prices remaining the same), the factory could be kept at work thirteen hours instead of eleven and a half, with an addition of about £2,600 to the circulating capital, the net profit would be more than doubled. On the other hand, if the hours of working were reduced by one hour per day (prices remaining the same), the net profit would be destroyed — if they were reduced by one hour and a half, even the gross profit would be destroyed."[10]

And the Professor calls this an "analysis!" If, giving credence to the out-cries of the manufacturers, he believed that the workmen spend the best part of the day in the production, i.e., the reproduction or replacement of the value of the buildings, machinery, cotton, coal, &c., then his analysis was superfluous. His answer would simply have been: — Gentlemen! if you work your mills for 10 hours instead of 11 1/2, then, other things being equal, the daily consumption of cotton, machinery, &c., will decrease in proportion. You gain just as much as you lose. Your work-people will in future spend one hour and a half less time in reproducing or replacing the capital that has been advanced. — If, on the other hand, he did not believe them without further inquiry, but, as being an expert in such matters, deemed an analysis necessary, then he ought, in a question that is concerned exclusively with the relations of net profit to the length of the working-day, before all things to have asked the manufacturers, to be careful not to lump together machinery, workshops, raw material, and labour, but to be good enough to place the constant capital, invested in buildings, machinery, raw material, &c., on one side of the account, and the capital advanced in wages on the other side. If the Professor then found, that in accordance with the calculation of the manufacturers, the workman reproduced or replaced his wages in 2 half-hours, in that case, he should have continued his analysis thus:

According to your figures, the workman in the last hour but one produces his wages, and in the last hour your surplus-value or net profit. Now, since in equal periods he produces equal values, the produce of the last hour but one, must have the same value as that of the last hour. Further, it is only while he labours that he produces any value at all, and the amount of his labour is measured by his labour-time. This you say, amounts to 11 1/2 hours a day. He employs one portion of these 11 1/2 hours, in producing or replacing his wages, and the remaining portion in producing your net profit. Beyond this he does absolutely nothing. But since, on your assumption, his wages, and the surplus-value he yields, are of equal value, it is clear that he produces his wages in 5 3/4 hours, and your net profit in the other 5 3/4 hours. Again, since the value of the yarn produced in 2 hours, is equal to the sum of the values of his wages and of your net profit, the measure of the value of this yarn must be 11 1/2 working-hours, of which 5 3/4 hours measure the value of the yarn produced in the last hour but one, and 5 3/4, the value of the yarn produced in the last hour. We now come to a ticklish point; therefore, attention! The last working-hour but one is, like the first, an ordinary working-hour, neither more nor less. How then can the spinner produce in one hour, in the shape of yarn, a value that embodies 5 3/4 hours' labour? The truth is that he performs no such miracle. The use-value produced by him in one hour, is a definite quantity of yarn. The value of this yarn is measured by 5 3/4 working-hours, of which 4 3/4 were, without any assistance from him, previously embodied in the means of production, in the cotton, the machinery, and so on; the remaining one hour alone is added by him. Therefore since his wages are produced in 5 3/4 hours, and the yarn produced in one hour also contains 5 3/4 hours' work, there is no witchcraft in the result, that the value created by his 5 3/4 hours' spinning, is equal to the value of the product spun in one hour. You are altogether on the wrong track, if you think that he loses a single moment of his working-day, in reproducing or replacing the values of the cotton, the machinery, and so on. On the contrary, it is because his labour converts the cotton and spindles into yarn, because he spins, that the values of the cotton and spindles go over to the yarn of their own accord. This result is owing to the quality of his labour, not to its quantity. It is true, he will in one hour transfer to the yarn more value, in the shape of cotton, than he will in half an hour; but that is only because in one hour he spins up more cotton than in half an hour. You see then, your assertion, that the workman produces, in the last hour but one, the value of his wages, and in the last hour your net profit, amounts to no more than this, that in the yarn produced by him in 2 working-hours, whether they are the 2 first or the 2 last hours of the working-day, in that yarn, there are incorporated 11 1/2 working-hours, or just a whole day's work, i.e., two hours of his own work and 9 1/2 hours of other people's. And my assertion that, in the first 5 3/4 hours, he produces his wages, and in the last 5 3/4 hours your net profit, amounts only to this, that you pay him for the former, but not for the latter. In speaking of payment of labour, instead of payment of labour-power, I only talk your own slang. Now, gentlemen, if you compare the working-time you pay for, with that which you do not pay for, you will find that they are to one another, as half a day is to half a day; this gives a rate of 100%, and a very pretty percentage it is. Further, there is not the least doubt, that if you make you "hands" toil for 13 hours, instead of 11 1/2, and, as may be expected from you, treat the work done in that extra one hour and a half, as pure surplus-labour, then the latter will be increased from 5 3/4 hours' labour to 7 1/4 hours' labour, and the rate of surplus-value from 100% to 126 2/23%. So that you are altogether too sanguine, in expecting that by such an addition of 1 1/2 hours to the working-day, the rate will rise from 100% to 200% and more, in other words that it will be "more than doubled." On the other hand-man's heart is a wonderful thing, especially when carried in the purse — you take too pessimist a view, when you fear, that with a reduction of the hours of labour from 11 1/2 to 10, the whole of your net profit will go to the dogs. Not at all. All other conditions remaining the same, the surplus-labour will fall from 5 3/4 hours to 4 3/4 hours, a period that still gives a very profitable rate of surplus-value, namely 82 14/23%. But this dreadful "last hour," about which you have invented more stories than have the millenarians about the day of judgment, is "all bosh." If it goes, it will cost neither you, your net profit, nor the boys and girls whom you employ, their "purity of mind." [11] Whenever your "last hour" strikes in earnest, think of the Oxford Professor. And now, gentlemen, "farewell, and may we meet again in yonder better world, but not before."

Senior invented the battle cry of the "last hour" in 1836. [12] In the London Economist of the 15th April, 1848, the same cry was again raised by James Wilson, an economic mandarin of high standing: this time in opposition to the 10 hours' bill.

Section 4.
Surplus-Produce

The portion of the product that represents the surplus-value, (one tenth of the 20 lbs., or 2 lbs. of yarn, in the example given in Sec. 2) we call "surplus-produce." Just as the rate of surplus-value is determined by its relation, not to the sum total of the capital, but to its variable part; in like manner, the relative quantity of surplus-produce is determined by the ratio that this produce bears, not to the remaining part of the total product, but to that part of it in which is incorporated the necessary labour. Since the production of surplus-value is the chief end and aim of capitalist production, it is clear, that the greatness of a man's or a nation's wealth should be measured, not by the absolute quantity produced, but by the relative magnitude of the surplus-produce. [13]

The sum of the necessary labour and the surplus-labour, i.e., of the periods of time during which the workman replaces the value of his labour-power, and produces the surplus-value, this sum constitutes the actual time during which he works, i.e., the working-day.

Footnotes

[1] "If we reckon the value of the fixed capital employed as a part of the advances, we must reckon the remaining value of such capital at the end of the year as a part of the annual returns." (Malthus, "Princ. of Pol. Econ." 2nd. ed., Lond., 1836, p. 269.)

[2] What Lucretius says is self-evident; "nil posse creari de nihilo," out of nothing, nothing can be created. Creation of value is transformation of labour-power into labour. Labourpower itself is energy transferred to a human organism by means of nourishing matter.

[3] In the same way that the English use the terms "rate of profit," "rate of interest." We shall see, in Book III, that the rate of profit is no mystery, so soon as we know the laws of surplus-value. If we reverse the process, we cannot comprehend either the one or the other.

[4] Note added in the 3rd German edition. — The author resorts here to the economic language in current use. It will be remembered that on p. 182 (present edition, p. 174) it was shown that in reality the labourer "advances" to the capitalist and not the capitalist to the labourer. — F. E.

[5] In this work, we have, up to now, employed the term "necessary labour-time," to designate the time necessary under given social conditions for the production of any commodity. Henceforward we use it to designate also the time necessary for the production of the particular commodity labour-power. The use of one and the same technical term in different senses is inconvenient, but in no science can it be altogether avoided. Compare, for instance, the higher with the lower branches of mathematics.

[6] Herr Wilhelm Thucydides Roscher has found a mare's nest. He has made the important discovery that if, on the one hand, the formation of surplus-value, or surplus-produce, and the consequent accumulation of capital, is now-a-days due to the thrift of the capitalist, on the other hand, in the lowest stages of civilisation it is the strong who compel the weak to economise. (l. c., p. 78.) To economise what? Labour? Or superfluous wealth that does not exist? What is it that makes such men as Roscher account for the origin of surplus-value, by a mere rechauffé of the more of less plausible excuses by the capitalist, for his appropriation of surplus-value? It is, besides their real ignorance, their apologetic dread of a scientific analysis of value and surplus-value, and of obtaining a result, possibly not altogether palatable to the powers that be.

[7] Although the rate of surplus-value is an exact expression for the degree of exploitation of labour-power, it is, in no sense, an expression for the absolute amount of exploitation. For example, if the necessary labour 5 hours and the surplus-labour = 5 hours, the degree of exploitation is 100%. The amount of exploitation is here measured by 5 hours. If, on the other hand, the necessary labour = 6 hours and the surplus-labour = 6 hours, the degree of exploitation remains, as before, 100%, while the actual amount of exploitation has increased 20%, namely from five hours to six.

[8] The above data, which may be relied upon, were given me by a Manchester spinner. In England the horse-power of an engine was formerly calculated from the diameter of its cylinder, now the actual horse-power shown by the indicator is taken.

[9] The calculations given in the text are intended merely as illustrations. We have in fact. assumed that prices = values. We shall, however, see, in Book Ill., that even in the case of average prices the assumption cannot be made in this very simple manner.

[10] Senior, l. c., pp. 12, 13. We let pass such extraordinary notions as are of no importance for our purpose; for instance, the assertion, that manufacturers reckon as part of their profit, gross or net, the amount required to make good wear and tear of machinery, or in other words, to replace a part of the capital. So, too, we pass over any question as to the accuracy of his figures. Leonard Homer has shown in "A Letter to Mr. Senior," &c., London, 1837, that they are worth no more than so-called "Analysis." Leonard Horner was one of the Factory Inquiry Commissioners in 1833, and Inspector, or rather Censor of Factories till 1859. He rendered undying service to the English working-class. He carried on a life-long contest, not only with the embittered manufacturers, but also with the Cabinet, to whom the number of votes given by the masters in the Lower

House, was a matter of far greater importance than the number of hours worked by the "hands" in the mills.

Apart from efforts in principle, Senior's statement is confused. What he really intended to say was this: The manufacturer employs the workman for 11 1/2 hours or for 23 half-hours daily. As the working-day, so, too, the working year, may be conceived to consist of 11 1/2 hours or 23 half-hours, but each multiplied by the number of working-days in the year. On this supposition, the 23 half-hours yield an annual product of £115,000; one half-hour yields 1/23 x £115,000; 20 half-hours yield 20/23 x £115,000 = £100,000, i.e., they replace no more than the capital advanced. There remain 3 half-hours, which yield 3/23 x £115,000 = £5,000 or the gross profit. Of these 3 half-hours, one yields 1/23 x £115,000 = £5,000; i.e., it makes up for the wear and tear of the machinery; the remaining 2 half-hours, i.e., the last hour, yield 2/23 x £115,000 = £10,000 or the net profit. In the text Senior converts the last 2/23 of the product into portions of the working-day itself.

[11] If, on the one hand, Senior proved that the net profit of the manufacturer, the existence of the English cotton industry, and England's command of the markets of the world, depend on "the last working-hour," on the other hand, Dr. Andrew Ure showed, that if children and young persons under 18 years of age, instead of being kept the full 12 hours in the warm and pure moral atmosphere of the factory, are turned out an hour sooner into the heartless and frivolous outer world, they will be deprived, by idleness and vice, of all hope of salvation for their souls. Since 1848, the factory inspectors have never tired of twitting the masters with this "last," this "fatal hour." Thus Mr. Hovell in his report of the 21st May, 1855: "Had the following ingenious calculation (he quotes Senior) been correct, every cotton factory in the United Kingdom would have been working at a loss since the year 1850." (Reports of the Insp. of Fact., for the half-year, ending 30th April, 1855, pp. 19, 20.) In the year 1848, after the passing of the 10 hours' bill, the masters of some flax spinning mills, scattered, few and far between, over the country on the borders of Dorset and Somerset, foisted a petition against the bill on to the shoulders of a few of their work-people. One of the clauses of this petition is as follows: "Your petitioners, as parents, conceive that an additional hour of leisure will tend more to demoralise the children than otherwise, believing that idleness is the parent of vice." On this the factory report of 31st Oct., 1848, says: The atmosphere of the flax mills, in which the children of these virtuous and tender parents work, is so loaded with dust and fibre from the raw material, that it is exceptionally unpleasant to stand even 10 minutes in the spinning rooms: for you are unable to do so without the most painful sensation, owing to the eyes, the ears, the nostrils, and mouth, being immediately filled by the clouds of flax dust from which there is no escape. The labour itself, owing to the feverish haste of the machinery, demands unceasing application of skill and movement, under the control of a watchfulness that never tires, and it seems somewhat hard, to let parents apply the term "idling" to their own children, who, after allowing for meal-times, are fettered for 10 whole hours to such an occupation, in such an atmosphere.... These children work longer than the labourers in the neighbouring villages.... Such cruel talk about "idleness and vice" ought to be branded as the purest cant, and the most shameless hypocrisy.... That portion of the public, who, about 12 years ago, were struck by the assurance with which, under the sanction of high authority, it was publicly and most earnestly proclaimed, that the whole net profit of the manufacturer flows from the labour of the last hour, and that, therefore, the reduction of the working-day by one hour, would destroy his net profit, that portion of the public, we say, will hardly believe its own eyes, when it now finds, that the original discovery of the virtues of "the last hour" has since been so far improved, as to include morals as well as profit; so that, if the duration of the labour of children, is reduced to a full 10 hours, their morals, together with the net profits of their employers, will vanish, both being dependent on this last, this fatal hour. (See Repts., Insp. of Fact., for 31st Oct., 1848, p. 101.) The same report then gives some examples of the morality and virtue of these same pure-minded manufacturers, of the tricks, the artifices, the cajoling, the threats, and the falsifications, they made use of, in order, first, to compel a few defenceless workmen to sign petitions of such a kind, and then to impose them upon Parliament as the petitions of a whole branch of industry, or a whole country. It is highly characteristic of the present status of so-called economic science, that neither Senior himself, who, at a later period, to his honour be it said, energetically supported the factory legislation, nor his opponents,

from first to last, have ever been able to explain the false conclusions of the "original discovery." They appeal to actual experience, but the why and wherefore remains a mystery.

[12] Nevertheless, the learned professor was not without some benefit from his journey to Manchester. In the "Letters on the Factory Act," he makes the whole net gains including "profit" and "interests" and even "something more," depend upon a single unpaid hour's work of the labourer. One year previously, in his "Outlines of Political Economy," written for the instruction of Oxford students and cultivated Philistines, he had also "discovered, in opposition to Ricardo's determination of value by labour, that profit is derived from the labour of the capitalist, and interest from his asceticism, in other words, from his abstinence." The dodge was an old one, but the word "abstinence " was new. Herr Roscher translates it rightly by "Enthaltung." Some of his countrymen, the Browns, Jones, and Robinsons, of Germany, not so well versed in Latin as he, have, monk-like, rendered it by "Entsagung" (renunciation).

[13] "To an individual with a capital of £20,000, whose profits were £2,000 per annum, it would be a matter quite indifferent whether his capital would employ a 100 or 1,000 men, whether the commodity produced sold for £10,000 or £20,000, provided, in all cases, his profit were not diminished below £2,000. Is not the real interest of the nation similar? Provided its net real income, its rent and profits, be the same, it is of no importance whether the nation consists of 10 or of 12 millions of inhabitants." (Ric. l. c.,.p. 416.) Long before Ricardo, Arthur Young, a fanatical upholder of surplus-produce, for the rest, a rambling, uncritical writer, whose reputation is in the inverse ratio of his merit, says, "Of what use, in a modem kingdom, would be a whole province thus divided [in the old Roman manner, by small independent peasants], however well cultivated, except for the mere purpose of breeding men, which taken singly is a most useless purpose?" (Arthur Young: "Political Arithmetic, &c." London, 1774, p. 47.)

Very curious is "the strong inclination... to represent net wealth as beneficial to the labouring class... though it is evidently not on account of being net." (Th . Hopkins, "On Rent of Land, &c." London, 1828, p. 126.)

Chapter Ten:
The Working-Day

Section 1:
The Limits of the Working-Day

We started with the supposition that labour-power is bought and sold at its value. Its value, like that of all other commodities, is determined by the working-time necessary to its production. If the production of the average daily means of subsistence of the labourer takes up 6 hours, he must work, on the average, 6 hours every day, to produce his daily labour-power, or to reproduce the value received as the result of its sale. The necessary part of his working-day amounts to 6 hours, and is, therefore, caeteris paribus, a given quantity. But with this, the extent of the working-day itself is not yet given.

Let us assume that the line A—-B represents the length of the necessary working-time, say 6 hours. If the labour be prolonged 1, 3, or 6 hours beyond A B, we have 3 other lines:

Working day I	Working day II	Working day III
A -- -- -->B -->C	A -- -- -->B -- -- >C	A -- -->B -- -- -->C

representing 3 different working-days of 7, 9, and 12 hours. The extension B C of the line A—-B represents the length of the surplus-labour. As the working-day is A B+B C or A C, it varies with the variable quantity B C. Since A B is constant, the ratio of B C to A B can always be calculated. In working-day I, it is 1/6, in working-day II, 3/6, in working day III 6/6 of A B. Since further the ratio surplus working-time/necessary working-time, determines the rate of the surplus-value, the latter is given by the ratio of B C to A B. It amounts in the 3 different working-days respectively to 16 2/3, 50 and 100 per cent. On the other hand, the rate of surplus-value alone would not give us the extent of the working-day. If this rate, e.g., were 100 per cent., the working-day might be of 8, 10, 12, or more hours. It would indicate that the 2 constituent parts of the working-day, necessary-labour and surplus-labour time, were equal in extent, but not how long each of these two constituent parts was.

The working-day is thus not a constant, but a variable quantity. One of its parts, certainly, is determined by the working-time required for the reproduction of the labour-power of the labourer himself. But its total amount varies with the duration of the surplus-labour. The working-day is, therefore, determinable, but is, per se, indeterminate. [1]

Although the working-day is not a fixed, but a fluent quantity, it can, on the other hand, only vary within certain limits. The minimum limit is, however, not determinable; of course, if we make the extension line B C or the surplus-labour = 0, we have a minimum limit, i.e., the part of the day which the labourer must necessarily work for his own maintenance. On the basis of capitalist production, however, this necessary labour can form a part only of the working-day; the working-day itself can never be reduced to this minimum. On the other hand, the working-day has a maximum limit. It cannot be prolonged beyond a certain point. This maximum limit is conditioned by two things. First, by the physical bounds of labour-power. Within the 24 hours of the natural day a man can expend only a definite quantity of his vital force. A horse, in like manner, can only work from day to day, 8 hours. During part of the day this force must rest, sleep; during another part the man has to satisfy other physical needs, to feed, wash, and clothe himself. Besides these purely physical limitations, the extension of the working-day encounters moral ones. The labourer needs time for satisfying his intellectual and social wants, the extent and number of which are conditioned by the general state of social advancement. The variation of the working-day fluctuates, therefore, within physical and social bounds. But both these limiting conditions are of a very elastic nature, and allow the greatest latitude. So we find working-days of 8, 10, 12, 14, 16, 18 hours, i.e., of the most different lengths.

The capitalist has bought the labour-power at its day-rate. To him its use-value belongs during one working-day. He has thus acquired the right to make the labourer work for him during one day. But, what is a working-day? [2]

pAt all events, less than a natural day. By how much? The capitalist has his own views of this ultima Thule, the necessary limit of the working-day. As capitalist, he is only capital personified. His soul is the soul of capital. But capital has one single life impulse, the tendency to create value and surplus-value, to make its constant factor, the means of production, absorb the greatest possible amount of surplus-labour. [3]

Capital is dead labour, that, vampire-like, only lives by sucking living labour, and lives the more, the more labour it sucks. The time during which the labourer works, is the time during which the capitalist consumes the labour-power he has purchased of him. [4]

If the labourer consumes his disposable time for himself, he robs the capitalist. [5]

The capitalist then takes his stand on the law of the exchange of commodities. He, like all other buyers, seeks to get the greatest possible benefit out of the use-value of his commodity. Suddenly the voice of the labourer, which had been stifled in the storm and stress of the process of production, rises:

The commodity that I have sold to you differs from the crowd of other commodities, in that its use creates value, and a value greater than its own. That is why you bought it. That which on your side appears a spontaneous expansion of capital, is on mine extra expenditure of labour-power. You and I know on the market only one law, that of the exchange of commodities. And the consumption of the commodity belongs not to the seller who parts with it, but to the buyer, who acquires it. To you, therefore, belongs the use of my daily labour-power. But by means of the price that you pay for it each day, I must be able to reproduce it daily, and to sell it again. Apart from natural exhaustion through age, &c., I must be able on the morrow to work with the same normal amount of force, health and freshness as to-day. You preach to me constantly the gospel of "saving" and "abstinence." Good! I will, like a sensible saving owner, husband my sole wealth, labour-power, and abstain from all foolish waste of it. I will each day spend, set in motion, put into action only as much of it as is compatible with pits normal duration, and healthy development. By an unlimited extension of the working-day, you may in one day use up a quantity of labour-power greater than I can restore in three. What you gain in labour I lose in substance. The use of my labour-power and the spoliation of it are quite different things. If the average time that (doing a reasonable amount of work) an average labourer can live, is 30 years, the value of my labour-power, which you pay me from day to day is $1 / 365 \times 30$ or $1 / 10950$ of its total value. But if you consume it in 10 years, you pay me daily $1 / 10950$ instead of $1 / 3650$ of its total value, i.e., only 1/3 of its daily value, and you rob me, therefore, every day of 2/3 of the value of my commodity. You pay me for one day's labour-power, whilst you use that of 3 days. That is against our contract and the law of exchanges. I demand, therefore, a working-day of normal length, and I demand it without any appeal to your heart, for in money matters sentiment is out of place. You may be a model citizen, perhaps a member of the Society for the Prevention of Cruelty to Animals, and in the odour of sanctity to boot; but the thing that you represent face to face with me has no heart in its breast. That which seems to throb there is my own heart-beating. I demand the normal working-day because I, like every other seller, demand the value of my commodity. [6]

We see then, that, apart from extremely elastic bounds, the nature of the exchange of commodities itself imposes no limit to the working-day, no limit to surplus-labour. The capitalist maintains his rights as a purchaser when he tries to make the working-day as long as possible, and to make, whenever possible, two working-days out of one. On the other hand, the peculiar nature of the commodity sold implies a limit to its consumption by the purchaser, and the labourer maintains his right as seller when he wishes to reduce the working-day to one of definite normal duration. There is here, therefore, an antinomy, right against right, both equally bearing the seal of the law of exchanges. Between equal rights force decides. Hence is it that in the history of capitalist production, the determination of what is a working-day, presents itself as the result of a struggle, a struggle between collective capital, i.e., the class of capitalists, and collective labour, i.e., the working-class.

Section 2: The Greed for Surplus-Labour. Manufacturer and Boyard

Capital has not invented surplus-labour. Wherever a part of society possesses the monopoly of the means of production, the labourer, free or not free, must add to the working-time necessary for his own maintenance an extra working-time in order to produce the means of subsistence for the owners of the means of production, 7 whether this proprietor be the Athenian xxxxx xxxxxxx, Etruscan theocrat, civis Romanus, Norman baron, American slave-owner, Wallachian Boyard, modern landlord or capitalist. 8 It is, however, clear that in any given economic formation of society, where not the exchange-value but the use-value of the product predominates, surplus-labour will be limited by a given set of wants which may be greater or less, and that here no boundless thirst for surplus-labour arises from the nature of the production itself. Hence in antiquity over-work becomes horrible only when the object is to obtain exchange-value in its specific independent money-form; in the production of gold and silver. Compulsory working to death is here the recognised form of over-work. Only read Diodorus Siculus. 9 Still these are exceptions in antiquity. But as soon as people, whose production still moves within the lower forms of slave-labour, corvée-labour, &c., are drawn into the whirlpool of an international market dominated by the capitalistic mode of production, the sale of their products for export becoming their principal interest, the civilised horrors of over-work are grafted on the barbaric horrors of slavery, serfdom, &c. Hence the negro labour in the Southern States of the American Union preserved something of a patriarchal character, so long as production was chiefly directed to immediate local consumption. But in proportion, as the export of cotton became of vital interest to these states, the over-working of the negro and sometimes the using up of his life in 7 years of labour became a factor in a calculated and calculating system. It was no longer a question of obtaining from him a certain quantity of useful products. It was now a question of production pof surplus-labour itself: So was it also with the corvée, e.g., in the Danubian Principalities (now Roumania).

The comparison of the greed for surplus-labour in the Danubian Principalities with the same greed in English factories has a special interest, because surplus-labour in the corvée has an independent and palpable form.

Suppose the working-day consists of 6 hours of necessary labour, and 6 hours of surplus-labour. Then the free labourer gives the capitalist every week 6 x 6 or 36 hours of surplus-labour. It is the same as if he worked 3 days in the week for himself, and 3 days in the week gratis for the capitalist. But this is not evident on the surface. Surplus-labour and necessary labour glide one into the other. I can, therefore, express the same relationship by saying, e.g., that the labourer in every minute works 30 seconds for himself, and 30 for the capitalist, etc. It is otherwise with the corvée. The necessary labour which the Wallachian peasant does for his own maintenance is distinctly marked off from his surplus-labour on behalf of the Boyard. The one he does on his own field, the other on the seignorial estate. Both parts of the labour-time exist, therefore, independently, side by side one with the other. In the corvée the surplus-labour is accurately marked off from the necessary labour. This, however, can make no difference with regard to the quantitative relation of surplus-labour to necessary labour. Three days' surplus-labour in the week remain three days that yield no equivalent to the labourer himself, whether it be called corvée or wage-labour. But in the capitalist the greed for surplus-labour appears in the straining after an unlimited extension of the working-day, in the Boyard more simply in a direct hunting after days of corvée. 10

In the Danubian Principalities the corvée was mixed up with rents in kind and other appurtenances of bondage, but it formed the most important tribute paid to the ruling class. Where this was the case, the corvée rarely arose from serfdom; serfdom much more frequently on the other hand took origin from the corvée. 11 This is what took place pin the Roumanian provinces. Their original mode of production was based on community of the soil, but not in the Slavonic or Indian form. Part of the land was cultivated in severalty as freehold by the members of the community, another part — ager publicus — was cultivated by them in common. The products of this common labour served partly as a reserve fund against bad harvests and other accidents, partly as a public store for providing the costs of war, religion, and other common expenses. In course of time military and clerical dignitaries usurped, along with the common land, the labour spent upon it. The labour of the free peasants on their common land was transformed into corvée for the thieves of the common land. This corvée soon developed into a servile relationship existing in point of fact, not in point of law, until Russia, the liberator of the world, made it legal under presence of abolishing serfdom. The code of the corvée, which the Russian General Kisseleff proclaimed in 1831, was of course dictated by the Boyards themselves. Thus Russia conquered with one blow the magnates of the Danubian provinces, and the applause of liberal cretins throughout Europe.

According to the "Réglement organique," as this code of the corvée is called, every Wallachian peasant owes to the so-called landlord, besides a mass of detailed payments in kind: (1), 12 days of general labour; (2), one day of field labour; (3), one day of wood carrying. In all, 14 days in the year. With deep insight into Political Economy, however, the working-day is not taken in its ordinary sense, but as the working-day necessary to the production of an average daily product; and that average daily product is determined in so crafty a way that no Cyclops would be done with it in 24 hours. In dry words, the Réglement itself declares with true Russian irony that by 12 working-days one must understand the product of the manual labour of 36 days, by 1 day of field labour 3 days, and by 1 day of wood carrying in like manner three times as much. In all, 42 corvée days. To this had to be added the so-called jobagie, service due to the lord for extraordinary occasions. In proportion to the size of its population, every village has to furnish annually a definite contingent to the jobagie. This additional corvée is estimated at 14 days for each Wallachian peasant. Thus the prescribed corvée amounts to 56 working-days yearly. But the agricultural year in Wallachia numbers in consequence of the severe climate only 210 days, of which 40 for Sundays and holidays, 30 on an average for bad weather, together 70 days, do not count. 140 working-days remain. The ratio of the corvée to the necessary labour 56/84 or 66 2/3 % gives a much smaller rate of surplus-value than that which regulates the labour of the English agricultural or factory labourer. This is, however, only the legally prescribed corvée. And in a spirit yet more "liberal" than pthe English Factory Acts, the "Réglement organique" has known how to facilitate its own evasion. After it has made 56 days out of 12, the nominal day's work of each of the 56 corvée days is again so arranged that a portion of it must fall on the ensuing day. In one day, e.g., must be weeded an extent of land, which, for this work, especially in maize plantations, needs twice as much time. The legal day's work for some kinds of agricultural labour is interpretable in such a way that the day begins in May and ends in October. In Moldavia conditions are still harder. "The 12 corvée days of the 'Réglement organique' cried a Boyard drunk with victory, amount to 365 days in the year." [12]

If the Réglement organique of the Danubian provinces was a positive expression of the greed for surplus-labour which every paragraph legalised, the English Factory Acts are the negative expression of the same greed. These acts curb the passion of capital for a limitless draining of labour-power, by forcibly limiting the working-day by state regulations, made by a state that is ruled by capitalist-and landlord. Apart from the working-class movement that daily grew more threatening, the limiting of factory labour was dictated by the same necessity which spread guano over the English fields. The same blind eagerness for plunder that in the one case exhausted the soil, had, in the other, torn up by the roots the living force of the nation. Periodical epidemics speak on this point as clearly as the diminishing military standard in Germany and France. [13]

The Factory Act of 1850 now in force (1867) allows for the average working-day 10 hours, i.e., for the first 5 days 12 hours from 6 a.m. to 6 p.m., including 1/2 an hour for breakfast, and an hour for dinner, and thus leaving 10 1/2 working-hours, and 8 hours for Saturday, from 6 a.m. to 2 p.m., of which 1/2 an hour is subtracted for breakfast. 60 working-hours are left, 10 1/2 for each of the first 5 days, 7 1/2 for the last. [14]

Certain guardians of these laws are appointed, Factory Inspectors, directly under the Home Secretary, whose reports are published half-yearly, by order of Parliament. They give regular and official statistics of the capitalistic greed for surplus-labour.

Let us listen, for a moment, to the Factory Inspectors. [15] "The fraudulent mill-owner begins work a quarter of an hour (sometimes more, sometimes less) before 6 a.m., and leaves off a quarter of an hour (sometimes more, sometimes less) after 6 p.m. He takes 5 minutes from the beginning and from the end of the half hour nominally allowed for breakfast, and 10 minutes at the beginning and end of the hour nominally allowed for dinner. He works for a quarter of an hour (sometimes more, sometimes less) after 2 p.m.

on Saturday. Thus his gain is —

```
Before 6 a.m., .................. 15 minutes.
   After 6 p.m., .................... 15 "
At breakfast time, .............. 10 "
  At dinner time, ................. 20 "
              ——————
Five days — 300 minutes, 60 "
```

```
On Saturday before 6 a.m., ...... 15 minutes.
      At breakfast time, .............. 10 "
         After 2 p.m., ................... 15 "
                   ——————
                  40 minutes.
```

Total weekly, ... 340 minutes.

pOr 5 hours and 40 minutes weekly, which multiplied by 50 working weeks in the year (allowing two for holidays and occasional stoppages) is equal to 27 working-days." [16]

"Five minutes a day's increased work, multiplied by weeks, are equal to two and a half days of produce in the year." [17]

"An additional hour a day gained by small instalments before 6 a.m., after 6 p.m., and at the beginning and end of the times nominally fixed for meals, is nearly equivalent to working 13 months in the year." [18]

Crises during which production is interrupted and the factories work "short time," i.e., for only a part of the week, naturally do not affect the tendency to extend the working-day. The less business there is, the more profit has to be made on the business done. The less time spent in work, the more of that time has to be turned into surplus labour-time.

Thus the Factory Inspector's report on the period of the crisis from 1857 to 1858:

"It may seem inconsistent that there should be any overworking at a time when trade is so bad; but that very badness leads to the transgression by unscrupulous men, they get the extra profit of it. ... In the last half year, says Leonard Homer, 122 mills in my district have been given up; 143 were found standing," yet, over-work is continued beyond the legal hours. [19]

"For a great part of the time," says Mr. Howell, "owing to the depression of trade, many factories were altogether closed, and a still greater number were working short time. I continue, however, to receive about the usual number of complaints that half, or three-quarters of an hour in the day, are snatched from the workers by encroaching upon the times professedly allowed for rest and refreshment." [20] The same phenomenon was reproduced on a smaller scale during the frightful cotton-crises from 1861 to 1865. [21] "It is sometimes advanced by way of excuse, when persons are found at work in a factory, either at a meal hour, or at some illegal time, that they will not leave the mill at the appointed hour, and that compulsion is necessary to force them to cease work [cleaning their machinery, &c.], especially on pSaturday afternoons. But, if the hands remain in a factory after the machinery has ceased to revolve ... they would not have been so employed if sufficient time had been set apart specially for cleaning, &c., either before 6 a.m. [sic.!] or before 2 p.m. on Saturday afternoons." [22]

"The profit to be gained by it (over-working in violation of the Act) appears to be, to many, a greater temptation than they can resist; they calculate upon the chance of not being found out; and when they see the small amount of penalty and costs, which those who have been convicted have had to pay, they find that if they should be detected there will still be a considerable balance of gain.... [23] In cases where the additional time is gained by a multiplication of small thefts in the course of the day, there are insuperable difficulties to the inspectors making out a case." [24]

These "small thefts" of capital from the labourer's meal and recreation time, the factory inspectors also designate as "petty pilferings of minutes," [25] "snatching a few minutes," [26] or, as the labourers technically called them, "nibbling and cribbling at meal-times." [27]

It is evident that in this atmosphere the formation of surplus-value by surplus-labour, is no secret. "If you allow me," said a highly respectable master to me, "to work only ten minutes in the day over-time, you put one thousand a year in my pocket." [28] "Moments are the elements of profit." [29]

Nothing is from this point of view more characteristic than the designation of the workers who work full time as "full-timers," and the children under 13 who are only allowed to work 6 hours as "half-timers." The worker is here nothing more than personified labour-time. All individual distinctions are merged in those of "full-timers" and "half-timers " [30]

Section 3
Branches of English Industry Without Legal Limits to Exploitation

We have hitherto considered the tendency to the extension of the working-day, the were-wolf's hunger for surplus-labour in a department where the monstrous exactions, not surpassed, says an English bourgeois economist, by the cruelties of the Spaniards to the American red-skins, [31] caused capital at last to be bound by the chains of legal regulations. Now, let us cast a glance at certain branches of production in which the exploitation of labour is either free from fetters to this day, or was so yesterday.

Mr. Broughton Charlton, county magistrate, declared, as chairman of a meeting held at the Assembly Rooms, Nottingham, on the 14th January, 1860, "that there was an amount of privation and suffering among that portion of the population connected with the lace trade, unknown in other parts of the kingdom, indeed, in the civilised world .... Children of nine or ten years are dragged from their squalid beds at two, three, or four o'clock in the morning and compelled to work for a bare subsistence until ten, eleven, or twelve at night, their limbs wearing away, their frames dwindling, their faces whitening, and their humanity absolutely sinking into a stone-like torpor, utterly horrible to contemplate.... We are not surprised that Mr. allett, or any other manufacturer, should stand forward and protest against discussion.... The system, as the Rev. Montagu Valpy describes it, is one of unmiti pgated slavery, socially, physically, morally, and spiritually.... What can be thought of a town which holds a public meeting to petition that the period of labour for men shall be diminished to eighteen hours a day? .... We declaim against the Virginian and Carolinian cotton-planters. Is their black-market, their lash, and their barter of human flesh more detestable than this slow sacrifice of humanity which takes place in order that veils and collars may be fabricated for the benefit of capitalists?" [32]

The potteries of Staffordshire have, during the last 22 years, been the subject of three parliamentary inquiries. The result is embodied in Mr. Scriven's Report of 1841 to the "Children's Employment Commissioners," in the report of Dr. Greenhow of 1860 published by order of the medical officer of the Privy Council (Public Health, 3rd Report, 112-113), lastly, in the report of Mr. Longe of 1862 in the "First Report of the Children's Employment Commission, of the 13th June, 1863." For my purpose it is enough to take, from the reports of 1860 and 1863, some depositions of the exploited children themselves. From the children we may form an opinion as to the adults, especially the girls and women, and that in a branch of industry by the side of which cotton-spinning appears an agreeable and healthful occupation. [33]

William Wood, 9 years old, was 7 years and 10 months when he began to work. He "ran moulds" (carried ready-moulded articles into the drying-room, afterwards bringing back the empty mould) from the beginning. He came to work every day in the week at 6 a.m., and left off about 9 p.m. "I work till 9 o'clock at night six days in the week. I have done so seven or eight weeks." Fifteen hours of labour for a child 7 years old! J. Murray, 12 years of age, says: "I turn jigger, and run moulds. I come at 6. Sometimes I come at 4. I worked all night last night, till 6 o'clock this morning. I have not been in bed since the night before last. There were eight or nine other boys working last night. All but one have come this morning. I get 3 shillings and sixpence. I do not get any more for working at night. I worked two nights last week." Fernyhough, a boy of ten: "I have not always an hour (for dinner). I have only half an hour sometimes; on Thursday, Friday, and Saturday. [34]

Dr. Greenhow states that the average duration of life in the pottery districts of Stoke-on-Trent, and Wolstanton is extraordinarily short. Although in the district of Stoke, only 36.6% and in Wolstanton only p30.4% of the adult male population above 20 are employed in the potteries, among the men of that age in the first district more than half, in the second, nearly 2/5 of the whole deaths are the result of pulmonary diseases among the potters. Dr. Boothroyd, a medical practitioner at Hanley, says: "Each successive generation of potters is more dwarfed and less robust than the preceding one." In like manner another doctor, Mr. M'Bean: "Since he began to practice among the potters 25 years ago, he had observed a marked degeneration especially shown in diminution of stature and breadth." These statements are taken from the report of Dr. Greenhow in 1860. [35]

From the report of the Commissioners in 1863, the following: Dr. J. T. Arledge, senior physician of the North Staffordshire Infirmary, says: "The potters as a class, both men and women, represent a degenerated population, both physically and morally. They are, as a rule, stunted in growth, ill-shaped, and frequently ill-formed in the chest; they become prematurely old, and are certainly short-lived; they are phlegmatic and bloodless, and exhibit their debility of constitution by obstinate attacks of dyspepsia, and disorders of the liver and kidneys, and by rheumatism. But of all diseases they are especially prone to chest-disease, to pneumonia, phthisis, bronchitis, and asthma. One form would appear peculiar to them, and is known as potter's asthma, or potter's consumption. Scrofula attacking the glands, or bones, or other parts of the body, is a disease of two-thirds or more of the potters .... That the 'degenerescence' of the population of this district is not even greater than it is, is due to the constant recruiting from the adjacent country, and intermarriages with more healthy races." [36]

Mr. Charles Parsons, late house surgeon of the same institution, writes in a letter to Commissioner Longe, amongst other things: "I can only speak from personal observation and not from statistical data, but I do not hesitate to assert that my indignation has been aroused again and again at the sight of poor children whose health has been sacrificed to gratify the avarice of either parents or employers." He enumerates the causes of the diseases of the potters, and sums them up in the phrase, "long hours." The report of the Commission trusts that "a manufacture which has assumed so prominent a place in the whole world, will not long be subject to the remark that its great success is accompanied with the physical deterioration, widespread bodily suffering, and early death of the workpeople ... by whose labour and pskill such great results have been achieved." [37] And all that holds of the potteries in England is true of those in Scotland. [38]

The manufacture of lucifer matches dates from 1833, from the discovery of the method of applying phosphorus to the match itself. Since 1845 this manufacture has rapidly developed in England, and has extended especially amongst the thickly populated parts of London as well as in Manchester, Birmingham, Liverpool, Bristol, Norwich, Newcastle and Glasgow. With it has spread the form of lockjaw, which a Vienna physician in 1845 discovered to be a disease peculiar to lucifer-matchmakers. Half the workers are children under thirteen, and young persons under eighteen. The manufacture is on account of its unhealthiness and unpleasantness in such bad odour that only the most miserable part of the labouring class, half-starved widows and so forth, deliver up their children to it, "the ragged, half-starved, untaught children." [39]

Of the witnesses that Commissioner White examined (1863), 270 were under 18, 50 under 10, 10 only 8, and 5 only 6 years old. A range of the working-day from 12 to 14 or 15 hours, night-labour, irregular meal-times, meals for the most part taken in the very workrooms that are pestilent with phosphorus. Dante would have found the worst horrors of his Inferno surpassed in this manufacture.

In the manufacture of paper-hangings the coarser sorts are printed by machine; the finer by hand (block-printing). The most active business months are from the beginning of October to the end of April. During this time the work goes on fast and furious without intermission from 6 a.m. to 10 p.m. or further into the night.

J. Leach deposes: "Last winter six out of nineteen girls were away from ill-health at one time from over-work. I have to bawl at them to keep them awake." W. Duffy: "I have seen when the children could none of them keep their eyes open for the work; indeed, none of us could." J. Lightbourne: "Am 13 We worked last winter till 9 (evening), and the winter before till 10. I used to cry with sore feet every night last winter." G. Apsden: "That boy of mine when he was 7 years old I used to carry him on my back to and fro through the snow, and he used to have 16 hours a day ... I have often knelt down to feed him as he stood by the machine, for he could not leave it or stop." Smith, the managing partner of a Manchester factory: "We (he means his "hands" who work for "us") work on with no stoppage for meals, so that day's work of 10 1/2 hours is finished by 4.30 p.m., and all pafter that is over-time." [40] (Does this Mr. Smith take no meals himself during 10 1/2 hours?) "We (this same Smith) seldom leave off working before 6 p.m. (he means leave off the consumption of "our" labour-power machines), so that we (iterum Crispinus) are really working over-time the whole year round For all these, children and adults alike (152 children and young persons and 140 adults), the average work for the last 18 months has been at the very least 7 days, 5 hours, or 78 1/2 hours a week. For the six weeks ending May 2nd this year (1862), the average was higher — 8 days or 84 hours a week." Still this same Mr. Smith, who is so extremely devoted to the pluralis majestatis, adds with a smile, "Machine-work is not great." So the employers in the block-printing say: "Hand labour is more healthy than machine work." On the whole, manufacturers declare with indignation against the proposal "to stop the machines at least during meal-times." A clause, says Mr. Otley, manager of a wall-paper factory in the Borough, "which allowed work between, say 6 a.m. and 9 p. in would suit us (!) very well, but the factory hours, 6 a.m. to 6 p.m., are not suitable. Our machine is always stopped for dinner. (What generosity!) There is no waste of paper and colour to speak of. But," he adds sympathetically, "I can understand the loss of time not being liked." The report of the Commission opines with naïvete that the fear of some "leading firms" of losing time, i.e., the time for appropriating the labour of others, and thence losing profit is not a sufficient reason for allowing children under 13, and young persons under 18, working 12 to 16 hours per day, to lose their dinner, nor for giving it to them as coal and water are supplied to the steam-engine, soap to wool, oil to the wheel — as merely auxiliary material to the instruments of labour, during the process of production itself. [41]

No branch of industry in England (we do not take into account the making of bread by machinery recently introduced) has preserved up to the present day a method of production so archaic, so — as we see from the poets of the Roman Empire — pre-christian, as baking. But capital, as was said earlier, is at first indifferent as to the ptechnical character of the labour-process; it begins by taking it just as it finds it.

The incredible adulteration of bread, especially in London, was first revealed by the House of Commons Committee "on the adulteration of articles of food" (1855-56), and Dr. Hassall's work, "Adulterations detected." [42] The consequence of these revelations was the Act of August 6th, 1860, "for preventing the adulteration of articles of food and drink," an inoperative law, as it naturally shows the tenderest consideration for every Free-trader who determines by the buying or selling of adulterated commodities "to turn an honest penny." [43] The Committee itself formulated more or less naïvely its conviction that Free-trade meant essentially trade with adulterated, or as the English ingeniously put it, "sophisticated" goods. In fact this kind of sophistry knows better than Protagoras how to make white black, and black white, and better than the Eleatics how to demonstrate ad oculos that everything is only appearance. [44]

At all events the Committee had directed the attention of the public to its "daily bread," and therefore to the baking trade. At the same time in public meetings and in petitions to Parliament rose the cry of the London journeymen bakers against their over-work, &c. The cry was so urgent that Mr. H. S. Tremenheere, also a member of the Commission of 1863 several times mentioned, was appointed Royal Commissioner of Inquiry. His report. [45] together with the evidence given, roused capitalist, or landlord, or sinecurist, is commanded to eat his bread in the sweat of his brow, but they did not know that he had to peat daily in his bread a certain quantity of human perspiration mixed with the discharge of abscesses, cobwebs, dead black-beetles, and putrid German yeast, without counting alum, sand, and other agreeable mineral ingredients. Without any regard to his holiness, Free-trade, the free baking-trade was therefore placed under the supervision of the State inspectors (Close of the Parliamentary session of 1863), and by the same Act of Parliament, work from 9 in the evening to 5 in the morning was forbidden for journeymen bakers under 18. The last clause speaks volumes as to the over-work in this old-fashioned, homely line of business.

"The work of a London journeyman baker begins, as a rule, at about eleven at night. At that hour he 'makes the dough,' — a laborious process, which lasts from half an hour to three quarters of an hour, according to the size of the batch or the labour bestowed upon it. He then lies down upon the kneading-board, which is also the covering of the trough in which the dough is 'made'; and with a sack under him, and another rolled up as a pillow, he sleeps for about a couple of hours. He is then engaged in a rapid and continuous labour for about five hours — throwing out the dough, 'scaling it off,' moulding it, putting it into the oven, preparing and baking rolls and fancy bread, taking the batch bread out of the oven, and up into the shop, &c., &c. The temperature of a bakehouse ranges from about 75 to upwards of 90 degrees, and in the smaller bakehouses approximates usually to the higher rather than to the lower degree of heat. When the business of making the bread, rolls, &c., is over, that of its distribution begins, and a considerable proportion of the journeymen in the trade, after working hard in the manner described during the night, are upon their legs for many hours during the day, carrying baskets, or wheeling hand-carts, and sometimes again in the bakehouse, leaving off work at various hours between 1 and 6 p.m. according to the season of the year, or the amount and nature of their master's business; while others are again engaged in the bakehouse in 'bringing out' more batches until late in the afternoon. [46] ... During what is called 'the London season,'the operatives belonging to the 'full-priced' bakers at the West End of the town, generally begin work at 11 p.m., and are engaged in making the bread, with one or two short (sometimes very short) intervals of rest, up to 8 o'clock the next morning. They are then engaged all day long, up to 4, 5, 6, and as late as 7 o'clock in the evening carrying out bread, or sometimes in the afternoon in the bakehouse again, assisting in the biscuit-baking. They may have, after they have done their work, sometimes five or six, sometimes only four or five hours' sleep before they begin again. On Fridays they always pbegin sooner, some about ten o'clock, and continue in some cases, at work, either in making or delivering the bread up to 8 p.m. on Saturday night, but more generally up to 4 or 5 o'clock, Sunday morning. On Sundays the men must attend twice or three times during the day for an hour or two to make preparations for the next day's bread.... The men employed by the underselling masters (who sell their bread under the 'full price,' and who, as already pointed out, comprise three-fourths of the London bakers) have not only to work on the average longer hours, but their work is almost entirely confined to the bakehouse. The underselling masters generally sell their bread... in the shop. If they send it out, which is not common, except as supplying chandlers' shops, they usually employ other hands for that purpose. It is not their practice to deliver bread from house to house. Towards the end of the week ... the men begin on Thursday night at 10 o'clock, and continue on with only slight intermission until late on Saturday evening." [47]

Even the bourgeois intellect understands the position of the "underselling" masters. "The unpaid labour of the men was made the source whereby the competition was carried on." [48] And the "full-priced" baker denounces his underselling competitors to the Commission of Inquiry as thieves of foreign labour and adulterators. "They only exist now by first defrauding the public, and next getting 18 hours' work out of their men for 12 hours' wages." [49]

The adulteration of bread and the formation of a class of bakers that sells the bread below the full price, date from the beginning of the 18th century, from the time when the corporate character of the trade was lost, and the capitalist in the form of the miller or flour-factor, rises behind the nominal master baker [50] Thus was laid the foundation of capitalistic production in this trade, of the unlimited extension of the working-day and of night-labour, although the latter only since 1824 gained a serious footing, even in London. [51]

After what has just been said, it will be understood that the Report of the Commission classes journeymen bakers among the short-lived plabourers, who, having by good luck escaped the normal decimation of the children of the working-class, rarely reach the age of 42. Nevertheless, the baking trade is always overwhelmed with applicants. The sources of the supply of these labour-powers to London are Scotland, the western agricultural districts of England, and Germany.

In the years 1858-60, the journeymen bakers in Ireland organised at their own expense great meetings to agitate against night and Sunday work. The public — e.g., at the Dublin meeting in May, 1860 — took their part with Irish warmth. As a result of this movement, day-labour alone was successfully established in Wexford, Kilkenny, Clonmel, Waterford, &c. "In Limerick, where the grievances of the journeymen are demonstrated to be excessive, the movement has been defeated by the opposition of the master bakers, the miller bakers being the greatest opponents. The example of Limerick led to a retrogression in Ennis and Tipperary. In Cork, where the strongest possible demonstration of feeling took place, the masters, by exercising their power of turning the men out of employment, have defeated the movement. In Dublin, the master bakers have offered the most determined opposition to the movement, and by discountenancing as much as possible the journeymen promoting it, have succeeded in leading the men into acquiescence in Sunday work and night-work, contrary to the convictions of the men." [52]

The Committee of the English Government, which Government, in Ireland, is armed to the teeth, and generally knows how to show it, remonstrates in mild, though funereal, tones with the implacable master bakers of Dublin, Limerick, Cork, &c.: "The Committee believe that the hours of labour are limited by natural laws, which cannot be violated with impunity. That for master bakers to induce their workmen, by the fear of losing employment, to violate their religious convictions and their better feelings, to disobey the laws of the land, and to disregard public opinion (this all refers to Sunday labour), is calculated to provoke ill-feeling between workmen and masters, ... and affords an example dangerous to religion, morality, and social order.... The Committee believe that any constant work beyond 12 hours a-day encroaches on the domestic and private life of the working-man, and so leads to disastrous moral results, interfering with each man's home, and the discharge of his family duties as a son, a brother, a husband, a father. That work beyond 12 hours has a tendency to undermine the health of the workingman, and so leads to premature old age and death, to the great injury of families of working-men, thus deprived of the care and support of the head of the family when most required." [53]

pSo far, we have dealt with Ireland. On the other side of the channel, in Scotland, the agricultural labourer, the ploughman, protests against his 13-14 hours' work in the most inclement climate, with 4 hours' additional work on Sunday (in this land of Sabbatarians!), [54] whilst, at the same time, three railway men are standing before a London coroner's jury — a guard, an engine-driver, a signalman. A tremendous railway accident has hurried hundreds of passengers into another world. The negligence of the employee is the cause of the misfortune. They declare with one voice before the jury that ten or twelve years before, their labour only lasted eight hours a-day. During the last five or six years it had been screwed up to 14, 18, and 20 hours, and under a specially severe pressure of holiday-makers, at times of excursion trains, it often lasted for 40 or 50 hours without a break. They were ordinary men, not Cyclops. At a certain point their labour-power failed. Torpor seized them. Their brain ceased to think, their eyes to see. The thoroughly "respectable" British jurymen answered by a verdict that sent them to the next assizes on a charge of manslaughter, and, in a gentle "rider" to their verdict, expressed the pious hope that the capitalistic magnates of the railways would, in future, be more extravagant in the purchase of a sufficient quantity of labour-power, and more "abstemious", more "self-denying," more "thrifty," in the draining of paid labour-power. [55]

From the motley crowd of labourers of all callings, ages, sexes, that press on us more busily than the souls of the slain on Ulysses, on whom — without referring to the Blue books under their arms — we see at a glance the mark of over-work, let us take two more figures whose striking contrast proves that before capital all men are alike — a milliner and a blacksmith.

In the last week of June, 1863, all the London daily papers published a paragraph with the "sensational" heading, "Death from simple over-work." It dealt with the death of the milliner, Mary Anne Walkley, 20 years of age, employed in a highly-respectable dressmaking establishment, exploited by a lady with the pleasant name of Elise. The old, often-told story, [56] was once more recounted. This girl worked, on an average, 16 1/2 hours, during the season often 30 hours, without a break, whilst her failing labour-power was revived by occasional supplies of sherry, port, or coffee. It was just now the height of the season. It was necessary to conjure up in the twinkling of an eye the gorgeous dresses for the noble ladies bidden to the ball in honour of the newly-imported Princess of Wales. Mary Anne Walkley had worked without intermission for 26 1/2 hours, with 60 other girls, 30 in one room, that only afforded 3 of the cubic feet of air required for them. At night, they slept in pairs in one of the stifling holes into which the bedroom was divided by partitions of board. [57] And this was one of the best mil plinery establishments in London. Mary Anne Walkley fell ill on the Friday, died on Sunday, without, to the astonishment of Madame Elise, having previously completed the work in hand. The doctor, r. Keys, called too late to the death-bed, duly bore witness before the coroner's jury that "Mary Anne Walkley had died from long hours of work in an over-crowded work-room, and a too small and badly ventilated bedroom." In order to give the doctor a lesson in good manners, the coroner's jury thereupon brought in a verdict that "the deceased had died of apoplexy, but there was reason to fear that her death had been accelerated by over-work in an over-crowded workroom, &c." "Our white slaves," cried the Morning Star, the organ of the Free-traders, Cobden and Bright, "our white slaves, who are toiled into the grave, for the most part silently pine and die." [58]

"It is not in dressmakers' rooms that working to death is the order of the day, but in a thousand other places; in every place I had almost said, where 'a thriving business' has to be done.... We will take the blacksmith as a type. If the poets were true, there is no man so hearty, so merry, as the blacksmith; he rises early and strikes his sparks before the sun; he eats and drinks and sleeps as no other man. Working in moderation, he is, in fact, in one of the best of human positions, physically speaking. But we follow him into the city or town, and we see the stress of work on that strong man, and what then is his position in the death-rate of his country. In Marylebone, blacksmiths die at the rate of 31 per thousand per annum, or 11 above the mean of the male adults pof the country in its entirety. The occupation, instinctive almost as a portion of human art, unobjectionable as a branch of human industry, is made by mere excess of work, the destroyer of the man. He can strike so many blows per day, walk so many steps, breathe so many breaths, produce so much work, and live an average, say of fifty years; he is made to strike so many more blows, to walk so many more steps, to breathe so many more breaths per day, and to increase altogether a fourth of his life. He meets the effort; the result is, that producing for a limited time a fourth more work, he dies at 37 for 50." [59]

Section 4
Day and Night Work. The Relay System.

Constant capital, the means of production, considered from the standpoint of the creation of surplus-value, only exist to absorb labour, and with every drop of labour a proportional quantity of surplus-labour. While they fail to do this, their mere existence causes a relative loss to the capitalist, for they represent during the time they lie fallow, a useless advance of capital. And this loss becomes positive and absolute as soon as the intermission of their employment necessitates additional outlay at the recommencement of work. The prolongation of the working-day beyond the limits of the natural day, into the night, only acts as a palliative. It quenches only in a slight degree the vampire thirst for the living blood of labour. To appropriate labour during all the 24 hours of the day is, therefore, the inherent tendency of capitalist production. But as it is physically impossible to exploit the same individual labour-power constantly during the night as well as the day, to overcome this physical hindrance, an alternation becomes necessary between the workpeople whose powers are exhausted by day, and those who are used up by night. This alternation may be effected in various ways; e.g., it may be so arranged that part of the workers are one week employed on day-work, the next week on night-work. It is well known that this relay system, this alternation of two sets of workers, held full sway in the full-blooded youth-time of the English cotton manufacture, and that at the present time it still flourishes, among others, in the cotton spinning of the Moscow district. This 24 hours' process of production exists to-day as a system in many of the branches of industry of Great Britain that are still "free," in the blast-furnaces, forges, plate-rolling mills, and other metallurgical establishments in England, Wales, and Scotland. The working-time here includes, besides the 24 hours of the 6 working-days, a great part also of the 24 hours of Sunday. The workers consist of men and women, adults and children pof both sexes. The ages of the children and young persons run through all intermediate grades, from 8 (in some cases from 6) to 18. [60]

In some branches of industry, the girls and women work through the night together with the males. [61]

Placing on one side the generally injurious influence of night-labour, [62] the duration of the process of production, unbroken during the 24 hours, offers very welcome opportunities of exceeding the limits of the normal working-day, e.g., in the branches of industry already mentioned, which are of an exceedingly fatiguing nature; the official working-day means for each worker usually 12 hours by night or day. But the over-work beyond this amount is in many cases, to use the words of the English official report, "truly fearful." [63]

"It is impossible," the report continues, "for any mind to realise the amount of work described in the following passages as being performed by boys of from 9 to 12 years of age ... without coming irresistibly to the conclusion that such abuses of the power of parents and of employers can no longer be allowed to exist." [64]

p"The practice of boys working at all by day and night turns either in the usual course of things, or at pressing times, seems inevitably to open the door to their not unfrequently working unduly long hours. These hours are, indeed, in some cases, not only cruelly but even incredibly long for children. Amongst a number of boys it will, of course, not unfrequently happen that one or more are from some cause absent. When this happens, their place is made up by one or more boys, who work in the other turn. That this is a well understood system is plain ... from the answer of the manager of some large rolling-mills, who, when I asked him how the place of the boys absent from their turn was made up, 'I daresay, sir, you know that as well as I do,' and admitted the fact." [65]

"At a rolling-mill where the proper hours were from 6 a.m. to 5 1/2 p.m., a boy worked about four nights every week till 8 1/2 p.m. at least ... and this for six months. Another, at 9 years old, sometimes made three 12-hour shifts running, and, when 10, has made two days and two nights running." A third, "now 10 ... worked from 6 a.m. till 12 p.m. three nights, and till 9 p.m. the other nights." "Another, now 13, ... worked from 6 p.m. till 12 noon next day, for a week together, and sometimes for three shifts together, e.g., from Monday morning till Tuesday night." "Another, now 12, has worked in an iron foundry at Stavely from 6 a.m. till 12 p.m. for a fortnight on end; could not do it any more." "George Allinsworth, age 9, came here as cellar-boy last Friday; next morning we had to begin at 3, so I stopped here all night. Live five miles off. Slept on the floor of the furnace, over head, with an apron under me, and a bit of a jacket over me. The two other days I have been here at 6 a.m. Aye! it is hot in here. Before I came here I was nearly a year at the same work at some works in the country. Began there, too, at 3 on Saturday morning — always did, but was very gain [near] home, and could sleep at home. Other days I began at 6 in the morning, and gi'en over at 6 or 7 in the evening," &c. [66]

pLet us now hear how capital itself regards this 24 hours' system. The extreme forms of the system, its abuse in the "cruel and incredible" extension of the working-day are naturally passed over in silence. Capital only speaks of the system in its "normal" form.

Messrs. Naylor & Vickers, steel manufacturers, who employ between 600 and 700 persons, among whom only 10 per cent are under 18, and of those, only 20 boys under 18 work in night sets, thus express themselves: "The boys do not suffer from the heat. The temperature is probably from 86° to 90°.... At the forges and in the rollingmills the hands work night and day, in relays, but all the other parts of the work are day-work, i.e., from 6 a.m. to 6 p.m. In the forge the hours are from 12 to 12. Some of the hands always work in the night, without any alternation of day and night work.... We do not find any difference in the health of those who work regularly by night and those who work by day, and probably people can sleep better if they have the same period of rest than if it is changed.... About 20 of the boys under the age of 18 work in the night sets.... We could not well do without lads under 18 working by night. The objection would be the increase in the cost of production.... Skilled hands and the heads in every department are difficult to get, but of lads we could get any number.... But from the small proportion of boys that we employ, pthe subject (i.e., of restrictions on night-work) is of little importance or interest to us." [67]

Mr. J. Ellis, one of the firm of Messrs. John Brown & Co., steel and iron works, employing about 3,000 men and boys, part of whose operations, namely, iron and heavier steel work, goes on night and day by relays, states "that in the heavier steel work one or two boys are employed to a score or two men." Their concern employs upwards of 500 boys under 18, of whom about 1/3 or 170 are under the age of 13. With reference to the proposed alteration of the law, Mr. Ellis says: "I do not think it would be very objectionable to require that no person under the age of 18 should work more than 12 hours in the 24. But we do not think that any line could be drawn over the age of 12, at which boys could be dispensed with for night-work. But we would sooner be prevented from employing boys under the age of 13, or even so high as 14, at all, than not be allowed to employ boys that we do have at night. Those boys who work in the day sets must take their turn in the night sets also. because the men could not work in the night sets only; it would ruin their health.... We think, however, that night-work in alternate weeks is no harm. (Messrs. Naylor & Vickers, on the other hand, in conformity with the interest of their business, considered that periodically changed night-labour might possibly do more harm than continual night-labour.) We find the men who do it, as well as the others who do other work only by day.... Our objections to not allowing boys under 18 to work at night, would be on account of the increase of expense, but this is the only reason. (What cynical naïveté!) We think that the increase would be more than the trade, with due regard to its being successfully carried out, could fairly bear. (What mealy-mouthed phraseology!) labour is scarce here, and might fall short if there were such a regulation." (i.e., Ellis Brown & Co. might fall into the fatal perplexity of being obliged to pay labour-power its full value.) [68]

The "Cyclops Steel and Iron Works," of Messrs. Cammell & Co., are concocted on the same large scale as those of the above-mentioned John Brown & Co. The managing director had handed in his evidence to the Government Commissioner, Mr. White, in writing. Later he found it convenient to suppress the MS. when it had been returned to him for revision. Mr. White, however, has a good memory. He remembered quite clearly that for the Messrs. Cyclops the forbidding of the night-labour of children and young persons "would be impossible, it would be tantamount to stopping their works," and yet their business pemploys little more than 6% of boys under 18, and less than 1% under 13. [69]

On the same subject Mr. E. F. Sanderson, of the firm of Sanderson, Bros., & Co., steel rolling-mills and forges, Attercliffe, says: "Great difficulty would be caused by preventing boys under 18 from working at night. The chief would be the increase of cost from employing men instead of boys. I cannot say what this would be, but probably it would not be enough to enable the manufacturers to raise the price of steel, and consequently it would fall on them, as of course the men (what queer-headed folk!) would refuse to pay it." Mr. Sanderson does not know how much he pays the children, but "perhaps the younger boys get from 4s. to 5s. a week.... The boys' work is of a kind for which the strength of the boys is generally ('generally,' of course not always) quite sufficient, and consequently there would be no gain in the greater strength of the men to counterbalance the loss, or it would be only in the few cases in which the metal is heavy. The men would not like so well not to have boys under them, as men would be less obedient. Besides, boys must begin young to learn the trade. Leaving day-work alone open to boys would not answer this purpose." And why not? Why could not boys learn their handicraft in the day-time? Your reason? "Owing to the men working days and nights in alternate weeks, the men would be separated half the time from their boys, and would lose half the profit which they make from them. The training which they give to. an apprentice is considered as part of the return for the boys' labour, and thus enables the man to get it at a cheaper rate. Each man would want half of this profit." In other words, Messrs. Sanderson would have to pay part of the wages of the adult men out of their own pockets instead of by the night-work of the boys. Messrs. Sanderson's profit would thus fall to some extent, and this is the good Sandersonian reason why boys cannot learn their handicraft in the day. [70] In addition to this, it would throw night-labour on those who worked instead of the boys, which they would not be able to stand. The difficulties in fact would be so great that they would very likely lead to the giving up of night-work altogether, and "as far as the work itself is concerned," says E. F. Sanderson, "this would suit as well, but — " But Messrs. Sanderson have something else to make besides steel. Steel-making is simply a pretext for surplus-value making. The smelting furnaces, rolling-mills, &c., the buildings, machinery, iron, coal, &c., have something more to do than transform themselves into steel. They are there to absorb surplus-labour, and naturally absorb more in 24 hours pthan in 12. In fact they give, by grace of God and law, the Sandersons a cheque on the working-time of a certain number of hands for all the 24 hours of the day, and they lose their character as capital, are therefore a pure loss for the Sandersons, as soon as their function of absorbing labour is interrupted. "But then there would be the loss from so much expensive machinery, Iying idle half the time, and to get through the amount of work which we are able to do on the present system, we should have to double our premises and plant, which would double the outlay." But why should these Sandersons pretend to a privilege not enjoyed by the other capitalists who only work during the day, and whose buildings, machinery, raw material, therefore lie "idle" during the night? E. F. Sanderson answers in the name of all the Sandersons: "It is true that there is this loss from machinery Iying idle in those manufactories in which work only goes on by day. But the use of furnaces would involve a further loss in our case. If they were kept up there would be a waste of fuel (instead of, as now, a waste of the living substance of the workers), and if they were not, there would be loss of time in laying the fires and getting the heat up (whilst the loss of sleeping time, even to children of 8 is a gain of working-time for the Sanderson tribe), and the furnaces themselves would suffer from the changes of temperature." (Whilst those same furnaces suffer nothing from the day and night change of labour.) [71]

<h1 align="center">Section 5
The Struggle for a Normal Working-Day.
Compulsory Laws for the Extension of the Working-Day from the Middle of the 14th to the End of the 17th Century</h1>

"What is a working-day? What is the length of time during which capital may consume the labour-power whose daily value it buys? How far may the working-day be extended beyond the working-time necessary for the reproduction of labour-power itself?" It has been seen that to these questions capital replies: the working-day contains the full 24 hours, with the deduction of the few hours of repose without which labour-power absolutely refuses its services again. Hence it is self-evident that the labourer is nothing else, his whole life through, than labour-power, that therefore all his disposable time is by nature and law labour-time, to be devoted to the self-expansion of capital. Time for education, for intellectual development, for the fulfilling of social functions and for social intercourse, for the free-play of his bodily and mental activity, even the rest time of Sunday (and that in a country of Sabbatarians!) [72] — moonshine! But in its blind unrestrainable passion, its were-wolf hunger for surplus-labour, capital oversteps not only the moral, but even the merely physical maximum bounds of the working-day. It usurps the time for growth, development, and healthy maintenance of the body. It steals the time required for the consumption of fresh air and sunlight. It higgles over a meal-time, incorporating it where possible with the process of production itself, so that food is given to the labourer as to a mere means of production, as coal is supplied to the boiler, grease and oil to the machinery. It reduces the sound sleep needed for the restoration, reparation, re pfreshment of the bodily powers to just so many hours of torpor as the revival of an organism, absolutely exhausted, renders essential. It is not the normal maintenance of the labour-power which is to determine the limits of the working-day; it is the greatest possible daily expenditure of labour-power, no matter how diseased, compulsory, and painful it may be, which is to determine the limits of the labourers' period of repose. Capital cares nothing for the length of life of labour-power. All that concerns it is simply and solely the maximum of labour-power, that can be rendered fluent in a working-day. It attains this end by shortening the extent of the labourer's life, as a greedy farmer snatches increased produce from the soil by robbing it of its fertility.

The capitalistic mode of production (essentially the production of surplus-value, the absorption of surplus-labour), produces thus, with the extension of the working-day, not only the deterioration of human labour-power by robbing it of its normal, moral and physical, conditions of development and function. It produces also the premature exhaustion and death of this labour-power itself. [73] It extends the labourer's time of production during a given period by shortening his actual life-time.

But the value of the labour-power includes the value of the commodities necessary for the reproduction of the worker, or for the keeping up of the working-class. If then the unnatural extension of the working-day, that capital necessarily strives after in its unmeasured passion for self-expansion, shortens the length of life of the individual labourer, and therefore the duration of his labour-power, the forces used up have to be replaced at a more rapid rate and the sum of the expenses for the reproduction of labour-power will be greater; just as in a machine the part of its value to be reproduced every day is greater the more rapidly the machine is worn out. It would seem therefore that the interest capital itself points in the direction of a normal working-day.

The slave-owner buys his labourer as he buys his horse. If he loses his slave, he loses capital that can only be restored by new outlay in the slave-mart. But "the rice-grounds of Georgia, or the swamps of the ississippi may be fatally injurious to the human constitution; but the waste of human life which the cultivation of these districts necessitates, is not so great that it cannot be repaired from the teeming preserves of

Virginia and Kentucky. Considerations of economy, moreover, which, under a natural system, afford some security for humane treatment by identifying the master's interest with the slave's preservation, when once trading in slaves is practiced, become reasons for racking to the uttermost the toil of the slave; for, when his place can at once be supplied from foreign preserves, the duration of his life becomes a matter of less moment than its productiveness while it lasts. It is accordingly a maxim of slave management, in slave-importing countries, that the most effective economy is that which takes out of the human chattel in the shortest space of time the utmost amount of exertion it is capable of putting forth. It is in tropical culture, where annual profits often equal the whole capital of plantations, that negro life is most recklessly sacrificed. It is the agriculture of the West Indies, which has been for centuries prolific of fabulous wealth, that has engulfed millions of the African race. It is in Cuba, at this day, whose revenues are reckoned by millions, and whose planters are princes, that we see in the servile class, the coarsest fare, the most exhausting and unremitting toil, and even the absolute destruction of a portion of its numbers every year." [74]

Mutato nomine de te fabula narratur. For slave-trade read labour-market, for Kentucky and Virginia, Ireland and the agricultural districts of England, Scotland, and Wales, for Africa, Germany. We heard how over-work thinned the ranks of the bakers in London. Nevertheless, the London labour-market is always over-stocked with German and other candidates for death in the bakeries. Pottery, as we saw, is one of the shortest-lived industries. Is there any want therefore of potters? Josiah Wedgwood, the inventor of modern pottery, himself originally a common workman, said in 1785 before the House of Commons that the whole trade employed from 15,000 to 20,000 people. [75] In the year 1861 the population alone of the town centres of this industry in Great Britain numbered 101,302. "The cotton trade has existed for ninety years.... It has existed for three generations of the English race, and I believe I may safely say that during that period it has destroyed nine generations of factory operatives." [76]

No doubt in certain epochs of feverish activity the labour-market shows significant gaps. In 1834, e.g. But then the manufacturers proposed to the Poor Law Commissioners that they should send the "surplus-population" of the agricultural districts to the north, with the explanation "that the manufacturers would absorb and use it up." [77] Agents were appointed with the consent of the Poor Law Commissioners. ... An office was set up in Manchester, to which lists were sent pof those workpeople in the agricultural districts wanting employment, and their names were registered in books. The manufacturers attended at these offices, and selected such persons as they chose; when they had selected such persons as their 'wants required', they gave instructions to have them forwarded to Manchester, and they were sent, ticketed like bales of goods, by canals, or with carriers, others tramping on the road, and many of them were found on the way lost and half-starved. This system had grown up unto a regular trade. This House will hardly believe it, but I tell them, that this traffic in human flesh was as well kept up, they were in effect as regularly sold to these [Manchester] manufacturers as slaves are sold to the cotton-grower in the United States.... In 1860, 'the cotton trade was at its zenith.' ... The manufacturers again found that they were short of hands.... They applied to the 'flesh agents, as they are called. Those agents sent to the southern downs of England, to the pastures of Dorsetshire, to the glades of Devonshire, to the people tending kine in Wiltshire, but they sought in vain. The surplus-population was 'absorbed.'" The Bury Guardian said, on the completion of the French treaty, that "10,000 additional hands could be absorbed by Lancashire, and that 30,000 or 40,000 will be needed." After the "flesh agents and sub-agents" had in vain sought through the agricultural districts, "a deputation came up to London, and waited on the right hon. gentleman [Mr. Villiers, President of the Poor Law Board] with a view of obtaining poor children from certain union houses for the mills of Lancashire." [78]

pWhat experience shows to the capitalist generally is a constant excess of population, i.e., an excess in relation to the momentary requirements of surplus-labour-absorbing capital, although this excess is made up of generations of human beings stunted, short-lived, swiftly replacing each other, plucked, so to say, before maturity. [79] And, indeed, experience shows to the intelligent observer with what swiftness and grip the capitalist mode of production, dating, historically speaking, only from yesterday, has seized the vital power of the people by the very root — shows how the degeneration of the industrial population is only retarded by the constant absorption of primitive and physically uncorrupted elements from the country — shows how even the country labourers, in spite of fresh air and the principle of natural selection, that works so powerfully amongst them, and only permits the survival of the strongest, are already beginning to die off. [80] Capital that has such good reasons for denying the sufferings of the legions of workers that surround it, is in practice moved as much and as little by the sight of the coming degradation and final depopulation of the human race, pas by the probable fall of the earth into the sun. In every stockjobbing swindle every one knows that some time or other the crash must come, but every one hopes that it may fall on the head of his neighbour, after he himself has caught the shower of gold and placed it in safety. Après moi le déluge! is the watchword of every capitalist and of every capitalist nation. Hence Capital is reckless of the health or length of life of the labourer, unless under compulsion from society. [81] To the out-cry as to the physical and mental degradation, the premature death, the torture of over-work, it answers: Ought these to trouble us since they increase our profits? But looking at things as a whole, all this does not, indeed, depend on the good or ill will of the individual capitalist. Free competition brings out the inherent laws of capitalist production, in the shape of external coercive laws having power over every individual capitalist. [82]

The establishment of a normal working-day is the result of centuries of struggle between capitalist and labourer. The history of this struggle shows two opposed tendencies. Compare, e.g., the English factory legislation of our time with the English labour Statutes from the 14th century to well into the middle of the 18th. [83] Whilst the modern Factory Acts compulsorily shortened the working-day, the earlier statutes ptried to lengthen it by compulsion. Of course the pretensions of capital in embryo — when, beginning to grow, it secures the right of absorbing a quantum sufficit of surplus-labour, not merely by the force of economic relations, but by the help of the State — appear very modest when put face to face with the concessions that, growling and struggling, it has to make in its adult condition. It takes centuries ere the "free" labourer, thanks to the development of capitalistic production, agrees, i.e., is compelled by social conditions, to sell the whole of his active life. his very capacity for work, for the price of the necessaries of life, his birth-right for a mess of pottage. Hence it is natural that the lengthening of the working-day, which capital, from the middle of the 14th to the end of the 17th century, tries to impose by State-measures on adult labourers, approximately coincides with the shortening of the working-day which, in the second half of the 19th century, has here and there been effected by the State to prevent the coining of children's blood into capital. That which to-day, e.g., in the State of Massachusetts, until recently the freest State of the North-American Republic, has been proclaimed as the statutory limit of the labour of children under 12, was in England, even in the middle of the 17th century, the normal working-day of able-bodied artisans, robust labourers, athletic blacksmiths. [84]

The first "Statute of Labourers" (23 Edward III., 1349) found its immediate pretext (not its cause, for legislation of this kind lasts centuries after the pretext for it has disappeared) in the great plague that decimated the people, so that, as a Tory writer says, "The difficulty of getting men to work on reasonable terms (i.e., at a price that left their employers a reasonable quantity of surplus-labour) grew to such a height as to be quite intolerable." [85] Reasonable wages were, therefore, fixed by plaw as well as the limits of the working-day. The latter point, the only one that here interests us, is repeated in the Statute of 1496 (Henry VII.). The working-day for all artificers and field labourers from March to September ought, according to this statute (which, however, could not be enforced), to last from 5 in the morning to between 7 and 8 in the evening. But the meal-times consist of 1 hour for breakfast, 1 1/2 hours for dinner, and 1/2 an hour for "noon-meate," i.e., exactly twice as much as under the factory acts now in force. [86] In winter, work was to last from 5 in the morning until dark, with the same intervals. A statute of Elizabeth of 1562 leaves the length of the working-day for all labourers "hired for daily or weekly wage" untouched, but aims at limiting the intervals to 2 1/2 hours in the summer, or to 2 in the winter. Dinner is only to last 1 hour, and the "afternoon-sleep of half an hour" is only allowed between the middle of May and the middle of August. For every hour of absence 1d. is to be subtracted from the wage. In practice, however, the conditions were much more favourable to the labourers than in the statute-book. William Petty, the father of Political Economy, and to some extent the founder of Statistics, says in a work that he published in the last third of the 17th century: "Labouring-men (then meaning field-labourers) work 10 hours per diem, and make 20 meals per week, viz., 3 a day for working-days, and 2 on Sundays; whereby it is plain, that if they could fast on Friday nights, and dine in one hour and an half, whereas they take two, from eleven to one; thereby thus working 1/20 more, and spending 1/20 less, the above-mentioned (tax) might be raised." [87] Was not Dr. Andrew Ure right in crying down the 12 hours' bill of 1833 as a retrogression to the times of the dark ages? It is true these regulations contained in the statute mentioned by Petty, apply also to apprentices. But the condition of child-labour, even at the end of the 17th century, is seen from the following complaint: "'Tis not their practice (in Germany) as with us in this kingdom, to bind an papprentice for seven years; three or four is their common standard: and the reason is, because they are educated from their cradle to something of employment, which renders them the more apt and docile, and consequently the more capable of attaining to a ripeness and quicker proficiency in business. Whereas our youth, here in England, being bred to nothing before they come to be apprentices, make a very slow progress and require much longer time wherein to reach the perfection of accomplished artists." [88]

Still, during the greater part of the 18th century, up to the epoch of Modern Industry and machinism, capital in England had not succeeded in seizing for itself, by the payment of the weekly value of labour-power, the whole week of the labourer, with the exception, however, of the agricultural labourers. The fact that they could live for a whole week on the wage of four days, did not appear to the labourers a sufficient reason that they should work the other two days for the capitalist. One party of English economists, in the interest of capital, denounces this obstinacy in the most violent manner, another party defends the labourers. Let us listen, e.g., to the contest between Postlethwayt whose Dictionary of Trade then had the same reputation as the kindred works of MacCulloch and MacGregor to-day, and the author (already quoted) of the "Essay on Trade and Commerce." [89]

pPostlethwayt says among other things: "We cannot put an end to those few observations, without noticing that trite remark in the mouth of too many; that if the industrious poor can obtain enough to maintain themselves in five days, they will not work the whole six. Whence they infer the necessity of even the necessaries of life being made dear by taxes, or any other means, to compel the working artisan and manufacturer to labour the whole six days in the week, without ceasing. I must beg leave to differ in sentiment from those great politicians, who contend for the perpetual slavery of the working people of this kingdom; they forget the vulgar adage, all work and no play. Have not the English boasted of the ingenuity and dexterity of her working artists and manufacturers which have heretofore given credit and reputation to British wares in general? What has this been owing to? To nothing more probably than the relaxation of the working people in their own way. Were they obliged to toil the year round, the whole six days in the week, in a repetition of the same work, might it not blunt their ingenuity, and render them stupid instead of alert and dexterous; and might not our workmen lose their reputation instead of maintaining it by such eternal slavery? ... And what sort of workmanship could we expect from such hard-driven animals? ... Many of them will execute as much work in four days as a Frenchman will in five or six. But if Englishmen are to be eternal drudges, 'tis to be feared they will degenerate below the Frenchmen. As our people are famed for bravery in war, do we not say that it is owing to good English roes t beef and pudding in their bellies, as well as their constitutional spirit of liberty? And why may not the superior ingenuity and dexterity of, our artists and manufacturers, be owing to that freedom and liberty to direct themselves in their own way, and I hope we shall never have them deprived of such privileges and that good living from whence their ingenuity no less than their courage may proceed."[90] Thereupon the author of the "Essay on Trade and Commerce" replies: "If the making of every seventh day an holiday is supposed to be of divine pinstitution, as it implies the appropriating the other six days to labour" (he means capital as we shall soon see) "surely it will not be thought cruel to enforce it .... That mankind in general, are naturally inclined to ease and indolence, we fatally experience to be true, from the conduct of our manufacturing populace, who do not labour, upon an average, above four days in a week, unless provisions happen to be very dear.... Put all the necessaries of the poor under one denomination; for instance, call them all wheat, or suppose that ... the bushel of wheat shall cost five shillings and that he (a manufacturer) earns a shilling by his labour, he then would be obliged to work five days only in a week. If the bushel of wheat should cost but four shillings, he would be obliged to work but four days; but as wages in this kingdom are much higher in proportion to the price of necessaries ... the manufacturer, who labours four days, has a surplus of money to live idle with the rest of the week . ... I hope I have said enough to make it appear that the moderate labour of six days in a week is no slavery. Our labouring people do this, and to all appearance are the happiest of all our labouring poor, [91] but the Dutch do this in manufactures, and appear to be a very happy people. The French do so, when holidays do not intervene. [92] But our populace have adopted a notion, that as Englishmen they enjoy a birthright privilege of being more free and independent than in any country in Europe. Now this idea, as far as it may affect the bravery of our troops, may be of some use; nut the less the manufacturing poor have of it, certainly the better for themselves and for the State. The labouring people should never) think themselves independent of their superiors.... It is extremely dangerous to encourage mobs in a commercial state like ours, where, perhaps, seven parts out of eight of the whole, are people with little or no property. The cure will not be perfect, till our manufacturing poor are contented to labour six days for the same sum which they now earn in four days." [93] To this end, and for "extirpating idleness debauchery and excess," promoting a spirit of industry, "lowering the price of labour in our manufactories, and easing the lands of the heavy burden of poor's rates," our "faithful Eckart" of capital proposes this approved device: to shut up such labourers as become dependent on ppublic support, in a word, paupers, in "an ideal workhouse." Such ideal workhouse must be made a "House of Terror," and not an asylum for the poor, "where they are to be plentifully fed, warmly and decently clothed, and where they do but little work." [94] In this "House of Terror," this "ideal workhouse, the poor shall work 14 hours in a day, allowing proper time for meals, in such manner that there shall remain 12 hours of neat-labour." [95]

Twelve working-hours daily in the Ideal Workhouse, in the "House of Terror" of 1770! 63 years later, in 1833, when the English Parliament reduced the working-day for children of 13 to 18, in four branches of industry to 12 full hours, the judgment day of English Industry had dawned! In 1852, when Louis Bonaparte sought to secure his position with the bourgeoisie by tampering with the legal working-day, the French working people cried out with one voice "the law that limits the working-day to 12 hours is the one good that has remained to us of the legislation of the Republic!" [96] At Zürich the work of children over 10, is limited to 12 hours; in Aargau in 1862, the work of children between 13 and 16, was reduced from 12 1/2 to 12 hours; in Austria in 1860, for children between 14 and 16, the same reduction was made. [97] "What a progress," since 1770! Macaulay would shout with exultation!

The "House of Terror" for paupers of which the capitalistic soul of 1770 only dreamed, was realised a few years later in the shape of a gigantic "Workhouse" for the industrial worker himself. It is called the Factory. And the ideal this time fades before the reality.

Section 6
The Struggle for the Normal Working-Day. Compulsory Limitation by Law of the Working-Time. The English Factory Acts, 1833 to 1864

After capital had taken centuries in extending the working-day to its normal maximum limit, and then beyond this to the limit of the natural day of 12 hours, [98] there followed on the birth of machinism and modern industry in the last third of the 18th century, a violent encroachment like that of an avalanche in its intensity and extent. All bounds of morals and nature, age and sex, day and night, were broken down. Even the ideas of day and night, of rustic simplicity in the old statutes, became so confused that an English judge, as late as 1860, needed a quite Talmudic sagacity to explain "judicially" what was day and what was night. [99] Capital celebrated its orgies.

As soon as the working-class, stunned at first by the noise and turmoil of the new system of production, recovered, in some measure, its senses, its resistance began, and first in the native land of machinism, in England. For 30 years, however, the concessions conquered by the workpeople were purely nominal. Parliament passed 5 labour Laws between 1802 and 1833, but was shrewd enough not to vote a penny for their carrying out, for the requisite officials, &c. [100]

They remained a dead letter. "The fact is, that prior to the Act of 1833, young persons and children were worked all night, all day, or both ad libitum." [101]

pA normal working-day for modern industry only dates from the Factory Act of 1833, which included cotton, wool, flax, and silk factories. Nothing is more characteristic of the spirit of capital than the history of the English Factory Acts from 1833 to 1864.

The Act of 1833 declares the ordinary factory working-day to be from half-past five in the morning to half-past eight in the evening and within these limits, a period of 15 hours, it is lawful to employ young persons (i.e., persons between 13 and 18 years of age), at any time of the day, provided no one individual young person should work more than 12 hours in any one day, except in certain cases especially provided for. The 6th section of the Act provided. "That there shall be allowed in the course of every day not less than one and a half hours for meals to every such person restricted as hereinbefore provided." The employment of children under 9, with exceptions mentioned later was forbidden; the work of children between 9 and 13 was limited to 8 hours a day, night-work, i.e., according to this Act, work between 8:30 p.m. and 5:30 a.m., was forbidden for all persons between 9 and 18.

The law-makers were so far from wishing to trench on the freedom of capital to exploit adult labour-power, or, as they called it, "the freedom of labour," that they created a special system in order to prevent the Factory Acts from having a consequence so outrageous.

"The great evil of the factory system as at present conducted," says the first report of the Central Board of the Commission of June 28th 1833, "has appeared to us to be that it entails the necessity of continuing the labour of children to the utmost length of that of the adults. The only remedy for this evil, short of the limitation of the labour of adults which would, in our opinion, create an evil greater than that which is sought to be remedied, appears to be the plan of working double sets of children." ... Under the name of System of Relays, this "plan" was therefore carried out, so that, e.g., from 5.30 a.m. until 1.30 in the afternoon, one set of children between 9 and 13, and from 1.30 p.m. to 8.30 in the evening another set were "put to," &c.

In order to reward the manufacturers for having, in the most barefaced way, ignored all the Acts as to children's labour passed during the last twenty-two years, the pill was yet further gilded for them. Parliament decreed that after March 1st, 1834, no child under 11, after March 1st 1835, no child under 12, and after March 1st, 1836, no child under 13 was to work more than eight hours in a factory. This "liberalism," so full of consideration for "capital," was the more noteworthy as. Dr. Farre, Sir A. Carlisle, Sir B. Brodie, Sir C. Bell, Mr. Guthrie, &c., in a word, the most distinguished physicians and surgeons in London, had declared in their evidence before the House of Commons, that there was danger in delay. Dr. Farre expressed himself still more coarse pIy. "Legislation is necessary for the prevention of death, in any form in which it can be prematurely inflicted, and certainly this (i.e., the factory method) must be viewed as a most cruel mode of inflicting it."

That same "reformed" Parliament, which in its delicate consideration for the manufacturers, condemned children under 13, for years to come, to 72 hours of work per week in the Factory Hell, on the other hand, in the Emancipation Act, which also administered freedom drop by drop, forbade the planters, from the outset, to work any negro slave more than 45 hours a week.

But in no wise conciliated, capital now began a noisy agitation that went on for several years. It turned chiefly on the age of those who, under the name of children, were limited to 8 hours' work, and were subject to a certain amount of compulsory education. According to capitalistic anthropology, the age of childhood ended at 10, or at the outside, at 11. The more nearly the time approached for the coming into full force of the Factory Act, the fatal year 1836, the more wildly raged the mob of manufacturers. They managed, in fact, to intimidate the government to such an extent that in 1835 it proposed to lower the limit of the age of childhood from 13 to 12. In the meantime the pressure from without grew more threatening. Courage failed the House of Commons. It refused to throw children of 13 under the Juggernaut Car of capital for more than 8 hours a day, and the Act of 1833 came into full operation. It remained unaltered until June, 1844.

In the ten years during which it regulated factory work, first in part, and then entirely, the official reports of the factory inspectors teem with complaints as to the impossibility of putting the Act into force. As the law of 1833 left it optional with the lords of capital during the 15 hours, from 5.30 a.m. to 8.30 p.m., to make every "young person," and "every child" begin, break off, resume, or end his 12 or 8 hours at any moment they liked, and also permitted them to assign to different persons, different times for meals, these gentlemen soon discovered a new "system of relays," by which the labour-horses were not changed at fixed stations, but were constantly re-harnessed at changing stations. We do not pause longer on the beauty of this system, as we shall have to return to it later. But this much is clear at the first glance: that this system annulled the whole Factory Act, not only in the spirit, but in the letter. How could factory inspectors, with this complex bookkeeping in respect to each individual child or young person, enforce the legally determined work-time and the granting of the legal mealtimes? In a great many of the factories, the old brutalities soon blossomed out again unpunished. In an interview with the Home Secretary (1844), the factory inspectors demonstrated the impossibility of any control punder the newly invented relay system. [102] In the meantime, however, circumstances had greatly changed. The factory hands, especially since 1838, had made the Ten Hours' Bill their economic, as they had made the Charter their political, election-cry. Some of the manufacturers, even, who had managed their factories in conformity with the Act of 1833, overwhelmed Parliament with memorials on the immoral competition of their false brethren whom greater impudence, or more fortunate local circumstances, enabled to break the law. Moreover, however much the individual manufacturer might give the rein to his old lust for gain, the spokesmen and political leaders of the manufacturing class ordered a change of front and of speech towards the workpeople. They had entered upon the contest for the repeal of the Corn Laws, and needed the workers to help them to victory. They promised therefore, not only a double-sized loaf of bread, but the enactment of the Ten Hours' Bill in the Free-trade millennium. [103] Thus they still less dared to oppose a measure intended only to make the law of 1833 a reality. Threatened in their holiest interest, the rent of land, the Tories thundered with philanthropic indignation against the "nefarious practices" [104] of their foes.

This was the origin of the additional Factory Act of June 7th, 1844. It came into effect on September 10th, 1844. It places under protection a new category of workers, viz., the women over 18. They were placed in every respect on the same footing as the young persons, their worktime limited to twelve hours, their night-labour forbidden, &c. For the first time, legislation saw itself compelled to control directly and officially the labour of adults. In the Factory Report of 1844-1845, it is said with irony: "No instances have come to my knowledge of adult women having expressed any regret at their rights being thus far interfered with." [105] The working-time of children under 13 was reduced to 6½, and in certain circumstances to 7 hours a-day. [106]

To get rid of the abuses of the "spurious relay system," the law established besides others the following important regulations: — "That the hours of work of children and young persons shall be reckoned from the time when any child or young person shall begin to work in the morning." So that if A, e.g., begins work at 8 in the morning, and B pat 10, B's work-day must nevertheless end at the same hour as A's. "The time shall be regulated by a public clock," for example, the nearest railway clock, by which the factory clock is to be set. The occupier is to hang up a "legible" printed notice stating the hours for the beginning and ending of work and the times allowed for the several meals. Children beginning work before 12 noon may not be again employed after I p.m. The afternoon shift must therefore consist of other children than those employed in the morning. Of the hour and a half for meal-times, "one hour thereof at the least shall be given before three of the clock in the afternoon ... and at the same period of the day. No child or young person shall be employed more than five hours before I p.m. without an interval for meal-time of at least 30 minutes. No child or young person [or female] shall be employed or allowed to remain in any room in which any manufacturing process is then [i.e., at mealtimes] carried on," &c.

It has been seen that these minutiae, which, with military uniformity, regulate by stroke of the clock the times, limits, pauses of the work were not at all the products of Parliamentary fancy. They developed gradually out of circumstances as natural laws of the modern mode of production. Their formulation, official recognition, and proclamation by the State, were the result of a long struggle of classes. One of their first consequences was that in practice the working-day of the adult males in factories became subject to the same limitations, since in most processes of production the co-operation of the children. young persons, and women is indispensable. On the whole, therefore, during the period from 1844 to 1847, the 12 hours' working-day became general and uniform in all branches of industry under the Factory Act.

The manufacturers, however, did not allow this "progress" without a compensating "retrogression." At their instigation the House of Commons reduced the minimum age for exploitable children from 9 to 8, in order to assure that additional supply of factory children which is due to capitalists, according to divine and human law. [107]

The years 1846-47 are epoch-making in the economic history of England. The Repeal of the Corn Laws, and of the duties on cotton and other raw material; Free-trade proclaimed as the guiding star of legislation; in a word, the arrival of the millennium. On the other hand, in the same years, the Chartist movement and the 10 hours' agitation reached their highest point. They found allies in the Tories panting for prevenge. Despite the fanatical opposition of the army of perjured Free-traders, with Bright and Cobden at their head, the Ten Hours' Bill, struggled for so long, went through Parliament.

The new Factory Act of June 8th, 1847, enacted that on July 1st, 1847, there should be a preliminary shortening of the working-day for "young persons" (from 13 to 18), and all females to 11 hours, but that on May 1st, 1848, there should be a definite limitation of the working-day to 10 hours. In other respects, the Act only amended and completed the Acts of 1833 and 1844.

Capital now entered upon a preliminary campaign in order to hinder the Act from coming into full force on May 1st, 1848. And the workers themselves, under the presence that they had been taught by experience, were to help in the destruction of their own work. The moment was cleverly chosen. "It must be remembered, too, that there has been more than two years of great suffering (in consequence of the terrible crisis of 1846-47) among the factory operatives, from many mills having worked short time, and many being altogether closed. A considerable number of the operatives must therefore be in very narrow circumstances many, it is to be feared, in debt; so that it might fairly have been presumed that at the present time they would prefer working the longer time, in order to make up for past losses, perhaps to pay off debts, or get their furniture out of pawn, or replace that sold, or to get a new supply of clothes for themselves and their families." [108]

The manufacturers tried to aggravate the natural effect of these circumstances by a general reduction of wages by 10%. This was done so to say, to celebrate the inauguration of the new Free-trade era. Then followed a further reduction of 8 1/3% as soon as the working-day was shortened to 11, and a reduction of double that amount as soon as it was finally shortened to 10 hours. Wherever, therefore, circumstances allowed it, a reduction of wages of at least 25% took place. [109] Under such favourably prepared conditions the agitation among the factory workers for the repeal of the Act of 1847 was begun. Neither lies, bribery, nor threats were spared in this attempt. But all was in vain. Concerning the half-dozen petitions in which workpeople were made to complain of "their oppression by the Act," the petitioners themselves declared under oral examination, that their signatures had been extorted from them. "They felt themselves oppressed, but not exactly by the Factory pAct." [110] But if the manufacturers did not succeed in making the workpeople speak as they wished, they themselves shrieked all the louder in press and Parliament in the name of the workpeople. They denounced the Factory Inspectors as a kind of revolutionary commissioners like those of the French National Convention ruthlessly sacrificing the unhappy factory workers to their humanitarian crotchet. This maneuvre also failed. Factory Inspector Leonard Homer conducted in his own person, and through his sub-inspectors, many examinations of witnesses in the factories of Lancashire. About 70% of the workpeople examined declared in favour of 10 hours, a much smaller percentage in favour of 11, and an altogether insignificant minority for the old 12 hours. [111]

Another "friendly" dodge was to make the adult males work 12 to 15 hours, and then to blazon abroad this fact as the best proof of what the proletariat desired in its heart of hearts. But the "ruthless" Factory Inspector Leonard Homer was again to the fore. The majority of the "over-times" declared: "They would much prefer working ten hours for less wages, but that they had no choice; that so many were out of employment (so many spinners getting very low wages by having to work as piecers, being unable to do better), that if they refused to work the longer time, others would immediately get their places, so that it was a question with them of agreeing to work the longer time, or of being thrown out of employment altogether." [112]

The preliminary campaign of capital thus came to grief, and the Ten Hours' Act came into force May 1st, 1848. But meanwhile the fiasco of the Chartist party whose leaders were imprisoned, and whose organisation was dismembered, had shaken the confidence of the English working-class in its own strength. Soon after this the June insurrection in Paris and its bloody suppression united, in England as on the Continent, all fractions of the ruling classes, landlords and capitalists, stock-exchange wolves and shop-keepers, Protectionists and Freetraders, government and opposition, priests and freethinkers, young whores and old nuns, under the common cry for the salvation of Property, pReligion, the Family and Society. The working-class was everywhere proclaimed, placed under a ban, under a virtual law of suspects. The manufacturers had no need any longer to restrain themselves. They broke out in open revolt not only against the Ten Hours' Act, but against the whole of the legislation that since 1833 had aimed at restricting in some measure the "free" exploitation of labour-power. It was a pro-slavery rebellion in miniature, carried on for over two years with a cynical recklessness, a terrorist energy all the cheaper because the rebel capitalist risked nothing except the skin of his "hands."

To understand that which follows we must remember that the Factory Acts of 1833, 1844, and 1847 were all three in force so far as the one did not amend the other: that not one of these limited the working-day of the male worker over 18, and that since 1833 the 15 hours from 5.30 a.m. to 8.30 p.m. had remained the legal "day," within the limits of which at first the 12, and later the 10 hours' labour of young persons and women had to be performed under the prescribed conditions.

The manufacturers began by here and there discharging a part of, in many cases half of the young persons and women employed by them, and then, for the adult males, restoring the almost obsolete night-work. The Ten Hours' Act, they cried, leaves no other alternative. [113]

Their second step dealt with the legal pauses for meals. Let us hear the Factory Inspectors. "Since the restriction of the hours of work to ten, the factory occupiers maintain, although they have not yet practically gone the whole length, that supposing the hours of work to be from 9 a.m. to 7 p.m. they fulfil the provisions of the statutes by allowing an hour before 9 a.m. and half an hour after 7 p.m. [for meals]. In some cases they now allow an hour, or half an hour for dinner, insisting at the same time, that they are not bound to allow any part of the hour and a half in the course of the factory working-day." [114] The manufacturers maintained therefore that the scrupulously strict provisions of the Act of 1844 with regard to meal-times only gave the operatives permission to eat and drink before coming into, and after leaving the factory — i.e., at home. And why should not the workpeople eat their dinner before 9 in the morning? The crown lawyers, however, decided that the prescribed meal-times "must be in the interval during the working-hours, and that it will not be lawful to work for 10 hours continuously, from 9 a.m. to 7 p.m., without any interval." [115]

After these pleasant demonstrations, Capital preluded its revolt by pa step which agreed with the letter of the law of 1844, and was therefore legal.

The Act of 1844 certainly prohibited the employment after 1 p.m. of such children, from 8 to 13, as had been employed before noon. But it did not regulate in any way the 6 1/2 hours' work of the children whose work-time began at 12 midday or later. Children of 8 might, if they began work at noon, be employed from 12 to 1, 1 hour; from 2 to 4 in the afternoon, 2 hours; from 5 to 8.30 in the evening, 3 1/2 hours; in all, the legal 6 1/2 hours. Or better still. In order to make their work coincide with that of the adult male labourers up to 8.30 p.m., the manufacturers only had to give them no work till 2 in the afternoon, they could then keep them in the factory without intermission till 8.30 in the evening. "And it is now expressly admitted that the practice exists in England from the desire of mill-owners to have their machinery at work for more than 10 hours a-day, to keep the children at work with male adults after all the young persons and women have left, and until 8.30 p.m. if the factory-owners choose." [116] Workmen and factory inspectors protested on hygienic and moral grounds, but Capital answered:

"My deeds upon my head! I crave the law,
The penalty and forfeit of my bond."

In fact, according to statistics laid before the House of Commons on July 26th, 1850, in spite of all protests, on July 15th, 1850, 3,742 children were subjected to this "practice" in 257 factories. [117]

Still, this was not enough. The Lynx eye of Capital discovered that the Act of 1844 did not allow 5 hours' work before mid-day without a pause of at least 30 minutes for refreshment, but prescribed nothing of the kind for work after mid-day. Therefore, it claimed and obtained the enjoyment not only of making children of 8 drudge without intermission from 2 to 8.30 p.m., but also of making them hunger during that time.

> "Ay, his heart.
> So says the bond."

This Shylock-clinging[118] to the letter of the law of 1844, so far as it regulated children's labour, was but to lead up to an open revolt against the same law, so far as it regulated the labour of "young persons and women." It will be remembered that the abolition of the "false relay system" was the chief aim and object of that law. The masters began their revolt with the simple declaration that the sections of the Act of 1844 which prohibited the ad libitum use of young persons and women in such short fractions of the day of 15 hours as the employer chose, were "comparatively harmless" so long as the work-time was fixed at 12 hours. But under the Ten Hours' Act they were a "grievous hardship."[119] They informed the inspectors in the coolest manner that they should place themselves above the letter of the law, and re-introduce the old system on their own account.[120] They were acting in the interests of the ill-advised operatives themselves, "in order to be able to pay them higher wages." "This was the only possible plan by which to maintain, under the Ten Hours' Act, the industrial supremacy of Great Britain." "Perhaps it may be a little difficult to detect irregularities under the relay system; but what of that? Is the great manufacturing interest of this country to be treated as a secondary matter in order to save some little trouble to Inspectors and Sub-Inspectors of Factories?"[121]

All these shifts naturally were of no avail. The Factory Inspectors appealed to the Law Courts. But soon such a cloud of dust in the way of petitions from the masters overwhelmed the Home Secretary, Sir George Grey, that in a circular of August 5th, 1848, he recommends the inspectors not "to lay informations against mill-owners for a breach of the letter of the Act, or for employment of young persons by relays in cases in which there is no reason to believe that such young persons have been actually employed for a longer period than that sanctioned by law." Hereupon, Factory Inspector J. Stuart allowed the so-called relay system during the 15 hours of the factory day throughout Scotland, where it soon flourished again as of old. The English Factory Inspectors, on the other hand, declared that the Home Secretary had no power dictatorially to suspend the law, and continued their legal proceedings against the pro-slavery rebellion.

pBut what was the good of summoning the capitalists when the Courts in this case the country magistrates — Cobbett's "Great Unpaid" — acquitted them? In these tribunals, the masters sat in judgment on themselves An example. One Eskrigge, cotton-spinner, of the firm of Kershaw, Leese, & Co., had laid before the Factory Inspector of his district the scheme of a relay system intended for his mill. Receiving a refusal, he at first kept quiet. A few months later, an individual named Robinson, also a cotton-spinner, and if not his Man Friday, at all events related to Eskrigge, appeared before the borough magistrates of Stockport on a charge of introducing the identical plan of relays invented by Eskrigge. Four Justices sat, among them three cottonspinners, at their head this same inevitable Eskrigge. Eskrigge acquitted Robinson, and now was of opinion that what was right for Robinson was fair for Eskrigge. Supported by his own legal decision, he introduced the system at once into his own factory.[122] Of course, the composition of this tribunal was in itself a violation of the law.[123] These judicial farces, exclaims Inspector Howell, "urgently call for a remedy — either that the law should be so altered as to be made to conform to these decisions, or that it should be administered by a less fallible tribunal, whose decisions would conform to the law ... when these cases are brought forward. I long for a stipendiary magistrate."[124]

The crown lawyers declared the masters' interpretation of the Act of 1848 absurd. But the Saviours of Society would not allow themselves to be turned from their purpose. Leonard Homer reports, "Having endeavoured to enforce the Act ... by ten prosecutions in seven magisterial divisions, and having been supported by the magistrates in one case only

... I considered it useless to prosecute more for this evasion of the law. That part of the Act of 1848 which was framed for securing uniformity in the hours of work, ... is thus no longer in force in my district (Lancashire). Neither have the sub-inspectors or myself any means of satisfying ourselves, when we inspect a mill working by shifts, that the young persons and women are not working more than 10 hours a-day.... In a return of the 30th April, ... of millowners working by shifts, the number amounts to 114, and has been for some time rapidly increasing. In general, the time of working the mill is extended to 13 1/2 hours' from 6 a.m. to 7 1/2 p.m., ... in some in pstances it amounts to 15 hours, from 5 1/2 a.m. to 8 1/2 p.m." [125] Already, in December, 1848, Leonard Homer had a list of 65 manufacturers and 29 overlookers who unanimously declared that no system of supervision could, under this relay system, prevent enormous over-work.[126] Now, the same children and young persons were shifted from the spinning-room to the weaving-room, now, during 15 hours, from one factory to another.[127] How was it possible to control a system which, "under the guise of relays, is some one of the many plans for shuffling 'the hands' about in endless variety, and shifting the hours of work and of rest for different individuals throughout the day, so that you may never have one complete set of hands working together in the same room at the same time."[128]

But altogether independently of actual over-work, this so-called relay system was an offspring of capitalistic fantasy, such as Fourier, in his humorous sketches of "Courses Seances," has never surpassed, except that the "attraction of labour" was changed into the attraction of capital. Look, for example, at those schemes of the masters which the "respectable" press praised as models of "what a reasonable degree of care and method can accomplish." The personnel of the workpeople was sometimes divided into from 12 to 14 categories, which themselves constantly changed and recharged their constituent parts. During the 15 hours of the factory day, capital dragged in the labourer now for 30 minutes, now for an hour, and then pushed him out again, to drag him into the factory and to thrust him out afresh, hounding him hither and thither, in scattered shreds of time, without ever losing hold of him until the full 10 hours' work was done. As on the stage, the same persons had to appear in turns in the different scenes of the different acts. But as an actor during the whole course of the play belongs to the stage, so the operatives, during 15 hours, belonged to the factory, without reckoning the time for going and coming. Thus the hours of rest were turned into hours of enforced idleness, which drove the youths to the pot-house, and the girls to the brothel. At every new trick that the capitalist, from day to day, hit upon for keeping his machinery going 12 or 15 hours without increasing the number of his hands, the worker had to swallow his meals now in this fragment of time, now in that. At the time of the 10 hours' agitation, the masters cried out that the working mob petitioned in the hope of obtaining 12 hours' wages for 10 hours' work. Now they reversed the medal. They paid 10 hours' pwages for 12 or 15 hours' lordship over labour-power.[129] This was the gist of the matter, this the masters' interpretation of the 10 hours' law! These were the same unctuous Free-traders, perspiring with the love of humanity, who for full 10 years, during the Anti-Corn Law agitation, had preached to the operatives, by a reckoning of pounds, shillings, and pence, that with free importation of corn, and with the means possessed by English industry, 10 hours' labour would be quite enough to enrich the capitalists.[130] This revolt of capital, after two years was at last crowned with victory by a decision of one of the four highest Courts of Justice in England, the Court of Exchequer, which in a case brought before it on February 8th, 1850, decided that the manufacturers were certainly acting against the sense of the Act of 1844, but that this Act itself contained certain words that rendered it meaningless. "By this decision, the Ten Hours' Act was abolished."[131] A crowd of masters, who until then had been afraid of using the relay system for young persons and women, now took it up heart and soul.[132]

But on this apparently decisive victory of capital, followed at once a revulsion. The workpeople had hitherto offered a passive, although inflexible and unremitting resistance. They now protested in Lancashire and Yorkshire in threatening meetings. The pretended Ten Hours' Act was thus simple humbug, parliamentary cheating, had never existed! The Factory Inspectors urgently warned the Government that the antagonism of classes had arrived at an incredible tension. Some of the masters themselves murmured: "On account of the contradictory decisions of the magistrates, a condition of things altogether abnormal and anarchical obtains. One law holds in another in its immediate neighbourhood. The manufacturer in large towns could evade the law, the manufacturer in country districts could not find the people necessary for the relay system, still less for the shifting of hands from one factory to another," &c. And the first birthright of capital is equal exploitation of labour-power by all capitalists.

Under these circumstances a compromise between masters and men pwas effected that received the seal of Parliament in the additional Factory Act of August 5th, 1850. The working-day for "young persons and women," was raised from 10 to 10 − hours for the first five days of the week, and shortened to 7 1/2 on the Saturday. The work was to go on between 6 a.m. and 6 p.m.,[133] with pauses of not less than 1 1/2 hours for meal-times, these meal-times to be allowed at one and the same time for all, and conformably to the conditions of 1844. By this an end was put to the relay system once for all.[134] For children's labour, the Act of 1844 remained in force.

One set of masters, this time as before, secured to itself special seigneurial rights over the children of the proletariat. These were the silk manufacturers. In 1833 they had howled out in threatening fashion, "if the liberty of working children of any age for 10 hours a day were taken away, it would stop their works."[135] It would be impossible for them to buy a sufficient number of children over 13. They extorted the privilege they desired. The pretext was shown on subsequent investigation to be a deliberate lie.[136] It did not, however, prevent them, during 10 years, from spinning silk 10 hours a day out of the blood of little children who had to be placed upon stools for the performance of their work.[137] The Act of 1844 certainly "robbed" them of the "liberty" of employing children under 11 longer than 6 1/2 hours a day. But it secured to them, on the other hand, the privilege of working children between 11 and 13, 10 hours a day, and of annulling in their case the education made compulsory for all other factory children. This time the pretext was "the delicate texture of the fabric in which they were employed, requiring a lightness of touch, only to be acquired by their early introduction to these factories."[138] The children were slaughtered out-and-out for the sake of their delicate fingers, as in Southern Russia the horned cattle for the sake of their hide and tallow. At length, in 1850, the privilege granted in 1844, was limited to the departments of silk-twisting and silk-winding. But here, to make amends to capital bereft of its "freedom," the work-lime for children from 11 to 13 was raised from 10 pto 10 1/2 hours. Pretext: "Labour in silk mills was lighter than in mills
for other fabrics, and less likely in other respects also to be prejudicial to health."[139] Official medical inquiries proved afterwards that, on the contrary, "the average death-rate is exceedingly high in the silk districts and amongst the female part of the population is higher even than it is in the cotton districts of Lancashire."[140] Despite the protests of the Factory Inspector, renewed every 6 months, the mischief continues to this hour.[141]

The Act of 1850 changed the 15 hours' time from 6 a.m. to 8.30 p.m., into the 12 hours from 6 a.m. to 6 p.m. for "young persons and women" only. It did not, therefore, affect children who could always be employed for half an hour before and 2 1/2 hours after this period, provided the pwhole of their labour did not exceed 6 1/2 hours. Whilst the bill was under discussion, the Factory Inspectors laid before Parliament statistics of the infamous abuses due to this anomaly. To no purpose. In the background lurked the intention of screwing up, during prosperous years, the working-day of adult males to 15 hours by the aid of the children. The experience of the three following years showed that such an attempt must come to grief against the resistance of the adult male operatives. The Act of 1850 was therefore finally completed in 1853 by forbidding the "employment of children in the morning before and in the evening after young persons and women." Henceforth with a few exceptions the Factory Act of 1850 regulated the working-day of all workers in the branches of industry that come under it.[142] Since the passing of the first Factory Act half a century had elapsed.[143]

Factory legislation for the first time went beyond its original sphere in the "Printworks' Act of 1845." The displeasure with which capital received this new "extravagance" speaks through every line of the Act. It limits the working-day for children from 8 to 13, and for women to 16 hours, between 6 a.m. and 10 p.m., without any legal pause for meal-times. It allows males over 13 to be worked at will day and night.[144] It is a Parliamentary abortion.[145]

However, the principle had triumphed with its victory in those great branches of industry which form the most characteristic creation of the modern mode of production. Their wonderful development from 1853 to 1860, hand-in-hand with the physical and moral regeneration of the factory workers, struck the most purblind. The masters from whom the plegal limitation and regulation had been wrung step by step after a civil war of half a century, themselves referred ostentatiously to the contrast with the branches of exploitation still "free."[146] The Pharisees of "Political Economy" now proclaimed the discernment of the necessity of a legally fixed working-day as a characteristic new discovery of their "science."[147] It will be easily understood that after the factory magnates had resigned themselves and become reconciled to the inevitable, the power of resistance of capital gradually weakened, whilst at the same time the power of attack of the working-class grew with the number of its allies in the classes of society not immediately interested in the question. Hence the comparatively rapid advance since 1860.

The dye-works and bleach-works all came under the Factory Act of 1850 in 1860;[148] lace and stocking manufactures in 1861.

In consequence of the first report of the Commission on the employment of children (1863) the same fate was shared by the manufacturers of all earthenwares (not merely pottery), Lucifer-matches, percussioncaps, cartridges, carpets, fustian-cutting, and many processes included under the name of "finishing." In the year 1863 bleaching in the open air[149] and baking were placed under special Acts, by which, in the former, pthe labour of young persons and women during the night-time (from 8 in the evening to 6 in the morning), and in the latter, the employment of journeymen bakers under 18, between 9 in the evening and 5 in the morning were forbidden. We shall return to the later proposals of the same Commission, which threatened to deprive of their "freedom" all the important branches of English Industry, with the exception of agriculture, mines, and the means of transport.[150]

Section 7
The Struggle for the Normal Working-Day.
Re-action of the English Factory Acts on Other Countries

The reader will bear in mind that the production of surplus-value, or the extraction of surplus-labour, is the specific end and aim, the sum and substance, of capitalist production, quite apart from any changes pin the mode of production, which may arise from the subordination of labour to capital. He will remember that as far as we have at present gone only the independent labourer, and therefore only the labourer legally qualified to act for himself, enters as a vendor of a commodity into a contract with the capitalist. If, therefore, in our historical sketch, on the one hand, modern industry, on the other, the labour of those who are physically and legally minors, play important parts, the former was to us only a special department, and the latter only a specially striking example of labour exploitation. Without, however, anticipating the subsequent development of our inquiry, from the mere connexion of the historic facts before us it follows:

First. The passion of capital for an unlimited and reckless extension of the working-day, is first gratified in the industries earliest revolutionised by water-power, steam, and machinery, in those first creations of the modern mode of production, cotton, wool, flax, and silk spinning, and weaving. The changes in the material mode of production, and the corresponding changes in the social relations of the producers[151] gave rise first to an extravagance beyond all bounds, and then in opposition to this, called forth a control on the part of Society which legally limits, regulates, and makes uniform the working-day and its pauses. This control appears, therefore, during the first half of the nineteenth century simply as exceptional legislation.[152] As soon as this primitive dominion of the new mode of production was conquered, it was found that, in the meantime, not only had many other branches of production been made to adopt the same factory system, but that manufactures with more or less obsolete methods, such as potteries, glass-making, &c., that old-fashioned handicrafts, like baking, and, finally, even that the so-called domestic industries, such as nail-making,[153] had long since fallen as completely under capitalist exploitation as the factories themselves. Legislation was, therefore, compelled to gradually get rid of its exceptional character, or where, as in England, it proceeds after the manner of the Roman Casuists, to declare any house in which work was done to be a factory. [154]

pSecond. The history of the regulation of the working-day in certain branches of production, and the struggle still going on in others in regard to this regulation, prove conclusively that the isolated labourer, the labourer as "free" vendor of his labour-power, when capitalist production has once attained a certain stage, succumbs without any power of resistance. The creation of a normal working-day is, therefore, the product of a protracted civil war, more or less dissembled, between the capitalist class and the working-class. As the contest takes place in the arena of modern industry, it first breaks out in the home of that industry — England.[155] The English factory workers were the champions, not only of the English, but of the modern working-class generally, as their theorists were the first to throw down the gauntlet to the theory of capital.[156] Hence, the philosopher of the Factory, Ure, denounces as an ineffable disgrace to the English working-class that they inscribed "the slavery of the Factory Acts" on the banner which they bore against capital, manfully striving for "perfect freedom of labour."[157]

France limps slowly behind England. The February revolution was necessary to bring into the world the 12 hours' law,[158] which is much more pdeficient than its English original. For all that, the French revolutionary method has its special advantages. It once for all commands the same limit to the working-day in all shops and factories without distinction, whilst English legislation reluctantly yields to the pressure of circumstances, now on this point, now on that, and is getting lost in a hopelessly bewildering tangle of contradictory enactments. [159] On the other hand, the French law proclaims as a principle that which in England was only won in the name of children, minors, and women, and has been only recently for the first time claimed as a general right.[160]

In the United States of North America, every independent movement of the workers was paralysed so long as slavery disfigured a part of the Republic. Labour cannot emancipate itself in the white skin where in the black it is branded. But out of the death of slavery a new life at once arose. The first fruit of the Civil War was the eight hours' agitation, that ran with the seven-leagued boots of the locomotive from the Atlantic to the Pacific, from New England to California. The General Congress of labour at Baltimore (August 16th, 1866) declared: "The first and great necessity of the present, to free the labour of this country from capitalistic slavery, is the passing of a law by which eight hours shall be the normal working-day in all States of the American Union. We are resolved to put forth all our strength until this glorious result is attained."[161] At the same time, the Congress of the International pWorking Men's Association at Geneva, on the proposition of the London General Council, resolved that "the limitation of the working-day is a preliminary condition without which all further attempts at improvement and emancipation must prove abortive... the Congress proposes eight hours as the legal limit of the working-day."

Thus the movement of the working-class on both sides of the Atlantic, that had grown instinctively out of the conditions of production themselves, endorsed the words of the English Factory Inspector, R. J. Saunders "Further steps towards a reformation of society can never be carried out with any hope of success, unless the hours of labour be limited, and the prescribed limit strictly enforced."[162]

It must be acknowledged that our labourer comes out of the process of production other than he entered. In the market he stood as owner of the commodity "labour-power" face to face with other owners of commodities, dealer against dealer. The contract by which he sold to the capitalist his labour-power proved, so to say, in black and white that he disposed of himself freely. The bargain concluded, it is discovered that he was no "free agent," that the time for which he is free to sell his labour-power is the time for which he is forced to sell it,[163] that in fact the vampire will not lose its hold on him "so long as there is a muscle, a nerve, a drop of blood to be exploited."[164] For "protection" against "the serpent of their agonies," the labourers must put their heads together, and, as a class, compel the passing of a law, an all-powerful social barrier that shall prevent the very workers from selling. by voluntary contract with capital, themselves and their families into slavery and death.[165] In place of the pompous catalogue of the "inalienable prights of man" comes the modest Magna Charta of a legally limited working-day, which shall make clear "when the time which the worker sells is ended, and when his own begins."[166] Quantum mutatus ab illo!

Footnotes

[1] "A day's labour is vague, it may be long or short." ("An Essay on Trade and Commerce, Containing Observations on Taxes, &c." London. 1770, p. 73.)

[2] This question is far more important than the celebrated question of Sir Robert Peel to the Birmingham Chamber of Commerce: What is a pound? A question that could only have been proposed, because Peel was as much in the dark as to the nature of money as the "little shilling men" of Birmingham.

[3] "It is the aim of the capitalist to obtain with his expended capital the greatest possible quantity of labour (d'obtenir du capital depense la plus forte somme de travail possible). J. G. Courcelle-Seneuil. "Traité théorique et pratique des entreprises industrielles." 2nd ed. Paris, 1857, p. 63.

[4] "An hour's labour lost in a day is a prodigious injury to a commercial State.... There is a very great consumption of luxuries among the labouring poor of this kingdom: particularly among the manufacturing populace, by which they also consume their time, the most fatal of consumptions." "An Essay on Trade and Commerce, &c.," p. 47, and 15 3.

[5] "Si le manouvrier libre prend un instant de repos, I'économie sordide qui le suit des yeux avec inquiétude, prétend qu'il la vole." N. Linguet, "Théorie des Lois Civiles. &c." London, 1767, t. II., p. 466.

[6] During the great strike of the London builders, 1860-61, for the reduction of the working-day to 9 hours, their Committee published a manifesto that contained, to some extent, the plea of our worker. The manifesto alludes, not without irony, to the fact, that the greatest profit-monger amongst the building masters, a certain Sir . Peto, was in the odour of sanctity (This same Peto, after 1867, came to an end a la Strousberg.)

[7] "Those who labour ... in reality feed both the pensioners ... [called the rich] and themselves." (Edmund Burke, l. c., p. 2.)

[8] Niebuhr in his "Roman History" says very naively: "It is evident that works like the Etruscan, which in their ruins astound us, pre-suppose in little (!) states lords and vassals." Sismondi says far more to the purpose that "Brussels lace" pre-supposes wage-lords and wage-slaves.

[9] "One cannot see these unfortunates (in the gold mines between Egypt, Ethiopia, and Arabia) who cannot even have their bodies dean, or their nakedness clothed, without pitying their miserable lot. There is no indulgence, no forbearance for the sick, the feeble, the aged, for woman's weakness. All must, forced by blows, work on until death puts an end to their sufferings and their distress." ("Diod. Sic. Bibl. Hist.," lib. 2, c. 13.)

[10] That which follows refers to the situation in the Roumanian provinces before the change effected since the Crimean war.

[11] This holds likewise for Germany, and especially for Prussia east of the Elbe. In the 15th century the German peasant was nearly everywhere a man, who, whilst subject to certain rents paid in produce and labour was otherwise at least practically free. The German colonists in Brandenburg, Pomerania, Silesia, and Eastern Prussia, were even legally acknowledged as free men. The victory of the nobility in the peasants' war put an end to that. Not only were the conquered South German peasants again enslaved. From the middle of the 16th century the peasants of Eastern Prussia, Brandenburg, Pomerania, and Silesia, and soon after the free peasants of Schleswig-Holstein were degraded to the condition of serfs. (Maurer, Fronhöfe iv. vol., — Meitzen, "Der Boden des preussischen Staats" — Hanssen, ``Leibeigenschaft in Schleswig-Holstein." — F. E.)

[12] Further details are to be found in E. Regnault's "Histoire politique et sociale des Principautés Danubiennes," Paris, 1855.

[13] "In general and within certain limits, exceeding the medium size of their kind, is evidence of the prosperity of organic beings. As to man, his bodily height lessens if his due growth is interfered with, either by physical or local conditions. In all European countries in which the conscription holds, since its introduction, the medium height of adult men, and generally their fitness for military service, has diminished. Before the revolution (1789), the minimum for the infantry in France was 165 centimetres; in 1818 (law of March 10th), 157; by the law of March 21, 1832, 156 c.m.; on the average in France more than half are rejected on account of deficient height or bodily weakness. The military standard in Saxony was in 1780, 178 c. m. It is now 155. In Prussia it is 157. According to the statement of Dr. Meyer in the Bavarian Gazette, ay 9th, 1862, the result of an average of 9 years is, that in Prussia out of 1,000 conscripts 716 were unfit for military service, 317 because of deficiency in height, and 399 because of bodily defects.... Berlin in 1858 could not provide

its contingent of recruits, it was 156 men short." J. von Liebig: "Die Chemie in ihrer Anwendung auf Agrikultur und Physiologie. 1862," 7th Ed., vol. 1, pp. 117, 118.

[14] The history of the Factory Act of 1850 will be found in the course of this chapter.

[15] I only touch here and there on the period from the beginning of modern industry in England to 1845. For this period I refer the reader to "Die Lage der arbeitenden Klasse in England," von Friedrich Engels, Leipzig, 1845. How completely Engels understood the nature of the capitalist mode of production is shown by the Factory Reports, Reports on Mines, &c., that have appeared since 1845, and how wonderfully he painted the circumstances in detail is seen on the most superficial comparison of his work with the off~-cial reports of the Children's Employment Commission, published 18 to 20 years later (1863-1867). These deal especially with the branches of industry in which the Factory Acts had not, up to 1862, been introduced, in fact are not yet introduced. Here, then, little or no alteration had been enforced, by authority, in the conditions painted by Engels. I borrow my examples chiefly from the Free-trade period after 1848, that age of paradise, of which the commercial travellers for the great firm of Free-trade, blatant as ignorant, tell such fabulous tales. For the rest England figures here in the foreground because she is the classic representative of capitalist production, and she alone has a continuous set of official ctatistics of the thin~s we are considerinR.

[16] "Suggestions, &c. by Mr. L. Homer, Inspector of Factories," in Factories Regulation Acts. Ordered by the House of Commons to be printed, 9th August, 1859, pp. 4, 5.

[17] Reports of the Inspector of Factories for the half year. October, 1856, p. 35.

[18] Reports, &c., 30th April, 1858, p. 9.

[19] Reports, &c., l. c., p. 43.

[20] Reports &c., l. c., p. 25.

[21] Reports &c., for the half year ending 30th April, 1861. See Appendix No. 2; Reports, &c., 31st October, 1862, pp. 7, 52, 53. The violations of the Acts became more numerous during the last half year 1863. Cf Reports, &c., ending 31st October, 1863, p. 7.

[22] Reports, &c., October 31st, 1860, p. 23. With what fanaticism, according to the evidence of manufacturers given in courts of law, their hands set themselves against every interruption in factory labour, the following curious circumstance shows. In the beginning of June, 1836, information reached the magistrates of Dewsbury (Yorkshire) that the owners of 8 large mills in the neighbourhood of Batley had violated the Factory Acts. Some of these gentlemen were accused of having kept at work 5 boys between 12 and 15 years of age, from 6 a.m. on Friday to 4 p.m. on the following Saturday, not allowing them any respite except for meals and one hour for sleep at midnight. And these children had to do this ceaseless labour of 30 hours in the "shoddyhole," as the hole is called, in which the woollen rags are pulled in pieces, and where a dense atmosphere of dust, shreds, &c., forces even the adult workman to cover his mouth continually with handkerchiefs for the protection of his lungs! The accused gentlemen affirm in lieu of taking an oath — as quakers they were too scrupulously religious to take an oath — that they had, in their great compassion for the unhappy children, allowed them four hours for sleep, but the obstinate children absolutely would not go to bed. The quaker gentlemen were mulcted in £20. Dryden anticipated these gentry:

Fox full fraught in seeming sanctity,
That feared an oath, but like the devil would lie,
That look'd like Lent, and had the holy leer,
And durst not sin! before he said his prayer!"

[23] Rep., 31st Oct., 1856, p. 34.

[24] l. c., p. 35.

[25] l. c., p. 48.

[26] l. c., p. 48.

[27] l. c., p. 48.

[28] l. c., p. 48.

[29] Report of the Insp. &c., 30th April 1860, p. 56.

[30] This is the official expression both in the factories and in the reports.

[31] "The cupidity of mill-owners whose cruelties in the pursuit of gain have hardly been exceeded by those perpetrated by the Spaniards on the conquest of America in the

pursuit of gold." John Wade, "History of the Middle and Working Classes," 3rd Ed. London, 1835, p. 114. The theoretical part of this book, a kind of hand-book of Political Economy, is, considering the time of its publication, original in some parts, e.g., on commercial crises. The historical part is, to a great extent, a shameless plagiarism of Sir F. M. Eden's ``The State of the Poor," London, 1797.

[32] Daily Telegraph, 1 7th January, 1860.

[33] Cf. F. Engels "Lage, etc." pp. 249-51.

[34] Children's Employment Commission. First report., etc., 1863. Evidence, p. 16, 19, 18

[35] Public Health, 3rd report, etc., pp. 102, 104, 105.

[36] Child. Empl. Comm. I. Report, p. 24.

[37] Children's Employment Commission, p. 22, and xi.

[38] l. c., p. xlvii.

[39] l. c., p. liv.

[40] This is not to be taken in the same sense as our surplus-labour time. These gentlemen consider 10 1/2 hours of labour as the normal working-day, which includes of course the normal surplus-labour. After this begins "over-time" which is paid a little better. It will be seen later that the labour expended during the so-called normal day is paid below its value, so that the over-time is simply a capitalist trick in order to extort more surplus-labour, which it would still be, everi if the labour-power expended during the normal working-day were properly paid.

[41] l. c., Evidence, pp. 123, 124, 125, 140, and 54.

[42] Alum finely powdered, or mixed with salt, is a normal article of commerce bearing the significant name of "bakers' stuff."

[43] Soot is a well-known and very energetic form of carbon, and forms a manure that capitalistic chimney-sweeps sell to English farmers. Now in 1862 the British juryman had in a law-suit to decide whether soot, with which, unknown to the buyer, 90% of dust and sand are mixed, is genuine soot in the commercial sense or adulterated soot in the legal sense. The "amis du commerce" decided it to be genuine commercial soot, and nonsuited the plaintiff farmer, who had in addition to pay the costs of the suit.

[44] The French chemist, Chevallier, in his treatise on the "sophistications" of commodities, enumerates for many of the 600 or more articles which he passes in review, 10, 20, 30 different methods of adulteration. He adds that he does not know all the methods and does not mention all that he knows. He gives 6 kinds of adulteration of sugar, 9 of olive oil, 10 of butter, 12 of salt, 19 of milk, 20 of bread, 23 of brandy, 24 of meal, 28 of chocolate, 30 of wine, 32 of coffee, etc. Even God Almighty does not escape this fate. See Rouard de Card, "On the Falsifications of the hlaterials of the Sacrament." ("De la falsification des substances sacramentelles," Paris, 1856.)

[45] "Report, &c., relating to the grievances complained of by the journeymen bakers, &c., London, 1862," and "Second Report, &c., London, 1863."

[46] l. c., First Report, &c., p. vi.

[47] l. c., p. lxxi.

[48] George Read, "The History of Baking," London, 1848, p. 16.

[49] Report (First) &c. Evidence of the "full-priced" baker Cheeseman, p. 108.

[50] George Read, l. c. At the end of the 17th and the beginning of the 18th centuries the factors (agents) that crowded into every possible trade were still denounced as "public nuisances." Thus the Grand Jury at the quarter session of the Justices of the Peace for the County of Somerset, addressed a presentment to the Lower House which, among other things, states, "that these factors of Blackwell Hall are a Public Nuisance and Prejudice to the Clothing Trade, and ought to be put down as a Nuisance." "The Case of our English Wool., &c.," London, 1685, pp. 6, 7.

[51] First Report, &c.

[52] Report of Committee on the Baking Trade in Ireland for 1861.

[53] l. c.

[54] Public meeting of agricultural labourers at Lasswade, near Edinburgh, January 5th, 1866. (See Workman's Advocate, January 13th, 1866.) The formation since the close of 1865 of a Trades' Union among the agricultural labourers at first in Scotland is a historic event. In one of the most oppressed agricultural districts of England, Buckinghamshire, the labourers, in March, 1867, made a ueat strike for the raising of their weekly wage from

9-10 shillings to 12 shillings. (It will be seen from the preceding passage that the movement of the English agricultural proletariat, entirely crushed since the suppression of its violent manifestations after 1830, and especially since the introduction of the new Poor Laws, begins again in the sixties, until it becomes finally epoch-making in 1872. I return to this in the 2nd volume, as well as to the Blue books that have appeared since 1867 on the position of the English land labourers. Addendum to the 3rd ea.)

[55] Reynolds' Newspaper, January, 1866. — Every week this same paper has, under the sensational headings, "Fearful and fatal accidents," "Appalling tragedies," &c., a whole list of fresh railway catastrophes. On these an employe on the North Staffordshire line comments: "Everyone knows the consequences that may occur if the driver and fireman of a locomotive engine are not continually on the look-out. How can that be expected from a man who has been at such work for 29 or 30 hours, exposed to the weather, and without rest. The following is an example which is of very frequent occurrence: — One fireman commenced work on the Monday morning at a very early hour. When he had finished what is called a day's work, he had been on duty 14 hours 50 minutes. Before he had time to get his tea, he was again called on for duty.... The next time he finished he had been on duty 14 hours 25 minutes, making a total of 29 hours 15 minutes without intermission. The rest of the week's work was made up as follows: — Wednesday. 15 hours: Thursday, 15 hours 35 minutes; Friday, 14 2 hours; Saturday, 14 hours 10 minutes, making a total for the week of 88 hours 40 minutes. Now, sir, fancy his astonishment on being paid 6 1/4 days for the whole. Thinking it was a mistake, he applied to the time-keeper,... and inquited what they considered a day's work, and was told 13 hours for a goods man (i.e., 78 hours).... He then asked for what he had made over and above the 78 hours per week, but was refused. However, he was at last told they would give him another quarter, i.e., 10 d.," l. c., 4th February. 1866.

[56] Cf F. Engels, l. c., pp. 253, 254.

[57] Dr. Letheby, Consulting Physician of the Board of Health, declared: "The minimum of air for each adult ought to be in a sleeping room 300, and in a dwelling room 500 cubic feet." Dr. Richardson, Senior Physician to one of the London Hospitals: "With needlewomen of all kinds, including milliners, dressmakers, and ordinary sempstresses, there are three miseries — over-work, deficient air, and either deficient food or deficient digestion.... Needlework, in the main, ... is infinitely better adapted to women than to men. But the mischiefs of the trade, in the metropolis especially, are that it is monopolised by some twenty-six capitalists, who, under the advantages that spring from capital, can bring in capital to force economy out of labour. This power tells throughout the whole class. If a dressmaker can get a little circle of customers, such is the competition that, in her home, she must work to the death to hold together, and this same over-work she must of necessity inflict on any who may assist her. If she fail, or do not try independently, she must join an establishment, where her labour is oot less, but where her money is safe. Placed thus, she becomes a mere slave. tossed about with the variations of society. Now at home, in one room, starving, or near to it, then engaged 15, 16, aye, even 18 hours out of the 24, in an air that is scarcely tolerable, and on food which, even if it be good, cannot be digested in the absence of pure air. On these victims, consumption, which is purely a disease of bad air, feeds." Dr. Richardson: "Work and Over-work," in "Social Science Review," 18th July, 1863.

[58] Morning Star, 23rd June, 1863. — The Times made useofthe circumstance to defend the American slave-owners against Bright, &c. "Very many of us think," says a leader of July 2nd, 1863, "that, while we work our own young women to death, using the scourge of starvation, instead of the crack of the whip, as the instrument of compulsion, we have scarcely a right to hound on fire and slaughter against families who were born slave-owners, and who, at least, feed their slaves well, and work them lightly." In the same manner, the Standard, a Tory organ, fell foul of the Rev. Newman Hall: "He excommunicated the slave-owners, but prays with the fine folk who, without remorse, make the omnibus drivers and conductors of London, &c., work 16 hours a-day for the wages of a dog." Finally, spake the oracle, Thomas Carlyle, of whom I wrote, in 1850, "Zum Teufel ist der Genius, der Kultus ist geblieben." In a short parable, he reduces the one great event of contemporary history, the American Civil War, to this level, that the Peter of the North wants to break the head of the Paul of the South with all his might, because the Peter of the North hires his labour by the day, and the Paul of the South hires his by the

life. ("Macmillan's Magazine." llias Americana in nuce. August, 1863.) Thus, the bubble of Tory sympathy for the urban workers — by no means for the rural — has burst at last. The sum of all is — slavery!

[59] Dr. Richardson, l. c.

[60] Children's Employment Commission. Third Report. London, 1864, pp. iv., v., vi.

[61] "Both in Staffordshire and in South Wales young girls and women are employed on the pit banks and on the coke heaps, not only by day but also by night. This practice has been often noticed in Reports presented to Parliament, as being attended with great and notorious evils. These females employed with the men, hardly distinguished from them in their dress, and begrimed with dirt and smoke, are exposed to the deterioration of character, arising from the loss of self-respect, which can hardly fail to follow from their unfeminine occupation." (l. c., 194, p. xxvi. Cf. Fourth Report (1865), 61, p. xiii.) It is the same in glass-works.

[62] A steel manufacturer who employs children in night-labour remarked: "It seems but natural that boys who work at night cannot sleep and get proper rest by day, but will be running about.' (l. c., Fourth Report, 63, p. xiii.) On the importance of sunlight for the maintenance and growth of the body, a physician writes: "Light also acts upon the tissues of the body directly in hardening them and supporting their elasticity. Tne muscles of animals, when they are deprived of a proper amount of light, become sofl and inelastic, the nenous power loses its tone from defective stimulation, and the daboration of all growth seems to be perverted.... In the case of children, constant access to plenty of light during the day, and to the direct rays of the sun for a part of it, is most essential to health. Light assists in the elaboration of good plastic blood, and hardens the fibre after it has been laid down. It also acts as a stimulus upon the organs of sips, and by this means brings about more activity in the various cerebral functions." Dr. W. Strange, Senior Physician of the Worcester General Hospital, from whose work on "Health" (1864) this passage is taken, writes in a letter to Mr. White, one of the commissioners: "I have had opportunities formerly, when in Lancashire, of observing the effects of nightwork upon children, and I have no hesitation in saying, contrary to what some employers were fond of asserting, those children who were subjected to it soon suffered in their health." (l. c., 284., p. 55.) That such a question should furnish the material of serious controversy, shows plainly how capitalist production acts on the brain-functions of capitalists and their retainers.

[63] l. c., 57, p. xii.

[64] l. c.. Fourth Report (1865). 58. p. xii.

[65] l. c.

[66] l. c., p. xiii. The degree of culture of these "labour-powers" must naturally be such as appears in the following dialogues with one of the commissioners: Jeremiah Haynes, age 12 — "Four times four is 8; 4 fours are 16. A king is him that has all the money and gold. We have aj king (told it is a Queen), they call her the Princess Alexandra. Told that she married the Queen's son. The Queen's son is the Princess Alexandra. A Princess is a man " William Turner, age 12 — "Don't live in England. Think it is a country, but didn't know before." John Morris, age 14 — "Have heard say that God made the world, and that all the people was drowndedbut one, heard say that one was a little bird." William Smith age 15 — ``God made man, man made woman." Edward Taylor, age 15 — "Do not know of London." Henry Matthewman, age 17 — "Had been to chapel, but missed a good many times lately. One name that they preached about was Jesus Christ, but I cannot say any others, and I cannot te~l anything about him. He was not killed, but died like other people. He was not the same as other people in some ways, because he was religious in some ways and others isn't." (l. c., p. xv.) "The devil is a good person. I don't know where he lives." ' Christ was a wicked man." "This girl spelt God as dog, and did not know the name of the queen." ("Ch. Employment Comm. V. Report, 1866 " p. 55, n. 278.) The same system obtains in the glass and paper works as in the metallurgical, already cited. In the paper factories, where the paper is made by machinery, nips-work is the rule for all processes, except rag-sorting. In some cases night-work, by relays, is carried on incessantly throup the whole week, usually from Sunday nipt until midnipt of the following Saturday. Those who are on day-work work 5 days of 12, and I day of 18 hours; those on nips-work 5 nipts of 12, and I of 6 hours in each week. In other cases each set works 24 hours consecutively on alternate days, one set working 6 hours on Monday, and 18 on Saturday to make up the 24 hours. In other cases an intermediate system prevails, by which all employed on the

paper-making machinery work 15 or 16 hours every day in the week. This system, says Commissioner Lord, "seems to combine all the evils of both the 12 hours' and the 24 hours' relays." Children under 13, young persons under 18, and women, work under this nipt system. Sometimes under the 12 hours' system they are obliged, on account of the non-appearance of those that oupt to relieve them, to work a double turn of 24 hours. The evidence proves that boys and girls very often work overtime, which, not unfrequently, extends to 24 or even 36 hours of uninterrupted toil. In the continuous and unvarying process of glazing are found girls of 12 who work the whole month 14 hours a day, "without any regular relief or cessation beyond 2 or, at most, 3 breaks of half an hour each for meals." In some mills. where regular nips-work has been entirely given up, over-work goes on to a terrible extent, "and that often in the dirtiest, and in the hottest, and in the most monotonous of the various processes." ("Ch. EmpIoyment Comm. Report IV., 1865," p. xxxviii, and xxxix.)

[67] Fourth Report, &c.. 1865, 79, p. xvi.

[68] l. c., 80. p. xvi.

[69] l. c., 82. p. xvii.

[70] In our reflecting and reasoning age a man is not worth much who cannot give a good reason for everything, no matter how bad or how crazy. Everything in the world that has been done wrong has been done wrong for the very best of reasons. (Hegel, l. c., p. 249)

[71] l. c., 85, p. xvii. To similar tender scruples of the glass manufacturers that regular meal-times for the children are impossible because as a consequence a certain quantity of heat, radiated by the furnaces, would be "a pure loss" or "wasted," Commissioner White makes answer. His answer.is unlike that of Ure, Senior, &c., and their puny German plagiarists.a la Roscher who are touched by the "abstinence," "self-denial," "saving," of the capitalists in the expenditure of their gold, and by their Timur-Tamerlanish prodigality of human life! "A certain amount of heat beyond what is usual at present might also be going to waste, if meal-times were secured in these cases, but it seems likely not equal in money-value to the waste of animal power now going on in glass-houses throughout the kingdom from growing boys not having enough quiet time to eat their meals at ease, with a little rest afterwards for digestion." (l. c., p. xiv.) And this in the year of progress 1865! Without considering the expenditure of strength in lifting and carrying, such a child, in the sheds where bottle and flint glass are made, walks during the performance of his work 15-20 miles in every 6 hours! And the work often lasts 14 or 15 hours! In many of these glass works, as in the Moscow spinning mills, the system of 6 hours' relays is in force. "During the working part of the week six hours is the utmost unbroken period ever attained at any one time for rest, and out of this has to come the time spent in coming and going to and from work, washing, dressing, and meals, leaving a very short period indeed for rest, and none for fresh air and play, unless at the expense of the sleep necessary for young boys, especially at such hot and fatiguing work.... Even the short sleep is obviously liable to be broken by a boy having to wake himself if it is night, or by the noise, if it is day." Mr. White gives cases where a boy worked 36 consecutive hours; others where,boys of 12 drudged on until 2 in the morning, and then slept in the works till 5 a.m. (3 hours!) only to resume their work. "The amount of work," say Tremenheere and Tufnell, who drafted the general report, "done by boys, youths, girls, and women, in the course of their daily or nightly spell of labour, is certainly extraordinary." (l. c., xliii. and xliv.) Meanwhile, late by night, self-denying Mr. Glass-Capital, primed with port-wine, reels out of his club homeward droning out idiotically. "Britons never, never shall be slaves!"

[72] In England even now occasionally in rural districts a labourer is condemned to imprisonment for desecrating the Sabbath, by working in his front garden. The same labourer is punished for breach of contract if he remains away from his metal, paper, or glass works on the Sunday, even if it be from a religious whim. The orthodox Parliament will hear nothing of Sabbath-breaking if it occurs in the process of expanding capital. A memorial (August 1863), in which the London day-labourers in fish and poultry shops asked for the abolition of Sunday labour, states that their work lasts for the first 6 days of the week on an average 15 hours a-day, and on Sunday 8-10 hours. From this same memorial we learn also that the delicate gourmands among the aristocratic hypocrita of Exeter Hall, especially encourage this "Sunday labour." These "holy ones," so zealous in cute curanda, show their Christianity by the humility with which they bear the overwork,

the privations, and the hunger of others. Obsequium ventris istis (the labourers) perniciosius est.

[73] "We have given in our previous reports the statements of several experienced manufacturers to the effect that over-hours ... certainly tend prematurely to exhaust the workine oower of the men." (l. c., 64. p. xiii.)

[74] Cairnes, "The Slave Power," pp. 110. 111.

[75] John Ward: "The Borough of Stoke-upon-Trent," London, 1843, p. 42.

[76] Ferrand's Speech in the House of Commons, 27th April, 1863.

[77] Those were the very words used by the cotton manufacturers." l. c.

[78] l. c. Mr. Villiers, despite the best of intentions on his part, was "legally" obliged to refuse the requests of the manufacturers. These gentlemen, however, attairied their end through the obliging nature of the local poor law boards. Mr. A. Redgrave, Inspector of Factories, asserts that this time the system under which orphans and pauper children were treated "legally" as apprentices "was not accompanied with the old abuses" (on these "abuses" see Engels, l. c.), although in one case there certainly was "abuse of this system in respect to a number of girls and young women brought from the agricultural districts of Scotland into Lancashire and Cheshire." Under this system the manufacturer entered into a contract with the workhouse authorities for a certain period. He fed, clothed and lodged the children, and gave them a small allowance of money. A remark of Mr. Redgrave to be quoted directly seems strange, especially if we consider that even among the years of prosperity of the English cotton trade, the year 1860 stands unparalleled, and that, besides, wages were exceptionally high. For this extraordinary demand for work had to contend with the depopulation of Ireland, with unexampled emigration from the English and Scotch agricultural districts to Australia and America, with an actual diminution of the population in some of the English agricultural districts, in cons'equence partly of an actual breakdown of the vital force of the labourers, partly of the already effected dispersion of the disposable population through the dealers in human flesh. Despite all this Mr. Redgrave says: "This kind of labour, however, would only be sought after when none other could be procured, for it is a high-priced labour. The ordinary wages of a boy of 13 would be about 4s. per week, but to lodge, to clothe, to feed, and to provide medical attendance and proper superintendence for 50 or 100 of these boys, and to set aside some remuneration for them, could not be accomplished for 4s. a-head per week." (Report of the Inspector of Factories for 30th April, 1860, p. 27.) Mr. Redgrave forgets to tell us how the labourer himself can do all this for his children out of their 4s. a-week wages, when the manufacturer cannot do it for the 50 or 100 children lodged, boarded, superintended all together. To guard against false conclusions from the text, I ought here to remark that the English cotton industry, since it was placed under the Factory Act of 1850 with its regulations of labour-time, &c., must be regarded as the model industry of England. The English cotton operative is in every respect better off than his Continental companion in misery. "The Prussian factory operative labours at least ten hours per week more than his English competitor, and if employed at his own loom in his bwn house, his labour is not restricted to even those additional hours. ("Rep. of Insp. of Fact.," 31st October, 1855, p. 103.) Redgrave, the Factory Inspector mentioned above, after the Industrial Exhibition in 1851, travelled on the Continent, especially in France and Germany, for the purpose of inquiring into the conditions of the factories. Of the Prussian operative he says: "He receives a remuneration sufficient to procure the simple fare, and to supply the slender comforts to which he has been accustomed ... he lives upon his coarse fare, and works hard, wherein his position is subordinate to that of the English operative." ("Rep. of Insp. of Fact." 31st Oct., 1855, p. 85.)

[79] The over-worked "die off with strange rapidity; but the places of those who perish are instantly filled, and a frequent change of persons makes no alteration in the scene." ("England and America." London, 1833, vol. I, p. 55. By E. G. Wakefield.)

[80] See "Public Health. Sixth Report of the Medical Officer of the Privy Council, 1863." Published in London 1864. This report deals especially with the agricultural labourers. "Sutherland ... is commonly represented as a highly improved county ... but ... recent inquiry has discovered that even there, in districts once famous for fine men and gallant soldiers, the inhabitants have degenerated into a meagre and stunted race. In the healthiest situations, on hill sides fronting the sea, the faces of their famished children are as pale as they could be in the foul atmosphere of a London alley." (W. Th. Thornton.

"Overpopulation and its Remedy." l. c., pp. 74, 75.) They resemble in fact the 30,000 "gallant Highlanders" whom Glasgow pigs together in its wynds and closes, with prostitutes and thieves.

[81] "But though the health of a population is so important a fact of the national capital, we are afraid it must be said that the class of employers of labour have not been the most forward to guard and cherish this treasure.... The consideration of the health of the operatives was forced upon the mill-owners." (Times, November 5th, 1861.) "The men of the West Riding became the clothiers of mankind ... the health of the workpeople was sacnficed, and the lace in a few generations must have degenerated. But a reaction set in. Lord Shaftesbury's Bill limited the hours of children's labour," &c. ("Report of the Registrar-General," for October 1861.)

[82] We, therefore, find, e.g., that in the beginning of 1863, 26 firms owning extensive potteries in Staffordshire, amongst others, Josiah Wedgwood, & Sons, petition in a memorial for "some legislative enactment." Competition with other capitalists permits them no voluntary timitation of working-ti me for children, &c. "Much as we deplore the evils before mentioned, it would not be possible to prevent them by any scheme of agreement between the manufacturers.~.. Taking all these points into consideration, we have come to the conviction that some legislative enactment is wanted." ("Children's Employment Comm." Rep. I, 1863, p. 322.) Most recently a much more striking example offers. The rise in the price of cotton during a period of feverish activity, had induced the manufacturers in Blackburn to shorten, by mutual consent, the working-time in their mills during a certain fixed period. This period terminated about the end of November, 1871. Meanwhile, the wealthier manufacturers, who combined spinning with weaving, used the diminution of production resulting from this agreement, to extend their own business and thus to make great profits at the expense of the small employers. The latter thereupon turned in their extremity to the operatives, urged them earnestly to agitate for the 9 hours' system, and promised contributions in money to this end.

[83] The labour Statutes, the like of which were enacted at the same time in France, the Netherlands, and elsewhere, were first formally repealed in England in 1813, long after the changes in n~ethods of production had rendered them obsolete.

[84] "No child under 12 years of age shall be employed in any manufacturing establishment more than 10 hours in one day." General Statutes of Massachusetts, 63, ch. 12. (The various Statutes were passed between 1836 and 1858.) "Labour performed during a period of 10 hours on any day in all cotton, woollen, silk, paper, glass, and flax factories, or in manufactories of iron and brass, shall be considered a legal day's labour. And be it enacted, that hereafter no minor engaged in any factory shall be holden or required to work more than 10 hours in any day,or 60 hours in any week; and that hereafter no minor shall be admitted as a worker under the age of 10 years in any factory within this State." State of New Jersey. An Act to limit the hours of labour, llLc., § I and 2. (Law of 18th March, 1851.) "No minor who has attained the age of 12 years, and is under the age of 15 years, shall be employed in any manufacturing atablishment more than 11 hours in any one day, nor before 5 o'clock in the morning, nor after 7.30 in the evening." ("Revised Statutes of the State of Rhode Island," &c., ch. 139, § 23, Ist July, 1857.)

[85] "Sophisms of Free Trade." 7th Ed. London, 1850, p. 205, 9th Ed., p. 253. This same Tory, moreover, admits that "Acts of Parliament regulating wages, but against the labourer and in favour of the master, lasted for the long period of 464 years. Population grew. These laws were then found, and really became, unnecessary and burdensome." (l. c., p. 206.)

[86] In reference to this statute, J. Wade with truth remarks: "From the statement above (i.e., with regard to the statute) it appears that in 1496 the diet was considered equivalent to one-third of the income of an artificer and one-half the income of a labourer, which indicates a greater degree of independence among the working-classes than prevails at present; for the board, both of labourers and artificers, would now be reckoned at a much higher proportion of their wages." (J. Wade, "History of the Middle and Working Classes, ' pp. 24, 25, and 577.) The opinion that this difference is due to the difference in the pricerelations between food and clothing then and now is refuted by the most cursory glance at "Chronicon Preciosum, Icc." By Bishop Fleetwood. Ist Ed., London, 1707; 2nd Ed., London, 1 745.

[87] W. Petty. ``Political Anatomy of Ireland, Verbum Sapienti," 1672, Ed. 1691, p. 10.

[88] "A Discourse on the necessity of encouraging Mechanick Industry," London, 1690, p. 13. Macaulay, who has falsified English history in the interests of the Whigs and the bourgeoisie, declares as follows: "The practice of setting children prematurely to work ... prevailed in the 17th century to an extent which, when compared with the extent of the manufacturing system, seems almost incredible. At Norwich, the chief seat of the clothing trade, a little creature of six years old was thought fit for labour. Several writers of that time, and among them some who were considered as eminently benevokot, mention with exultation the fact that in that single city, boys and girls of very tender age create wealth exceeding what was necessary for their own subsistence by twelve thousand pounds a year. The more carefully we examine the history of the past, the more reason shall we find to dissent from those who imagine that our age has been fruitful of new social evils.... That which is new is the intelligence and the humanity which remedies them." ("History of England," vol. 1., p. 417.) Macaulay might have reported further that "extremely welldisposed" amfs du commerce in the 17th century, narrate with "exultation" how in a poorhouse in Holland a child of four was employed, and that this example of "vertu m~se en praflque" passes muster in all the humanitarian works, d la Macaulay, to the time of Adam Smith. It is true that with the substitution of manufacture for handicrafts, traces of the exploitation of children begin to appear. This exploitation existed always to a certain extent among peasants, and was the more dkvdoped, the heavier the yoke pressing on the husbandman. The tendency of capital is there unmistakably; but the facts themselves are still as isolated as the phenomena of two-headed children. Hence they were noted "with exultation" as especially worthy of remark and as wonders by the far-seeing "amds du commerce," and recommended as modds for their own time and for posterity. This same Scotch sycophant and fine talker, Macaulay, says: "We hear to-day only of retrogression and see only progress." What eyes, and especially what ears!

[89] Among the accusers of the workpeopk, the most angry is the anonymous author quoted in the text of "An Essay on Trade and Commerce, containing Observations on Taxes, &c.," London, 1770. He had already dealt with this subject in his earlier work: "Considerations on Taxes." London, 1765. Gn the same side follows Polonius Arthur Young, the unutterable statistical prattler. Among the defenders of the working-classes the foremost are: Jacob Vanderlint, in: "Money Answers all Things." London, 1734 the Rev. Nathaniel Forster, D. D., in "An Enquiry into the Causes of the Present High Price of Provisions,,' London, 1767; Dr. Price, and especially Postlethwayt, as well in the supplement to his ``Universal Dictionary of Trade and Commerce," as in his "Great Bntain's Commercial Interest explained and improved." 2nd Edition, 1755. The facts themselves are confirmed by many other writers of the time, among others by Josiah Tucker

[90] Postlethwayt, l. c., "First Preliminary Discourse," p. 14.

[91] "An Essay," &c. He himself relates on p. 96 wherein the "happiness" of the English agricultural labourer already in 1770 consisted. "Their powers are always upon the stretch, they cannot live cheaper than they do, nor work harder."

[92] Protestantism, by changing almost all the traditional holidays into workdays, plays an important pan in the genesis of capital.

[93] "An Essay," 4c., pp. 15, 41, 96, 97, 55, 57, 69. — Jacob Vanderlint, as early as 1734, declared that the secret of the out-cry of the capitalists as to the laziness of the working people was simply that they claimed for the same wages 6 days' labour instead of 4.

[94] l. c., p. 242.

[95] l. c. "The French," he says, "laugh at our enthusiastic ideas of liberty." l. c., p. 78.

[96] "They especially objected to work beyond the 12 hours per day, because the law which fixed those hours, is the only good which remains to them of the legislation of the Republic." ("Rep. of Insp. of Fact.", 31 st October, 1856, p. 80.) The French Twelve Hours' Bill of September 5th, 1850, a bourgeois edition of the decree of the Provisional Government of March 2nd, 1848, holds in all workshops without exceptions. Before this law the working-day in France was without definite limit. It lasted in the factories 14, 15, or more hours. See &'Des classes ouvrieres en France, pendant l'annee 1848. Par M. Blanqui." M. Blanqui the economist, not the Revolutionist, had been entrusted by the Government with an inquiry into the condition of the working-class.

[97] Belgium is the model bourgeois state in regard to the regulation of the working-day. Lord Howard of Welden, English Plenipotentiary at Brussels, reports to the Foreign Office May 12th, 1862: "M. Rogier, the minister, informed me that children's labour is limited neither by a general law nor by any local regulations; that the Government, during the last three years, intended in every session to propose a bill on the subject, but always found an insuperable obstacle in the jealous opposition to any legislation in contradiction with the principle of perfect freedom of labour."

[98] It is certainly much to be regretted that any class of persons should toil 12 hours a day, which, including the time for their meals and for going to and returning from their work, amounts, in fact, to 14 of the 24 hours.... Without entering into the question of health, no one will hesitate, I think, to admit that, in a moral point of view, so entire an absorption of the time of the working-classes, without intermission, from the early age of 13, and in trades not subject to restriction, much younger, must be extremely prejudicial, and is an evil greatly to be deplored.... For the sake, therefore, of public morals. of bringing up an orderly population, and of giving the great body of the people a reasonable enjoyment of life, it is much to be desired that in all trades some portion of every working-day should be reserved for rest and leisure." (Leonard Homer in ``Reports of Insp. of Fact. for 31st Dec., 1841.")

[99] See "Judgment of Mr. J. H. Otway, Belfast. Hilary Sessions, County Antrim, 1860."

[100] It is very characteristic of the regime of Louis Philippe, the bourgeois king, that the one Factory Act passed during his reign, that of March 22nd, 1841, was never put in force. And this law only dealt with child-labour. It fixed 8 hours a day for children between 8 and 12, 12 hours for children between 12 and 16, &c., with many exceptions which allow night-work even for children 8 years old. The supervision and enforcement of this law are, in a country where every mouse is under police administration, left to the good-will of the amis du commerce. Only since 1853, in one single department — the Departement du Nord — has a paid government inspector been appointed. Not less characteristic of the development of French society, generally, is the fact, that Louis Philippe~s law stood solitary among the all-embracing mass of French laws, till the Revolution of 1848.

[101] Report of Insn. of Fact." 30th April, 1860, p. 50.

[102] "Rept. of Insp. of Fact.," 31st October, 1849, p. 6.

[103] "Rept. of Insp. of Fact.," 31st October, 1848, p. 98.

[104] Leonard Homer uses the expression "nefarious practices" in his official reports. ("Report of Insp. of Fact.," 31st October, 1859, p. 7.)

[105] "Rept.," &c., 30th Sept., 1844, p. 15.

[106] The Act allows children to be employed for 10 hours if they do not work day after day, but only on alternate days. In the main, this clause remained inoperative.

[107] "As a reduction in their hours of work would cause a larger number (of children) to be employed, it was thought that the additional supply of children from 8 to 9 years oi age would meet the increased demand" (l. c., p. 13).

[108] "Rep. of Insp. of Fact.," 31st Oct., 1848, p. 16.

[109] "I found that men who had been getting lOs. a week, had had Is. taken off for a reduction in the rate of 10 per cent, and Is. 6d. off the remaining 9s. for the reduction in time, together 2s. 6d.. and notwithstanding this, many of them said they would rather work 10 hours." l. c.

[110] "Though I signed it [the petition!, I said at the time I was putting my hand to a wrong thing.' 'Then why did you put your hand to it?' 'Because I should have been turned off if I had refused.' Whence it would appear that this petitioner felt himself 'oppressed,' but not exactly by the Factory Act." l. c., p. 102.

[111] p. 17, l. c. In Mr. Homer's district 10,270 adult male labourers were thus examined in 181 factories. Their evidence is to be found in the appendix to the Factory Reports for the half-year ending October 1848. These examinations furnish valuable material in other connexions also.

[112] l. c. See the evidence collected by Leonard Homer himself, Nos. 69, 70, 71, 72, 92, 93, and that collected by Sub-lnspector A., Nos. 51, 52, 58, 59, 62, 70, of the Appendix. One manufacturer, too, tells the plain truth. See No. 14, and No. 265, l. c.

[113] Reports, &c., for 31st October, 1848, pp. 133, 134.

[114] Reports, &c., for 30th April, 1848, p. 47.

[115] Reports, &c., for 31st October, 1848, p. 130.

[116] Reports, &c., l. c., p. 142.

[117] Reports &c., for 31st October, 1850, pp. 5, 6.

[118] The nature of capital remains the same in its developed as in its undeveloped form. In the code which the influence of the slave-owners, shortly before the outbreak of the American Civil War, imposed on the territory of New Mexico, it is said that the labourer, in as much as the capitalist has bought his labour-power, "is his (the capitalist's) money." The same view was current among the Roman patricians. The money they had advanced to the plebeian debtor had been transformed via the means of subsistence into the flesh and blood of the debtor. This "flesh and blood" were, therefore, "their money." Hence, the Shylock-law of the Ten Tables. Linguet's hypothesis that the patrician creditors from time to time prepared, beyond the Tiber, bunquets of debtors' flesh, may remain as undecided as that of Daumer on the Christian Euchanst.

[119] Reports, &c.. for 30th April, 1848, p. 28.

[120] Thus, among others, Philanthropist Ashworth to Leonard Homer, in a disgusting Quaker letter. (Reports, &c., April, 1849, p. 4.)

[121] l. c., p. 140.

[122] Reports, &c., for 30th April, 1849, pp. 21, 22. Cf like examples ibid., pp. 4. 5.

[123] By I. and II. Will. IV., ch. 24, s. 10, known as Sir John Wobhouse's Factory Act, it was forbidden to any owner of a cotton-spinning or weaving mill, or the father, son, or brother of such owner, to act as Justice of the Peace in any inquiries that concerned the Factory Act.

[124] l. c.

[125] Reports, &c., for 30th April, 1849, p. S.

[126] Reports, &c., for 31st October, 1849, p. 6.

[127] Reports, &c., for 30th April, 1849, p. 21.

[128] Reports, &c., for 31st October, 1848, p. 95.

[129] See Reports, &c., for 30th April, 1849, p. 6, and the detailed explanation of the "shifting system," by Factory Inspectors Howell and Saunders, in "Reports, &c., for 31st October, 1848." See also the petition to the Queen from the clergy of Ashton and vicinity, in the spring of 1849, against the shift system."

[130] Cf. for example, ·'The Factory Question and the Ten Hours' gill.', By R. H. Greg, 1837.

[131] F. Engels: 'The English Ten Hours' Bill." (In the "Neue Rheinische Zeitung. Politisch-oekonomische Revue." Edited by K. Marx. April number, 1850, p. 13.) The same "high" Court of Justice discovered, during the American Civil War, a verbal ambiguity which exactly reversed the meaning of the law against the arming of pirate ships.

[132] Rep., &c., for 30th April, 1850.

[133] In winter, from 7 a.m. to 7 p.m. may be substituted.

[134] "The present law (of 1850) was a compromise whereby the employed surrendered the benefit of the Ten Hours' Act for the advantage of one uniform period for the commencement and termination of the labour of those whose labour is restricted." (Reports, &c., for 30th April, 1852, p. 14.)

[135] Reports, &c., for Sept., 1844, p. 13.

[136] l. c.

[137] l. c.

[138] l. c.

[139] "Reports, &c., for 31st Oct., 1846," p. 20.

[140] l. c.,p. 27. On the whole the working population, subject to the Factory Act, has greatly improved physically. All medical testimony agrees on this point, and personal obsenation at different times has convinced me of it. Nevertheless, and exclusive of the terrible death-rate of children in the first years of their life, the official reports of Dr. Greenhow show the unfavourable health condition of the manufacturing districts as compared with "agricultural districts of normal health." As evidence, take the following table from his 1861 report:

Percentage of Adult Males engaged in manufactures	Death-rate from Pulmonary Affections per 100,000 Males	Name of District	Death-rate from Pulmonary Affections per 100,000 Females	Percentage of Adult Females engaged in manufactures	Kind of Female Occupation
14.9	598	Wigan	644	18.0	Cotton
42.6	708	Blackburn	734	44.9	Do.
37.3	547	Halifax	564	20.4	Worsted
41.9	611	Bradford	603	30.0	Do.
31.0	691	Macclesfield	804	26.0	Silk
14.9	588	Leek	705	17.2	Do.
36.6	721	Stoke-upon-Trent	665	19.3	Earthen ware
30.4	726	Woolstanton	727	13.9	Do.
	305	Eight healthy agricultural districts	340		

[141] It is well known with what reluctance the English "Free-traders," gave up the protective duty on the silk manufacture. Instead of the protection against French importation, the absence of protection to English factory children now senes their turn.

[142] During 1859 and 1860, the zenith years of the English cotton industry, some manufacturer3 tried, by the decoy bait of higher wages forover-time,to reconcile the adult male operatives to an extension of the working-day. The hand-mule spinners and self-actor mincers put an end to the experiment by a petition to their employers in which they say, "Plainly speaking, our lives are to us a burthen; and, while we are confined to the mills nearly two days a week more than the other operatives of the country, we feel like helots in the land, and that we are perpetuating a system injurious to ourselves and future generations.... This, therefore, is to give you most respectful notice that when we commence work again after the Christmas and New Year's holidays, we shall work 60 hours per week, and no more, or from six to six, with one hour and a half out." (Reports, &rc., for 30th April, 1860, p. 30.)

[143] On the means that the wording of this Act afforded for its violation cf the Parliamentary Return "Factories Regulation Act" (6th August, 1859), and in it Leonard Homer's "Suggestions for amending the Factory Acts to enable the Inspectors to prevent illegal working, now becoming very prevalent."

[144] "Children of the age of 8 years and upwards, have, indeed, been employed from 6 a.m. to 9 p.m. during the last half year in my district." (Reports, &c., for 31st October, 1857, p. 39.)

[145] "The Printworks' Act is admitted to be a failure both with reference to its educational and protective provisions." (Reports, &c., for 31st October, 1862, p. 52.)

[146] Thus, e.g., E. Potter in a letter to the Times of March 24th, 1863. The Times reminded him of the maoufacturers' revolt against the Ten Hours' Bill.

[147] Thus, among others, Mr. W. Newmarch, collaborator and editor of Tooke's "History of Prices." Is it a scientific advance to make cowardly concessions to public opinion?

[148] The Act passed in 1860, determined that, in regard to dye and bleachworks, the working-day should be fixed on August Ist, 1861, provisionally at 12 hours, and definitely on August Ist, 1862, at 10 hours, i.e., at 10 1/2 hours for ordinary days, and 7 1/2 for Saturday. Now, when the fatal year, 1862, came, the old farce was repeated. Besides, the manufacturers petitioned Parliament to allow the employment of young persons and

women for 12 hours during one year longer. "In the existing condition of the trade (the time of the cotton famine), it was ueatly to the advantage of the operatives to work 12 hours per day, and make wages when they could." A bill to this effect had been brought in, "and it was mainly due to the action of the operative bleachers in Scotland that the bill was abandoned." (Reports, &:c., for 31st October, 1862, pp. 14-15.) Thus defeated by-the very workpeople, in whose name it pretended to speak Capital discovered, with the help of lawyer spectacles, that the Act of 1860, drawn up, I;ke all the Acts of Parliament for the "protection of labour," in equivocal phrases, gave them a pretext to exclude from its working the calenderers and finishers. English jurisprudence, ever the faithful servant of capital, sanctioned in the COun of Common Pleas this piece of pettifogging. "The operatives have been greatly disappointed ... they have comphined of over-work, and it is greatly to be regretted that the clear intention of the legislature should have failed by reason of a faulty definition." (l. c., p. 18.)

[149] The "open-air bleachers" had evaded the law of 1860, by means of the lie that no women worked at it in the night. The lie was exposed by the Fwtory Inspectors, and at the same time Parliament was, by petitions ffom the operatives, bereft of its notions as to the cool meadow-fragrance, in which bleaching in the open-air was reported to take place. In this aerial bleaching, drying-rooms were used at temperatures of from 90° to 100° Fahrenheit, in which the work was done for the most part by girls. "Cooling" is the technical expression for their occasional escape from the drying-rooms into the fresh air. "Fifteen girls in stoves. Heat from 80° to 90° for linens, and 100° and upwards for cambrics. Twelve girls ironing and doing-up in a small room about 10 feet square, in the centre of which is a close stove. The girls stand round the stove, which throws out a terrific heat, and dries the cambrics rapidly for the ironers. The hours of work for these hands are unlimited. If busy, they work till 9 or 12 at night for successive nights." (Reports, &c., for 31st October, 1862, p. 56.) A medical man states: "No special hours are allowed for cooling, but if the temperature gets too high, or the workers' hands get soiled from perspiration, they are allowed to go out for a few minutes.... My experience, which is considerable, in treating the diseases of stove workers, compels me to express the opinion that their sanitary condition is by no means so high as that of the operatives in a spinning factory (and Capital, in its memorials to Parliament, had painted them as floridly healthy after the manner of Rubens.) The diseases most observable amongst them are phthisis, bronchitis, irregularity of uterine functions, hysteria in its most aggravated forms, and rheumatism. All of these, I believe, are either directly or indirectly induced by the impure, overheated air of the apartments in which the hands are employed and the want of sufficient comfortable clothing to protect them from the cold, damp atmosphere, in winter, when going to their homes." (l. c., pp. 56-57.) The Factory Inspectors remarked on the supplementary law of 1860, torn from these open-air bleachers: "The Act has not only failed to afford that protection to the workers which it appears to offer, but contains a clause ... apparently so worded that, unless persons are detected working after 8 o'clock at night they appear to come under no protective provisions at all, and if they do so work the mode of proof is so doubtful that a conviction can scarcely follow." (l. c., p. 52.) "To all intents and purposes, therefore, as an Act for any benevolent or educational purpose, it is a failure; since it can scarcely be called benevolent to permit, which is tantamount to compelling, women and children to work 14 hours a day with or without meals, as the case may be, and perhaps for longer hours than these, without limit as to age, without reference to sex, and without regard to the social habits of the families of the neighbourhood, in which such works (bleaching and dyeing) are situated." (Reports, &c., for 30th April, 1863, p. 40.)

[150] Note to the 2nd Ed. Since 1866, when I wrote the above passages, a reaction has again set in.

[151] "The conduct of each of these classes (capitalists and workmen) has been the result of the relative situatico in which they have been placed." (Reports, &c., for 31st October, 1848, p. 113.)

[152] "The employments, placed under restriction, were connected with the manufacture of textile fabrics by the aid of steam or water-power There were two conditions to which an employment must be subject to cause it to be inspected, viz., the use of steam or waterpower, and the manufacture of certain specified fibr=." (Reports, &c., f.or 31st October, 1864, p. 8.)

[153] On the condition of so-called domestic industries, specially valuable materials are to be found in the latfft reports of the Children's Employment Commission.

[154] "The Acts of last Session (1864) ... embrace a diversity of occupations, the customs in which differ greatly, and the use of mechanical power to give motion to machinery is no longer one of the elements necessary. as formerly, to constitute, in legal phrase, a 'Factory.'" (Reports, &c., for 31st October, 1864, p. 8.)

[155] Belgium, the paradise of Continental Liberalism, shows no trace of this movement. Even in the coal and metal mines labourers of both sexes, and all ages, are consumed, in perfect "freedom" at any period and through any length of time. Of every 1,000 persons employed there, 733 are men, 88 women. 135 boys, and 44 girls under 16; in the blast furnaces, &c., of every 1,000, 668 are men, 149 women, 98 boys, and 85 girls under 16. Add to this the low wages for the enormous exploitafion of mature and immature labour-power. The average daily pay for a man is 2s. 8d.. for a woman, 1s. 8d.. for a boy. 1s. 2 1/2 d. As a result, Belgium had in 1863, as compared with 1850, nearly doubled both the amount and the value of its exports of coal, iron, &c.

[156] Robert Owen, soon after 1810, not only maintained the necessity of a limitation of the working-day in theory, but actually introduced the 10 hours' day into his factory at New Lanark. This was laughed at as a communistic Utopia; so were his "Combination of children s education with productive labour and the Co-operative Societies of workingmen. first called into being by him. To-day. the first Utopia is a Factory Act, the second figures as an official phrase in all Factory Acts, the third is already being used as a cloak for reactionary humbug.

[157] Ure: "French translation, Philosophie des Manufactures." Paris, 1836, Vol. II, pp. 39, 40, 67, 77, &c.

[158] In the Compte Rendu of the International Statistical Congress at Paris, 1855, it is stated: "The French law, which limits the length of daily labour in factories and workshops to 12 hours, does not confine this work to definite fixed hours. For children's labour only the work-time is prescabed as between 5 a.m. and 9 p.m. Therefore, some of the masters use the nght which this fatal silence gives them to keep their works going, without intermission, day in, day out, possibly with the exception of Sunday. For this purpose they use two different sets of workers, of whom neither is in the workshop more than 12 hours at a time, but the work of the establishment lasts day and night. The law is satisfied, but is humanity?" Besides "the destructive influence or night-labour on the human organism," stress is also laid upon "the fatal influence of the association of the two sexes by night in the same badly-lighted workshops."

[159] "For instance, there is within my district one occupier who, within the same curtilage, is at the same time a bleacher and dyer under the Bleaching and Dyeing Works Act, a printer under the Print Works Act, and a finisher under the Factory Act." (Repon of Mr. Baker, in Reports, lic., for October 31st, 1861, p. 20.) Afler enumerating the different provisions of these Acts,and the complications arising from them, Mr. Baker says: "It will hence appear that it must be very difficult to secure the execution of these three Acts of Parliament where the occupier chooses to evade the law." But what is assured to the lawyers by this is law-suits.

[160] Thus the Factory Inspectors at last venture to say: "These objections (of capital to the legal limitation of the working-day) must succumb before the broad principle of the rights of labour.... There is a time when the master's right in his workman's labour ceases, and his time becomes his own, even if there were no exhaustion in the question." (Reports, 8cc., for 31 st Oct., 1862, p. 54.)

[161] "We, the workers of Dunkirk, declare that the length of time of labour required under the present system is too great, and that, far from leaving the worker time for rest and educatioo, it plunges him into a coodition of servitude but little better than slavery. That is why we decide that 8 hours are enough for a working-day, and ought to be legally recognised as enough; why we call to our help that powerful lever, the press; ... and why we shall consider all those that refuse us this help as enemies of the reform of labour and of the rights of the labourer." (Resolution of the Working Men of Dunkirk, New York State, 1866.)

[162] Reports, &c., for Oct., 1848, p. 112.

[163] "The proceedings (the manoeuvres of capital, e.g., from 1848-50) have afforded, moreover, incontrovertible proof of the fallacy of the assertion so often advanced, that operatives need no protection, but may be considered as free agents in the disposal of the only property which they possess — the labour of their hands and the sweat of their brows." (Reports, &c., for April 30th, 1850, p. 45.) "Free labour (if so it may be termed) even in a free country, requires the strong arm of the law to protect it." (Reports, &c., forOctober31st, 1864, p. 34.) "To permit, which is tantamount to compelling ... to work 14 hours a day with or without meals," &c. (Repts., &c., for April 30th, 1863, p. 40.)

[164] Friedrich Engels, l. c., p. 5

[165] The 10 Hours' Act has, in the branches of industry that come under it, "put an end to the premature decrepitude of the former long-hour workers." (Reports, &c., for 31st Oct., 1859, p. 47.) "Capital (in factories) can never be employed in keeping the machinery in motion beyond a limited time, without certain injury to the health and morals of the labourers employed; and they are not in a position to protect themselves." l. c., p. 8)

[166] "A still greater boon is the distinction at last made clear between the worker's own time and his master's. The worker knows now when that which he sells is ended, and when his own begins; and by possessing a sure foreknowledge of this, is enabled to prearrange his own minutes for his own purposes." (l. c., p. 52.) "By making them masters of their own time (the Factory Acts) have given them a moral energy which is directing them to the eventual possession of political power" (l. c., p. 47). With suppressed irony, and in very well weighed words, the Factory Inspectors hint that the actual law also frees the capitalist from some of the brutality natural to a man who is a mere embodiment of capital, and that it has given him time for a little "culture." "Formerly the master had no time for anything but money; the servant had no time for anything but labour" (l. c., p. 48).

Chapter Eleven
Rate and Mass of Surplus Value

In this chapter, as hitherto, the value of labour-power, and therefore the part of the workingday necessary for the reproduction or maintenance of that labour-power, are supposed to be given, constant magnitudes.

This premised, with the rate, the mass is at the same time given of the surplusvalue that the individual labourer furnishes to the capitalist in a definite period of time. If, e.g., the necessary labour amounts to 6 hours daily, expressed in a quantum of gold = 3 shillings, then 3s. is the daily value of one labour-power or the value of the capital advanced in the buying of one labour-power. If, further, the rate of surplusvalue be = 100%, this variable capital of 3s. produces a mass of surplusvalue of 3s., or the labourer supplies daily a mass of surpluslabour equal to 6 hours.

But the variable capital of a capitalist is the expression in money of the total value of all the labour-powers that he employs simultaneously. Its value is, therefore, equal to the average value of one labour-power, multiplied by the number of labour-powers employed. With a given value of labour-power, therefore, the magnitude of the variable capital varies directly as the number of labourers employed simultaneously. If the daily value of one labour-power = 3s., then a capital of 300s. must be advanced in order to exploit daily 100 labour-powers, of n times 3s., in order to exploit daily n labour-powers.

In the same way, if a variable capital of 3s., being the daily value of one labour-power, produce a daily surplusvalue of 3s., a variable capital of 300s. will produce a daily surplusvalue of 300s., and one of n times 3s. a daily surplusvalue of n x 3s. The mass of the surplusvalue produced is therefore equal to the surplusvalue which the workingday of one labourer supplies multiplied by the number of labourers employed. But as further the mass of surplusvalue which a single labourer produces, the value of labour-power being given, is determined by the rate of the surplusvalue, this law follows: the mass of the surplusvalue produced is equal to the amount of the variable capital advanced, multiplied by the rate of surplusvalue, in other words: it is determined by the compound ratio between the number of labour-powers exploited simultaneously by the same capitalist and the degree of exploitation of each individual labour-power.

Let the mass of the surplusvalue be S, the surplusvalue supplied by the individual labourer in the average day s the variable capital daily advanced in the purchase of one individual labour-power v, the sum total of the variable capital V, the value of an average labour-power P, its degree of exploitation

a'	(surplus-labor)
a	(necessary-labor)

and the number of labourers employed n; we have:

		{	s/v	×	V
S	=	{			
		{	P	×	a'/a	n

It is always supposed, not only that the value of an average labour-power is constant, but that the labourers employed by a capitalist are reduced to average labourers. There are exceptional cases in which the surplusvalue produced does not increase in proportion to the number of labourers exploited, but then the value of the labour-power does not remain constant.

In the production of a definite mass of surplusvalue, therefore the decrease of one factor may be compensated by the increase of the other. If the variable capital diminishes, and at the same time the rate of surplusvalue increases in the same ratio, the mass of surplusvalue produced remains unaltered. If on our earlier assumption the capitalist must advance 300s., in order to exploit 100 labourers a day, and if the rate of surplusvalue amounts to 50%, this variable capital of 300s. yields a surplusvalue of 150s. or of 100 x 3 workinghours. If the rate of surplusvalue doubles, or the workingday, instead of being extended from 6 to 9, is extended from 6 to 12 hours and at the same time variable capital is lessened by half, and reduced to 150s., it yields also a surplus-value of 150s. or 50 x 6 workinghours. Diminution of the variable capital may therefore be compensated by a proportionate rise in the degree of exploitation of labour-power, or the decrease in the number of the labourers employed by a proportionate extension of the workingday. Within certain limits therefore the supply of labour exploitable by capital is independent of the supply of labourers. [1] On the contrary, a fall in the rate of surplusvalue leaves unaltered the mass of the surplus-value produced, if the amount of the variable capital, or number of the labourers employed, increases in the same proportion.

Nevertheless, the compensation of a decrease in the number of labourers employed, or of the amount of variable capital advanced by a rise in the rate of surplusvalue. or by the lengthening of the working-day, has impassable limits. Whatever the value of labour-power may be, whether the workingtime necessary for the maintenance of the labourer is 2 or 10 hours, the total value that a labourer can produce, day in, day out, is always less than the value in which 24 hours of labour are embodied, less than 12s., if 12s. is the money expression for 24 hours of realised labour. In our former assumption, according to which 6 workinghours are daily necessary in order to reproduce the labour-power itself or to replace the value of the capital advanced in its purchase, a variable capital of 1,500s., that employs 500 labourers at a rate of surplusvalue of 100% with a 12 hours' workingday, produces daily a surplusvalue of 1,500s. or of 6 x 500 workinghours. A capital of 300s. that employs 100 labourers a day with a rate of surplusvalue of 200% or with a workingday of 18 hours, produces only a mass of surplusvalue of 600s. or 12 x 100 workinghours; and its total value-product, the equivalent of the variable capital advanced plus the surplus-value, can, day in, day out, never reach the sum of 1,200s. or 24 x 100 workinghours. The absolute limit of the average workingday -- ; this being by nature always less than 24 hours -- ; sets an absolute limit to the compensation of a reduction of variable capital by a higher rate of surplusvalue, or of the decrease of the number of labourers exploited by a higher degree of exploitation of labour-power. This palpable law is of importance for the clearing up of many phenomena, arising from a tendency (to be worked out later on) of capital to reduce as much as possible the number of labourers employed by it, or its variable constituent transformed into labour-power, in contradiction to its other tendency to produce the greatest possible mass of surplusvalue. On the other hand, if the mass of labour-power employed, or the amount of variable capital, increases, but not in proportion to the fall in the rate of surplusvalue, the mass of the surplusvalue produced, falls.

A third law results from the determination, of the mass of the surplus-value produced, by the two factors: rate of surplusvalue and amount of variable capital advanced. The rate of surplusvalue, or the degree of exploitation of labour-power, and the value of labour-power, or the amount of necessary workingtime being given, it is selfevident that the greater the variable capital, the greater would be the mass of the value produced and of the surplus value. If the limit of the working-day is given, and also the limit of its necessary constituent, the mass of value and surplusvalue that an individual capitalist produces, is clearly exclusively dependent on the mass of labour that he sets in motion. But this, under the conditions supposed above, depends on the mass of labour-power, or the number of labourers whom he exploits, and this number in its turn is determined by the amount of the variable capital advanced. With a given rate of surplusvalue, and a given value of labour-power, therefore, the masses of surplusvalue produced vary directly as the amounts of the variable capitals advanced. Now we know that the capitalist divides his capital into two parts. One part he lays out in means of production. This is the constant part of his capital. The other part he lays out in living labour-power. This part forms his variable capital. On the basis of the same mode of social production, the division of capital into constant and variable differs in different branches of production, and within the same branch of production, too, this relation changes with changes in the technical conditions and in the social combinations of the processes of production. But in whatever proportion a given capital breaks up into a constant and a variable part, whether the latter is to the former as 1:2 or 1:10 or 1:x, the law just laid down is not affected by this. For, according to our previous analysis, the value of the constant capital reappears in the value of the product, but does not enter into the newly produced value, the newly created valueproduct. To employ 1,000 spinners, more raw material, spindles, &c., are, of course, required, than to employ 100. The value of these additional means of production however may rise, fall, remain unaltered, be large or small; it has no influence on the process of creation of surplusvalue by means of the labour-powers that put them in motion. The law demonstrated above now, therefore, takes this form: the masses of value and of surplusvalue produced by different capitals — the value of labour-power being given and its degree of exploitation being equal — vary directly as the amounts of the variable constituents of these capitals, i.e., as their constituents transformed into living labour-power.

This law clearly contradicts all experience based on appearance. Everyone knows that a cotton spinner, who, reckoning the percentage on the whole of his applied capital, employs much constant and little variable capital, does not, on account of this, pocket less profit or surplusvalue than a baker, who relatively sets in motion much variable and little constant capital. For the solution of this apparent contradiction, many intermediate terms are as yet wanted, as from the standpoint of elementary algebra many intermediate terms are wanted to understand that 0/0 may represent an actual magnitude. Classical economy, although not formulating the law, holds instinctively to it, because it is a necessary consequence of the general law of value. It tries to rescue the law from collision with contradictory phenomena by a violent abstraction. It will be seen later[2] how the school of Ricardo has come to grief over this stumblingblock. Vulgar economy which, indeed, "has really learnt nothing," here as everywhere sticks to appearances in opposition to the law which regulates and explains them. In opposition to Spinoza, it believes that "ignorance is a sufficient reason."

The labour which is set in motion by the total capital of a society, day in, day out, may be regarded as a single collective workingday. If, e.g., the number of labourers is a million, and the average working-day of a labourer is 10 hours, the social workingday consists of ten million hours. With a given length of this workingday, whether its limits are fixed physically or socially, the mass of surplusvalue can only be increased by increasing the number of labourers, i.e., of the labouring population. The growth of population here forms the mathematical limit to the production of surplusvalue by the total social capital. On the contrary, with a given amount of population, this limit is formed by the possible lengthening of the workingday.[3] It will, however, be seen in the following chapter that this law only holds for the form of surplusvalue dealt with up to the present.

From the treatment of the production of surplusvalue, so far, it follows that not every sum of money, or of value, is at pleasure transformable into capital. To effect this transformation, in fact, a certain minimum of money or of exchangevalue must be presupposed in the hands of the individual possessor of money or commodities. The minimum of variable capital is the cost price of a single labour-power, employed the whole year through, day in, day out, for the production of surplusvalue. If this labourer were in possession of his own means of production, and were satisfied to live as a labourer, he need not work beyond the time necessary for the reproduction of his means of subsistence, say 8 hours a day. He would, besides, only require the means of production sufficient for 8 workinghours. The capitalist, on the other hand, who makes him do, besides these 8 hours, say 4 hours' surplus-labour, requires an additional sum of money for furnishing the additional means of production. On our supposition, however, he would have to employ two labourers in order to live, on the surplusvalue appropriated daily, as well as, and no better than a labourer, i.e., to be able to satisfy his necessary wants. In this case the mere maintenance of life would be the end of his production, not the increase of wealth; but this latter is implied in capitalist production. That he may live only twice as well as an ordinary labourer, and besides turn half of the surplusvalue produced into capital, he would have to raise, with the number of labourers, the minimum of the capital advanced 8 times. Of course he can, like his labourer, take to work himself, participate directly in the process of production, but he is then only a hybrid between capitalist and labourer, a "small master." A certain stage of capitalist production necessitates that the capitalist be able to devote the whole of the time during which he functions as a capitalist, i.e., as personified capital, to the appropriation and therefore control of the labour of others, and to the selling of the products of this labour.[4] The guilds of the middle ages therefore tried to prevent by force the transformation of the master of a trade into a capitalist, by limiting the number of labourers that could be employed by one master within a very small maximum. The possessor of money or commodities actually turns into a capitalist in such cases only where the minimum sum advanced for production greatly exceeds the maximum of the middle ages. Here, as in natural science, is shown the correctness of the law discovered by Hegel (in his "Logic"), that merely quantitative differences beyond a certain point pass into qualitative changes.[5]

The minimum of the sum of value that the individual possessor of money or commodities must command, in order to metamorphose himself into a capitalist, changes with the different stages of development of capitalist production, and is at given stages different in different spheres of production, according to their special and technical conditions. Certain spheres of production demand, even at the very outset of capitalist production, a minimum of capital that is not as yet found in the hands of single individuals. This gives rise partly to state subsidies to private persons, as in France in the time of Clobber, and as in many German states up to our own epoch, partly to the formation of societies with legal monopoly for the exploitation of certain branches of industry and commerce, the forerunners of our modern jointstock companies.[6]

Within the process of production, as we have seen, capital acquired the command over labour, i.e., over functioning labour-power or the labourer himself. Personified capital, the capitalist takes care that the labourer does his work regularly and with the proper degree of intensity.

Capital further developed into a coercive relation, which compels the workingclass to do more work than the narrow round of its own lifewants prescribes. As a producer of the activity of others, as a pumper-out of surpluslabour and exploiter of labour-power, it surpasses in energy, disregard of bounds, recklessness and efficiency, all earlier systems of production based on directly compulsory labour.

At first, capital subordinates labour on the basis of the technical conditions in which it historically finds it. It does not, therefore, change immediately the mode of production. The production of surplusvalue — in the form hitherto considered by us — by means of simple extension of the workingday, proved, therefore, to be independent of any change in the mode of production itself. It was not less active in the oldfashioned bakeries than in the modern cotton factories.

If we consider the process of production from the point of view of the simple labourprocess, the labourer stands in relation to the means of production, not in their quality as capital, but as the mere means and material of his own intelligent productive activity. In tanning, e.g., he deals with the skins as his simple object of labour. It is not the capitalist whose skin he tans. But it is different as soon as we deal with the process of production from the point of view of the process of creation of surplusvalue. The means of production are at once changed into means for the absorption of the labour of others. It is now no longer the labourer that employs the means of production, but the means of production that employ the labourer. Instead of being consumed by him as material elements of his productive activity, they consume him as the ferment necessary to their own lifeprocess, and the lifeprocess of capital consists only in its movement as value constantly expanding, constantly multiplying itself. Furnaces and workshops that stand idle by night, and absorb no living labour, are "a mere loss" to the capitalist. Hence, furnaces and workshops constitute lawful claims upon the nightlabour of the work-people. The simple transformation of money into the material factors of the process of production, into means of production, transforms the latter into a title and a right to the labour and surpluslabour of others. An example will show, in conclusion, how this sophistication, peculiar to and characteristic of capitalist production, this complete inversion of the relation between dead and living labour, between value and the force that creates value, mirrors itself in the consciousness of capitalists. During the revolt of the English factory lords between 1848 and 1850, "the head of one of the oldest and most respectable houses in the West of Scotland, Messrs. Carlile Sons & Co., of the linen and cotton thread factory at Paisley, a company which has now existed for about a century, which was in operation in 1752, and four generations of the same family have conducted it" ... this "very intelligent gentleman" then wrote a letter[7] in the Glasgow Daily Mail of April 25th, 1849, with the title, "The relay system," in which among other things the following grotesquely naïve passage occurs: "Let us now ... see what evils will attend the limiting to 10 hours the working of the factory.... They amount to the most serious damage to the millowner's prospects and property. If he (i.e., his "hands") worked 12 hours before,and is limited to 10, then every 12 machines or spindles in his establishment shrink to 10, and should the works be disposed of, they will be valued only as 10, so that a sixth part would thus be deducted from the value of every factory in the country."[8]

To this West of Scotland bourgeois brain, inheriting the accumulated capitalistic qualities of "four generations." the value of the means of production, spindles, &c., is so inseparably mixed up with their property, as capital, to expand their own value, and to swallow up daily a definite quantity of the unpaid labour of others, that the head of the firm of Carlile & Co. actually imagines that if he sells his factory, not only will the value of the spindles be paid to him, but, in addition, their power of annexing surplusvalue, not only the labour which is embodied in them, and is necessary to the production of spindles of this kind, but also the surpluslabour which they help to pump out daily from the brave Scots of Paisley, and for that very reason he thinks that with the shortening of the workingday by 2 hours, the sellingprice of 12 spinning machines dwindles to that of 10!

Footnotes

[1] This elementary law appears to be unknown to the vulgar economists, who, upside-down Archimedes, in the determination of the market-price of labour by supply and demand, imagine they have found the fulcrum by means of which, not to move the world, but to stop its motion.

[2] Further particulars will be given in Book IV.

[3] "The Labour, that is the economic time, of society, is a given portion, say ten hours a day of a million of people, or ten million hours.... Capital has its boundary of increase. This boundary may, at any given period, be attained in the actual extent of economic time employed." ("An Essay on the Political Economy of Nations." London, 1821, pp. 47, 49.)

[4] "The farmer cannot rely on his own labour, and if he does, I will maintain that he is a loser by it. His employment should be a general attention to the whole: his thresher must be watched, or he will soon lose his wages in corn not threshed out, his mowers reapers, &c., must be looked after; he must constantly go round his fences; he must see there is no neglect; which would be the case if he was confined to any one spot." ("`An Inquiry into the Connexion between the Present Price of Provisions and the Size of Farms, &c. By a Farmer." London, 1773, p. 12.) This book is very interesting. In it the genesis of the "capitalist farmer" or "merchant farmer," as he is explicitly called, may be studied, and his selfglorification at the expense of the small farmer who has only to do with bare subsistence, be noted. "The class of capitalists are from the first partially, and they become ultimately completely, discharged from the necessity of the manual labour." ("Textbook of Lectures on the Political Economy of Nations. By the Rev. Richard Jones." Hertford 1852. Lecture III., p. 39.)

[5] The molecular theory of modern chemistry first scientifically worked out by Laurent and Gerhardt rests on no other law. (Addition to 3rd Edition.) For the explanation of this statement, which is not very clear to nonchemists, we remark that the author speaks here of the homologous series of carbon compounds, first so named by C. Gerhardt in 1843, each series of which has its own general algebraic formula. Thus the series of paraffins: $CnH_{2n}+2$, that of the normal alcohols: $CnH_{2n}+2O$; of the normal fatty acids: $CnH_{2n}O_2$ and many others. In the above examples, by the simply quantitative addition of CH_2 to the molecular formula, a qualitatively different body is each time formed. On the share (overestimated by Marx) of Laurent and Gerhardt in the determination of this important fact see Kopp, "Entwicklung der Chemie." Munchen, 1873, pp. 709, 716, and Schorkmmer, 'The Rise and Development of Organic Chemistry." London, 1879, p. 54. — F. E.

[6] Martin Luther calls these kinds of institutions: "The Company Monopolia."

[7] Reports of Insp. of Fact., April 30th, 1849, p. 59.

[8] l. c., p. 60. Factory Inspector Stuart, himself a Scotchman, and in contrast to the English Factory Inspectors, quite taken captive by the capitalistic method of thinking, remarks expressly on this letter which he incorporates in his report that it is "the most useful of the communications which any of the factoryowners working with relays have

given to those engaged in the same trade, and which is the most calculated to remove the prejudices of such of them as have scruples respecting any change of the arrangement of the hours of work."

Part IV:
Production of Relative Surplus Value

Chapter Twelve:
The Concept of Relative Surplus-Value

That portion of the working-day which merely produces an equivalent for the value paid by the capitalist for his labour-power, has, up to this point, been treated by us as a constant magnitude, and such in fact it is, under given conditions of production and at a given stage in the economic development of society. Beyond this, his necessary labour-time, the labourer, we saw, could continue to work for 2, 3, 4, 6, &c., hours. The rate of surplus-value and the length of the working-day depended on the magnitude of this prolongation. Though the necessary labour-time was constant, we saw, on the other hand, that the total working-day was variable. Now suppose we have a working-day whose length, and whose apportionment between necessary labour and surplus-labour, are given. Let the whole line a c, abc represent, for example, a working-day of 12 hours; the portion of a b 10 hours of necessary labour, and the portion b c 2 hours of surplus-labour. How now can the production of surplus-value be increased, i.e., how can the surplus-labour be prolonged, without, or independently of, any prolongation of a c?

Although the length of a c is given, b c appears to be capable of prolongation, if not by extension beyond its end c, which is also the end of the working-day a c, yet, at all events, by pushing back its starting-point b in the direction of a. Assume that b'b in the line ab'bc is equal to half of b c or to one hour's labour-time. If now, in a c, the working-day of 12 hours, we move the point b to b', b c becomes b' c; the surplus-labour increases by one half, from 2 hours to 3 hours, although the working-day remains as before at 12 hours. This extension of the surplus labour-time from b c to b' c, from 2 hours to 3 hours, is, however, evidently impossible, without a simultaneous contraction of the necessary labour-time from a b into a b', from 10 hours to 9 hours. The prolongation of the surplus-labour would correspond to a shortening of the necessary labour; or a portion of the labour-time previously consumed, in reality, for the labourer's own benefit, would be converted into labour-time for the benefit of the capitalist. There would be an alteration, not in the length of the working-day, but in its division into necessary labour-time and surplus labour-time.

On the other hand, it is evident that the duration of the surplus-labour is given, when the length of the working-day, and the value of labour-power, are given. The value of labour-power, i.e., the labour-time requisite to produce labour-power, determines the labour-time necessary for the reproduction of that value. If one working-hour be embodied in sixpence, and the value of a day's labour-power be five shillings, the labourer must work 10 hours a day, in order to replace the value paid by capital for his labour-power, or to produce an equivalent for the value of his daily necessary means of subsistence. Given the value of these means of subsistence, the value of his labour-power is given;[1] and given the value of his labour-power, the duration of his necessary labour-time is given. The duration of the surplus-labour, however, is arrived at, by subtracting the necessary labour-time from the total working-day. Ten hours subtracted from twelve, leave two, and it is not easy to see, how, under the given conditions, the surplus-labour can possibly be prolonged beyond two hours. No doubt, the capitalist can, instead of five shillings, pay the labourer four shillings and sixpence or even less. For the reproduction of this value of four shillings and sixpence, nine hours' labour-time would suffice; and consequently three hours of surplus-labour, instead of two, would accrue to the capitalist, and the surplus-value would rise from one shilling to eighteen-pence. This result, however, would be obtained only by lowering the wages of the labourer below the value of his labour-power. With the four shillings and sixpence which he produces in nine hours, he commands one-tenth less of the necessaries of life than before, and consequently the proper reproduction of his labour-power is crippled. The surplus-labour would in this case be prolonged only by an overstepping of its normal limits; its domain would be extended only by a usurpation of part of the domain of necessary labour-time. Despite the important part which this method plays in actual practice, we are excluded from considering it in this place, by our assumption, that all commodities, including labour-power, are bought and sold at their full value. Granted this, it follows that the labour-time necessary for the production of labour-power, or for the reproduction of its value, cannot be lessened by a fall in the labourer's wages below the value of his labour-power, but only by a fall in this value itself. Given the length of the working-day, the prolongation of the surplus-labour must of necessity originate in the curtailment of the necessary labour-time; the latter cannot arise from the former. In the example we have taken, it is necessary that the value of labour-power should actually fall by one-tenth, in order that the necessary labour-time may be diminished by one-tenth, i.e., from ten hours to nine, and in order that the surplus labour may consequently be prolonged from two hours to three.

Such a fall in the value of labour-power implies, however, that the same necessaries of life which were formerly produced in ten hours, can now be produced in nine hours. But this is impossible without an increase in the productiveness of labour. For example, suppose a shoe-maker, with given tools, makes in one working-day of twelve hours, one pair of boots. If he must make two pairs in the same time, the productiveness of his labour must be doubled; and this cannot be done, except by an alteration in his tools or in his mode of working, or in both. Hence, the conditions of production, i.e., his mode of production, and the labour-process itself, must be revolutionised. By increase in the productiveness of labour, we mean, generally, an alteration in the labour-process, of such a kind as to shorten the labour-time socially necessary for the production of a commodity, and to endow a given quantity of labour with the power of producing a greater quantity of use-value. [2] Hitherto in treating of surplus-value, arising from a simple prolongation of the working-day, we have assumed the mode of production to be given and invariable. But when surplus-value has to be produced by the conversion of necessary labour into surplus-labour, it by no means suffices for capital to take over the labour-process in the form under which it has been historically handed down, and then simply to prolong the duration of that process. The technical and social conditions of the process, and consequently the very mode of production must be revolutionised, before the productiveness of labour can be increased. By that means alone can the value of labour-power be made to sink, and the portion of the working-day necessary for the reproduction of that value, be shortened.

The surplus-value produced by prolongation of the working-day, I call absolute surplus-value. On the other hand, the surplus-value arising from the curtailment of the necessary labour-time, and from the corresponding alteration in the respective lengths of the two components of the working-day, I call relative surplus-value.

In order to effect a fall in the value of labour-power, the increase in the productiveness of labour must seize upon those branches of industry whose products determine the value of labour-power, and consequently either belong to the class of customary means of subsistence, or are capable of supplying the place of those means. But the value of a commodity is determined, not only by the quantity of labour which the labourer directly bestows upon that commodity, but also by the labour contained in the means of production. For instance, the value of a pair of boots depends not only on the cobbler's labour, but also on the value of the leather, wax, thread, &c. Hence, a fall in the value of labour-power is also brought about by an increase in the productiveness of labour, and by a corresponding cheapening of commodities in those industries which supply the instruments of labour and the raw material, that form the material elements of the constant capital required for producing the necessaries of life. But an increase in the productiveness of labour in those branches of industry which supply neither the necessaries of life, nor the means of production for such necessaries, leaves the value of labour-power undisturbed.

The cheapened commodity, of course, causes only a pro tanto fall in the value of labour-power, a fall proportional to the extent of that commodity's employment in the reproduction of labour-power. Shirts, for instance, are a necessary means of subsistence, but are only one out of many. The totality of the necessaries of life consists, however, of various commodities, each the product of a distinct industry; and the value of each of those commodities enters as a component part into the value of labour-power. This latter value decreases with the decrease of the labour-time necessary for its reproduction; the total decrease being the sum of all the different curtailments of labour-time effected in those various and distinct industries. This general result is treated, here, as if it were the immediate result directly aimed at in each individual case. Whenever an individual capitalist cheapens shirts, for instance, by increasing the productiveness of labour he by no means necessarily aims at reducing the value of labour-power and shortening, pro tanto<300> the necessary labour-time. But it is only in so far as he ultimately contributes to this result, that he assists in raising the general rate of surplus-value.[3] The general and necessary tendencies of capital must be distinguished from their forms of manifestation.

It is not our intention to consider, here, the way in which the laws, immanent in capitalist production, manifest themselves in the movements of individual masses of capital, where they assert themselves as coercive laws of competition, and are brought home to the mind and consciousness of the individual capitalist as the directing motives of his operations. But this much is clear; a scientific analysis of competition is not possible, before we have a conception of the inner nature of capital, just as the apparent motions of the heavenly bodies are not intelligible to any but him, who is acquainted with their real motions, motions which are not directly perceptible by the senses. Nevertheless, for the better comprehension of the production of relative surplus-value, we may add the following remarks, in which we assume nothing more than the results we have already obtained.

If one hour's labour is embodied in sixpence, a value of six shillings will be produced in a working-day of 12 hours. Suppose, that with the prevailing productiveness of labour, 12 articles are produced in these 12 hours. Let the value of the means of production used up in each article be sixpence. Under these circumstances, each article costs one shilling: sixpence for the value of the means of production, and sixpence for the value newly added in working with those means. Now let some one capitalist contrive to double the productiveness of labour, and to produce in the working-day of 12 hours, 24 instead of 12 such articles. The value of the means of production remaining the same, the value of each article will fall to ninepence, made up of sixpence for the value of the means of production and threepence for the value newly added by the labour. Despite the doubled productiveness of labour, the day's labour creates, as before, a new value of six shillings and no more, which, however, is now spread over twice as many articles. Of this value each article now has embodied in it 1/24th, instead of 1/12th, threepence instead of sixpence; or, what amounts to the same thing, only half an hour's instead of a whole hour's labour-time, is now added to the means of production while they are being transformed into each article. The individual value of these articles is now below their social value; in other words, they have cost less labour-time than the great bulk of the same article produced under the average social conditions. Each article costs, on an average, one shilling, and represents 2 hours of social labour; but under the altered mode of production it costs only ninepence, or contains only 1½ hours' labour. The real value of a commodity is, however, not its individual value, but its social value; that is to say, the real value is not measured by the labour-time that the article in each individual case costs the producer, but by the labour-time socially required for its production. If therefore, the capitalist who applies the new method, sells his commodity at its social value of one shilling, he sells it for threepence above its individual value, and thus realises an extra surplus-value of threepence. On the other hand, the working-day of 12 hours is, as regards him, now represented by 24 articles instead of 12. Hence, in order to get rid of the product of one working-day, the demand must be double what it was, i.e., the market must become twice as extensive. Other things being equal, his commodities can command a more extended market only by a diminution of their prices. He will therefore sell them above their individual but under their social value, say at tenpence each. By this means he still squeezes an extra surplus-value of one penny out of each. This augmentation of surplus-value is pocketed by him, whether his commodities belong or not to the class of necessary means of subsistence that participate in determining the general value of labour-power. Hence, independently of this latter circumstance, there is a motive for each individual capitalist to cheapen his commodities, by increasing the productiveness of labour.

Nevertheless, even in this case, the increased production of surplus-value arises from the curtailment of the necessary labour-time, and from the corresponding prolongation of the surplus-labour.[4] Let the necessary labour-time amount to 10 hours, the value of a day's labour-power to five shillings, the surplus labour-time to 2 hours, and the daily surplus-value to one shilling. But the capitalist now produces 24 articles, which he sells at tenpence a-piece, making twenty shillings in all. Since the value of the means of production is twelve shillings, 14 2/5 of these articles merely replace the constant capital advanced. The labour of the 12 hours' working-day is represented by the remaining 9 3/5 articles. Since the price of the labour-power is five shillings, 6 articles represent the necessary labour-time, and 3 3/5 articles the surplus-labour. The ratio of the necessary labour to the surplus-labour, which under average social conditions was 5:1, is now only 5:3. The same result may be arrived at in the following way. The value of the product of the working-day of 12 hours is twenty shillings. Of this sum, twelve shillings belong to the value of the means of production, a value that merely re-appears. There remain eight shillings, which are the expression in money, of the value newly created during the working-day. This sum is greater than the sum in which average social labour of the same kind is expressed: twelve hours of the latter labour are expressed by six shillings only. The exceptionally productive labour operates as intensified labour; it creates in equal periods of time greater values than average social labour of the same kind. (See Ch. I. Sect 1. p. 11.) But our capitalist still continues to pay as before only five shillings as the value of a day's labour-power. Hence, instead of 10 hours, the labourer need now work only 7½ hours, in order to reproduce this value. His surplus-labour is, therefore, increased by 2½ hours, and the surplus-value he produces grows from one, into three shillings. Hence, the capitalist who applies the improved method of production, appropriates to surplus-labour a greater portion of the working-day, than the other capitalists in the same trade. He does individually, what the whole body of capitalists engaged in producing relative surplus-value, do collectively. On the other hand, however, this extra surplus-value vanishes, so soon as the new method of production has become general, and has consequently caused the difference between the individual value of the cheapened commodity and its social value to vanish. The law of the determination of value by labour-time, a law which brings under its sway the individual capitalist who applies the new method of production, by compelling him to sell his goods under their social value, this same law, acting as a coercive law of competition, forces his competitors to adopt the new method.[5] The general rate of surplus-value is, therefore, ultimately affected by the whole process, only when the increase in the productiveness of labour, has seized upon those branches of production that are connected with, and has cheapened those commodities that form part of, the necessary means of subsistence, and are therefore elements of the value of labour-power.

The value of commodities is in inverse ratio to the productiveness of labour. And so, too, is the value of labour-power, because it depends on the values of commodities. Relative surplus-value is, on the contrary, directly proportional to that productiveness. It rises with rising and falls with falling productiveness. The value of money being assumed to be constant, an average social working-day of 12 hours always produces the same new value, six shillings, no matter how this sum may be apportioned between surplus-value and wages. But if, in consequence of increased productiveness, the value of the necessaries of life fall, and the value of a day's labour-power be thereby reduced from five shillings to three, the surplus-value increases from one shilling to three. Ten hours were necessary for the reproduction of the value of the labour-power; now only six are required. Four hours have been set free, and can be annexed to the domain of surplus-labour. Hence there is immanent in capital an inclination and constant tendency, to heighten the productiveness of labour, in order to cheapen commodities, and by such cheapening to cheapen the labourer himself.[6]

The value of a commodity is, in itself, of no interest to the capitalist. What alone interests him, is the surplus-value that dwells in it, and is realisable by sale. Realisation of the surplus-value necessarily carries with it the refunding of the value that was advanced. Now, since relative surplus-value increases in direct proportion to the development of the productiveness of labour, while, on the other hand, the value of commodities diminishes in the same proportion; since one and the same process cheapens commodities, and augments the surplus-value contained in them; we have here the solution of the riddle: why does the capitalist, whose sole concern is the production of exchange-value, continually strive to depress the exchange-value of commodities? A riddle with which Quesnay, one of the founders of Political Economy, tormented his opponents, and to which they could give him no answer. "You acknowledge," he says, "that the more expenses and the cost of labour can, in the manufacture of industrial products, be reduced without injury to production, the more advantageous is such reduction, because it diminishes the price of the finished article. And yet, you believe that the production of wealth, which arises from the labour of the workpeople, consists in the augmentation of the exchange-value of their products."[7]

The shortening of the working-day is, therefore, by no means what is aimed at, in capitalist production, when labour is economised by increasing its productiveness.[8] It is only the shortening of the labour-time, necessary for the production of a definite quantity of commodities, that is aimed at. The fact that the workman, when the productiveness of his labour has been increased, produces, say 10 times as many commodities as before, and thus spends one-tenth as much labour-time on each, by no means prevents him from continuing to work 12 hours as before, nor from producing in those 12 hours 1,200 articles instead of 120. Nay, more, his working-day may be prolonged at the same time, so as to make him produce, say 1,400 articles in 14 hours. In the treatises, therefore, of economists of the stamp of MacCulloch, Ure, Senior, and tutti quanti, we may read upon one page, that the labourer owes a debt of gratitude to capital for developing his productiveness, because the necessary labour-time is thereby shortened, and on the next page, that he must prove his gratitude by working in future for 15 hours instead of 10. The object of all development of the productiveness of labour, within the limits of capitalist production, is to shorten that part of the working-day, during which the workman must labour for his own benefit, and by that very shortening, to lengthen the other part of the day, during which he is at liberty to work gratis for the capitalist. How far this result is also attainable, without cheapening commodities, will appear from an examination of the particular modes of producing relative surplus-value, to which examination we now proceed.

Footnotes

[1] The value of his average daily wages is determined by what the labourer requires "so as to live, labour, and generate." (Wm. Petty: "Political Anatomy of Ireland," 1672, p. 64.) "The price of Labour is always constituted of the price of necessaries ... whenever ... the labouring man's wages will not, suitably to his low rank and station, as a labouring man, support such a family as is often the lot of many of them to have," he does not receive proper wages. (J. Vanderlint, l. c., p. 15.) "Le simple ouvrier, qui n'a que ses bras et son industries, n'a rien qu'autant qu'il parvient à vendre à d'autres sa peine... En tout genre de travail il doit arriver, et il arrive en effet, que le salaire de l'ouvrier se borne à ce qui lui est nécessaire pour lui procurer sa subsistance." (Turgot, "Réflexions, &c.," Oeuvres, éd. Daire t. I, p. 10.) "The price of the necessaries of life is, in fact, the cost of producing labour." (Malthus, "Inquiry into, &c., Rent," London, 1815, p. 48, note.)

[2] "Quando si perfezionano le arti, che non è altro che la scoperta di nuove vie, onde si possa compiere una manufattura con meno gente o (che è lo stesso) in minor tempo di prima." (Galiani, l. c., p. 159.) "L'économie sur les frais de production ne peu donc être autre chose que l'économie sur la quantité de travail employé pour produire. " (Sismondi, "Etudes," t. I. p. 22.)

[3] "Let us suppose ... the products ... of the manufacturer are doubled by improvement in machinery ... he will be able to clothe his workmen by means of a smaller proportion of the entire return ... and thus his profit will be raised. But in no other way will it be influenced." (Ramsay, l. c., pp. 168, 169.)

[4] "A man's profit does not depend upon his command of the produce of other men's labour, but upon his command of labour itself. If he can sell his goods at a higher price, while his workmen's wages remain unaltered, he is clearly benefited.... A smaller proportion of what he produces is sufficient to put that labour into motion, and a larger proportion consequently remains for himself." ("Outlines of Pol. Econ." London, 1832, pp. 49, 50.)

[5] "If my neighbour by doing much with little labour, can sell cheap, I must contrive to sell as cheap as he. So that every art, trade, or engine, doing work with labour of fewer hands, and consequently cheaper, begets in others a kind of necessity and emulation, either of using the same art, trade, or engine, or of inventing something like it, that every man may be upon the square, that no man may be able to undersell his neighbour." ("The Advantages of the East India Trade to England", London, 1720, p. 67.)

[6] "In whatever proportion the expenses of a labourer are diminished, in the same proportion will his wages be diminished, if the restraints upon industry are at the same time taken off." ("Considerations Concerning Taking off the Bounty on Corn Exported," &c., London, 1753, p. 7.) "The interest of trade requires, that corn and all provisions should be as cheap as possible; for whatever makes them dear, must make labour dear also ... in all countries, where industry is not restrained, the price of provisions must affect the price of labour. This will always be diminished when the necessaries of life grow cheaper." (I. c., p. 3.) "Wages are decreased in the same proportion as the powers of production increase. Machinery, it is true, cheapens the necessaries of life, but it also cheapens the labourer." ("A Prize Essay on the Comparative erits of Competition and Co-operation." London, 1834, p. 27.)

[7] "Ils conviennent que plus on peut, sans préjudice, épargner de frais ou de travaux dispendieux dans la fabrication des ouvrages des artisans, plus cette épargne est profitable par la diminution des prix de ces ouvrages. Cependant ils croient que la production de richesse qui résulte des travaux des artisans consiste dans l'augmentation de la valeur vénale de leurs ouvrages." (Quesnay: "Dialogues sur le Commerce et les Travaux des Artisans." pp. 188, 189.)

[8] "Ces spéculateurs si économes du travail des ouvriers qu'il faudrait qu'ils payassent." (J. N. Bidaut: "Du Monopole qui s'établit dans les arts industriels et le commerce." Paris, 1828, p. 13.) "The employer will be always on the stretch to economise time and labour." (Dugald Stewart: Works ed. by Sir W. Hamilton, Edinburgh, v., viii., 1855. "Lectures on Polit. Econ.," p. 318.) "Their (the capitalists') interest is that the productive powers of the labourers they employ should be the greatest possible. On promoting that power their attention is fixed and almost exclusively fixed." (R. Jones: l. c., Lecture III.)

Chapter Thirteen:
Co-Operation

Capitalist production only then really begins, as we have already seen, when each individual capital employs simultaneously a comparatively large number of labourers; when consequently the labour-process is carried on on an extensive scale and yields, relatively, large quantities of products. A greater number of labourers working together, at the same time, in one place (or, if you will, in the same field of labour), in order to produce the same sort of commodity under the mastership of one capitalist, constitutes, both historically and logically, the starting-point of capitalist production. With regard to the mode of production itself, manufacture, in its strict meaning, is hardly to be distinguished, in its earliest stages, from the handicraft trades of the guilds, otherwise than by the greater number of workmen simultaneously employed by one and the same individual capital. The workshop of the medieval master handicraftsman is simply enlarged.

At first, therefore, the difference is purely quantitative. We have shown that the surplus-value produced by a given capital is equal to the surplus-value produced by each workman multiplied by the number of workmen simultaneously employed. The number of workmen in itself does nor affect, either the rate of surplus-value, or the degree of exploitation of labour-power. If a working-day of 12 hours be embodied in six shillings, 1,200 such days will be embodied in 1,200 times 6 shillings. In one case 12 x 1,200 working-hours, and in the other 12 such hours are incorporated in the product. In the production of value a number of workmen rank merely as so many individual workmen; and it therefore makes no difference in the value produced whether the 1,200 men work separately, or united under the control of one capitalist.

Nevertheless, within certain limits, a modification takes place. The labour realised in value, is labour of an average social quality; is consequently the expenditure of average labour-power. Any average magnitude, however, is merely the average of a number of separate magnitudes all of one kind, but differing as to quantity. In every industry, each individual labourer, be he Peter or Paul, differs from the average labourer. These individual differences, or "errors" as they are called in mathematics, compensate one another, and vanish, whenever a certain minimum number of workmen are employed together. The celebrated sophist and sycophant, Edmund Burke, goes so far as to make the following assertion, based on his practical observations as a farmer; viz., that "in so small a platoon" as that of five farm labourers, all individual differences in the labour vanish, and that consequently any given five adult farm labourers taken together, will in the same time do as much work as any other five.[1] But, however that may be, it is clear, that the collective working-day of a large number of workmen simultaneously employed, divided by the number of these workmen, gives one day of average social labour. For example, let the working-day of each individual be 12 hours. Then the collective working-day of 12 men simultaneously employed, consists of 144 hours; and although the labour of each of the dozen men may deviate more or less from average social labour, each of them requiring a different time for the same operation, yet since the working-day of each is one-twelfth of the collective working-day of 144 hours, it possesses the qualities of an average social working-day. From the point of view, however, of the capitalist who employs these 12 men, the working-day is that of the whole dozen. Each individual man's day is an aliquot part of the collective working-day, no matter whether the 12 men assist one another in their work, or whether the connexion between their operations consists merely in the fact, that the men are all working for the same capitalist. But if the 12 men are employed in six pairs, by as many different small masters, it will be quite a matter of chance, whether each of these masters produces the same value, and consequently whether he realises the general rate of surplus-value. Deviations would occur in individual cases. If one workman required considerably more time for the production of a commodity than is socially necessary, the duration of the necessary labour-time would, in his case, sensibly deviate from the labour-time socially necessary on an average; and consequently his labour would not count as average labour, nor his labour-power as average labour-power. It would either be not saleable at all, or only at something below the average value of labour-power. A fixed minimum of efficiency in all labour is therefore assumed, and we shall see, later on, that capitalist production provides the means of fixing this minimum. Nevertheless, this minimum deviates from the average, although on the other hand the capitalist has to pay the average value of labour-power. Of the six small masters, one would therefore squeeze out more than the average rate of surplus-value, another less. The inequalities would be compensated for the society at large, but not for the individual masters. Thus the laws of the production of value are only fully realised for the individual producer, when he produces as a capitalist, and employs a number of workmen together, whose labour, by its collective nature, is at once stamped as average social labour.[2]

Even without an alteration in the system of working, the simultaneous employment of a large number of labourers effects a revolution in the material conditions of the labour-process. The buildings in which they work, the store-houses for the raw material, the implements and utensils used simultaneously or in turns by the workmen; in short, a portion of the means of production, are now consumed in common. On the one hand, the exchange-value of these means of production is not increased; for the exchange-value of a commodity is not raised by its use-value being consumed more thoroughly and to greater advantage. On the other hand, they are used in common, and therefore on a larger scale than before. A room where twenty weavers work at twenty looms must be larger than the room of a single weaver with two assistants. But it costs less labour to build one workshop for twenty persons than to build ten to accommodate two weavers each; thus the value of the means of production that are concentrated for use in common on a large scale does not increase in direct proportion to the expansion and to the increased useful effect of those means. When consumed in common, they give up a smaller part of their value to each single product; partly because the total value they part with is spread over a greater quantity of products, and partly because their value, though absolutely greater, is, having regard to their sphere of action in the process, relatively less than the value of isolated means of production. Owing to this, the value of a part of the constant capital falls, and in proportion to the magnitude of the fall, the total value of the commodity also falls. The effect is the same as if the means of production had cost less. The economy in their application is entirely owing to their being consumed in common by a large number of workmen. oreover, this character of being necessary conditions of social labour, a character that distinguishes them from the dispersed and relatively more costly means of production of isolated, independent labourers, or small masters, is acquired even when the numerous workmen assembled together do not assist one another, but merely work side by side. A portion of the instruments of labour acquires this social character before the labour-process itself does so.

Economy in the use of the means of production has to be considered under two aspects. First, as cheapening commodities, and thereby bringing about a fall in the value of labour-power. Secondly, as altering the ratio of the surplus-value to the total capital advanced, i.e., to the sum of the values of the constant and variable capital. The latter aspect will not be considered until we come to the third book, to which, with the object of treating them in their proper connexion, we also relegate many other points that relate to the present question. The march of our analysis compels this splitting up of the subject-matter, a splitting up that is quite in keeping with the spirit of capitalist production. For since, in this mode of production, the workman finds the instruments of labour existing independently of him as another man's property, economy in their use appears, with regard to him, to be a distinct operation, one that does not concern him, and which, therefore, has no connexion with the methods by which his own personal productiveness is increased.

When numerous labourers work together side by side, whether in one and the same process, or in different but connected processes, they are said to co-operate, or to work in co-operation.[3]

Just as the offensive power of a squadron of cavalry, or the defensive power of a regiment of infantry is essentially different from the sum of the offensive or defensive powers of the individual cavalry or infantry soldiers taken separately, so the sum total of the mechanical forces exerted by isolated workmen differs from the social force that is developed, when many hands take part simultaneously in one and the same undivided operation, such as raising a heavy weight, turning a winch, or removing an obstacle. [4] In such cases the effect of the combined labour could either not be produced at all by isolated individual labour, or it could only be produced by a great expenditure of time, or on a very dwarfed scale. Not only have we here an increase in the productive power of the individual, by means of co-operation, but the creation of a new power, namely, the collective power of masses.[5]

Apart from the new power that arises from the fusion of many forces into one single force, mere social contact begets in most industries an emulation and a stimulation of the animal spirits that heighten the efficiency of each individual workman. Hence it is that a dozen persons working together will, in their collective working-day of 144 hours, produce far more than twelve isolated men each working 12 hours, or than one man who works twelve days in succession.[6] The reason of this is that man is, if not as Aristotle contends, a political,[7] at all events a social animal.

Although a number of men may be occupied together at the same time on the same, or the same kind of work, yet the labour of each, as a part of the collective labour, may correspond to a distinct phase of the labour-process, through all whose phases, in consequence of co-operation, the subject of their labour passes with greater speed. For instance, if a dozen masons place themselves in a row, so as to pass stones from the foot of a ladder to its summit, each of them does the same thing; nevertheless, their separate acts form connected parts of one total operation; they are particular phases, which must be gone through by each stone; and the stones are thus carried up quicker by the 24 hands of the row of men than they could be if each man went separately up and down the ladder with his burden. [8] The object is carried over the same distance in a shorter time. Again, a combination of labour occurs whenever a building, for instance, is taken in hand on different sides simultaneously; although here also the co-operating masons are doing the same, or the same kind of work. The 12 masons, in their collective working-day of 144 hours, make much more progress with the building than one mason could make working for 12 days, or 144 hours. The reason is, that a body of men working in concert has hands and eyes both before and behind, and is, to a certain degree, omnipresent. The various parts of the work progress simultaneously.

In the above instances we have laid stress upon the point that the men do the same, or the same kind of work, because this, the most simple form of labour in common, plays a great part in co-operation, even in its most fully developed stage. If the work be complicated, then the mere number of the men who co-operate allows of the various operations being apportioned to different hands, and, consequently, of being carried on simultaneously. The time necessary for the completion of the whole work is thereby shortened. [9]

In many industries, there are critical periods, determined by the nature of the process, during which certain definite results must be obtained. For instance, if a flock of sheep has to be shorn, or a field of wheat to be cut and harvested, the quantity and quality of the product depends on the work being begun and ended within a certain time. In these cases, the time that ought to be taken by the process is prescribed, just as it is in herring fishing. A single person cannot carve a working-day of more than, say 12 hours, out of the natural day, but 100 men co-operating extend the working-day to 1,200 hours. The shortness of the time allowed for the work is compensated for by the large mass of labour thrown upon the field of production at the decisive moment. The completion of the task within the proper time depends on the simultaneous application of numerous combined working-days; the amount of useful effect depends on the number of labourers; this number, however, is always smaller than the number of isolated labourers required to do the same amount of work in the same period. [10] It is owing to the absence of this kind of co-operation that, in the western part of the United States, quantities of corn, and in those parts of East India where English rule has destroyed the old communities, quantities of cotton, are yearly wasted.[11]

On the one hand, co-operation allows of the work being carried on over an extended space; it is consequently imperatively called for in certain undertakings, such as draining, constructing dykes, irrigation works, and the making of canals, roads and railways. On the other hand, while extending the scale of production, it renders possible a relative contraction of the arena. This contraction of arena simultaneous with, and arising from, extension of scale, whereby a number of useless expenses are cut down, is owing to the conglomeration of labourers, to the aggregation of various processes, and to the concentration of the means of production. [12]

The combined working-day produces, relatively to an equal sum of isolated working-days, a greater quantity of use-values, and, consequently, diminishes the labour-time necessary for the production of a given useful effect. Whether the combined working-day, in a given case, acquires this increased productive power, because it heightens the mechanical force of labour, or extends its sphere of action over a greater space, or contracts the field of production relatively to the scale of production, or at the critical moment sets large masses of labour to work, or excites emulation between individuals and raises their animal spirits, or impresses on the similar operations carried on by a number of men the stamp of continuity and many-sidedness, or performs simultaneously different operations, or economises the means of production by use in common, or lends to individual labour the character of average social labour whichever of these be the cause of the increase, the special productive power of the combined working-day is, under all circumstances, the social productive power of labour, or the productive power of social labour. This power is due to co-operation itself. When the labourer co-operates systematically with others, he strips off the fetters of his individuality, and develops the capabilities of his species.[13]

As a general rule, labourers cannot co-operate without being brought together: their assemblage in one place is a necessary condition of their co-operation. Hence wage-labourers cannot co-operate, unless they are employed simultaneously by the same capital, the same capitalist, and unless therefore their labour-powers are bought simultaneously by him. The total value of these labour-powers, or the amount of the wages of these labourers for a day, or a week, as the case may be, must be ready in the pocket of the capitalist, before the workmen are assembled for the process of production. The payment of 300 workmen at once, though only for one day, requires a greater outlay of capital, than does the payment of a smaller number of men, week by week, during a whole year. Hence the number of the labourers that co-operate, or the scale of co-operation, depends, in the first instance, on the amount of capital that the individual capitalist can spare for the purchase of labour-power; in other words, on the extent to which a single capitalist has command over the means of subsistence of a number of labourers.

And as with the variable, so it is with the constant capital. For example, the outlay on raw material is 30 times as great, for the capitalist who employs 300 men, as it is for each of the 30 capitalists who employ 10 men. The value and quantity of the instruments of labour used in common do not, it is true, increase at the same rate as the number of workmen, but they do increase very considerably. Hence, concentration of large masses of the means of production in the hands of individual capitalists, is a material condition for the co-operation of wage-labourers, and the extent of the co-operation or the scale of production, depends on the extent of this concentration.

We saw in a former chapter, that a certain minimum amount of capital was necessary, in order that the number of labourers simultaneously employed, and, consequently, the amount of surplus-value produced, might suffice to liberate the employer himself from manual labour, to convert him from a small master into a capitalist, and thus formally to establish capitalist production. We now see that a certain minimum amount is a necessary condition for the conversion of numerous isolated and independent processes into one combined social process.

We also saw that at first, the subjection of labour to capital was only a formal result of the fact, that the labourer, instead of working for himself, works for and consequently under the capitalist. By the co-operation of numerous wage-labourers, the sway of capital develops into a requisite for carrying on the labour-process itself, into a real requisite of production. That a capitalist should command on the field of production, is now as indispensable as that a general should command on the field of battle.

All combined labour on a large scale requires, more or less, a directing authority, in order to secure the harmonious working of the individual activities, and to perform the general functions that have their origin in the action of the combined organism, as distinguished from the action of its separate organs. A single violin player is his own conductor; an orchestra requires a separate one. The work of directing, superintending, and adjusting, becomes one of the functions of capital, from the moment that the labour under the control of capital, becomes co-operative. Once a function of capital, it acquires special characteristics.

The directing motive, the end and aim of capitalist production, is to extract the greatest possible amount of surplus-value,[14] and consequently to exploit labour-power to the greatest possible extent. As the number of the co-operating labourers increases, so too does their resistance to the domination of capital, and with it, the necessity for capital to overcome this resistance by counterpressure. The control exercised by the capitalist is not only a special function, due to the nature of the social labour-process, and peculiar to that process, but it is, at the same time, a function of the exploitation of a social labour-process, and is consequently rooted in the unavoidable antagonism between the exploiter and the living and labouring raw material he exploits.

Again, in proportion to the increasing mass of the means of production, now no longer the property of the labourer, but of the capitalist, the necessity increases for some effective control over the proper application of those means.[15] Moreover, the co-operation of wage-labourers is entirely brought about by the capital that employs them. Their union into one single productive body and the establishment of a connexion between their individual functions, are matters foreign and external to them, are not their own act, but the act of the capital that brings and keeps them together. Hence the connexion existing between their various labours appears to them, ideally, in the shape of a preconceived plan of the capitalist, and practically in the shape of the authority of the same capitalist, in the shape of the powerful will of another, who subjects their activity to his aims. If, then, the control of the capitalist is in substance two-fold by reason of the two-fold nature of the process of production itself, which, on the one hand, is a social process for producing use-values, on the other, a process for creating surplus-value in form that control is despotic. As co-operation extends its scale, this despotism takes forms peculiar to itself. Just as at first the capitalist is relieved from actual labour so soon as his capital has reached that minimum amount with which capitalist production, as such, begins, so now, he hands over the work of direct and constant supervision of the individual workmen, and groups of workmen, to a special kind of wage-labourer. An industrial army of workmen, under the command of a capitalist, requires, like a real army, officers (managers), and sergeants (foremen, overlookers), who, while the work is being done, command in the name of the capitalist. The work of supervision becomes their established and exclusive function. When comparing the mode of production of isolated peasants and artisans with production by slave-labour, the political economist counts this labour of superintendence among the faux frais of production.[16] But, when considering the capitalist mode of production, he, on the contrary, treats the work of control made necessary by the co-operative character of the labour-process as identical with the different work of control, necessitated by the capitalist character of that process and the antagonism of interests between capitalist and labourer.[17] It is not because he is a leader of industry that a man is a capitalist; on the contrary, he is a leader of industry because he is a capitalist. The leadership of industry is an attribute of capital, just as in feudal times the functions of general and judge, were attributes of landed property.[18]

The labourer is the owner of his labour-power until he has done bargaining for its sale with the capitalist; and he can sell no more than what he has i.e., his individual, isolated labour-power. This state of things is in no way altered by the fact that the capitalist, instead of buying the labour-power of one man, buys that of 100, and enters into separate contracts with 100 unconnected men instead of with one. He is at liberty to set the 100 men to work, without letting them co-operate. He pays them the value of 100 independent labour-powers, but he does not pay for the combined labour-power of the hundred. Being independent of each other, the labourers are isolated persons, who enter into relations with the capitalist, but not with one another. This co-operation begins only with the labour-process, but they have then ceased to belong to themselves. On entering that process, they become incorporated with capital. As co-operators, as members of a working organism, they are but special modes of existence of capital. Hence, the productive power developed by the labourer when working in co-operation, is the productive power of capital. This power is developed gratuitously, whenever the workmen are placed under given conditions, and it is capital that places them under such conditions. Because this power costs capital nothing, and because, on the other hand, the labourer himself does not develop it before his labour belongs to capital, it appears as a power with which capital is endowed by Nature a productive power that is immanent in capital.

The colossal effects of simple co-operation are to be seen in the gigantic structures of the ancient Asiatics, Egyptians, Etruscans, &c. "It has happened in times past that these Oriental States, after supplying the expenses of their civil and military establishments, have found themselves in possession of a surplus which they could apply to works of magnificence or utility and in the construction of these their command over the hands and arms of almost the entire non-agricultural population has produced stupendous monuments which still indicate their power. The teeming valley of the Nile ... produced food for a swarming non-agricultural population, and this food, belonging to the monarch and the priesthood, afforded the means of erecting the mighty monuments which filled the land.... In moving the colossal statues and vast masses of which the transport creates wonder, human labour almost alone, was prodigally used.... The number of the labourers and the concentration of their efforts sufficed. We see mighty coral reefs rising from the depths of the ocean into islands and firm land, yet each individual depositor is puny, weak, and contemptible. The non-agricultural labourers of an Asiatic monarchy have little but their individual bodily exertions to bring to the task, but their number is their strength, and the power of directing these masses gave rise to the palaces and temples, the pyramids, and the armies of gigantic statues of which the remains astonish and perplex us. It is that confinement of the revenues which feed them, to one or a few hands, which makes such undertakings possible." [19] This power of Asiatic and Egyptian kings, Etruscan theocrats, &c., has in modern society been transferred to the capitalist, whether he be an isolated, or as in joint-stock companies, a collective capitalist.

Co-operation, such as we find it at the dawn of human development, among races who live by the chase,[20] or, say, in the agriculture of Indian communities, is based, on the one hand, on ownership in common of the means of production, and on the other hand, on the fact, that in those cases, each individual has no more torn himself off from the navel-string of his tribe or community, than each bee has freed itself from connexion with the hive. Such co-operation is distinguished from capitalistic co-operation by both of the above characteristics. The sporadic application of co-operation on a large scale in ancient times, in the middle ages, and in modern colonies, reposes on relations of dominion and servitude, principally on slavery. The capitalistic form, on the contrary, pre-supposes from first to last, the free wage-labourer, who sells his labour-power to capital. Historically, however, this form is developed in opposition to peasant agriculture and to the carrying on of independent handicrafts whether in guilds or not.[21] From the standpoint of these, capitalistic co-operation does not manifest itself as a particular historical form of co-operation, but co-operation itself appears to be a historical form peculiar to, and specifically distinguishing, the capitalist process of production.

Just as the social productive power of labour that is developed by co-operation, appears to be the productive power of capital, so co-operation itself, contrasted with the process of production carried on by isolated independent labourers, or even by small employers, appears to be a specific form of the capitalist process of production. It is the first change experienced by the actual labour-process, when subjected to capital. This change takes place spontaneously. The simultaneous employment of a large number of wage-labourers, in one and the same process, which is a necessary condition of this change, also forms the starting-point of capitalist production. This point coincides with the birth of capital itself. If then, on the one hand, the capitalist mode of production presents itself to us historically, as a necessary condition to the transformation of the labour-process into a social process, so, on the other hand, this social form of the labour-process presents itself, as a method employed by capital for the more profitable exploitation of labour, by increasing that labour's productiveness.

In the elementary form, under which we have hitherto viewed it, co-operation is a necessary concomitant of all production on a large scale, but it does not, in itself, represent a fixed form characteristic of a particular epoch in the development of the capitalist mode of production. At the most it appears to do so, and that only approximately, in the handicraft-like beginnings of manufacture,[22] and in that kind of agriculture on a large scale, which corresponds to the epoch of manufacture, and is distinguished from peasant agriculture, mainly by the number of the labourers simultaneously employed, and by the mass of the means of production concentrated for their use. Simple co-operation is always the prevailing form, in those branches of production in which capital operates on a large scale, and division of labour and machinery play but a subordinate part.

Co-operation ever constitutes the fundamental form of the capitalist mode of production, nevertheless the elementary form of co-operation continues to subsist as a particular form of capitalist production side by side with the more developed forms of that mode of production.

Footnotes

[1] "Unquestionably, there is a good deal of difference between the value of one man's labour and that of another from strength, dexterity, and honest application. But I am quite sure, from my best observation, that any given five men will, in their total, afford a proportion of labour equal to any other five within the periods of life I have stated; that is, that among such five men there will be one possessing all the qualifications of a good workman, one bad, and the other three middling, and approximating to the first, and the last. So that in so small a platoon as that of even five, you will find the full complement of all that five men can earn." (E. Burke, l. c., pp. 15, 16.) Compare Quételet on the average individual.

[2] Professor Roscher claims to have discovered that one needlewoman employed by Mrs. Roscher during two days, does more work than two needlewomen employed together during one day. The learned professor should not study the capitalist process of production in the nursery, nor under circumstances where the principal personage, the capitalist, is wanting.

[3] "Concours de forces." (Destutt de Tracy, l. c., p. 80.)

[4] There are numerous operations of so simple a kind as not to admit a division into parts, which cannot be performed without the co-operation of many pairs of hands. I would instance the lifting of a large tree on to a wain .., everything, in short, which cannot be done unless a great many pairs of hands help each other in the same undivided employment and at the same time." (E. G. Wakefield: "A View of the Art of Colonisation." London, 1849, p. 168.)

[5] "As one man cannot, and ten men must strain to lift a ton of weight, yet 100 men can do it only by the strength of a finger of each of them." (John Betters: "Proposals for Raising a Colledge of Industry." London, 1696, p. 21.)

[6] "There is also" (when the same number of men are employed by one farmer on 300 acres, instead of by ten farmers with 30 acres a piece) "an advantage in the proportion of servants, which will not so easily be understood but by practical men; for it is natural to say, as 1 is to 4, so are 3 to 12; but this will not hold good in practice; for in harvest time and many other operations which require that kind of despatch by the throwing many hands together, the work is better and more expeditiously done: f i. in harvest, 2 drivers, 2 loaders, 2 pitchers, 2 rakers, and the rest at the rick, or in the barn, will despatch double the work that the same number of hands would do if divided into different gangs on different farms." ("An Inquiry into the Connexion between the Present Price of Provisions and the Size of Farms." By a Farmer. London, 1773, pp. 7, 8.)

[7] Strictly, Aristotle's definition is that man is by nature a town-citizen. This is quite as characteristic of ancient classical society as Franklin's definition of man, as a tool-making animal, is characteristic of Yankeedom.

[8] "On doit encore remarquer que cette division partielle de travail peut se faire quand même les ouvriers sont occupes d'une même besogne. Des maçons par exemple, occupés à faire passer de mains en mains des briques à un échafaudage supérieur, font tous la même besogne, et pourtant il existe parmi eux une espèce de division de travail, qui consiste en ce que chacun d'eux fait passer la brique par un espace donné, et que tous ensemble la font parvenir beaucoup plus promptement à l'endroit marque qu'ils ne le feraient si chacun d'eux portait sa brique séparément jusqu'à l'échafaudage supérieur." (F. Skarbek: "Théorie des richesses sociales." Paris, 1839, t. I, pp. 97, 98.)

[9] "Est-il question d'exécuter un travail compliqué, plusieurs choses doivent être faites simultanément. L'un en fait une pendant que l'autre en fait une autre, et tous contribuent à l'effet qu'un sent homme n'aurait pu produire. L'un rame pendant que l'autre tient le gouvernail, et qu'un troisième jette le filet on harponne le poisson, et la pêche a un succès impossible sans ce concours." (Destutt de Tracy, l. c.)

[10] "The doing of it (agricultural work) at the critical juncture is of so much the greater consequence." ("An Inquiry into the Connexion between the Present Price," &c., p.

9.) "In agriculture, there is no more important factor than that of time." (Liebig: "Ueber Theorie und Praxis in der Landwirtschaft." 1856, p. 23.)

[11] "The next evil is one which one would scarcely expect to find in a country which exports more labour than any other in the world, with the exception, perhaps, of China and England the impossibility of procuring a sufficient number of hands to clean the cotton. The consequence of this is that large quantities of the crop are left unpicked, while another portion is gathered from the ground when it has fallen, and is of course discoloured and partially rotted, so that for want of labour at the proper season the cultivator is actually forced to submit to the loss of a large part of that crop for which England is so anxiously looking." ("Bengal Hurkaru." Bi-Monthly Overland Summary of News, 22nd July, 1861.)

[12] In the progress of culture "all, and perhaps more than all, the capital and labour which once loosely occupied 500 acres, are now concentrated for the more complete tillage of 100." Although "relatively to the amount of capital and labour employed, space is concentrated, it is an enlarged sphere of production, as compared to the sphere of production formerly occupied or worked upon by one single independent agent of production." (R. Jones: "An Essay on the Distribution of Wealth," part I. On Rent. London, 1831. p. 191.)

[13] "La forza di ciascuno uomo è minima, ma la riunione delle minime forze forma una forza totale maggiore anche della somma delle forze medesime fino a che le forze per essere riunite possono diminuere il tempo ed accrescere lo spazio della loro azione." (G. R. Carli, Note to P. Verri, l. c., t. xv., p. 196.)

[14] "Profits ... is the sole end of trade." (J. Vanderlint, l. c., p. 11.)

[15] That Philistine paper, the Spectator, states that after the introduction of a sort of partnership between capitalist and workmen in the "Wirework Company of Manchester," "the first result was a sudden decrease in waste, the men not seeing why they should waste their own property any more than any other master's, and waste is, perhaps, next to bad debts, the greatest source of manufacturing loss." The same paper finds that the main defect in the Rochdale co-operative experiments is this: "They showed that associations of workmen could manage shops, mills, and almost all forms of industry with success, and they immediately improved the condition of the men; but then they did not leave a clear place for masters." Quelle horreur!

[16] Professor Cairnes, after stating that the superintendence of labour is a leading feature of production by slaves in the Southern States of North America, continues: "The peasant proprietor (of the North), appropriating the whole produce of his toil, needs no other stimulus to exertion. Superintendence is here completely dispensed with." (Cairnes, l. c., pp. 48, 49.)

[17] Sir James Steuart, a writer altogether remarkable for his quick eye for the characteristic social distinctions between different modes of production, says: "Why do large undertakings in the manufacturing way ruin private industry, but by coming nearer to the simplicity of slaves?" ("Prin. of Pol. Econ.," London, 1767, v. I., pp. 167, 168.)

[18] Auguste Comte and his school might therefore have shown that feudal lords are an eternal necessity in the same way that they have done in the case of the lords of capital.

[19] R. Jones. "Textbook of Lectures," &c., pp. 77, 78. The ancient Assyrian, Egyptian, and other collections in London, and in other European capitals, make us eye-witnesses of the modes of carrying on that co-operative labour.

[20] Linguet is improbably right, when in his "Théorie des Lois Civiles," he declares hunting to be the first form of co-operation, and man-hunting (war) one of the earliest forms of hunting.

[21] Peasant agriculture on a small scale, and the carrying on of independent handicrafts, which together form the basis of the feudal mode of production, and after the dissolution of that system, continue side by side with the capitalist mode, also form the economic foundation of the classical communities at their best, after the primitive form of ownership of land in common had disappeared, and before slavery had seized on production in earnest.

[22] "Whether the united skill, industry, and emulation of many together on the same work be not the way to advance it? And whether it had been otherwise possible for England, to have carried on her Woollen Manufacture to so great a perfection?" (Berkeley. "The Querist." London, 1751, p. 56, par. 521.)

Chapter Fourteen:
Division of Labour and Manufacture

Section 1
Two-Fold Origin of Manufacture

That co-operation which is based on division of labour, assumes its typical form in manufacture, and is the prevalent characteristic form of the capitalist process of production throughout the manufacturing period properly so called. That period, roughly speaking, extends from the middle of the 16th to the last third of the 18th century.

Manufacture takes its rise in two ways:

(1.) By the assemblage, in one workshop under the control of a single capitalist, of labourers belonging to various independent handicrafts, but through whose hands a given article must pass on its way to completion. A carriage, for example, was formerly the product of the labour of a great number of independent artificers, such as wheelwrigths, harness-makers, tailors, locksmiths, upholsterers, turners, fringe-makers, glaziers, painters, polishers, gilders, &c. In the manufacture of carriages, however, all these different artificers are assembled in one building where they work into one another's hands. It is true that a carriage cannot be gilt before it has been made. But if a number of carriages are being made simultaneously, some may be in the hands of the gilders while others are going through an earlier process. So far, we are still in the domain of simple co-operation, which finds its materials ready to hand in the shape of men and things. But very soon an important change takes place. The tailor, the locksmith, and the other artificers, being now exclusively occupied in carriage-making, each gradually loses, through want of practice, the ability to carry on, to its full extent, his old handicraft. But, on the other hand, his activity now confined in one groove, assumes the form best adapted to the narrowed sphere of action. At first, carriage manufacture is a combination of various independent handicrafts. By degrees, it becomes the splitting up of carriage-making into its various detail processes, each of which crystallises into the exclusive function of a particular workman, the manufacture, as a whole, being carried on by the men in conjunction. In the same way, cloth manufacture, as also a whole series of other manufactures, arose by combining different handicrafts together under the control of a single capitalist.[1]

(2.) Manufacture also arises in a way exactly the reverse of this namely, by one capitalist employing simultaneously in one workshop a number of artificers, who all do the same, or the same kind of work, such as making paper, type, or needles. This is co-operation in its most elementary form. Each of these artificers (with the help, perhaps, of one or two apprentices), makes the entire commodity, and he consequently performs in succession all the operations necessary for its production. He still works in his old handicraft-like way. But very soon external circumstances cause a different use to be made of the concentration of the workmen on one spot, and of the simultaneousness of their work. An increased quantity of the article has perhaps to be delivered within a given time. The work is therefore re-distributed. Instead of each man being allowed to perform all the various operations in succession, these operations are changed into disconnected, isolated ones, carried on side by side; each is assigned to a different artificer, and the whole of them together are performed simultaneously by the co-operating workmen. This accidental repartition gets repeated, develops advantages of its own, and gradually ossifies into a systematic division of labour. The commodity, from being the individual product of an independent artificer, becomes the social product of a union of artificers, each of whom performs one, and only one, of the constituent partial operations. The same operations which, in the case of a papermaker belonging to a German Guild, merged one into the other as the successive acts of one artificer, became in the Dutch paper manufacture so many partial operations carried on side by side by numerous co-operating labourers. The needlemaker of the Nuremberg Guild was the cornerstone on which the English needle manufacture was raised. But while in Nuremberg that single artificer performed a series of perhaps 20 operations one after another, in England it was not long before there were 20 needlemakers side by side, each performing one alone of those 20 operations, and in consequence of further experience, each of those 20 operations was again split up, isolated, and made the exclusive function of a separate workman.

The mode in which manufacture arises, its growth out of handicrafts, is therefore two-fold. On the one hand, it arises from the union of various independent handicrafts, which become stripped of their independence and specialised to such an extent as to be reduced to mere supplementary partial processes in the production of one particular commodity. On the other hand, it arises from the co-operation of artificers of one handicraft; it splits up that particular handicraft into its various detail operations, isolating, and making these operations independent of one another up to the point where each becomes the exclusive function of a particular labourer. On the one hand, therefore, manufacture either introduces diversion of labour into a process of production, or further develops that division; on the other hand, it unites together handicrafts that were formerly separate. But whatever may have been its particular starting-point, its final form is invariably the same a productive mechanism whose parts are human beings.

For a proper understanding of the division of labour in manufacture, it is essential that the following points be firmly grasped. First, the decomposition of a process of production into its various successive steps coincides, here, strictly with the resolution of a handicraft into its successive manual operations. Whether complex or simple, each operation has to be done by hand, retains the character of a handicraft, and is therefore dependent on the strength, skill, quickness, and sureness, of the individual workman in handling his tools. The handicraft continues to be the basis. This narrow technical basis excludes a really scientific analysis of any definite process of industrial production, since it is still a condition that each detail process gone through by the product must be capable of being done by hand and of forming, in its way, a separate handicraft. It is just because handicraft skill continues, in this way, to be the foundation of the process of production, that each workman becomes exclusively assigned to a partial function, and that for the rest of his life, his labour-power is turned into the organ of this detail function.

Secondly, this division of labour is a particular sort of co-operation, and many of its disadvantages spring from the general character of co-operation, and not from this particular form of it.

Section 2:
The Detail Labourer and his Implements

If we now go more into detail, it is, in the first place, clear that a labourer who all his life performs one and the same simple operation, converts his whole body into the automatic, specialised implement of that operation. Consequently, he takes less time in doing it, than the artificer who performs a whole series of operations in succession. But the collective labourer, who constitutes the living mechanism of manufacture, is made up solely of such specialised detail labourers. Hence, in comparison with the independent handicraft, more is produced in a given time, or the productive power of labour is increased.[2] of one person, the methods it employs become perfected. The workman's continued repetition of the same simple act, and the concentration of his attention on it, teach him by experience how to attain the desired effect with the minimum of exertion. But since there are always several generations of labourers living at one time, and working together at the manufacture of a given article, the technical skill, the tricks of the trade thus acquired, become established, and are accumulated and handed down.[3]

Manufacture, in fact, produces the skill of the detail labourer, by reproducing, and systematically driving to an extreme within the workshop, the naturally developed differentiation of trades which it found ready to hand in society at large. On the other hand, the conversion of fractional work into the life-calling of one man, corresponds to the tendency shown by earlier societies, to make trades hereditary; either to petrify them into castes, or whenever definite historical conditions beget in the individual a tendency to vary in a manner incompatible with the nature of castes, to ossify them into guilds. Castes and guilds arise from the action of the same natural law, that regulates the differentiation of plants and animals into species and varieties, except that, when a certain degree of development has been reached, the heredity of castes and the exclusiveness of guilds are ordained as a law of society.[4]

"The muslins of Dakka in fineness, the calicoes and other piece goods of Coromandel in brilliant and durable colours, have never been surpassed. Yet they are produced without capital, machinery, division of labour, or any of those means which give such facilities to the manufacturing interest of Europe. The weaver is merely a detached individual, working a web when ordered of a customer, and with a loom of the rudest construction, consisting sometimes of a few branches or bars of wood, put roughly together. There is even no expedient for rolling up the warp; the loom must therefore be kept stretched to its full length, and becomes so inconveniently large, that it cannot be contained within the hut of the manufacturer, who is therefore compelled to ply his trade in the open air, where it is interrupted by every vicissitude of the weather."[5] It is only the special skill accumulated from generation to generation, and transmitted from father to son, that gives to the Hindu, as it does to the spider, this proficiency. And yet the work of such a Hindu weaver is very complicated, compared with that of a manufacturing labourer.

An artificer, who performs one after another the various fractional operations in the production of a finished article, must at one time change his place, at another his tools. The transition from one operation to another interrupts the flow of his labour, and creates, so to say, gaps in his working-day. These gaps close up so soon as he is tied to one and the same operation all day long; they vanish in proportion as the changes in his work diminish. The resulting increased productive power is owing either to an increased expenditure of labour-power in a given time i.e., to increased intensity of labour or to a decrease in the amount of labour-power unproductively consumed. The extra expenditure of power, demanded by every transition from rest to motion, is made up for by prolonging the duration of the normal velocity when once acquired. On the other hand, constant labour of one uniform kind disturbs the intensity and flow of a man's animal spirits, which find recreation and delight in mere change of activity.

The productiveness of labour depends not only on the proficiency of the workman, but on the perfection of his tools. Tools of the same kind, such as knives, drills, gimlets. hammers, &c., may be employed in different processes; and the same tool may serve various purposes in a single process. But so soon as the different operations of a labour-process are disconnected the one from the other, and each fractional operation acquires in the hands of the detail labourer a suitable and peculiar form, alterations become necessary in the implements that previously served more than one purpose. The direction taken by this change is determined by the difficulties experienced in consequence of the unchanged form of the implement. anufacture is characterised by the differentiation of the instruments of labour a differentiation whereby implements of a given sort acquire fixed shapes, adapted to each particular application, and by the specialisation of those instruments, giving to each special implement its full play only in the hands of a specific detail labourer. In Birmingham alone 500 varieties of hammers are produced, and not only is each adapted to one particular process, but several varieties often serve exclusively for the different operations in one and the same process. The manufacturing period simplifies, improves, and multiplies the implements of labour, by adapting them to the exclusively special functions of each detail labourer.[6] It thus creates at the same time one of the material conditions for the existence of machinery, which consists of a combination of simple instruments.

The detail labourer and his implements are the simplest elements of manufacture. Let us now turn to its aspect as a whole.

Section 3:
The Two Fundamental Forms of Manufacture: Heterogeneous Manufacture, Serial Manufacture

The organisation of manufacture has two fundamental forms which, in spite of occasional blending, are essentially different in kind, and, moreover, play very distinct parts in the subsequent transformation of manufacture into modern industry carried on by machinery. This double character arises from the nature of the article produced. This article either results from the mere mechanical fitting together of partial products made independently, or owes its completed shape to a series of connected processes and manipulations.

A locomotive, for instance, consists of more than 5,000 independent parts. It cannot, however, serve as an example of the first kind of genuine manufacture, for it is a structure produced by modern mechanical industry. But a watch can; and William Petty used it to illustrate the division of labour in manufacture. Formerly the individual work of a Nuremberg artificer, the watch has been transformed into the social product of an immense number of detail labourers, such as mainspring makers, dial makers, spiral spring makers, jewelled hole makers, ruby lever makers, hand makers, case makers, screw makers, gilders, with numerous subdivisions, such as wheel makers (brass and steel separate), pin makers, movement makers, acheveur de pignon (fixes the wheels on the axles, polishes the facets, &c.), pivot makers, planteur de finissage (puts the wheels and springs in the works), finisseur de barillet (cuts teeth in the wheels, makes the holes of the right size, &c.), escapement makers, cylinder makers for cylinder escapements, escapement wheel makers, balance wheel makers, raquette makers (apparatus for regulating the watch), the planteur d'échappement (escapement maker proper); then the repasseur de barillet (finishes the box for the spring, &c.), steel polishers, wheel polishers, screw polishers, figure painters, dial enamellers (melt the enamel on the copper), fabricant de pendants (makes the ring by which the case is hung), finisseur de charnière (puts the brass hinge in the cover, &c.), faiseur de secret (puts in the springs that open the case), graveur, ciseleur, polisseur de boite, &c., &c., and last of all the repasseur, who fits together the whole watch and hands it over in a going state. Only a few parts of the watch pass through several hands; and all these membra disjecta come together for the first time in the hand that binds them into one mechanical whole. This external relation between the finished product, and its various and diverse elements makes it, as well in this case as in the case of all similar finished articles, a matter of chance whether the detail labourers are brought together in one workshop or not. The detail operations may further be carried on like so many independent handicrafts, as they are in the Cantons of Vaud and Neufchâtel; while in Geneva there exist large watch manufactories where the detail labourers directly co-operate under the control of a single capitalist. And even in the latter case the dial, the springs, and the case, are seldom made in the factory itself. To carry on the trade as a manufacture, with concentration of workmen, is, in the watch trade, profitable only under exceptional conditions, because competition is greater between the labourers who desire to work at home, and because the splitting up of the work into a number of heterogeneous processes, permits but little use of the instruments of labour in common, and the capitalist, by scattering the work, saves the outlay on workshops, &c.[7] Nevertheless the position of this detail labourer who, though he works at home, does so for a capitalist (manufacturer, établisseur), is very different from that of the independent artificer, who works for his own customers.[8]

The second kind of manufacture, its perfected form, produces articles that go through connected phases of development, through a series of processes step by step, like the wire in the manufacture of needles, which passes through the hands of 72 and sometimes even 92 different detail workmen.

In so far as such a manufacture, when first started, combines scattered handicrafts, it lessens the space by which the various phases of production are separated from each other. The time taken in passing from one stage to another is shortened, so is the labour that effectuates this passage.[9] In comparison with a handicraft, productive power is gained, and this gain is owing to the general co-operative character of manufacture. On the other hand, division of labour, which is the distinguishing principle of manufacture, requires the isolation of the various stages of production and their independence of each other. The establishment and maintenance of a connexion between the isolated functions necessitates the incessant transport of the article from one hand to another, and from one process to another. From the standpoint of modern mechanical industry, this necessity stands forth as a characteristic and costly disadvantage, and one that is immanent in the principle of manufacture.[10]

If we confine our attention to some particular lot of raw materials, of rags, for instance, in paper manufacture, or of wire in needle manufacture, we perceive that it passes in succession through a series of stages in the hands of the various detail workmen until completion. On the other hand, if we look at the workshop as a whole, we see the raw material in all the stages of its production at the same time. The collective labourer, with one set of his many hands armed with one kind of tools, draws the wire, with another set, armed with different tools, he, at the same time, straightens it, with another, he cuts it, with another, points it, and so on. The different detail processes, which were successive in time, have become simultaneous, go on side by side in space. Hence, production of a greater quantum of finished commodities in a given time.[11] This simultaneity, it is true, is due to the general co-operative form of the process as a whole; but Manufacture not only finds the conditions for co-operation ready to hand, it also, to some extent, creates them by the sub-division of handicraft labour. On the other hand, it accomplishes this social organisation of the labour-process only by riveting each labourer to a single fractional detail.

Since the fractional product of each detail labourer is, at the same time, only a particular stage in the development of one and the same finished article, each labourer, or each group of labourers, prepares the raw material for another labourer or group. The result of the labour of the one is the starting-point for the labour of the other. The one workman therefore gives occupation directly to the other. The labour-time necessary in each partial process, for attaining the desired effect, is learnt by experience; and the mechanism of Manufacture, as a whole, is based on the assumption that a given result will be obtained in a given time. It is only on this assumption that the various supplementary labour-processes can proceed uninterruptedly, simultaneously, and side by side. It is clear that this direct dependence of the operations, and therefore of the labourers, on each other, compels each one of them to spend on his work no more than the necessary time, and thus a continuity, uniformity, regularity, order, [12] and even intensity of labour, of quite a different kind, is begotten than is to be found in an independent handicraft or even in simple co-operation. The rule, that the labour-time expended on a commodity should not exceed that which is socially necessary for its production, appears, in the production of commodities generally, to be established by the mere effect of competition; since, to express ourselves superficially, each single producer is obliged to sell his commodity at its market-price. In Manufacture, on the contrary, the turning out of a given quantum of product in a given time is a technical law of the process of production itself.[13]

Different operations take, however, unequal periods, and yield therefore, in equal times unequal quantities of fractional products. If, therefore, the same labourer has, day after day, to perform the same operation, there must be a different number of labourers for each operation; for instance, in type manufacture, there are four founders and two breakers to one rubber: the founder casts 2,000 type an hour, the breaker breaks up 4,000, and the rubber polishes 8,000. Here we have again the principle of co-operation in its simplest form, the simultaneous employment of many doing the same thing; only now, this principle is the expression of an organic relation. The division of labour, as carried out in Manufacture, not only simplifies and multiplies the qualitatively different parts of the social collective labourer, but also creates a fixed mathematical relation or ratio which regulates the quantitative extent of those parts i.e., the relative number of labourers, or the relative size of the group of labourers, for each detail operation. It develops, along with the qualitative sub-division of the social labour-process, a quantitative rule and proportionality for that process.

When once the most fitting proportion has been experimentally established for the numbers of the detail labourers in the various groups when producing on a given scale, that scale can be extended only by employing a multiple of each particular group.[14] There is this to boot, that the same individual can do certain kinds of work just as well on a large as on a small scale; for instance, the labour of superintendence, the carriage of the fractional product from one stage to the next, &c. The isolation of such functions, their allotment to a particular labourer, does not become advantageous till after an increase in the number of labourers employed; but this increase must affect every group proportionally.

The isolated group of labourers to whom any particular detail function is assigned, is made up of homogeneous elements, and is one of the constituent parts of the total mechanism. In many manufactures, however, the group itself is an organised body of labour, the total mechanism being a repetition or multiplication of these elementary organisms. Take, for instance, the manufacture of glass bottles. It may be resolved into three essentially different stages. First, the preliminary stage, consisting of the preparation of the components of the glass, mixing the sand and lime, &c., and melting them into a fluid mass of glass.[15] Various detail labourers are employed in this first stage, as also in the final one of removing the bottles from the drying furnace, sorting and packing them, &c. In the middle, between these two stages, comes the glass melting proper, the manipulation of the fluid mass. At each mouth of the furnace, there works a group, called "the hole," consisting of one bottlemaker or finisher, one blower, one gatherer, one putter-up or whetter-off, and one taker-in. These five detail workers are so many special organs of a single working organism that acts only as a whole, and therefore can operate only by the direct co-operation of the whole five. The whole body is paralysed if but one of its members be wanting. But a glass furnace has several openings (in England from 4 to 6), each of which contains an earthenware melting-pot full of molten glass, and employs a similar five-membered group of workers. The organisation of each group is based on division of labour, but the bond between the different groups is simple co-operation, which, by using in common one of the means of production, the furnace, causes it to be more economically consumed. Such a furnace, with its 4-6 groups, constitutes a glass house; and a glass manufactory comprises a number of such glass houses, together with the apparatus and workmen requisite for the preparatory and final stages.

Finally, just as Manufacture arises in part from the combination of various handicrafts, so, too, it develops into a combination of various manufactures. The larger English glass manufacturers, for instance, make their own earthenware melting-pots, because, on the quality of these depends, to a great extent, the success or failure of the process. The manufacture of one of the means of production is here united with that of the product. On the other hand, the manufacture of the product may be united with other manufactures, of which that product is the raw material, or with the products of which it is itself subsequently mixed. Thus, we find the manufacture of flint glass combined with that of glass cutting and brass founding; the latter for the metal settings of various articles of glass. The various manufactures so combined form more or less separate departments of a larger manufacture, but are at the same time independent processes, each with its own division of labour. In spite of the many advantages offered by this combination of manufactures, it never grows into a complete technical system on its own foundation. That happens only on its transformation into an industry carried on by machinery.

Early in the manufacturing period, the principle of lessening the necessary labour-time in the production of commodities,[16] was accepted and formulated: and the use of machines, especially for certain simple first processes that have to be conducted on a very large scale, and with the application of great force, sprang up here and there. Thus, at an early period in paper manufacture, the tearing up of the rags was done by paper-mills; and in metal works, the pounding of the ores was effected by stamping mills.[17] The Roman Empire had handed down the elementary form of all machinery in the water-wheel.[18]

The handicraft period bequeathed to us the great inventions of the compass, of gunpowder, of type-printing, and of the automatic clock. But, on the whole, machinery played that subordinate part which Adam Smith assigns to it in comparison with division of labour.[19] The sporadic use of machinery in the 17th century was of the greatest importance, because it supplied the great mathematicians of that time with a practical basis and stimulant to the creation of the science of mechanics.

The collective labourer, formed by the combination of a number of detail labourers, is the machinery specially characteristic of the manufacturing period. The various operations that are performed in turns by the producer of a commodity, and coalesce one with another during the progress of production, lay claim to him in various ways. In one operation he must exert more strength, in another more skill, in another more attention; and the same individual does not possess all these qualities in an equal degree. After Manufacture has once separated, made independent, and isolated the various operations, the labourers are divided, classified, and grouped according to their predominating qualities. If their natural endowments are, on the one hand, the foundation on which the division of labour is built up, on the other hand, Manufacture, once introduced, develops in them new powers that are by nature fitted only for limited and special functions. The collective labourer now possesses, in an equal degree of excellence, all the qualities requisite for production, and expends them in the most economical manner, by exclusively employing all his organs, consisting of particular labourers, or groups of labourers, in performing their special functions.[20] The one-sidedness and the deficiencies of the detail labourer become perfections when he is a part of the collective labourer.[21] The habit of doing only one thing converts him into a never failing instrument, while his connexion with the whole mechanism compels him to work with the regularity of the parts of a machine.[22]

Since the collective labourer has functions, both simple and complex, both high and low, his members, the individual labour-powers, require different degrees of training, and must therefore have different values. Manufacture, therefore, develops a hierarchy of labour-powers, to which there corresponds a scale of wages. If, on the one hand, the individual labourers are appropriated and annexed for life by a limited function; on the other hand, the various operations of the hierarchy are parcelled out among the labourers according to both their natural and their acquired capabilities.[23] Every process of production, however, requires certain simple manipulations, which every man is capable of doing. They too are now severed from their connexion with the more pregnant moments of activity, and ossified into exclusive functions of specially appointed labourers. Hence, Manufacture begets, in every handicraft that it seizes upon, a class of so-called unskilled labourers, a class which handicraft industry strictly excluded. If it develops a one-sided speciality into a perfection, at the expense of the whole of a man's working capacity, it also begins to make a speciality of the absence of all development. Alongside of the hierarchic gradation there steps the simple separation of the labourers into skilled and unskilled. For the latter, the cost of apprenticeship vanishes; for the former, it diminishes, compared with that of artificers, in consequence of the functions being simplified. In both cases the value of labour-power falls.[24] An exception to this law holds good whenever the decomposition of the labour-process begets new and comprehensive functions, that either had no place at all, or only a very modest one, in handicrafts. The fall in the value of labour-power, caused by the disappearance or diminution of the expenses of apprenticeship, implies a direct increase of surplus-value for the benefit of capital; for everything that shortens the necessary labour-time required for the reproduction of labour-power, extends the domain of surplus-labour.

Section 4
Division of Labour in Manufacture, and Division of Labour in Society

We first considered the origin of Manufacture, then its simple elements, then the detail labourer and his implements, and finally, the totality of the mechanism. We shall now lightly touch upon the relation between the division of labour in manufacture, and the social division of labour, which forms the foundation of all production of commodities.

If we keep labour alone in view, we may designate the separation of social production into its main divisions or genera — viz., agriculture, industries, &c., as division of labour in general, and the splitting up of these families into species and sub-species, as division of labour in particular, and the division of labour within the workshop as division of labour in singular or in detail.[25]

Division of labour in a society, and the corresponding tying down of individuals to a particular calling, develops itself, just as does the division of labour in manufacture, from opposite starting-points. Within a family,[26] and after further development within a tribe, there springs up naturally a division of labour, caused by differences of sex and age, a division that is consequently based on a purely physiological foundation, which division enlarges its materials by the expansion of the community, by the increase of population, and more especially, by the conflicts between different tribes, and the subjugation of one tribe by another. On the other hand, as I have before remarked, the exchange of products springs up at the points where different families, tribes, communities, come in contact; for, in the beginning of civilisation, it is not private individuals but families, tribes, &c., that meet on an independent footing. Different communities find different means of production, and different means of subsistence in their natural environment. Hence, their modes of production, and of living, and their products are different. It is this spontaneously developed difference which, when different communities come in contact, calls forth the mutual exchange of products, and the consequent gradual conversion of those products into commodities. Exchange does not create the differences between the spheres of production, but brings what are already different into relation, and thus converts them into more or less inter-dependent branches of the collective production of an enlarged society. In the latter case, the social division of labour arises from the exchange between spheres of production, that are originally distinct and independent of one another. In the former, where the physiological division of labour is the starting-point, the particular organs of a compact whole grow loose, and break off, principally owing to the exchange of commodities with foreign communities, and then isolate themselves so far, that the sole bond, still connecting the various kinds of work, is the exchange of the products as commodities. In the one case, it is the making dependent what was before independent; in the other case, the making independent what was before dependent.

The foundation of every division of labour that is well developed, and brought about by the exchange of commodities, is the separation between town and country.[27] It may be said, that the whole economic history of society is summed up in the movement of this antithesis. We pass it over, however, for the present.

Just as a certain number of simultaneously employed labourers are the material pre-requisites for division of labour in manufacture, so are the number and density of the population, which here correspond to the agglomeration in one workshop, a necessary condition for the division of labour in society.[28] Nevertheless, this density is more or less relative. A relatively thinly populated country, with well-developed means of communication, has a denser population than a more numerously populated country, with badly-developed means of communication; and in this sense the Northern States of the American Union, for instance, are more thickly populated than India.[29]

Since the production and the circulation of commodities are the general pre-requisites of the capitalist mode of production, division of labour in manufacture demands, that division of labour in society at large should previously have attained a certain degree of development. Inversely, the former division reacts upon and develops and multiplies the latter. Simultaneously, with the differentiation of the instruments of labour, the industries that produce these instruments, become more and more differentiated.[30] If the manufacturing system seize upon an industry, which, previously, was carried on in connexion with others, either as a chief or as a subordinate industry, and by one producer, these industries immediately separate their connexion, and become independent. If it seize upon a particular stage in the production of a commodity, the other stages of its production become converted into so many independent industries. It has already been stated, that where the finished article consists merely of a number of parts fitted together, the detail operations may re-establish themselves as genuine and separate handicrafts. In order to carry out more perfectly the division of labour in manufacture, a single branch of production is, according to the varieties of its raw material, or the various forms that one and the same raw material may assume, split up into numerous, and to some extent, entirely new manufactures. Accordingly, in France alone, in the first half of the 18th century, over 100 different kinds of silk stuffs were woven, and, in Avignon, it was law, that "every apprentice should devote himself to only one sort of fabrication, and should not learn the preparation of several kinds of stuff at once." The territorial division of labour, which confines special branches of production to special districts of a country, acquires fresh stimulus from the manufacturing system, which exploits every special advantage.[31] The Colonial system and the opening out of the markets of the world, both of which are included in the general conditions of existence of the manufacturing period, furnish rich material for developing the division of labour in society. It is not the place, here, to go on to show how division of labour seizes upon, not only the economic, but every other sphere of society, and everywhere lays the foundation of that all engrossing system of specialising and sorting men, that development in a man of one single faculty at the expense of all other faculties, which caused A. Ferguson, the master of Adam Smith, to exclaim: "We make a nation of Helots, and have no free citizens." [32]

But, in spite of the numerous analogies and links connecting them, division of labour in the interior of a society, and that in the interior of a workshop, differ not only in degree, but also in kind. The analogy appears most indisputable where there is an invisible bond uniting the various branches of trade. For instance the cattle-breeder produces hides, the tanner makes the hides into leather, and the shoemaker, the leather into boots. Here the thing produced by each of them is but a step towards the final form, which is the product of all their labours combined. There are, besides, all the various industries that supply the cattle-breeder, the tanner, and the shoemaker with the means of production. Now it is quite possible to imagine, with Adam Smith, that the difference between the above social division of labour, and the division in manufacture, is merely subjective, exists merely for the observer, who, in a manufacture, can see with one glance, all the numerous operations being performed on one spot, while in the instance given above, the spreading out of the work over great areas, and the great number of people employed in each branch of labour, obscure the connexion.[33] But what is it that forms the bond between the independent labours of the cattle-breeder, the tanner, and the shoemaker? It is the fact that their respective products are commodities. What, on the other hand, characterises division of labour in manufactures? The fact that the detail labourer produces no commodities.[34] It is only the common product of all the detail labourers that becomes a commodity.[35] Division of labour in society is brought about by the purchase and sale of the products of different branches of industry, while the connexion between the detail operations in a workshop, is due to the sale of the labour-power of several workmen to one capitalist, who applies it as combined labour-power. The division of labour in the workshop implies concentration of the means of production in the hands of one capitalist; the division of labour in society implies their dispersion among many independent producers of commodities. While within the workshop, the iron law of proportionality subjects definite numbers of workmen to definite functions, in the society outside the workshop, chance and caprice have full play in distributing the producers and their means of production among the various branches of industry. The different spheres of production, it is true, constantly tend to an equilibrium: for, on the one hand, while each producer of a commodity is bound to produce a use-value, to satisfy a particular social want, and while the extent of these wants differs quantitatively, still there exists an inner relation which settles their proportions into a regular system, and that system one of spontaneous growth; and, on the other hand, the law of the value of commodities ultimately determines how much of its disposable working-time society can expend on each particular class of commodities. But this constant tendency to equilibrium, of the various spheres of production, is exercised, only in the shape of a reaction against the constant upsetting of this equilibrium. The a priori system on which the division of labour, within the workshop, is regularly carried out, becomes in the division of labour within the society, an a posteriori, nature-imposed necessity, controlling the lawless caprice of the producers, and perceptible in the barometrical fluctuations of the market-prices. Division of labour within the workshop implies the undisputed authority of the capitalist over men, that are but parts of a mechanism that belongs to him. The division of labour within the society brings into contact independent commodity-producers, who acknowledge no other authority but that of competition, of the coercion exerted by the pressure of their mutual interests; just as in the animal kingdom, the bellum omnium contra omnes more or less preserves the conditions of existence of every species. The same bourgeois mind which praises division of labour in the workshop, life-long annexation of the labourer to a partial operation, and his complete subjection to capital, as being an organisation of labour that increases its productiveness that same bourgeois mind denounces with equal vigour every conscious attempt to socially control and regulate the process of production, as an inroad upon such sacred things as the rights of property, freedom and unrestricted play for the bent of the individual capitalist. It is very characteristic that the enthusiastic apologists of the factory system have nothing more damning to urge against a general organisation of the labour of society, than that it would turn all society into one immense factory.

If, in a society with capitalist production, anarchy in the social division of labour and despotism in that of the workshop are mutual conditions the one of the other, we find, on the contrary, in those earlier forms of society in which the separation of trades has been spontaneously developed, then crystallised, and finally made permanent by law, on the one hand, a specimen of the organisation of the labour of society, in accordance with an approved and authoritative plan, and on the other, the entire exclusion of division of labour in the workshop, or at all events a mere dwarflike or sporadic and accidental development of the same.[36]

Those small and extremely ancient Indian communities, some of which have continued down to this day, are based on possession in common of the land, on the blending of agriculture and handicrafts, and on an unalterable division of labour, which serves, whenever a new community is started, as a plan and scheme ready cut and dried. Occupying areas of from 100 up to several thousand acres, each forms a compact whole producing all it requires. The chief part of the products is destined for direct use by the community itself, and does not take the form of a commodity. Hence, production here is independent of that division of labour brought about, in Indian society as a whole, by means of the exchange of commodities. It is the surplus alone that becomes a commodity, and a portion of even that, not until it has reached the hands of the State, into whose hands from time immemorial a certain quantity of these products has found its way in the shape of rent in kind. The constitution of these communities varies in different parts of India. In those of the simplest form, the land is tilled in common, and the produce divided among the members. At the same time, spinning and weaving are carried on in each family as subsidiary industries. Side by side with the masses thus occupied with one and the same work, we find the "chief inhabitant," who is judge, police, and tax-gatherer in one; the book-keeper, who keeps the accounts of the tillage and registers everything relating thereto; another official, who prosecutes criminals, protects strangers travelling through and escorts them to the next village; the boundary man, who guards the boundaries against neighbouring communities; the water-overseer, who distributes the water from the common tanks for irrigation; the Brahmin, who conducts the religious services; the schoolmaster, who on the sand teaches the children reading and writing; the calendar-Brahmin, or astrologer, who makes known the lucky or unlucky days for seed-time and harvest, and for every other kind of agricultural work; a smith and a carpenter, who make and repair all the agricultural implements; the potter, who makes all the pottery of the village; the barber, the washerman, who washes clothes, the silversmith, here and there the poet, who in some communities replaces the silversmith, in others the schoolmaster. This dozen of individuals is maintained at the expense of the whole community. If the population increases, a new community is founded, on the pattern of the old one, on unoccupied land. The whole mechanism discloses a systematic division of labour; but a division like that in manufactures is impossible, since the smith and the carpenter, &c., find an unchanging market, and at the most there occur, according to the sizes of the villages, two or three of each, instead of one.[37] The law that regulates the division of labour in the community acts with the irresistible authority of a law of Nature, at the same time that each individual artificer, the smith, the carpenter, and so on, conducts in his workshop all the operations of his handicraft in the traditional way, but independently, and without recognising any authority over him. The simplicity of the organisation for production in these self-sufficing communities that constantly reproduce themselves in the same form, and when accidentally destroyed, spring up again on the spot and with the same name[38] this simplicity supplies the key to the secret of the unchangeableness of Asiatic societies, an unchangeableness in such striking contrast with the constant dissolution and refounding of Asiatic States, and the never-ceasing changes of dynasty. The structure of the economic elements of society remains untouched by the storm-clouds of the political sky.

The rules of the guilds, as I have said before, by limiting most strictly the number of apprentices and journeymen that a single master could employ, prevented him from becoming a capitalist. Moreover, he could not employ his journeymen in many other handicrafts than the one in which he was a master. The guilds zealously repelled every encroachment by the capital of merchants, the only form of free capital with which they came in contact. A merchant could buy every kind of commodity, but labour as a commodity he could not buy. He existed only on sufferance, as a dealer in the products of the handicrafts. If circumstances called for a further division of labour, the existing guilds split themselves up into varieties, or founded new guilds by the side of the old ones; all this, however, without concentrating various handicrafts in a single workshop. Hence, the guild organisation, however much it may have contributed by separating, isolating, and perfecting the handicrafts, to create the material conditions for the existence of manufacture, excluded division of labour in the workshop. On the whole, the labourer and his means of production remained closely united, like the snail with its shell, and thus there was wanting the principal basis of manufacture, the separation of the labourer from his means of production, and the conversion of these means into capital.

While division of labour in society at large, whether such division be brought about or not by exchange of commodities, is common to economic formations of society the most diverse, division of labour in the workshop, as practised by manufacture, is a special creation of the capitalist mode of production alone.

Section 5:
The Capitalistic Character of Manufacture

An increased number of labourers under the control of one capitalist is the natural starting-point, as well of co-operation generally, as of manufacture in particular. But the division of labour in manufacture makes this increase in the number of workmen a technical necessity. The minimum number that any given capitalist is bound to employ is here prescribed by the previously established division of labour. On the other hand, the advantages of further division are obtainable only by adding to the number of workmen, and this can be done only by adding multiples of the various detail groups. But an increase in the variable component of the capital employed necessitates an increase in its constant component, too, in the workshops, implements, &c., and, in particular, in the raw material, the call for which grows quicker than the number of workmen. The quantity of it consumed in a given time, by a given amount of labour, increases in the same ratio as does the productive power of that labour in consequence of its division. Hence, it is a law, based on the very nature of manufacture, that the minimum amount of capital, which is bound to be in the hands of each capitalist, must keep increasing; in other words, that the transformation into capital of the social means of production and subsistence must keep extending.[39]

In manufacture, as well as in simple co-operation, the collective working organism is a form of existence of capital. The mechanism that is made up of numerous individual detail labourers belongs to the capitalist. Hence, the productive power resulting from a combination of labours appears to be the productive power of capital. Manufacture proper not only subjects the previously independent workman to the discipline and command of capital, but, in addition, creates a hierarchic gradation of the workmen themselves. While simple co-operation leaves the mode of working by the individual for the most part unchanged, manufacture thoroughly revolutionises it, and seizes labour-power by its very roots. It converts the labourer into a crippled monstrosity, by forcing his detail dexterity at the expense of a world of productive capabilities and instincts; just as in the States of La Plata they butcher a whole beast for the sake of his hide or his tallow. Not only is the detail work distributed to the different individuals, but the individual himself is made the automatic motor of a fractional operation,[40] and the absurd fable of Menenius Agrippa, which makes man a mere fragment of his own body, becomes realised.[41] If, at first, the workman sells his labour-power to capital, because the material means of producing a commodity fail him, now his very labour-power refuses its services unless it has been sold to capital. Its functions can be exercised only in an environment that exists in the workshop of the capitalist after the sale. By nature unfitted to make anything independently, the manufacturing labourer develops productive activity as a mere appendage of the capitalist's workshop.[42] As the chosen people bore in their features the sign manual of Jehovah, so division of labour brands the manufacturing workman as the property of capital.

The knowledge, the judgement, and the will, which, though in ever so small a degree, are practised by the independent peasant or handicraftsman, in the same way as the savage makes the whole art of war consist in the exercise of his personal cunning these faculties are now required only for the workshop as a whole. Intelligence in production expands in one direction, because it vanishes in many others. What is lost by the detail labourers, is concentrated in the capital that employs them.[43] It is a result of the division of labour in manufactures, that the labourer is brought face to face with the intellectual potencies of the material process of production, as the property of another, and as a ruling power. This separation begins in simple co-operation, where the capitalist represents to the single workman, the oneness and the will of the associated labour. It is developed in manufacture which cuts down the labourer into a detail labourer. It is completed in modern industry, which makes science a productive force distinct from labour and presses it into the service of capital. [44]

In manufacture, in order to make the collective labourer, and through him capital, rich in social productive power, each labourer must be made poor in individual productive powers. "Ignorance is the mother of industry as well as of superstition. Reflection and fancy are subject to err; but a habit of moving the hand or the foot is independent of either. anufactures, accordingly, prosper most where the mind is least consulted, and where the workshop may ... be considered as an engine, the parts of which are men."[45] As a matter of fact, some few manufacturers in the middle of the 18th century preferred, for certain operations that were trade secrets, to employ half-idiotic persons.[46]

"The understandings of the greater part of men," says Adam Smith, "are necessarily formed by their ordinary employments. The man whose whole life is spent in performing a few simple operations ... has no occasion to exert his understanding... He generally becomes as stupid and ignorant as it is possible for a human creature to become." After describing the stupidity of the detail labourer he goes on: "The uniformity of his stationary life naturally corrupts the courage of his mind... It corrupts even the activity of his body and renders him incapable of exerting his strength with vigour and perseverance in any other employments than that to which he has been bred. His dexterity at his own particular trade seems in this manner to be acquired at the expense of his intellectual, social, and martial virtues. But in every improved and civilised society, this is the state into which the labouring poor, that is, the great body of the people, must necessarily fall."[47] For preventing the complete deterioration of the great mass of the people by division of labour, A. Smith recommends education of the people by the State, but prudently, and in homeopathic doses. G. Garnier, his French translator and commentator, who, under the first French Empire, quite naturally developed into a senator, quite as naturally opposes him on this point. Education of the masses, he urges, violates the first law of the division of labour, and with it "our whole social system would be proscribed." "Like all other divisions of labour," he says, "that between hand labour and head labour[48] is more pronounced and decided in proportion as society (he rightly uses this word, for capital, landed property and their State) becomes richer. This division of labour, like every other, is an effect of past, and a cause of future progress... ought the government then to work in opposition to this division of labour, and to hinder its natural course? Ought it to expend a part of the public money in the attempt to confound and blend together two classes of labour, which are striving after division and separation?" [49]

Some crippling of body and mind is inseparable even from division of labour in society as a whole. Since, however, manufacture carries this social separation of branches of labour much further, and also, by its peculiar division, attacks the individual at the very roots of his life, it is the first to afford the materials for, and to give a start to, industrial pathology.[50]

"To subdivide a man is to execute him, if he deserves the sentence, to assassinate him if he does not... The subdivision of labour is the assassination of a people."[51]

Co-operation based on division of labour, in other words, manufacture, commences as a spontaneous formation. So soon as it attains some consistence and extension, it becomes the recognised methodical and systematic form of capitalist production. History shows how the division of labour peculiar to manufacture, strictly so called, acquires the best adapted form at first by experience, as it were behind the backs of the actors, and then, like the guild handicrafts, strives to hold fast that form when once found, and here and there succeeds in keeping it for centuries. Any alteration in this form, except in trivial matters, is solely owing to a revolution in the instruments of labour. Modern manufacture wherever it arises I do not here allude to modern industry based on machinery either finds the disjecta membra poetae ready to hand, and only waiting to be collected together, as is the case in the manufacture of clothes in large towns, or it can easily apply the principle of division, simply by exclusively assigning the various operations of a handicraft (such as book-binding) to particular men. In such cases, a week's experience is enough to determine the proportion between the numbers of the hands necessary for the various functions.[52]

By decomposition of handicrafts, by specialisation of the instruments of labour, by the formation of detail labourers, and by grouping and combining the latter into a single mechanism, division of labour in manufacture creates a qualitative gradation, and a quantitative proportion in the social process of production; it consequently creates a definite organisation of the labour of society, and thereby develops at the same time new productive forces in the society. In its specific capitalist form and under the given conditions, it could take no other form than a capitalistic one manufacture is but a particular method of begetting relative surplus-value, or of augmenting at the expense of the labourer the self-expansion of capital usually called social wealth, "Wealth of Nations," &c. It increases the social productive power of labour, not only for the benefit of the capitalist instead of for that of the labourer, but it does this by crippling the individual labourers. It creates new conditions for the lordship of capital over labour. If, therefore, on the one hand, it presents itself historically as a progress and as a necessary phase in the economic development of society, on the other hand, it is a refined and civilised method of exploitation.

Political Economy, which as an independent science, first sprang into being during the period of manufacture, views the social division of labour only from the standpoint of manufacture,[53] and sees in it only the means of producing more commodities with a given quantity of labour, and, consequently, of cheapening commodities and hurrying on the accumulation of capital. In most striking contrast with this accentuation of quantity and exchange-value, is the attitude of the writers of classical antiquity, who hold exclusively by quality and use-value.[54] In consequence of the separation of the social branches of production, commodities are better made, the various bents and talents of men select a suitable field,[55] and without some restraint no important results can be obtained anywhere.[56] Hence both product and producer are improved by division of labour. If the growth of the quantity produced is occasionally mentioned, this is only done with reference to the greater abundance of use-values. There is not a word alluding to exchange-value or to the cheapening of commodities. This aspect, from the standpoint of use-value alone, is taken as well by Plato,[57] who treats division of labour as the foundation on which the division of society into classes is based, as by Xenophon, [58] who with characteristic bourgeois instinct, approaches more nearly to division of labour within the workshop. Plato's Republic, in so far as division of labour is treated in it, as the formative principle of the State, is merely the Athenian idealisation of the Egyptian system of castes, Egypt having served as the model of an industrial country to many of his contemporaries also, amongst others to Isocrates,[59] and it continued to have this importance to the Greeks of the Roman Empire.[60]

During the manufacturing period proper, i.e., the period during which manufacture is the predominant form taken by capitalist production, many obstacles are opposed to the full development of the peculiar tendencies of manufacture. Although manufacture creates, as we have already seen, a simple separation of the labourers into skilled and unskilled, simultaneously with their hierarchic arrangement in classes, yet the number of the unskilled labourers, owing to the preponderating influence of the skilled, remains very limited. Although it adapts the detail operations to the various degrees of maturity, strength, and development of the living instruments of labour, thus conducing to exploitation of women and children, yet this tendency as a whole is wrecked on the habits and the resistance of the male labourers. Although the splitting up of handicrafts lowers the cost of forming the workman, and thereby lowers his value, yet for the more difficult detail work, a longer apprenticeship is necessary, and, even where it would be superfluous, is jealously insisted upon by the workmen. In England, for instance, we find the laws of apprenticeship, with their seven years' probation, in full force down to the end of the manufacturing period; and they are not thrown on one side till the advent of Modern Industry. Since handicraft skill is the foundation of manufacture, and since the mechanism of manufacture as a whole possesses no framework, apart from the labourers themselves, capital is constantly compelled to wrestle with the insubordination of the workmen. "By the infirmity of human nature," says friend Ure, "it happens that the more skilful the workman, the more self-willed and intractable he is apt to become, and of course the less fit a component of a mechanical system in which ... he may do great damage to the whole."[61] Hence throughout the whole manufacturing period there runs the complaint of want of discipline among the workmen.[62] And had we not the testimony of contemporary writers, the simple facts, that during the period between the 16th century and the epoch of Modern Industry, capital failed to become the master of the whole disposable working-time of the manufacturing labourers, that manufactures are short-lived, and change their locality from one country to another with the emigrating or immigrating workmen, these facts would speak volumes. "Order must in one way or another be established," exclaims in 1770 the oft-cited author of the "Essay on Trade and Commerce." "Order," re-echoes Dr. Andrew Ure 66 years later, "Order" was wanting in manufacture based on "the scholastic dogma of division of labour," and "Arkwright created order."

At the same time manufacture was unable, either to seize upon the production of society to its full extent, or to revolutionise that production to its very core. It towered up as an economic work of art, on the broad foundation of the town handicrafts, and of the rural domestic industries. At a given stage in its development, the narrow technical basis on which manufacture rested, came into conflict with requirements of production that were created by manufacture itself.

One of its most finished creations was the workshop for the production of the instruments of labour themselves, including especially the complicated mechanical apparatus then already employed. A machine-factory, says Ure, "displayed the division of labour in manifold gradations the file, the drill, the lathe, having each its different workman in the order of skill." (P. 21.) This workshop, the product of the division of labour in manufacture, produced in its turn machines. It is they that sweep away the handicraftsman's work as the regulating principle of social production. Thus, on the one hand, the technical reason for the life-long annexation of the workman to a detail function is removed. On the other hand, the fetters that this same principle laid on the dominion of capital, fall away.

Footnotes

[1] To give a more modern instance: The silk spinning and weaving of Lyon and Nîmes "est toute patriarcale; elle emploie beaucoup de femmes et d'enfants, mais sans les épuiser ni les corrompre; elle les laisse dans leur belles valises de la Drôme, du Var, de l'Isère, de Vaucluse, pour y élever des vers et dévider leurs cocons; jamais elle n'entre dans une véritable fabrique. Pour être aussi bien observe ... le principe de la division du travail s'y revêt d'un caractère spécial. Il y a bien des dévideuses, des moulineurs, des teinturiers, des encolleurs, puis des tisserands; mais ils ne sont pas réunis dans un même établissement, ne dépendent pas d'un même maître, tous ils sont indépendants" (A. Blanqui: "Cours, d'Econ. Industrielle." Recueilli par A. Blaise. Paris, 1838-39, p. 79.) Since Blanqui wrote this, the various independent labourers have, to some extent, been united in factories. [And since Marx wrote the above, the power-loom has invaded these factories, and is now 1886 rapidly superseding the hand-loom. (Added in the 4th German edition. The Krefeld silk industry also has its tale to tell anent this subject.) F. E.]

[2] The more any manufacture of much variety shall be distributed and assigned to different artists, the same must needs be better done and with greater expedition, with less loss of time and labour." ("The Advantages of the East India Trade," Lond., 1720, p. 71.)

[3] "Easy labour is transmitted skill." (Th. Hodgskin, "Popular Political Economy," p. 48.)

[4] "The arts also have ... in Egypt reached the requisite degree of perfection. For it is the only country where artificers may not in any way meddle with the affairs of another class of citizens, but must follow that calling alone which by law is hereditary in their clan.... In other countries it is found that tradesmen divide their attention between too many objects. At one time they try agriculture, at another they take to commerce, at another they busy themselves with two or three occupations at once. In free countries, they mostly frequent the assemblies of the people.... In Egypt, on the contrary, every artificer is severely punished if he meddles with affairs of State, or carries on several trades at once. Thus there is nothing to disturb their application to their calling.... oreover, since, they inherit from their forefathers numerous rules, they are eager to discover fresh advantages" (Diodorus Siculus: Bibl. Hist. I. 1. c., 74.)

[5] "Historical and descriptive account of Brit. India, &c.," by Hugh Murray and James Wilson, &c., Edinburgh 1832, v. II., p. 449. The Indian loom is upright, i.e., the warp is stretched vertically.

[6] Darwin in his epoch-making work on the origin of species, remarks, with reference to the natural organs of plants and animals: "So long as one and the same organ has different kinds of work to perform, a ground for its changeability may possibly be found in this, that natural selection preserves or suppresses each small variation of form less carefully than if that organ were destined for one special purpose alone. Thus, knives that are adapted to cut all sorts of things, may, on the whole, be of one shape; but an implement destined to be used exclusively in one way must have a different shape for every different use."

[7] In the year 1854 Geneva produced 80,000 watches, which is not one-fifth of the production in the Canton of Neufchâtel. La Chaux-de-Fond alone, which we may look

upon as a huge watch manufactory, produces yearly twice as many as Geneva. From 1850-61 Geneva produced 720,000 watches. See "Report from Geneva on the Watch Trade" in "Reports by H. .'s Secretaries of Embassy and Legation on the Manufactures, Commerce, &c., No. 6, 1863." The want of connexion alone, between the processes into which the production of articles that merely consist of parts fitted together is split up, makes it very difficult to convert such a manufacture into a branch of modem industry carried on by machinery; but in the case of a watch there are two other impediments in addition, the minuteness and delicacy of its parts, and its character as an article of luxury. Hence their variety, which is such, that in the best London houses scarcely a dozen watches are made alike in the course of a year. The watch manufactory of Messrs. Vacheron & Constantin, in which machinery has been employed with success, produces at the most three or four different varieties of size and form.

[8] In watchmaking, that classical example of heterogeneous manufacture, we may study with great accuracy the above-mentioned differentiation and specialisation of the instruments of labour caused by the sub-division of handicrafts.

[9] "In so close a cohabitation of the people, the carriage must needs be less." ("The Advantages of the East India Trade," p. 106.)

[10] "The isolation of the different stages of manufacture, consequent upon the employment of manual labour, adds immensely to the cost of production, the loss mainly arising from the mere removals from one process to another." ("The Industry of Nations." Lond., 1855, Part II, p. 200.)

[11] "It (the division of labour) produces also an economy of time by separating the work into its different branches, all of which may be carried on into execution at the same moment.... By carrying on all the different processes at once, which an individual must have executed separately, it becomes possible to produce a multitude of pins completely finished in the same time as a single pin might have been either cut or pointed." (Dugald Stewart, l. c., p. 319.)

[12] "The more variety of artists to every manufacture... the greater the order and regularity of every work, the same must needs be done in less time, the labour must be less.' ("The Advantages," &c., p. 68.)

[13] Nevertheless, the manufacturing system, in many branches of industry, attains this result but very imperfectly, because it knows not how to control with certainty the general chemical and physical conditions of the process of production.

[14] "When (from the peculiar nature of the produce of each manufactory), the number of processes into which it is most advantageous to divide it is ascertained, as well as the number of individuals to be employed, then all other manufactories which do not employ a direct multiple of this number will produce the article at a greater cost.... Hence arises one of the causes of the great size of manufacturing establishments." (C. Babbage. 'On the Economy of Machinery," 1st ed. London. 1832. Ch. xxi, pp. 172-73.)

[15] In England, the melting-furnace is distinct from the glass-furnace in which the glass is manipulated. In Belgium, one and the same furnace serves for both processes.

[16] This can be seen from W. Petty, John Bellers, Andrew Yarranton, "The Advantages of the East India Trade," and J. Vanderlint, not to mention others.

[17] Towards the end of the 16th century, mortars and sieves were still used in France for pounding and washing ores.

[18] The whole history of the development of machinery can be traced in the history of the corn mill. The factory in England is still a "mill". In German technological works of the first decade of this century, the term "Mühle" is still found in use, not only for all machinery driven by the forces of Nature, but also for all manufactures where apparatus in the nature of machinery is applied.

[19] As will be seen more in detail in the fourth book of this work, Adam Smith has not established a single new proposition relating to division of labour. What, however, characterises him as the political economist par excellence of the period of Manufacture, is the stress he lays on division of labour. The subordinate part which he assigns to machinery gave occasion in the early days of modern mechanical industry to the polemic of Lauderdale, and, at a later period, to that of Ure. A. Smith also confounds differentiation of the instruments of labour, in which the detail labourers themselves took an active part, with the invention of machinery; in this latter, it is not the workmen in

manufactories, but learned men, handicraftsman, and even peasants (Brindley), who play a part.

[20] "The master manufacturer, by dividing the work to be executed into different processes, each requiring different degrees of skill or of force, can purchase exactly that precise quantity of both which is necessary for each process; whereas, if the whole work were executed by one workman, that person must possess sufficient skill to perform the most difficult, and sufficient strength to execute the most laborious of the operations into which the article is divided." (Ch. Babbage, l. c., ch. xix.)

[21] For instance, abnormal development of some muscles, curvature of bones, &c.

[22] The question put by one of the Inquiry Commissioners, How the young persons are kept steadily to their work, is very correctly answered by Mr. Wm. Marshall, the general manager of a glass manufactory: "They cannot well neglect their work; when they once begin, they must go on; they are just the same as parts of a machine." ("Children's Empl. Comm.," 4th Rep., 1865, p. 247.)

[23] Dr. Ure, in his apotheosis of Modern Mechanical Industry, brings out the peculiar character of manufacture more sharply than previous economists, who had not his polemical interest in the matter, and more sharply even than his contemporaries Babbage, e.g., who, though much his superior as a mathematician and mechanician, treated mechanical industry from the standpoint of manufacture alone. Ure says, "This appropriation ... to each, a workman of appropriate value and cost was naturally assigned, forms the very essence of division of labour." On the other hand, he describes this division as "adaptation of labour to the different talents of men," and lastly, characterises the whole manufacturing system as "a system for the division or gradation of labour," as "the division of labour into degrees of skill," &c. (Ure, l. c., pp. 19-23 passim.)

[24] "Each handicraftsman being ... enabled to perfect himself by practice in one point, became ... a cheaper workman." (Ure, l. c., p. 19.)

[25] "Division of labour proceeds from the separation of professions the most widely different to that division, where several labourers divide between them the preparation of one and the same product, as in manufacture." (Storch: "Cours d'Econ. Pol.," Paris Edn. t. I., p. 173.) "Nous rencontrons chez les peuples parvenus à un certain degré de civilisation trois genres de divisions d'industrie: la première, que nous nommerons générale, amène la distinction des producteurs en agriculteurs, manufacturiers et commerçants, elle se rapporte aux trois principales branches d'industrie nationale; la seconder qu'on pourrait appeler spéciale, est la division de chaque genre d'industrie en espèces ... la troisième division d'industrie, celle enfin qu'on devrait qualifier de division de la besogne on de travail proprement dit, est celle qui s'établit dans les arts et les métiers séparés ... qui s'établit dans la plupart des manufactures et des ateliers." (Skarbek, l. c., pp. 84, 85.)

[26] Note to the third edition. Subsequent very searching study of the primitive condition of man, led the author to the conclusion, that it was not the family that originally developed into the tribe, but that, on the contrary, the tribe was the primitive and spontaneously developed form of human association, on the basis of blood relationship, and that out of the first incipient loosening of the tribal bonds, the many and various forms of the family were afterwards developed. F. E.

[27] Sir James Steuart is the economist who has handled this subject best. How little his book, which appeared ten years before the "Wealth of Nations," is known, even at the present time, may be judged from the fact that the admirers of Malthus do not even know that the first edition of the latter's work on population contains, except in the purely declamatory part, very little but extracts from Steuart, and in a less degree, from Wallace and Townsend.

[28] "There is a certain density of population which is convenient, both for social intercourse, and for that combination of powers by which the produce of labour is increased." (James Mill, l. c., p. 50.) "As the number of labourers increases, the productive power of society augments in the compound ratio of that increase, multiplied by the effects of the division of labour." (Th. Hodgskin, l. c., pp. 125, 126.)

[29] In consequence of the great demand for cotton after 1861, the production of cotton, in some thickly populated districts of India, was extended at the expense of rice cultivation. In consequence there arose local famines, the defective means of communication not permitting the failure of rice in one district to be compensated by importation from another.

[30] Thus the fabrication of shuttles formed as early as the 17th century, a special branch of industry in Holland.

[31] Whether the woollen manufacture of England is not divided into several parts or branches appropriated to particular places, where they are only or principally manufactured; fine cloths in Somersetshire, coarse in Yorkshire, long ells at Exeter, soies at Sudbury, crapes at Norwich, linseys at Kendal, blankets at Whitney, and so forth." (Berkeley: "The Querist," 1751, § 520.)

[32] A. Ferguson: "History of Civil Society." Edinburgh, 1767; Part iv, sect. ii., p. 285.

[33] In manufacture proper, he says, the division of labour appears to be greater, because "those employed in every different branch of the work can often be collected into the same workhouse, and placed at once under the view of the spectator. In those great manufactures, (!) on the contrary, which are destined to supply the great wants of the great body of the people, every different branch of the work employs so great a number of workmen, that it is impossible to collect them all into the same workhouse ... the division is not near so obvious." (A. Smith: "Wealth of Nations," bk. i, ch. i.) The celebrated passage in the same chapter that begins with the words, "Observe the accommodation of the most common artificer or day-labourer in a civilised and thriving country," &c., and then proceeds to depict what an enormous number and variety of industries contribute to the satisfaction of the wants of an ordinary labourer, is copied almost word for word from B. de Mandeville's Remarks to his "Fable of the Bees, or Private Vices, Publick Benefits." (First ed., without the remarks, 1706; with the remarks, 1714.)

[34] "There is no longer anything which we can call the natural reward of individual labour. Each labourer produces only some part of a whole, and each part, having no value or utility in itself, there is nothing on which the labourer can seize, and say: It is my product, this I will keep to myself." ("Labour Defended against the Claims of Capital." Lond., 1825, p. 25.) The author of this admirable work is the Th. Hodgskin I have already cited.

[35] One of the new taxes devised at Washington during the civil war, was the duty of 6% "on all industrial products." Question: What is an industrial product? Answer of the legislature: A thing is produced "when it is made," and it is made when it is ready for sale. Now, for one example out of many. They entered as separate commodities into the umbrella manufactory, where they were fitted together. The Yankees have given to articles thus fitted together, the name of "assembled articles," a name they deserve, for being an assemblage of taxes. Thus the umbrella "assembles," first, 6% on the price of each of its elements, and a further 6% on its own total price.

[36] "On peut... établir en règle générale, que moins l'autorité préside à la division du travail dans l'intérieur de la société, plus la division du travail se développe dans l'intérieur de l'atelier, et plus elle y est soumise à I'autorité d'un seul. Ainsi I'autorité dans l'atelier et celle dans la société, par rapport à la division du travail, sont en raison inverse l'une de I'autre." (Karl Marx, "Misère," &c., pp. 130-131.)

[37] Lieut.-Col. Mark Wilks: "Historical Sketches of the South of India." Lond., 1810-17, v. I., pp. 118-20. A good description of the various forms of the Indian communities is to be found in George Campbell's "Modern India." Lond., 1852.

[38] "Under this simple form ... the inhabitants of the country have lived from time immemorial. The boundaries of the villages have been but seldom altered; and though the villages themselves have been sometimes injured, and even desolated by war, famine, and disease, the same name, the same limits, the same interests, and even the same families, have continued for ages. The inhabitants give themselves no trouble about the breaking up and division of kingdoms; while the village remains entire, they care not to what power it is transferred, or to what sovereign it devolves; its Internal economy remains unchanged." (Th. Stamford Raffles, late Lieut. Gov. of Java: "The History of Java." Lond., 1817, Vol. I., p. 285.)

[39] "It is not sufficient that the capital" (the writer should have said the necessary means of subsistence and of production) "required for the subdivision of handicrafts should be in readiness in the society: it must also be accumulated in the hands of the employers in sufficiently large quantities to enable them to conduct their operations on a large scale.... The more the division increases, the more does the constant employment of a given number of labourers require a greater outlay of capital in tools, raw material, &c." (Storch: "Cours d'Econ. Polit." Paris Ed., t. I., pp. 250, 251.) "La concentration des

instruments de production et la division du travail sont aussi inséparables l'une de I'autre que le sont, dans le régime politique, la concentration des pouvoirs publics et la division des intérêts privés." (Karl arx, l. c., p. 134.)

[40] Dugald Stewart calls manufacturing labourers "living automatons ... employed in the details of the work." (I. c., p. 318.)

[41] In corals, each individual is, in fact, the stomach of the whole group; but it supplies the group with nourishment, instead of, like the Roman patrician, withdrawing it.

[42] "L'ouvrier qui porte dans ses bras tout un métier, peut aller partout exercer son industrie et trouver des moyens de subsister: l'autre (the manufacturing labourer) n'est qu'un accessoire qui, séparé de ses confrères, n'a plus ni capacité, ni indépendance, et qui se trouve force d'accepter la loi qu'on juge à propos de lui imposer." (Storch, l. c., Petersb. edit., 1815, t. I., p. 204.)

[43] A. Ferguson, l. c., p. 281: "The former may have gained what the other has lost."

[44] "The man of knowledge and the productive labourer come to be widely divided from each other, and knowledge, instead of remaining the handmaid of labour in the hand of the labourer to increase his productive powers ... has almost everywhere arrayed itself against labour ... systematically deluding and leading them (the labourers) astray in order to render their muscular powers entirely mechanical and obedient." (W. Thompson: "An Inquiry into the Principles of the Distribution of Wealth." London, 1824, p. 274.)

[45] A. Ferguson, l. c., p. 280.

[46] J. D. Tuckett: "A History of the Past and Present State of the Labouring Population." Lond., 1846.

[47] A. Smith: "Wealth of Nations," Bk. v., ch. i, art. ii. Being a pupil of A. Ferguson who showed the disadvantageous effects of division of labour, Adam Smith was perfectly clear on this point. In the introduction to his work, where he ex professo praises division of labour, he indicates only in a cursory manner that it is the source of social inequalities. It is not till the 5th Book, on the Revenue of the State, that he reproduces Ferguson. In my "Misère de la Philosophie," I have sufficiently explained the historical connexion between Ferguson, A. Smith, Lemontey, and Say, as regards their criticisms of Division of Labour, and have shown, for the first time, that Division of Labour as practised in manufactures, is a specific form of the capitalist mode of production.

[48] Ferguson had already said, l. c., p. 281: "And thinking itself, in this age of separations, may become a peculiar craft."

[49] G. Garnier, vol. V. of his translation of A. Smith, pp. 4-5.

[50] Ramazzini, professor of practical medicine at Padua, published in 1713 his work "De morbis artificum," which was translated into French 1781, reprinted 1841 in the "Encyclopédie des Sciences Médicales. 7me Dis. Auteurs Classiques." The period of Modern Mechanical Industry has, of course, very much enlarged his catalogue of labour's diseases. See "Hygiène physique et morale de l'ouvrier dans les grandes villes en général et dans la ville de Lyon en particulier. Par le Dr. A. L. Fonteret, Paris, 1858," and "Die Krankheiten, welche verschiednen Ständen, Altern und Geschlechtern eigenthümlich sind. 6 Vols. Ulm, 1860," and others. In 1854 the Society of Arts appointed a Commission of Inquiry into industrial pathology. The list of documents collected by this commission is to be seen in the catalogue of the "Twickenham Economic Museum." Very important are the official "Reports on Public Health." See also Eduard Reich, M. D. "Ueber die Entartung des Menschen," Erlangen, 1868.

[51] (D. Urquhart: "Familiar Words." Lond., 1855, p. 119.) Hegel held very heretical views on division of labour. In his "Rechtsphilosophie" he says: "By well educated men we understand in the first instance, those who can do everything that others do."

[52] The simple belief in the inventive genius exercised a priori by the individual capitalist in division of labour, exists now-a-days only among German professors, of the stamp of Herr Roscher, who, to recompense the capitalist from whose Jovian head division of labour sprang ready formed, dedicates to him "various wages" (diverse Arbeitslöhne). The more or less extensive application of division of labour depends on length of purse, not on greatness of genius.

[53] The older writers, like Petty and the anonymous author of "Advantages of the East India Trade," bring out the capitalist character of division of labour as applied in manufacture more than A. Smith does.

[54] Amongst the moderns may be excepted a few writers of the 18th century, like Beccaria and James Harris, who with regard to division of labour almost entirely follow the ancients. Thus, Beccaria: "Ciascuno prova coll'esperienza, che applicando la mano e l'ingegno sempre allo stesso genere di opere e di produtte, egli più facili, più abbondanti e migliori ne traca risultati, di quello che se ciascuno isolatamente le cose tutte a se necessarie soltanto facesse.... Dividendosi in tal maniera per la comune e privata utilità gli uomini in varie classi e condizioni." (Cesare Beccaria: "Elementi di Econ: Pubblica," ed. Custodi, Parte Moderna, t. xi, p. 29.) James Harris, afterwards Earl of Malmesbury, celebrated for the "Diaries" of his embassy at St. Petersburg, says in a note to his "Dialogue Concerning Happiness," Lond., 1741, reprinted afterwards in "Three Treatises, 3 Ed., Lond., 1772: "The whole argument to prove society natural (i.e., by division of employments) ... is taken from the second book of Plato's Republic."

[57] With Plato, division of labour within the community is a development from the multifarious requirements, and the limited capacities of individuals. The main point with him is, that the labourer must adapt himself to the work, not the work to the labourer; which latter is unavoidable, if he carries on several trades at once, thus making one or the other of them subordinate. [Greek: "Ou gar ethelei to prattomenon ten tou prattonios scholen perimenein, all' anagke ton prattonta to prattomeno epakoloothein me en parergou merei. Anagke. Ek de touton pleio te ekasta gignetai kai kallion kai raon, otan eis en kaia physin kai en kairo scholen ton allon agon, pratte."] (Rep. 1. 2. Ed. Baiter, Orelli, &c.) So in Thucydides, l. c., c. 142: "Seafaring is an art like any other, and cannot, as circumstances require, be carried on as a subsidiary occupation; nay, other subsidiary occupations cannot be carried on alongside of this one." If the work, says Plato, has to wait for the labourer, the critical point in the process is missed and the article spoiled, [Greek: "ergou kairon diollytai."] The same Platonic idea is found recurring in the protest of the English bleachers against the clause in the Factory Act that provides fixed mealtimes for all operatives. Their business cannot wait the convenience of the workmen, for "in the various operations of singeing, washing, bleaching, mangling, calendering, and dyeing, none of them can be stopped at a given moment without risk of damage ... to enforce the same dinner hour for all the workpeople might occasionally subject valuable goods to the risk of danger by incomplete operations." Le platonisme où va-t-il se nicher!

[58] Xenophon says, it is not only an honour to receive food from the table of the King of Persia, but such food is much more tasty than other food. "And there is nothing wonderful in this, for as the other arts are brought to special perfection in the great towns, so the royal food is prepared in a special way. For in the small towns the same man makes bedsteads, doors, ploughs, and tables: often, too, he builds houses into the bargain, and is quite content if he finds custom sufficient for his sustenance. It is altogether impossible for a man who does so many things to do them all well. But in the great towns, where each can find many buyers, one trade is sufficient to maintain the man who carries it on. Nay, there is often not even need of one complete trade, but one man makes shoes for men, another for women. Here and there one man gets a living by sewing, another by cutting out shoes; one does nothing but cut out clothes, another nothing but sew the pieces together. It follows necessarily then, that he who does the simplest kind of work, undoubtedly does it better than anyone else. So it is with the art of cooking." (Xen. Cyrop. I. viii., c. 2.) Xenophon here lays stress exclusively upon the excellence to be attained in use-value, although he well knows that the gradations of the division of labour depend on the extent of the market.

[59] He (Busiris) divided them all into special castes ... commanded that the same individuals should always carry on the same trade, for he knew that they who change their occupations become skilled in none; but that those who constantly stick to one occupation bring it to the highest perfection. In truth, we shall also find that in relation to the arts and handicrafts, they have outstripped their rivals more than a master does a bungler; and the contrivances for maintaining the monarchy and the other institutions of their State are so admirable that the most celebrated philosophers who treat of this subject praise the constitution of the Egyptian State above all others. (Isocrates, Busiris, c. 8.)